Target Practice:
Painting Under Attack 1949–78

There is not such a great difference between construction and destruction. What I'm trying to do is to create poetry through destruction and I think it is beautiful.

—Niki de Saint Phalle

Harry Shunk, *Niki de Saint Phalle shooting at Old Master with a .22 rifle, Impasse Rousin, June 15, 1961*, 1961 (detail). Gelatin silver print, 8 x 10 in. (20.3 x 25.4 cm). Collection Niki Charitable Art Foundation, California, USA.
(catalogue only)

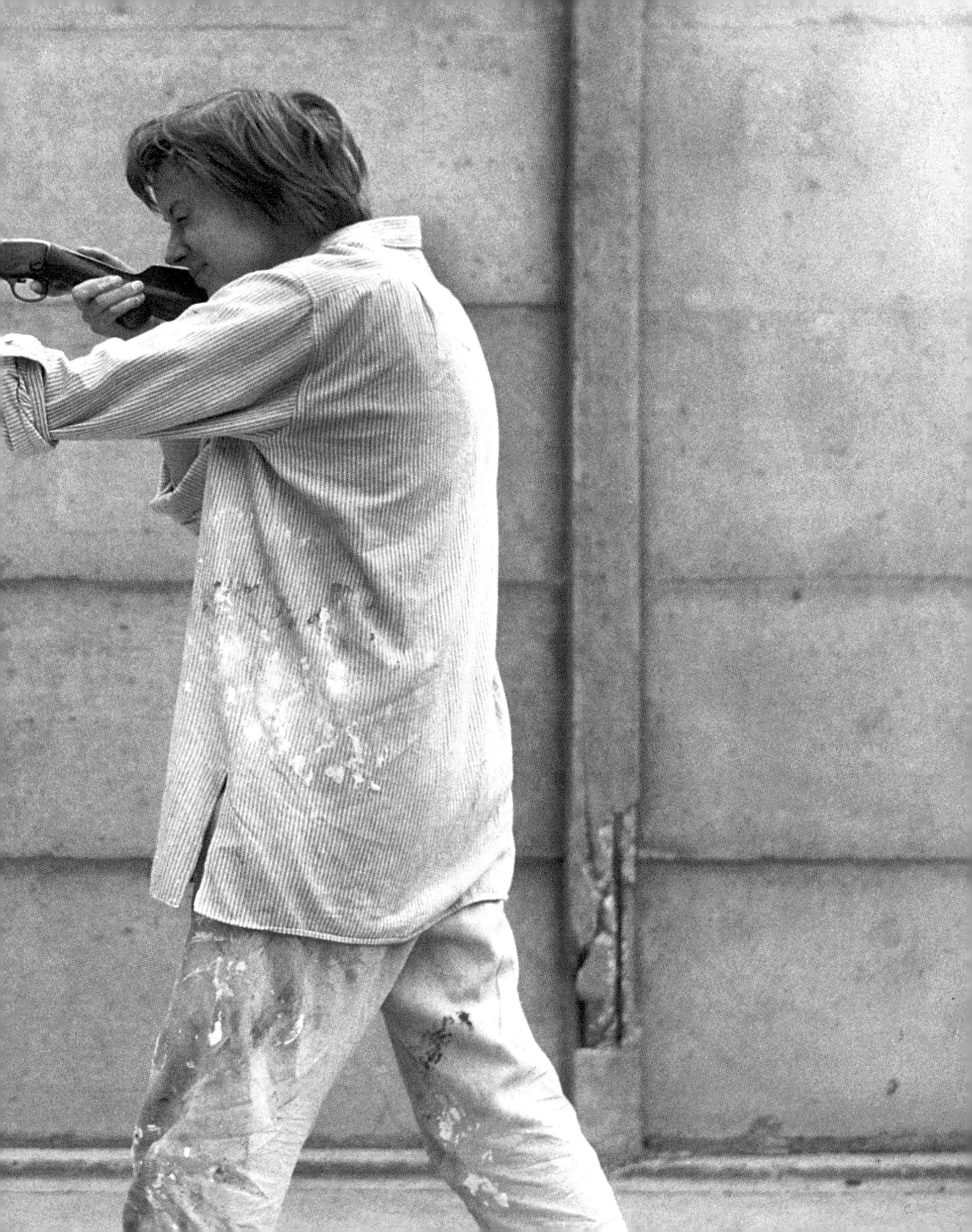

Published on the occasion of *Target Practice: Painting Under Attack 1949–78*
at the Seattle Art Museum, June 25–September 7, 2009.

The exhibition was organized by the Seattle Art Museum. Generous support is provided by Jon & Mary
Shirley, the Seattle Mayor's Office of Arts and Cultural Affairs, The Paul G. Allen Family Foundation,
The Seattle Foundation, and the National Endowment for the Arts.

Every effort has been made to locate the copyright holders for the images used in this book.
We apologize for any omissions.

Dimensions for the works included in the exhibition are listed in the checklist on pages 146–49.

Exhibition Curator: Michael Darling
Senior Manager Exhibitions/Curatorial Publications: Zora Hutlova Foy
Exhibitions and Publications Coordinator: Heather Pederson
Copy editor: Michelle Piranio
Proofreader: Sharon Rose Vonasch
Book designer: Derek Barnett for Information Office
Printing: Capital Offset Company Inc.

Published by Seattle Art Museum
1300 First Avenue, Seattle, WA 98101
www.seattleartmuseum.org

Cover: Harry Shunk, *Niki de Saint Phalle shooting at Old Master with a .22 rifle, Impasse Rousin,
June 15, 1961*, 1961 (detail). Gelatin silver print, 8 x 10 in. (20.3 x 25.4 cm). Collection Niki Charitable
Art Foundation, California, USA.

Library of Congress Cataloging-in-Publication Data

Target practice : painting under attack, 1949–78 / edited by Michael Darling.
   p. cm.
Published on the occasion of an exhibition held at the Seattle Art Museum, June 25–Sept. 7, 2009.
Includes bibliographical references.
ISBN 978-0-932216-64-9 (alk. paper)
1. Painting, Modern—20th century—Themes, motives—Exhibitions.
   I. Darling, Michael. II. Seattle Art Museum. III. Title: Painting under attack, 1949–78.
ND195.T37 2009
759.06'074797772—dc22
                                        009008422

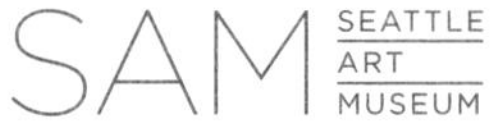

Edited by Michael Darling

Target Practice: Painting Under Attack 1949–78

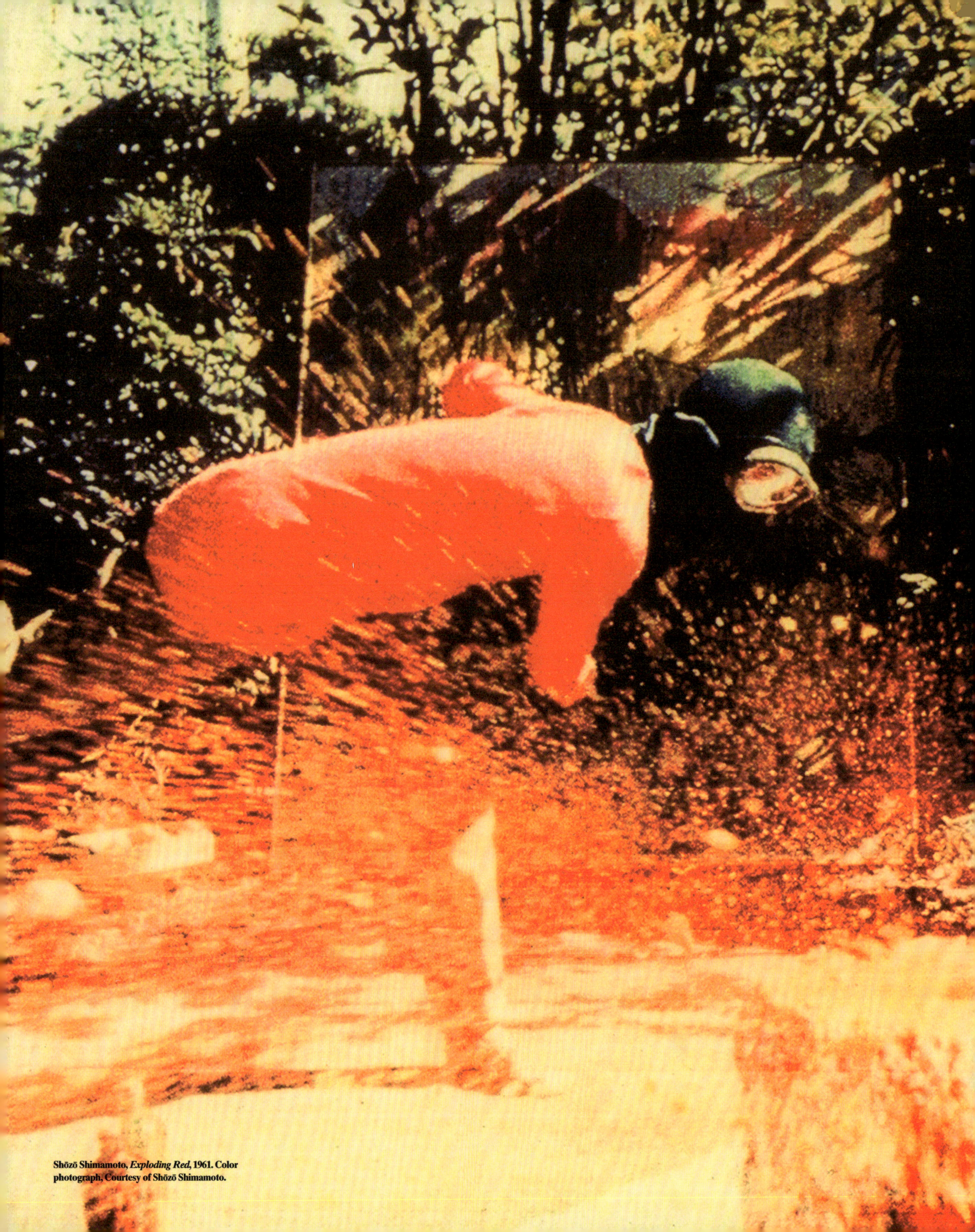

Shōzō Shimamoto, *Exploding Red*, 1961. Color photograph. Courtesy of Shōzō Shimamoto.

Contents

Ugo Mulas, *Lucio Fontana*, 1964. Gelatin silver print. Archivio Ugo Mulas, Milan.

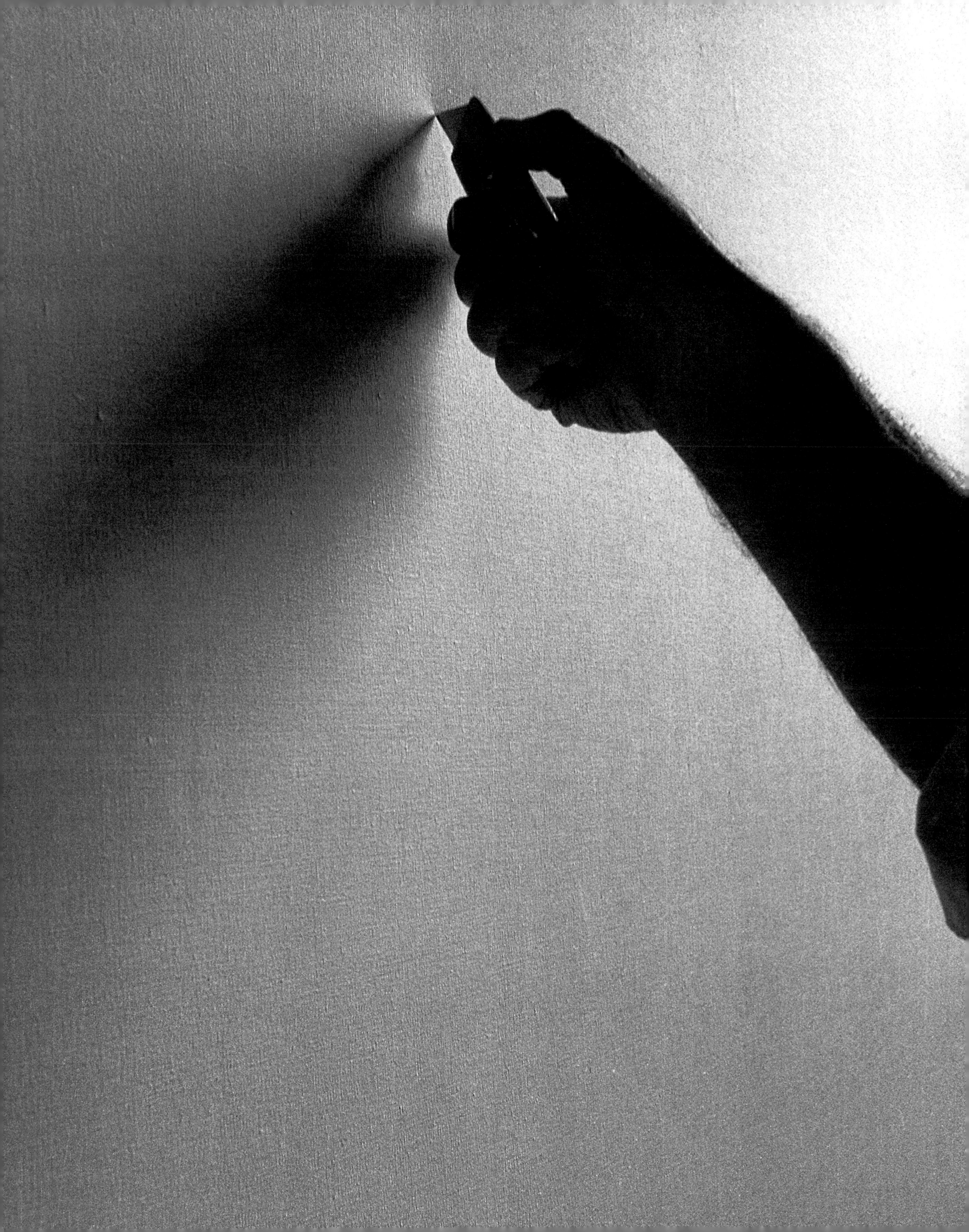

Foreword

The contemporary art world moves with such fervor and pace that it is often difficult, even for those thoroughly immersed in it, to keep up. New trends pop up with increasing speed, while rankings of artist influence bob up and down constantly in response to what are deemed the pressing issues of our day. Such is a history that is still relatively new and has yet to thoroughly sort itself out with the passage of time and the accumulation of critical distance. Though consensus is still forming, certain artists such as Lucio Fontana, Jasper Johns, Roy Lichtenstein, Robert Rauschenberg, and Andy Warhol have come to be regarded as immovable stalwarts of recent art history. As such, however, it is easy to forget just how radical their work must have appeared in that period, and we must remind ourselves of the milieus from which they emerged in order to keep their achievements in focus. *Target Practice: Painting Under Attack 1949–78* offers Seattle audiences a glimpse of a rambunctious and important period during which no-holds-barred critiques of painting were being launched all across the globe. The exhibition brings together well-known and little-recognized artists from the United States, Germany, France, Italy, Austria, Poland, Brazil, Japan, Canada, Belgium, Denmark, and Korea to re-create the iconoclastic energy of those decades, when painting had found itself at the center of an international artistic crisis that demanded to be addressed.

The exhibition was conceived by Michael Darling, the Jon and Mary Shirley Curator of Modern and Contemporary Art at the Seattle Art Museum, who is immensely thoughtful and perceptive about the art of our time and its precedents. Michael deserves our highest praise for the caliber of this exhibition and publication. The project has special relevance in a city that is rich with postwar painting. The museum's collection, built up over the years by numerous generous gifts from our unparalleled collecting community, teems with top-flight examples by the masters of American art after 1945, including Arshile Gorky, Jackson Pollock, Willem de Kooning, Mark Rothko, and Franz Kline (to name only a few), not to mention their successors Johns, Lichtenstein, Rauschenberg, and Warhol. But many of the Asian, European, and South American peers of these artists have rarely been shown in Seattle, and *Target Practice* aims to present the exciting fomentation of ideas and practices during this period with a wide-angle view.

Michael has been supported throughout the planning process by the museum's highly professional staff. We thank each and every staff member for their commitment and efforts. We are grateful for the generous support of this project by Jon and Mary Shirley, who stepped forward with a lead gift to ensure its realization To that were added other instrumental gifts by the Seattle Mayor's Office of Arts and Cultural Affairs, The Paul G. Allen Family Foundation, the Seattle Foundation, and the National Endowment for the Arts.

It is hoped that this powerful and tightly focused exhibition, and its thoughtful and engaging publication, will enable Seattle audiences to gain new insights into a field that can be perplexing at times, but also immensely rewarding. Contemporary art is the art of our time, and the Seattle Art Museum's core mission is to connect art to life. Efforts such as *Target Practice* are crucial if we are to fulfill our responsibilities to our audiences in this city, the broader region, and beyond.

Mimi Gardner Gates
Illsley Ball Nordstrom Director

Ugo Mulas, *Lucio Fontana*, 1964. Gelatin silver print. Archivio Ugo Mulas, Milan.

Acknowledgments

For an exhibition as wide-ranging and ambitious as *Target Practice: Painting Under Attack 1949–78*, it is no surprise that a host of friends, advisers, and colleagues helped to bring it into being. I owe its genesis to the encouragement and commitment of Seattle Art Museum director Mimi Gates and deputy director for art Chiyo Ishikawa, who immediately embraced my idea for the exhibition upon my arrival at SAM in 2006. Jon and Mary Shirley's crucial early contribution gave us the momentum to go forward, and the further support of deputy director Maryann Jordan and chief financial officer Bob Cundall ensured its realization. It is a show that builds on the great collection of postwar painting at SAM, and also within the extensive collections in Seattle, allowing us to revisit the radicality of many of these works, but also to see them alongside major works by international peers, both known and underrecognized, that have never been shown in Seattle before.

The courage to take on such a topic was surely forged under my former mentor Paul Schimmel, at the Museum of Contemporary Art, Los Angeles, who encouraged this very type of broad historical survey among his curators and led by example with exhibitions such as *Out of Actions: Between Performance and the Object, 1949–1979*, a clear touchstone for this project, even though its focus is more specifically on a teleology of painting. As I built the framework of the exhibition, I was helped by numerous people who introduced me to artists and specific artworks that would amplify and enrich my checklist. Included in this group of advisers are: Nicholas Baume, Tiffany Bell, Ian Berry, Janet Bishop, Stefania Bortolami, Karen Carson, Aimee Chang, Michael Clifton, Stuart Comer, Francesco Conz, Claudia Defendi, Maddalena Disch, Anne Ellegood, Rosamund Felsen, Ariane Pereira de Figueiredo, Regina Fiorito, Piero Golia, Nicolas Guagnini, Bruce Guenther, Geoffrey Hendricks, Jon Hendricks, Paulo Herkenhoff, Brad Hudson, Lyn Katsumoto, Kasper Koenig, Steven Leiber, Andrea Mardegan, Midori Matsui, David Moos, Lars Nittve, Cesar Oiticica, Barbara Piowarska, Andrzej Przywara, Ricardo Rego, Barry Rosen, Mary Sabbatino, Kim Schoenstadt, Allan Schwartzman, Noriko Shinohara, Katy Siegel, Tom Solomon, Sarah Taggart, and Philippe Vergne. Editorial guidance in the early stages of the book was offered by Russell Ferguson, Elizabeth Mangini, Lisa Gabrielle Mark, Christine Mehring, Scott Rothkopf, Reid Shier, and later perfected under the watchful eye of editor Michelle Piranio, who is directly responsible for the increased clarity of all our texts. I also had the great fortune of having research help from Fionn Meade, who was able to track down articles and essays that greatly informed my writings and helped to define the arguments of the exhibition. Marisa C. Sanchez took on the task of locating some of the more obscure loans and oversaw the creation of loan forms. Monica Giudici was indispensable in the early stages of the book production by corresponding with artists and gathering images, and Heather Pederson ably picked up where Monica left off to bring the contents of the book to fruition with extraordinary diligence and good cheer. They all worked under the guidance of the indefatigable Zora Hutlova Foy, who looked after all practical aspects of the exhibition's development, including the catalogue. I am pleased that we were able to commission insightful writings by three promising young scholars of contemporary art—Graham Bader, Elizabeth Mangini, and Mika Yoshitake; their contributions add new perspectives to the works on view. I am grateful to Derek Barnett for his thoughtful and sensitive design of the catalogue, especially because the publication will allow the project to reach audiences beyond the single exhibition venue of Seattle.

In this day and age when artworks by recognized contemporary masters have achieved great value and rarity, I am especially humbled by the generosity of the many lenders who have graciously shared their treasures with us on this occasion. They include: Diane L. Ackerman and Kelly L. Ackerman; Archivio Conz; Archivio Ugo Mulas; Ashiya City Museum of Art & History; John Baldessari; Iain Baxter; Lynda Benglis; Bortolami Gallery; Jeffrey and Susan Brotman; Daniel Buren; Ivan Cardoso; Cheim & Read; Corkin Gallery; Jim Dine, Barney A. Ebsworth; Electronic Arts Intermix; Fondazione Lucio Fontana; Gagosian Gallery; Howard Greenberg Gallery; Guild Hall Museum; Hauser & Wirth; Hessischer Rundfunk; Hirshhorn Museum and Sculpture Garden; Richard Jackson; Jasper Johns; Anton Kern Gallery; Yves Klein Archives; Pamela and Richard Kramlich; KwieKulik; Yayoi Kusama; James and Christina Lockwood; Los Angeles County Museum of Art; Estate of Lee Lozano; Paul McCarthy; Hirata Minoru; Victoria Miro Gallery; Mott-Warsh Collection; Musée d'Art Moderne et Contemporain de Strasbourg; Museum of Contemporary Art, Los Angeles; Museum of Contemporary Art, San Diego; Museum of Contemporary Art, Tokyo; Museum of Modern Art, New York; Niki Charitable Art Foundation; Cesar and Claudio Oiticica Collection; Yoko Ono; Ota Fine Arts; Pace Wildenstein; Nam June Paik Art Center; Portland Art Museum; Projeto Lygia Pape; The Rachofsky Collection; Regen Projects; San Francisco Museum of Modern Art; Shōzō Shimamoto; Gilbert and Lila Silverman Fluxus Collection; Charles Simonyi; Sragow Gallery; Tate Modern; Titze Collection; Vancouver Art Gallery; Walker Art Center; Lawrence Weiner; Whitney Museum of American Art; Merrill Wright; Virginia and Bagley Wright; and others who wish to remain anonymous. It goes without saying that the lending of artworks by individuals and institutions is crucial to the development of projects like this, and we hope the resulting scholarship is worth the sacrifice.

The beauty of the installation is owed to the expertise of the SAM staff, headed up by Michael McCafferty and also including Jamie Andrews, Charles Friedman, Ken Leback, Chris Manojlovic, Paul Martinez, and Dennis Meyer. Registrarial oversight by Phil Stoiber and Lauren Mellon has been crucial, and the effective marketing campaign has been ably led by Matthew Renton and his team. The ever difficult task of fundraising has been spearheaded by Jennifer Aydelott, Laura Hopkins, Carol Mabbott, and Linda Morrison, which resulted in important private, corporate, and foundation support. The Seattle Art Museum has a tremendous staff who all helped in countless ways both large and small to make this exhibition such a success, and for them and the great environment they create on a daily basis for presenting art I am thankful.

Michael Darling
The Jon and Mary Shirley Curator of Modern and Contemporary Art

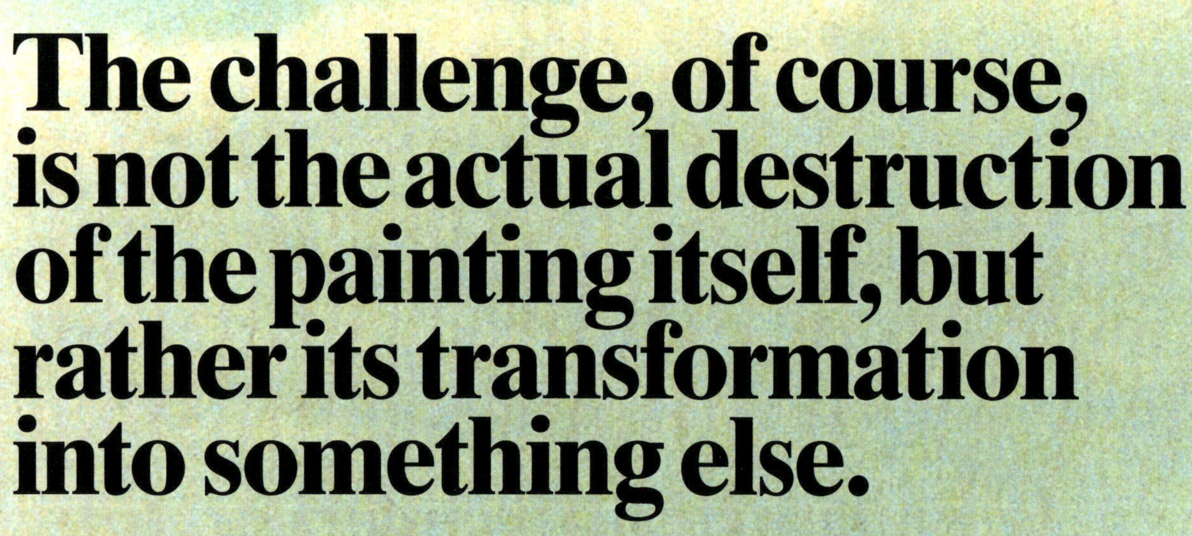

The challenge, of course, is not the actual destruction of the painting itself, but rather its transformation into something else.

—Hélio Oiticica

Still from Ivan Cardoso, *H.O.*, 1979. Film transferred to DVD. Courtesy of Ivan Cardoso.

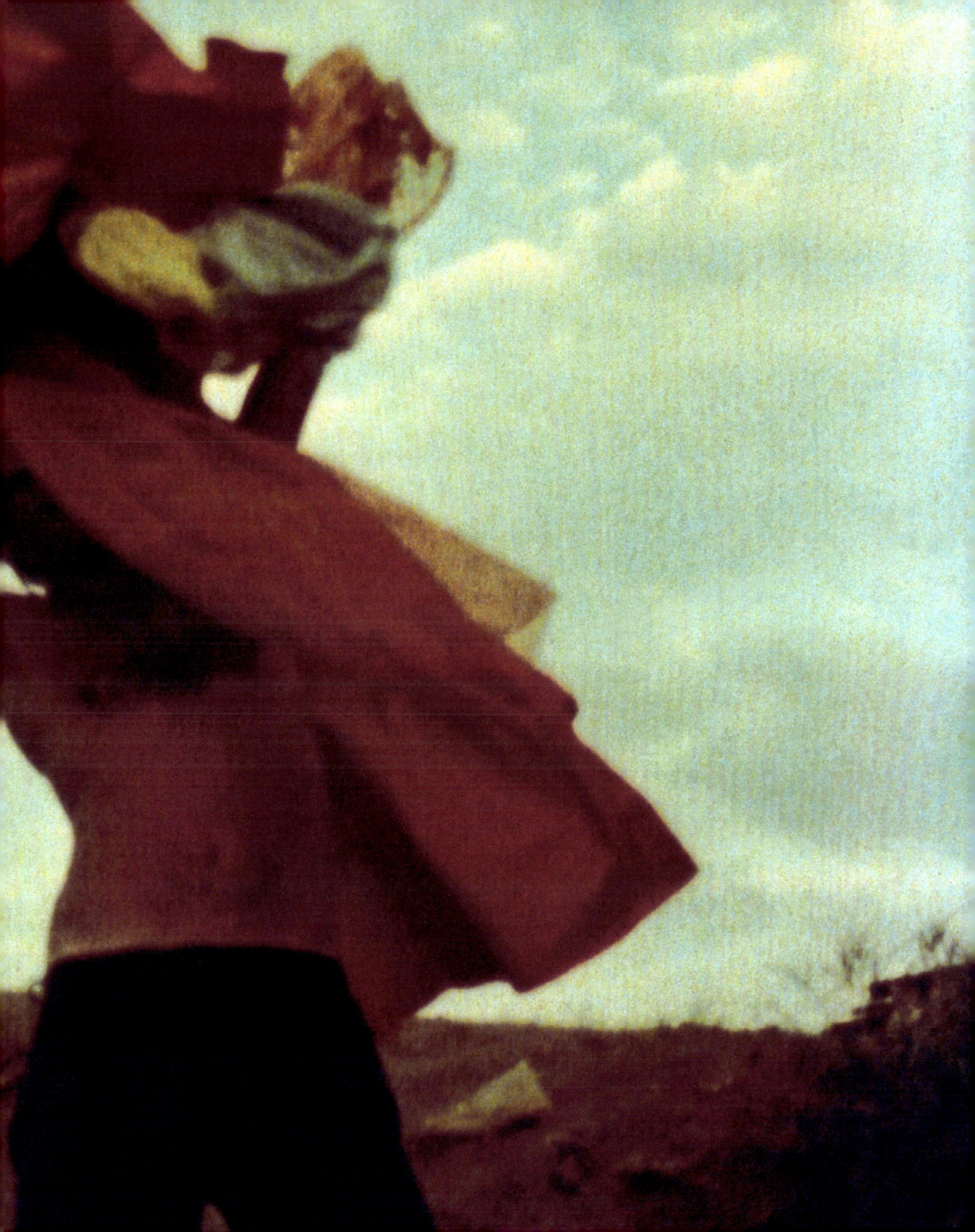

Target Practice:
Painting Under Atta[ck]

Michael Darling

ck 1949–78

The practice of putting paint on canvas is arguably the most hallowed of artistic traditions. Miles and miles of museum walls are devoted to it, millions of pages of text have been written about it, billions of dollars have been spent collecting it, and countless artists over the years have chosen it as their preferred means of expression. Any artist today who wields a brush must contend with the highly stratified history— and burden—of a tradition that has piled up to form a massive impasto of stroke and counterstroke, leading many artists over the centuries to foment revolutions in order to shake up convention and start anew. Looking back over just the past two hundred years, movements and trends as far-reaching as Romanticism, Realism, Impressionism, Fauvism, Post-Impressionism, Cubism, Futurism, Constructivism, Dadaism, Surrealism, Abstract Expressionism, Art Informel, Arte Povera, conceptualism, postmodernism, and many others have had at their core a dissatisfaction with the status quo of painting and a desire to find a way out of the comfort zone of acceptability. Many have been about regeneration and redirection; a few— such as Constructivism in the hands of Kazimir Malevich, or Dadaism in the work of Marcel Duchamp—have portended an end to painting that never quite came to pass, as detailed in the essay herein by Graham Bader. Today, painting is still alive and well, but just after the end of World War II a series of convulsions began that revealed that artists across continents had reached a collective frustration with the medium's limitations, formats, and processes. Seeking to steer a new course, they would bring painting the closest it had ever come to extinction.

In this work, which sprang up and built momentum in Europe, Asia, South America, and North America and cut across movements as diverse as Art Informel, Pop, Minimalism, Arte Povera, Neo-Concretism, and conceptualism, a new sort of violence was directed toward wall-mounted, rectangular sheets of fabric onto which paint was applied with a brush. Though groundwork had been laid by previous generations to develop and hone an important criticality around the making of paintings, which led to such breakthroughs as Jackson Pollock's nonhierarchical, allover skeins made on the floor rather than on an easel, there remained a basic adherence to

certain rules, one of which was that the surface remained whole and intact. It is the crossing of that threshold, and the newfound freedom that such a step opened up, that this exhibition and book seek to trace. *Target Practice: Painting Under Attack 1949–78* takes as its starting point the fateful year that Lucio Fontana punctured the taut surface of the support, calling stark attention to the nagging illusionism of painting within a windowlike frame.[1]

Fontana's first *Concetto spaziale* (Spatial Concept) pieces in 1949 introduced a new realism in painting that treated the surface— in this case paper mounted to canvas—as the vulnerable material it is, not as a sacrosanct veil on which the genius of the artist's hand is recorded. Through the simple yet intrinsically violent gesture of poking holes (*buchi*) through the support, he brought the space behind the painting into play, reasserting painting as an object, not just an image. After spending the war years in his native Argentina, Fontana returned to Italy in 1947. The stark realism offered in the *Buchi* had its counterpart in the war-torn physical environment he found there and in the shattered veneer of civilization that accompanies the destruction of buildings. Furthermore, the "bodily harm" done to painting in these works— Fontana wrote in 1948 that "art is eternal but not immortal"[2]—resonates with longstanding techniques for shaking up spiritual reverie: one need only think of the story of Doubting Thomas touching the wound of Christ to believe he is a man or Northern Renaissance depictions of extreme suffering on the cross that were meant to inspire a physical empathy toward Christ's

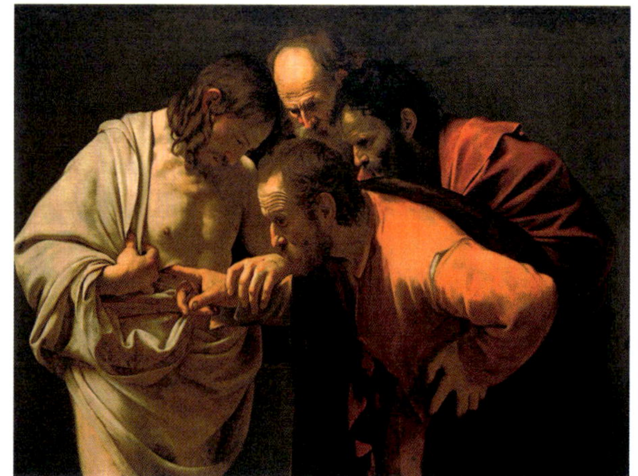

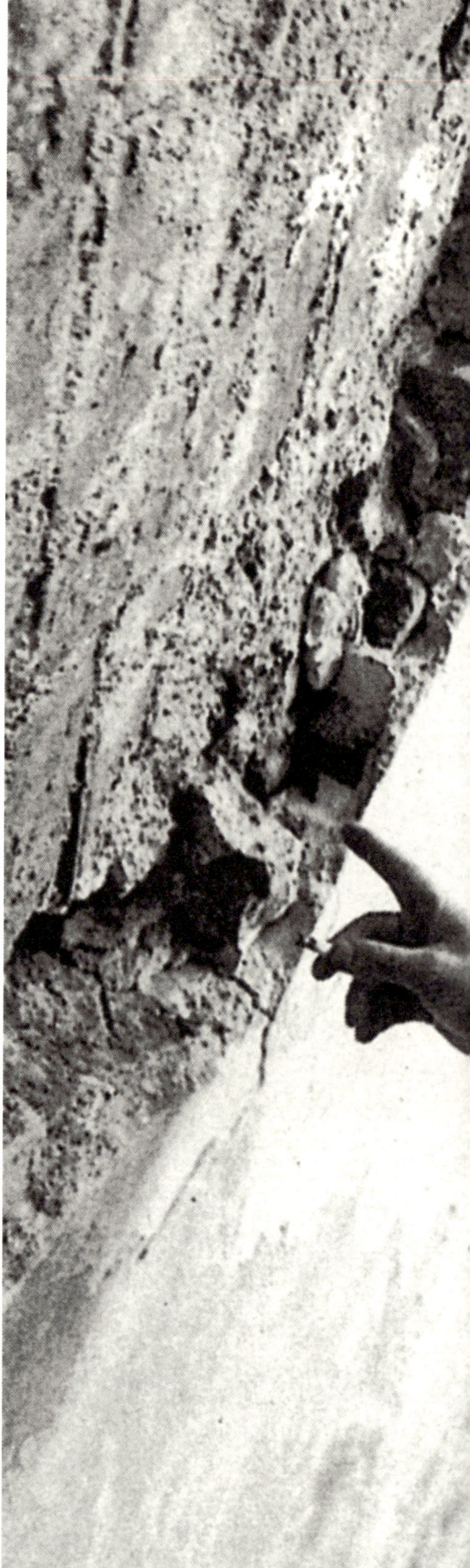

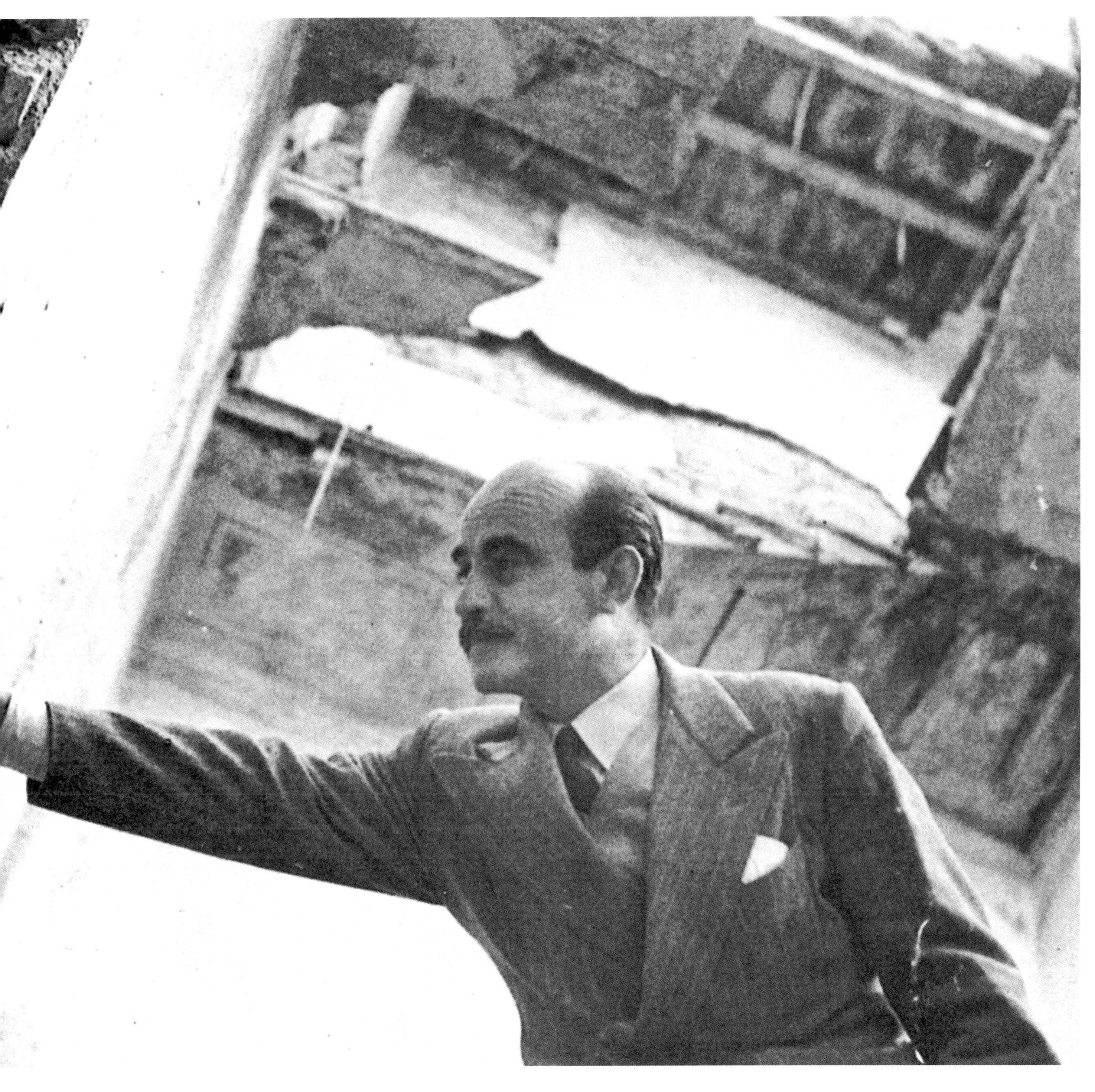

plight and sacrifice. Planting seeds of doubt, and trying to answer them with facts, seemed to have been exactly on Fontana's mind around the time he made his first *Buchi.* As he stated in 1949:

> For centuries artists have followed the techniques of painting, for the last few months a group of artists have conceived a new evolution of art, spatial art, I assure you that on the moon we won't be doing painting, we'll be doing spatial art.… The spatial environment gives me the exact sensation of a discovery, now I remain in terrible doubt.[3]

The artists Fontana mentions were a group with whom he coauthored three manifestos on "Spatialism," which certainly paved the way for his critical approach toward painting. In the second manifesto, published in March 1948, Fontana and his cohorts were already calling to free painting "from its frame," and this salvo would be the first of many that riddled cherished notions of painting, opening it up to rigorous investigation and promoting doubt and skepticism.[4] To doubt painting means to move away from belief in it, to dismiss it as something ideal and sacred. Likewise, by zeroing in on the surface of the canvas, Fontana began a sequence of enunciations that allowed artists to systematically dismantle the component parts of painting: medium, gesture, composition, support, orientation, and presence. Elizabeth Mangini elsewhere in this volume delves deeper into this development.

A fascinating aspect of this story is that even though Fontana may have taken the first step, he was not alone, and other artists in other parts of the world were moving simultaneously toward similar conclusions, as if guided by a shared zeitgeist. In another war-torn country, where reality came crashing down in the form of an atom bomb, the Japanese artist Shōzō Shimamoto, surely without prior knowledge of Fontana's activities, made similarly outrageous perforations to a paper-based, rectangular support. With the same dispassionate skepticism, coming out of a milieu of like-minded artists who eschewed romantic attachments to the making of art by generically titling their output *Work*, he made a series of punctured paintings in about 1950. When seen together

with an amazing sequence of iconoclastic and radical gestures that came out of Japan's Gutai Art Association, of which he was a member, Shimamoto's canvases are not anomalous. But when viewed in the context of Fontana's similar gestures half a world away, they represent an uncanny coincidence that suggests a sort of art-historical destiny. As Alexandra Munroe has written: "On a human level, World War II was a defeat for everyone. Perhaps, the Japanese were the first to accept the price of this defeat, which [architect] Isozaki Arata has called 'the death of history.' If that is so, Japanese artists have been in a special position to respond to the meaning of creation and destruction."[5] As Mika Yoshitake discusses in her essay, the Gutai artists borrowed every conceivable method for defiling art, and particularly painting, including ripping, punching, burning,

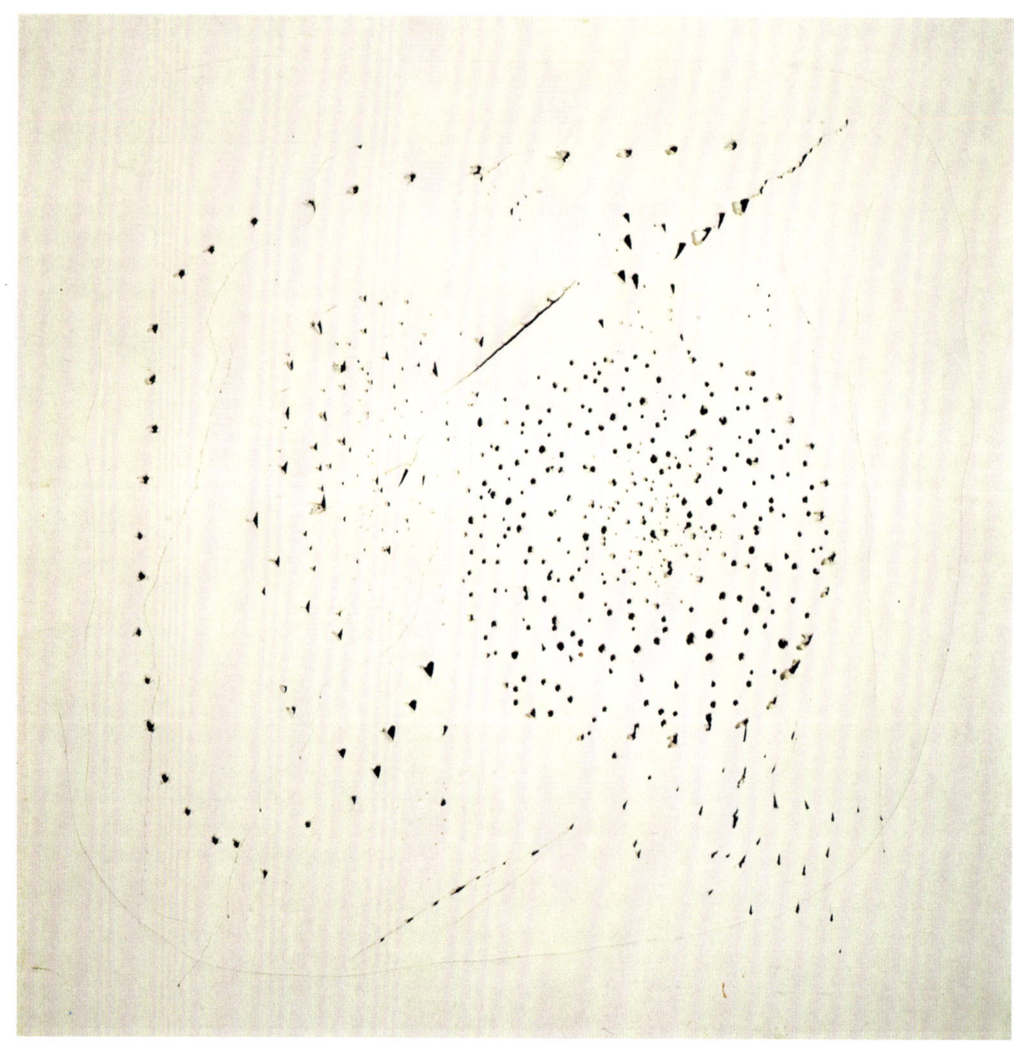

Page 18: Michelangelo Merisi da Caravaggio, *Doubting Thomas*, 1602–4. Oil on canvas, 57½ x 42 in. (146 x 107 cm). Prussian Palaces and Gardens Foundation, Berlin-Brandenburg. (catalogue only)

Page 19: Lucio Fontana, Milan, 1947. Fondazione Lucio Fontana, Milan. (catalogue only)

Above: Lucio Fontana, *Concetto spaziale (C.49B2)*, 1949. White paper mounted on canvas. Fondazione Lucio Fontana, Milan.

Opposite: Shōzō Shimamoto, *Work (Holes)*, ca. 1950. Paint and pencil on newspaper. Museum of Contemporary Art, Tokyo.

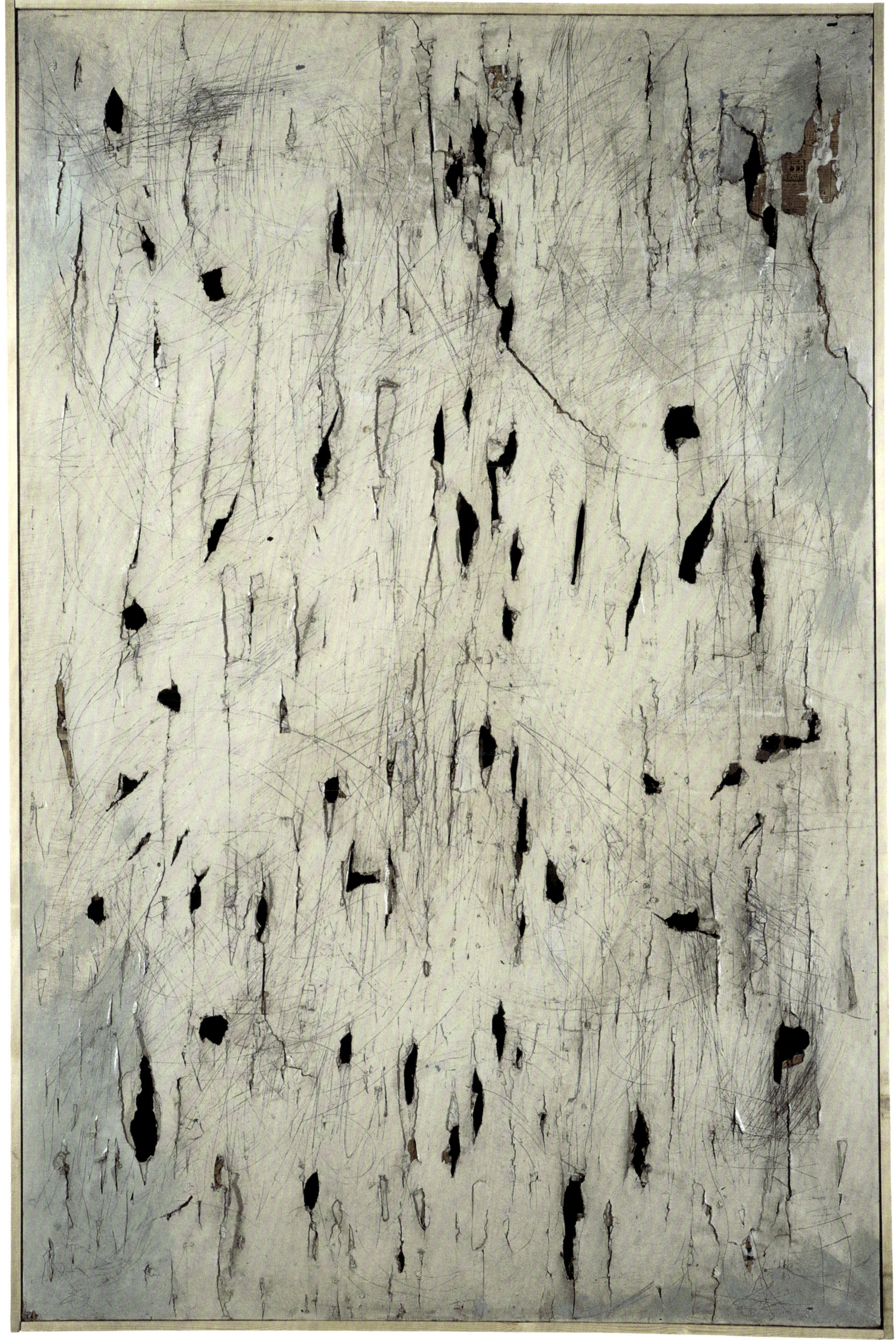

smashing, and shooting. Similar activities were occurring in studios and galleries around the world, suggesting a breaking point for painting. *Target Practice* looks at these varied approaches by category rather than by geography or chronology in order to emphasize just how widespread and exhaustive this thorough shake-up of painting was during the almost thirty-year period covered by the exhibition.

Literal and Figurative Targets

When looking at the pocked, violated surfaces of Fontana's and Shimamoto's works, which suggest the same residue of violence that a bullet-ridden wall or a shredded target would, one cannot help but think of gunfire. Some of Fontana's *Concetto spaziale* paintings even have circular patterns that are evocative of targets, and when viewed next to works by younger peers such as Jasper Johns and Niki de Saint Phalle that allude more directly to shooting, their implicit aggression is heightened. Johns's famous *Target* paintings have often been discussed as readymade images that belong in the same category as his flags and numbers, but the artist's choice of this particular motif carries with it a tremendous symbolism and directness; as fellow artist Robert Morris has retrospectively said of Johns's target paintings: "Looking is conflated with a .30-caliber weapon."[6] Describing this motif (and others) further in militaristic terms, Morris writes: "Half a century ago a recently discharged, young army veteran began his cultural assaults. In a decade-long campaign he raised the *Flag*, dared them to fire at his *Target*, *Numbered* the prisoners taken *O through 9, Mapped* out a strategy, and *Dived* from a height heretofore not attempted."[7] Johns had indeed served in the army from May 1951 to May 1953, an experience that may have provided an unconscious prompt for his series of *Target* paintings; but these works also fit more broadly within the "cultural assaults" that he and other artists were undertaking on painting, assaults that recur strategically and consistently throughout this exhibition.

The target, as a motif, is a culturally accepted cue to fix the gaze and attention, bringing a notion of scrutiny to the gallery experience that arguably did not exist before. Jeffrey Weiss has spoken of Johns's target as "an instrument of vision through deep space" and of such "seeing through space as a form of violation" that focuses the eye on a concentric vortex like no other painting in history.[8] It was appreciated as such from the beginning; a reviewer of Johns's 1958 show at Leo Castelli Gallery, which included several target paintings, described how they "compel your attentiveness,"[9] and the critic Leo Steinberg separately wrote that "the posture of aiming at a Johns target is no less sane than was genuflection before an icon. Because the subject in [his] art has regained real presence."[10] Presence, here, is achieved by making the subject and the object one and the same, denying the separate existence of an "image within a frame" in a way that recalls what Fontana and Shimamoto accomplished when they broke through the support and made the painting participate in real space.

The target, or at least the practice of shooting for the bull's-eye, is also equated with accuracy, a foreign concept for art, but one that Johns himself raised as a pursuit in his early works.[11] Such a notion, which can also be interpreted as a striving for objectivity, corresponds to other preoccupations in his paintings at the time such as measuring (thermometers, rulers, teaspoons) and numbering, creating a strategic foil against the *subjective* aspirations of the Abstract Expressionists. Johns's target, especially as painted in red, yellow, and blue—the traditional colors of targets used on a gun or archery practice range—or in early versions with hinged boxes on top, implies a use value that is anathema to abstract art and alludes to the "domain of the shooting gallery" rather than the art gallery.[12] Despite all of this inference, no shooting actually takes place in canvases by Johns at this time, consistent with his cool remove and conceptual distance. He did fire at a painting by Saint Phalle from around this period, however: a vertical diptych she made in homage to Johns that included a white monochrome target at the top and a gray combine with Johnsian objects such as a coat hanger, a lightbulb, and a paint can at the bottom. In *Tir de Jasper Johns, June 20, 1961*, Saint Phalle took the use value of the target to its logical conclusion, as she did in many other pieces she called *Tirs*, or shooting paintings. Part performance, part bricolage, but with a decidedly destructive bent, the *Tirs* released expressionistic

Right: Jasper Johns, *Target*, 1958. Oil and collage on canvas. Collection of the artist.

Page 24: Niki de Saint Phalle, *Tir neuf trous*, 1964. Paint, plaster, and plastic on plywood. Private collection.

Page 25: Niki de Saint Phalle, *Hors-d'oeuvre (Portrait of My Lover/Portrait of Myself)*, 1960. Paint, plaster, and various objects (dartboard, darts, man's white shirt, buttons, metal objects) on plywood. Collection Niki Charitable Foundation, California, USA.

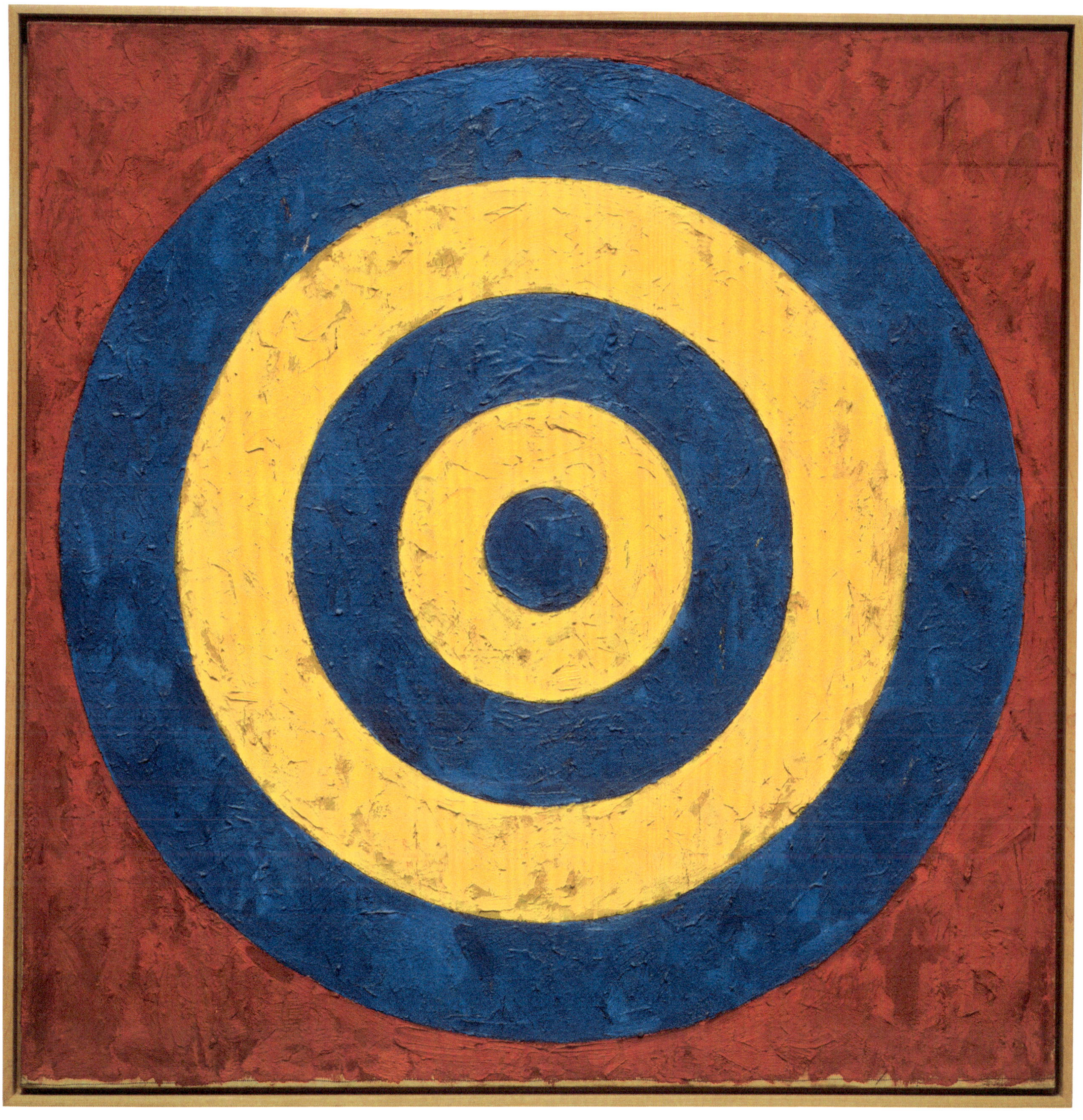

drips from the bullet-inflicted wounds in the canvas, equating the surface once again with the body and mortality and ushering it from idealism to a newfound realism.

Guns are symbols of freedom, violence, and revolution. The French Symbolist poet Charles Baudelaire found himself during the 1848 French uprisings brandishing "a beautiful, gleaming, pristine double-barreled gun and a marvelous equally pristine light brown leather cartridge belt."[13] He later wrote about the experience: "My intoxication of 1848, what kind of intoxication was it at the time? A taste for revenge. The natural enjoyment of demolishing, a literary intoxication, fed by memories of books."[14] More than a hundred years later, Saint Phalle described a similar liberation, this time from the perceived tyranny of the history of painting:

> There is not such a great difference between construction and destruction. What I'm trying to do is to create poetry through destruction and I think it is beautiful. Oil painting is finished, finished now because we are concerned with other problems. We're concerned with death. We're concerned with objects, with the end of things. We want to find a renewal. We want to find beauty in a new way. Making my paintings is life itself. The shooting is magic. The shooting is the moment. It's the only thing that lives because everything is dead afterwards. Nothing lives. Cézanne, Rembrandt, everything will be dead in the end. And the shooting is that one moment in which the miracle happens.[15]

Such creatively destructive artistic acts proliferated in Japan at the time as well, as in Saburō Murakami's *At One Moment Opening Six Holes* (1955; page 115), Shimamoto's *Work (Created by a Cannon)* (1956; page 117), and Kazuo Shiraga's *Cho Gendai Sanbansou (Sanbansou Super Modern)* (1957), which was created by shooting arrows at a canvaslike support. Ushio Shinohara, another of the Gutai artists, also reveled in iconoclastic approaches to painting, as is evident in the now-lost documentation of a 1958 performance in which he attacked a

canvas with both knife and brush while a jazz band was playing, or his equally direct *Boxing Painting Action* (1961–62; page 119), made by pummeling a support with paint-soaked "boxing gloves." Shinohara recounted sticking a knife into the heart of a traditional painting of a nude he had done in art school, saying, "I

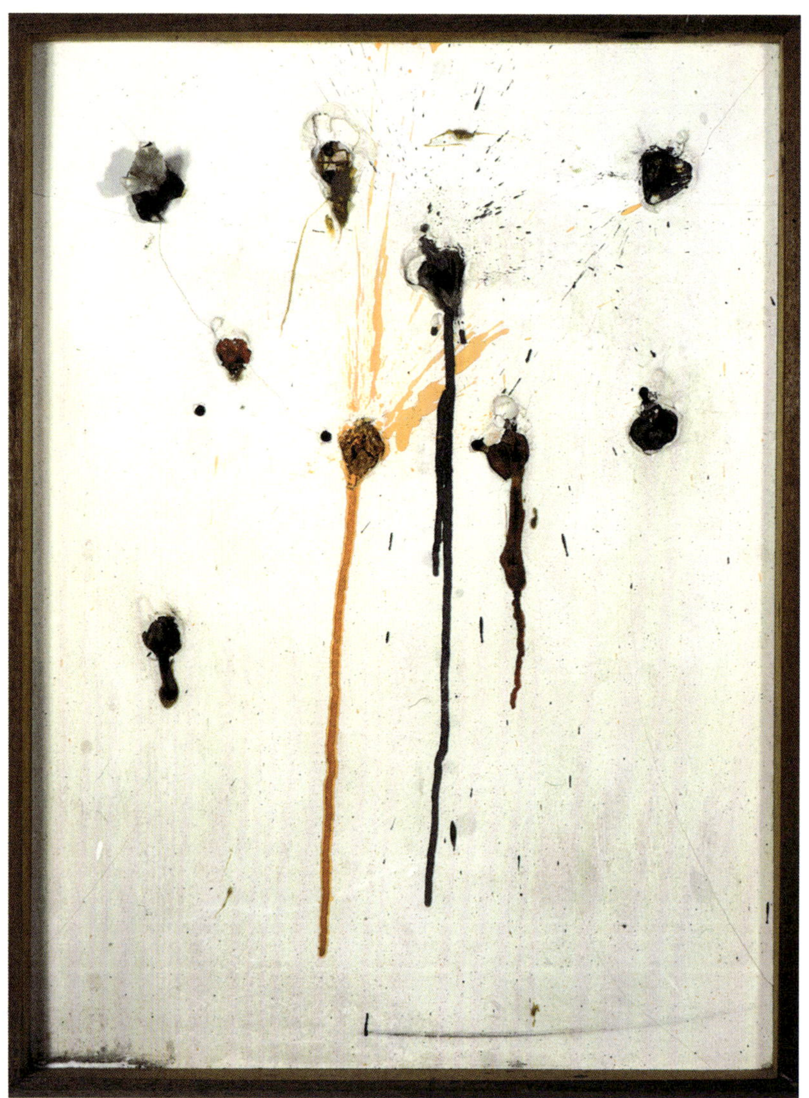

rejected the pursuit of a vague 'eternal beauty' like Mona Lisa, and tried to nail down a modern absoluteness by means of the dagger and the nude."[16] Throughout the period covered by *Target Practice*, artists all over the world found ways to degrade and debase painting, creating a virtual catalogue of actions that could be pursued to bring it in line with real life.

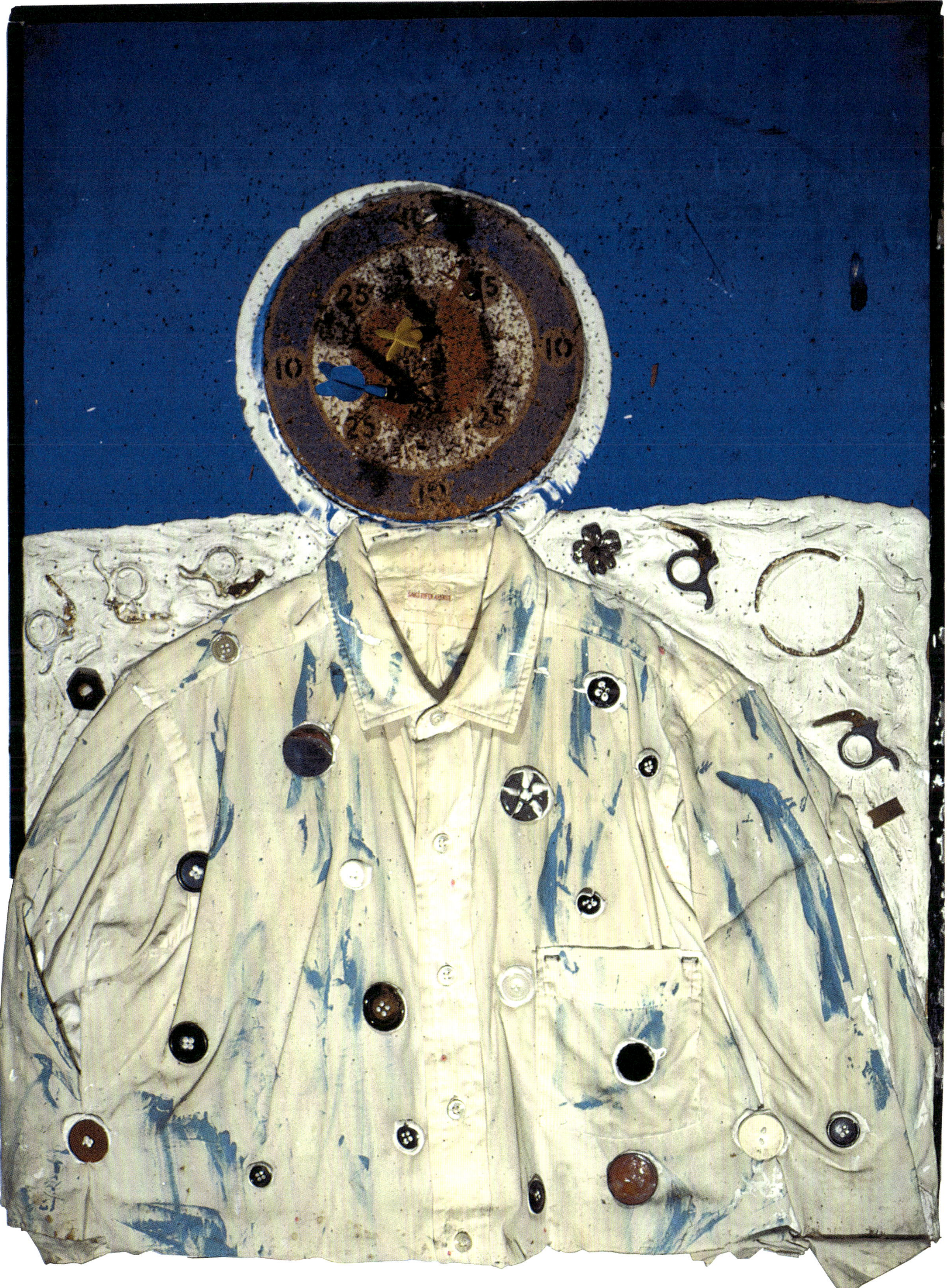
SAKS FIFTH AVENUE

Physical Abuse

One of the most famous acts of painterly patricide occurred not on canvas but on paper. In a directly Oedipal gesture that posited one generation's lionized leader against a young upstart, Robert Rauschenberg in 1953 procured from Willem de Kooning a drawing by the older master that he then methodically erased. While in reality this interchange was undertaken with a high degree of respect, as well as sanctioning by the "victim," it symbolized for both parties a passing of the torch and the beginning of a new way of thinking about painting. A stand-alone gesture within Rauschenberg's oeuvre, *Erased de Kooning Drawing* nevertheless resonated with his similarly iconoclastic series of White Paintings (1951) and Black Paintings (1951–53) in their pursuit of a nihilistic emptiness, followed by the visually richer but no less critical combine paintings, which he started making in 1953–54. The artist did other ones around this time that negated preexisting works, including transforming one of his own early collages (*Should Love Come First?,* from about 1951)—without its owner's knowledge—into a Black Painting (*Untitled [small black painting],* 1953)[17] and using a drawing by Roberto Matta as the ground for his preliminary study for *Minutiae* (1954).[18] But the motivation behind his erasing of the de Kooning and the three-week process required to accomplish it seem much more explicit. *Erased de Kooning Drawing* set in motion a litany of negating actions undertaken by artists during this critical period that, when seen all together, represent an onslaught of physical abuse toward painting. Among the works in *Target Practice* one can witness the results of artists erasing, burning, cutting, nailing into, stepping on, piercing, torturing, perforating, and pissing on paintings, not to mention the shots fired by Johns and Saint Phalle.

Just as the physical realities of postwar Italy provided a plausible context for Fontana's stark realism to have taken root, the impoverishment and sacrifices of the war years can be felt in his countryman Alberto Burri's *Sacco* (Sack) works, begun in 1949, with their use of discarded burlap, sutured tears, and charred surfaces. *Sacco* (1955; page 95) is held together only tentatively as a whole; rent with tears, scorched by burns, and feebly bolstered with cardboard, it is an evocation of the distressed state of painting at the time. Fontana added to his iconoclastic repertoire in 1958 when he used a utility knife to make cuts in his canvases (pages 96, 97). These cuts (*tagli*) were as violent as the *buchi*, as can be seen in the great series of photographs by Ugo Mulas that show the artist slicing open a canvas like a surgeon (pages 9, 11). However, there is also an elegance to the cuts that some have equated with the primacy and uniqueness of the painterly gesture, noting that the cuts are "as unrepeatable as the brushstroke" and "perpetuate the moment as East Asiatic ink painting does."[19] Fontana, however, would hold onto a more radical interpretation of his cuts to the end of his life: "I make a hole in the canvas in order to leave behind me the old pictorial formulae, the painting and the traditional view of art as I escape symbolically, but also materially, from the prison of the flat surface."[20]

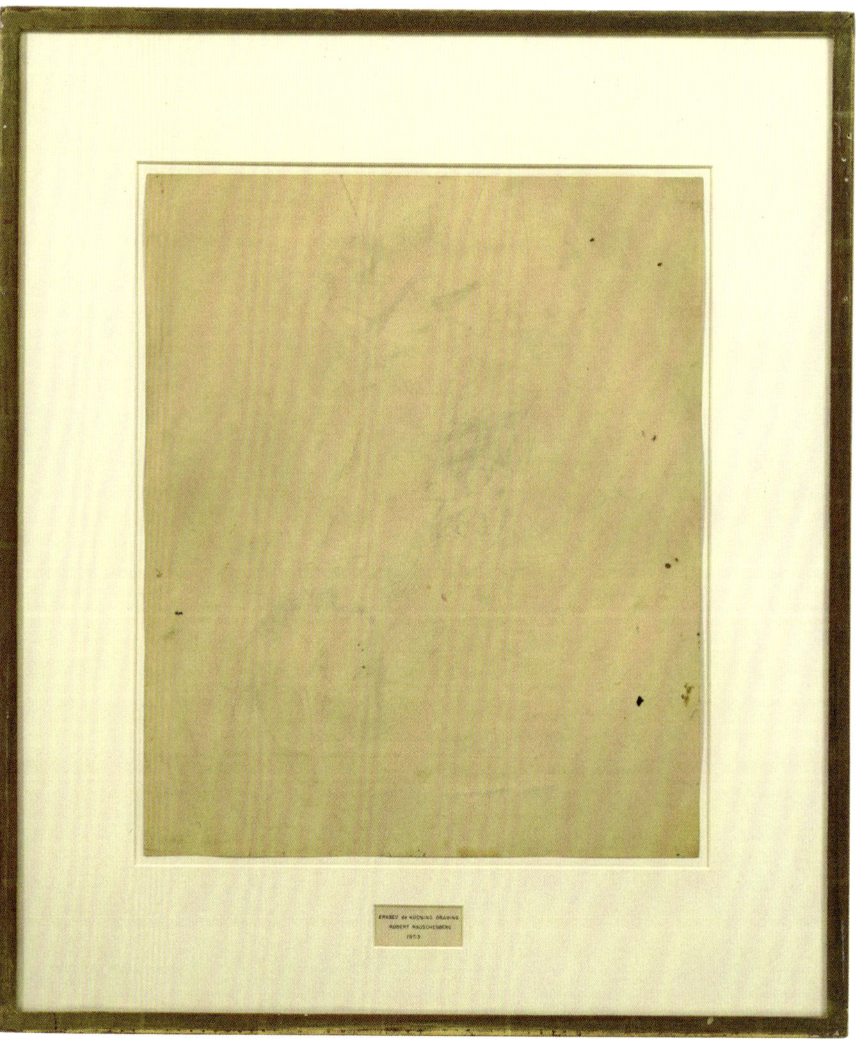

Below: Robert Rauschenberg, *Erased de Kooning Drawing*, 1953. Traces of ink and crayon on paper with mat and label on gold-leaf frame. San Francisco Museum of Modern Art, Purchased through a gift of Phyllis Wattis.

Right: Günter Brus, *Selbstbemalung* (detail), 1964. Nine gelatin silver prints. Archivio Conz, Verona.

Similar motivations (and resulting by-products) propelled other artists from Southern Europe, such as Salvatore Scarpitta, Manolo Millares, and Antoni Tàpies, as well as the German Michael Buthe, but the hotbed for transgressive approaches to painting in the 1960s was Vienna. Bloody, performative actions by Günter Brus, Otto Muehl, Hermann Nitsch, Rudolf Schwarzkogler, and others made gruesome connections between painting and mutilation, often leaving only photographic documentation of these ephemeral activities or, rarely, tortured artifacts such as Muehl's *Untitled* (1963; page 137). In 1961 Muehl began a systematic movement away from conventional painterly rules, attacking the component parts in often violent ways.[21] In this same year, he also created an installation in his Vienna apartment whose title revealed his stance toward painting: *The Overcoming of the Easel Picture by Representation of Its Destruction Process.*[22] Such works are powerful, visceral, but not particularly pretty communicators of painting's complicity in bourgeois culture, and these artists sought to transfer the discontent so prevalent in the streets and universities to the precincts of art. The German Günther Uecker, on the other hand, straddled the line that Fontana often found himself on, between beauty and rebellion. Uecker's signature canvases studded with nails have a certain iconoclastic bearing, alluding to crucifixion or perhaps the story of Saint Sebastian in a manner similar to Fontana's riddled surfaces, but they are also possessed of a graceful kineticism as the fields of nails swell and move according to the viewer's position

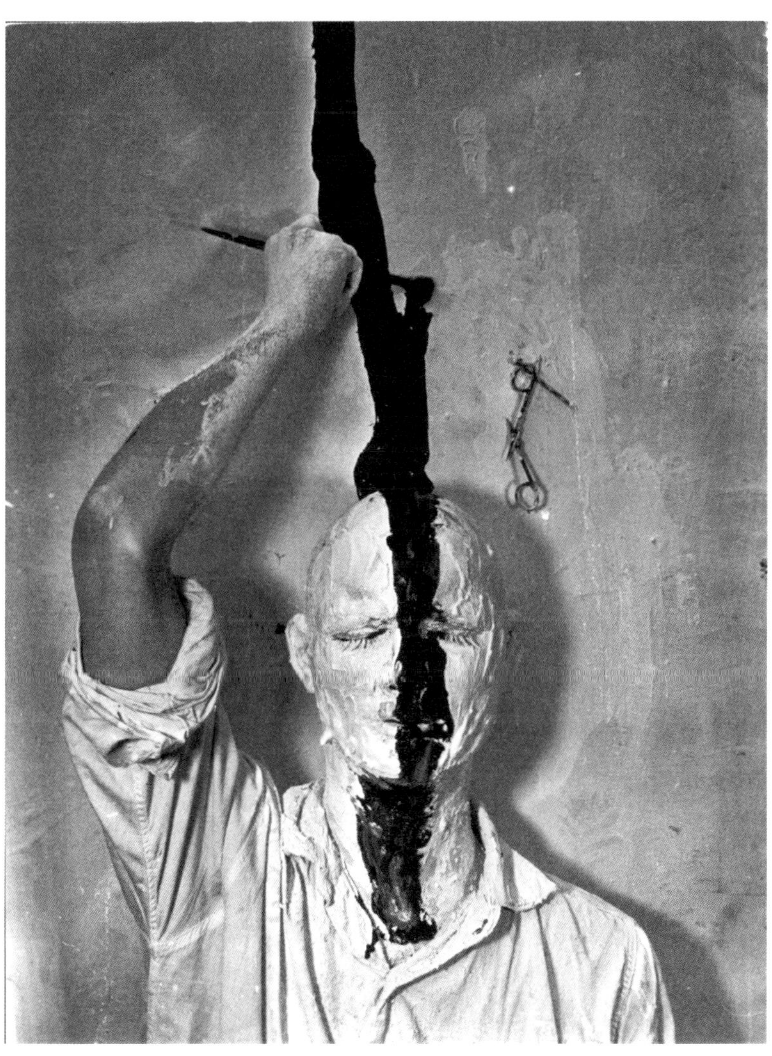

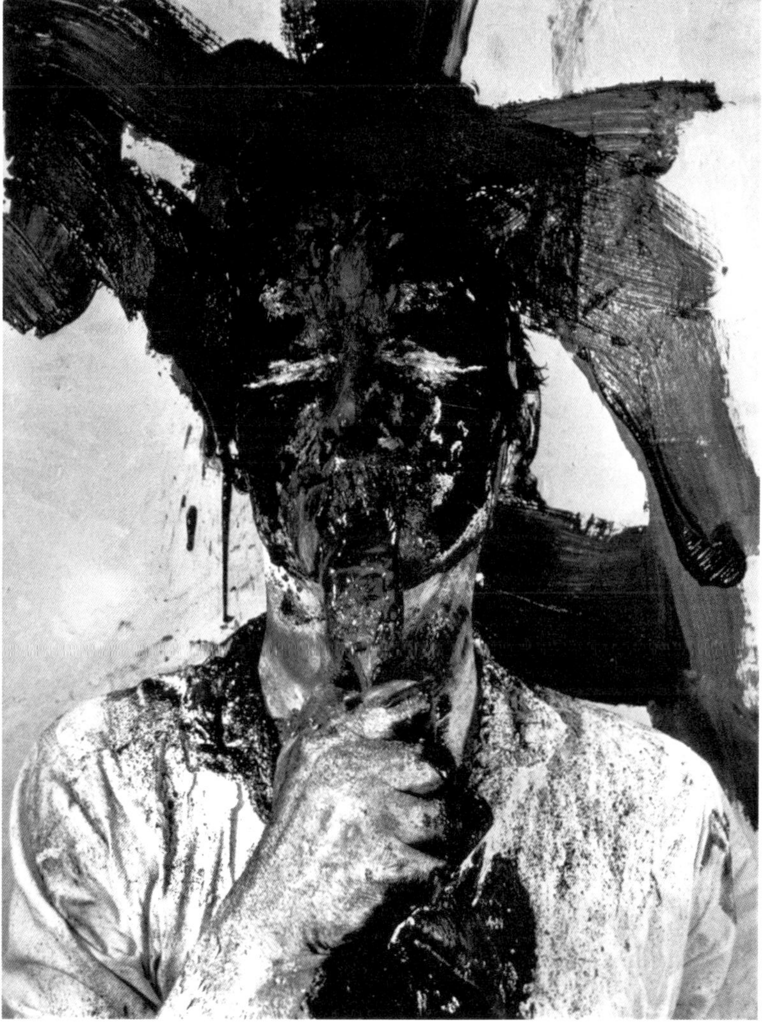

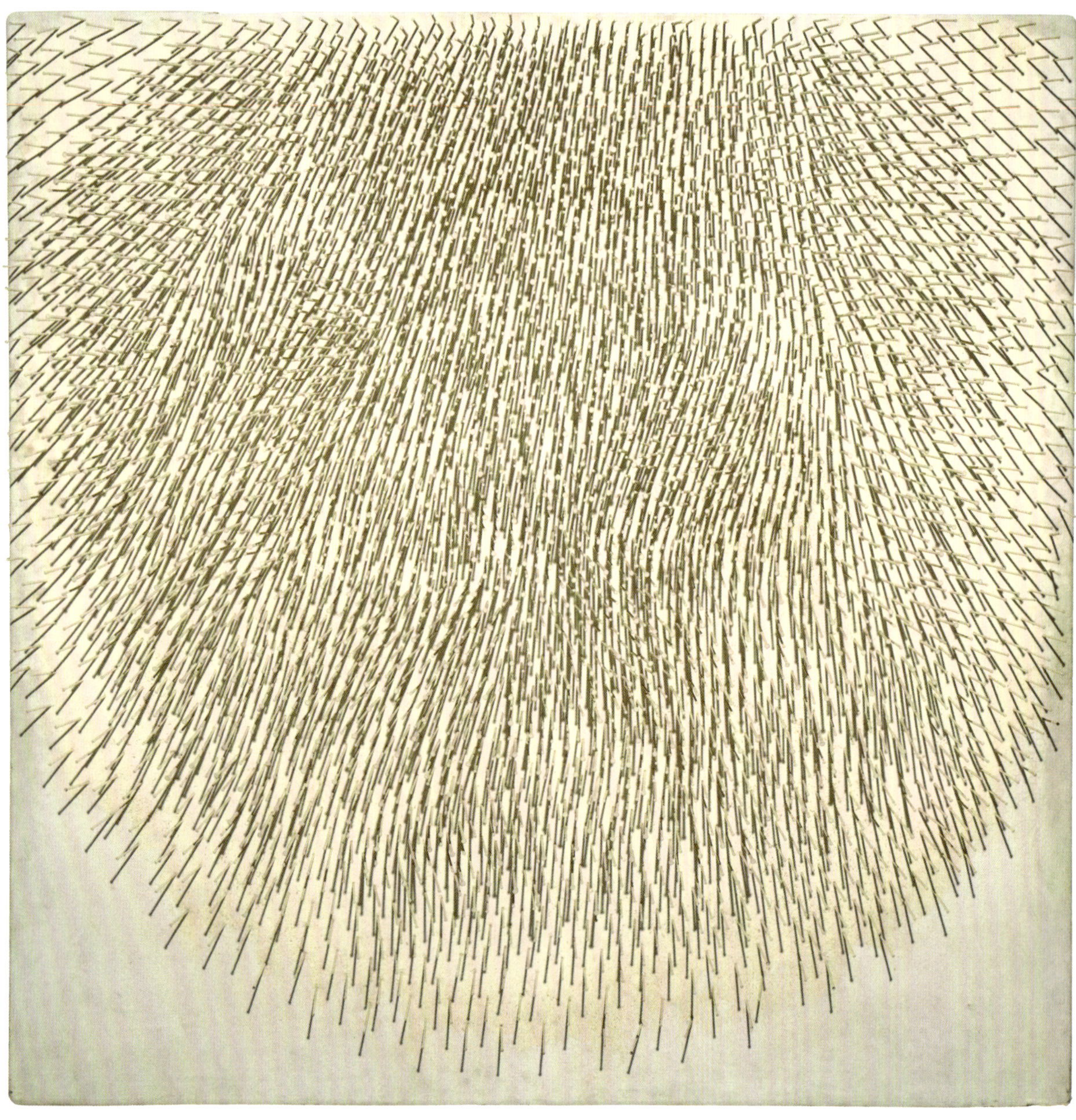

relative to the work. Such is the case when standing before *Grosse Wolke* (Big Cloud) from 1965, a work that has both a maniacal, destructive energy and something of the grandeur of nature.

In the United States, Yoko Ono also made use of the aggressive symbolism of nails in her explicit *Painting to Hammer a Nail* (1961), an instruction piece that has been realized on many subsequent occasions. Rather than having the artist be solely responsible for the violation of the canvas, the work is designed to be participatory, with the audience being invited to pick up a nail and cathartically pound it into a white monochrome. Her related *Painting to Be Stepped On* (first proposed in 1960; page 120), like its successor, could not be clearer in its antagonism toward the precious status of paintings within museum and gallery settings, and it turns the tables in a decidedly revolutionary manner. Other American artists took up similarly blatant attacks on the physical body of painting, including Jim Dine, who in his work of the early 1960s suggested that the field of a painting might as well be a tool

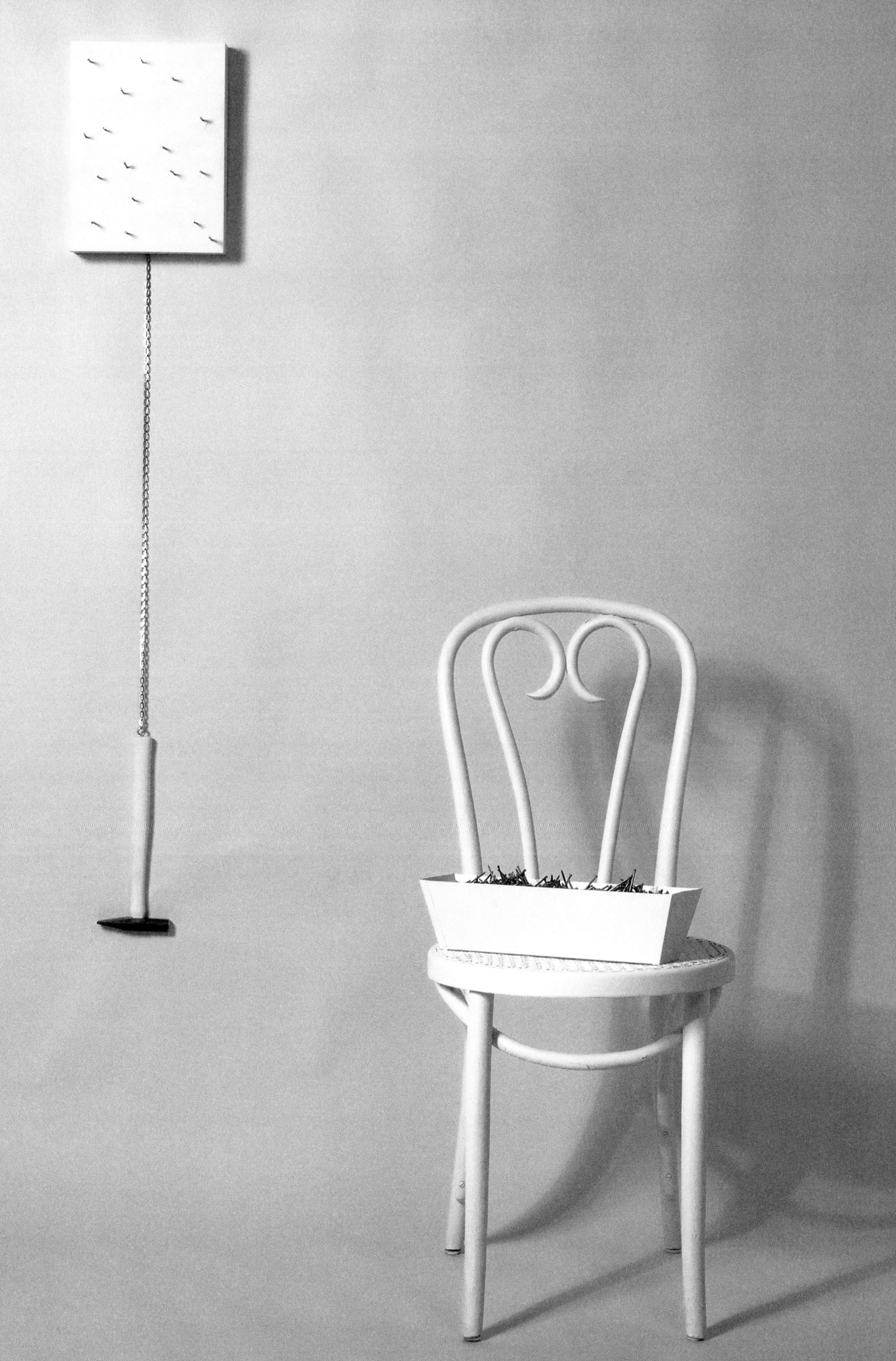

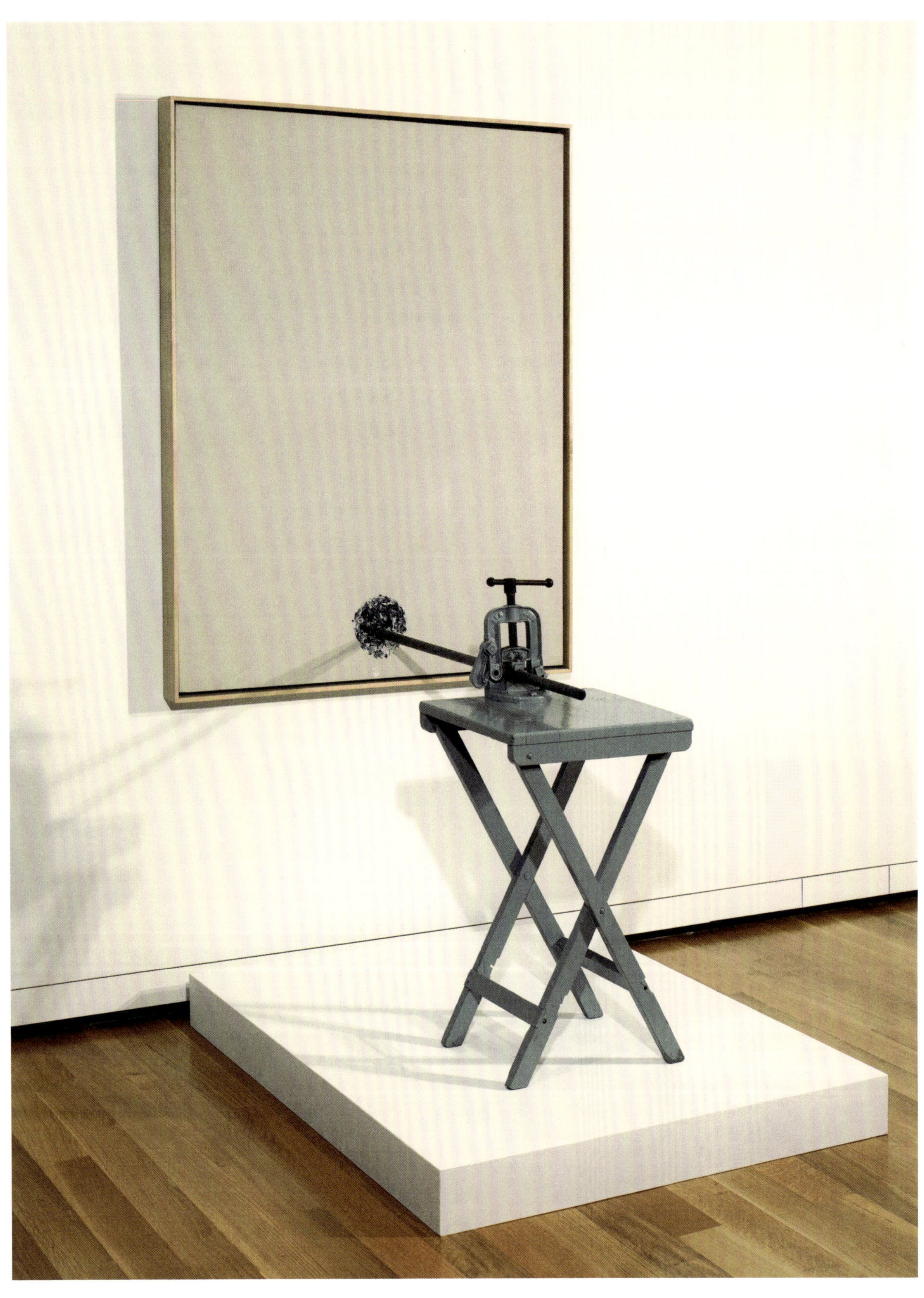

shed, a bathroom wall, or a child's bedroom, and in so doing demystified and debased it. In *Vise* (1962), he performs a related operation, piercing the canvas with a metal pipe to both connect painting to the world around it and substitute an object-oriented realism for illusionism. Edward Ruscha took a different approach in his canvases of the time, using illusionistic techniques that played within the rules of tradition to terrorize the cherished precincts of painting. As such, he set a match to one of his hometown museums (*The Los Angeles County Museum on Fire*, 1965–68), torched other "norms" and "standards" (*Norms, La Cienega on Fire*, 1964, and *Burning Gas Station*, 1965–66),[23] and raised the specter that a treasured painting could be harmed (*Damage*, 1964). In *Damage*, not only does Ruscha put the viewer

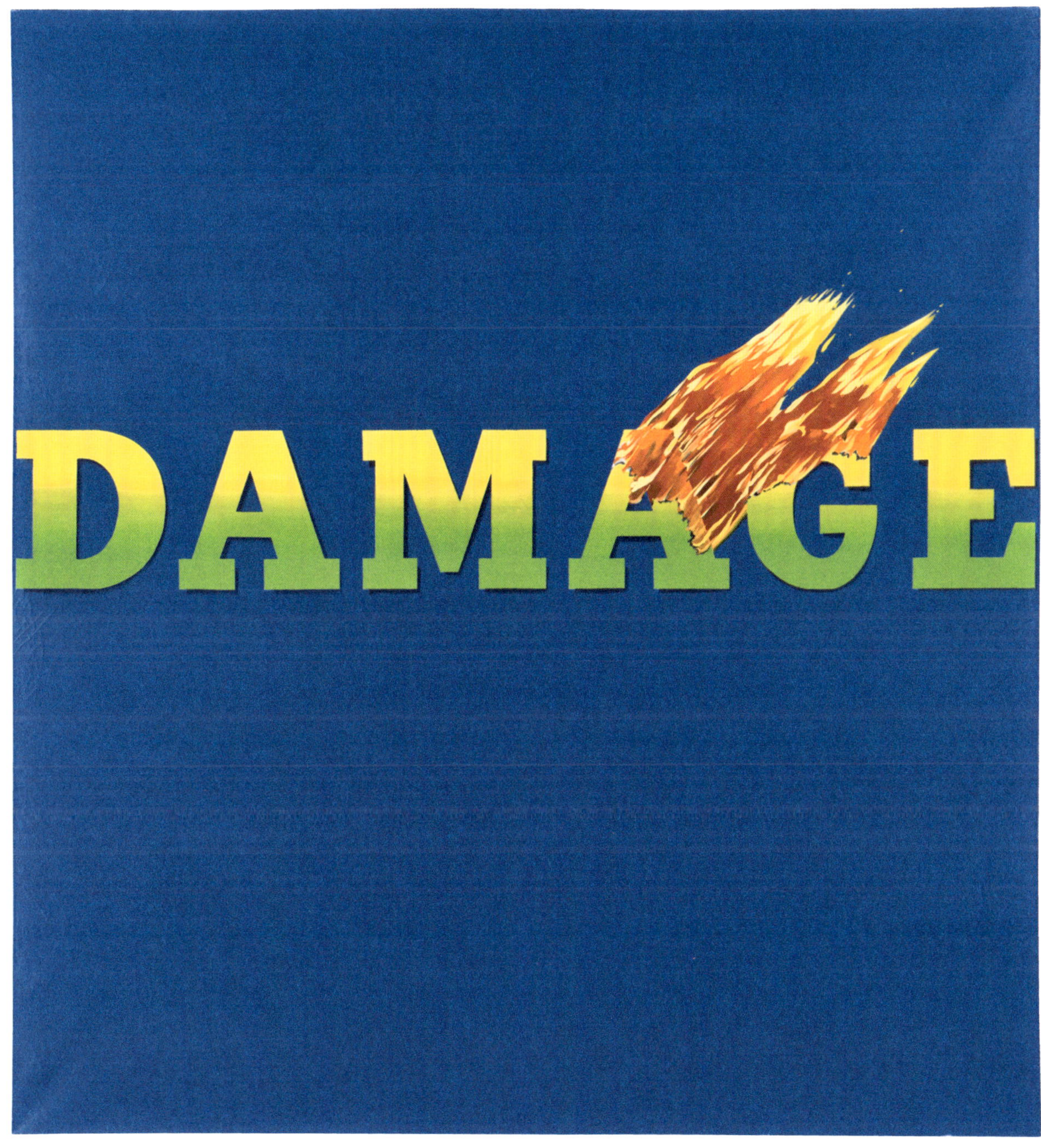

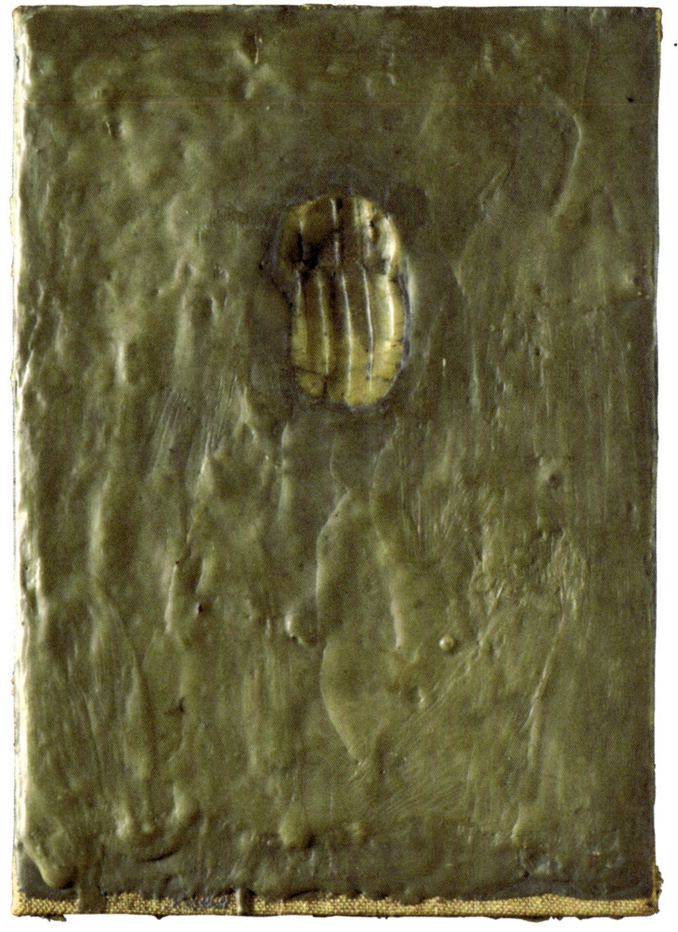

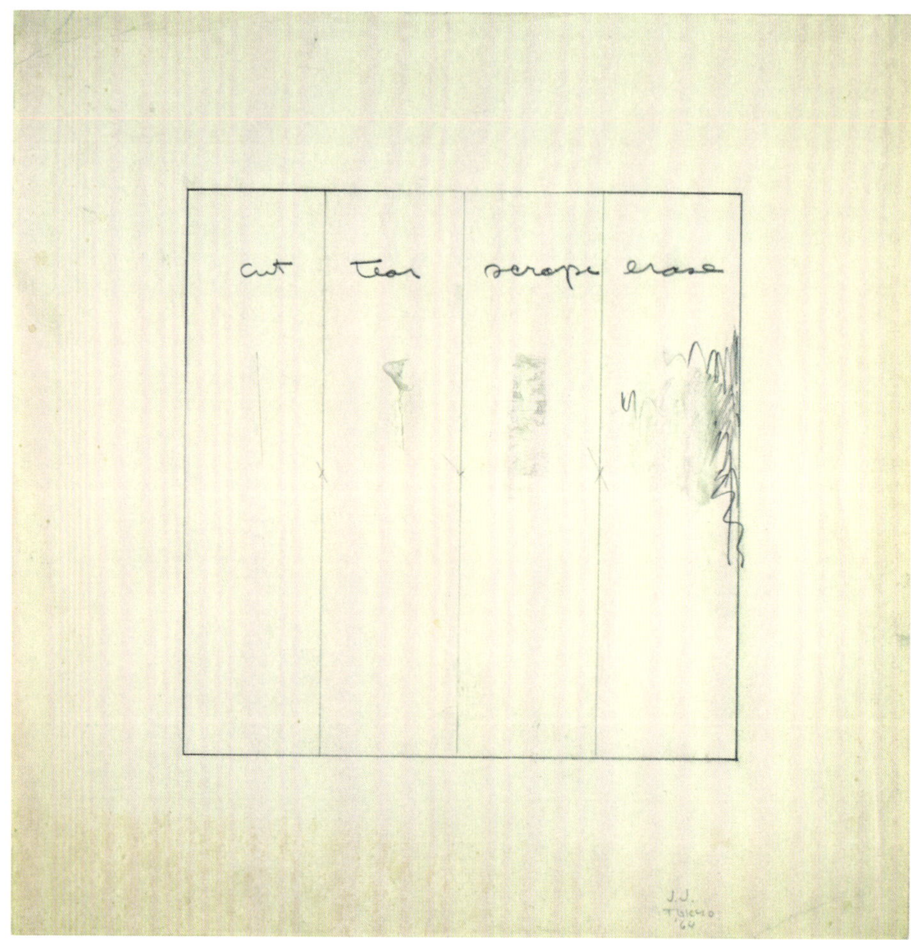

on edge by invoking the unspeakable in big, advertising-derived letters, but he also sets the word ablaze as if it were burning through the canvas support. This sentiment could not be farther from established attitudes toward art.

One of the artists who set Ruscha on his path of painterly mischief was Johns,[24] who not only suggested violence toward the wall-mounted canvas in the form of the target but also occasionally acted on those impulses himself. For example, *Painting Bitten by a Man* (1961) is a diminutive encaustic monochrome that the artist attacked with his own teeth, leaving little doubt as to his position vis-à-vis orthodoxy. In 1964, while in Tokyo, Johns made numerous works that were antagonistic to customary notions of painting, including *Souvenir 2* (1964), a canvas that was turned away from the viewer, and two works titled *No* (both 1964) that depict a ruler scraping wet paint from the surface. Also while in Japan he made a telling drawing, *Untitled (Cut, Tear, Scrape, Erase)* (1964), that coolly catalogues what could be called nonproductive approaches to painting or drawing. Indeed, as Weiss has written on the work, "As violations or subtractions, such demonstrations stand apart from the application of a medium to a support— apart, that is, from the means through which the artist *produces* an image. What they represent are modes of addressing the art object as such—as an object."[25] Weiss also astutely noted of this work that "conspicuous in its absence is the word 'mark' or 'deposit' or anything that references addition rather than subtraction."[26]

That powerfully neutralizing and objectifying notion of subtraction can be felt in Lee Lozano's *No Title* (1970), in which the deconstructive gestures of Fontana, Johns, and Muehl are carried out with an assassin-like clarity, eating away at the structural integrity of the canvas with two conflicting grid systems until wall and stretcher bar achieve an almost equal status with painted canvas in terms of the composition. Lozano was deeply invested

Above left: Jasper Johns, *Painting Bitten by Man*, 1961. Encaustic on canvas mounted on type plate, 9½ x 6⅞ in. (24.1 x 17.5 cm). The Museum of Modern Art, New York, Gift of Jasper Johns in Memory of Kirk Varnedoe, Chief Curator of the Department of Painting and Sculpture, 1989–2001. (catalogue only)

Above right: Jasper Johns, *Untitled (Cut, Tear, Scrape, Erase)*, 1964. Graphite pencil on paper. Collection of the artist.

Opposite: Lee Lozano, *No title*, 1970. Gesso with graphite and perforations on canvas. The Estate of Lee Lozano. Courtesy of Hauser & Wirth, Zurich and London.

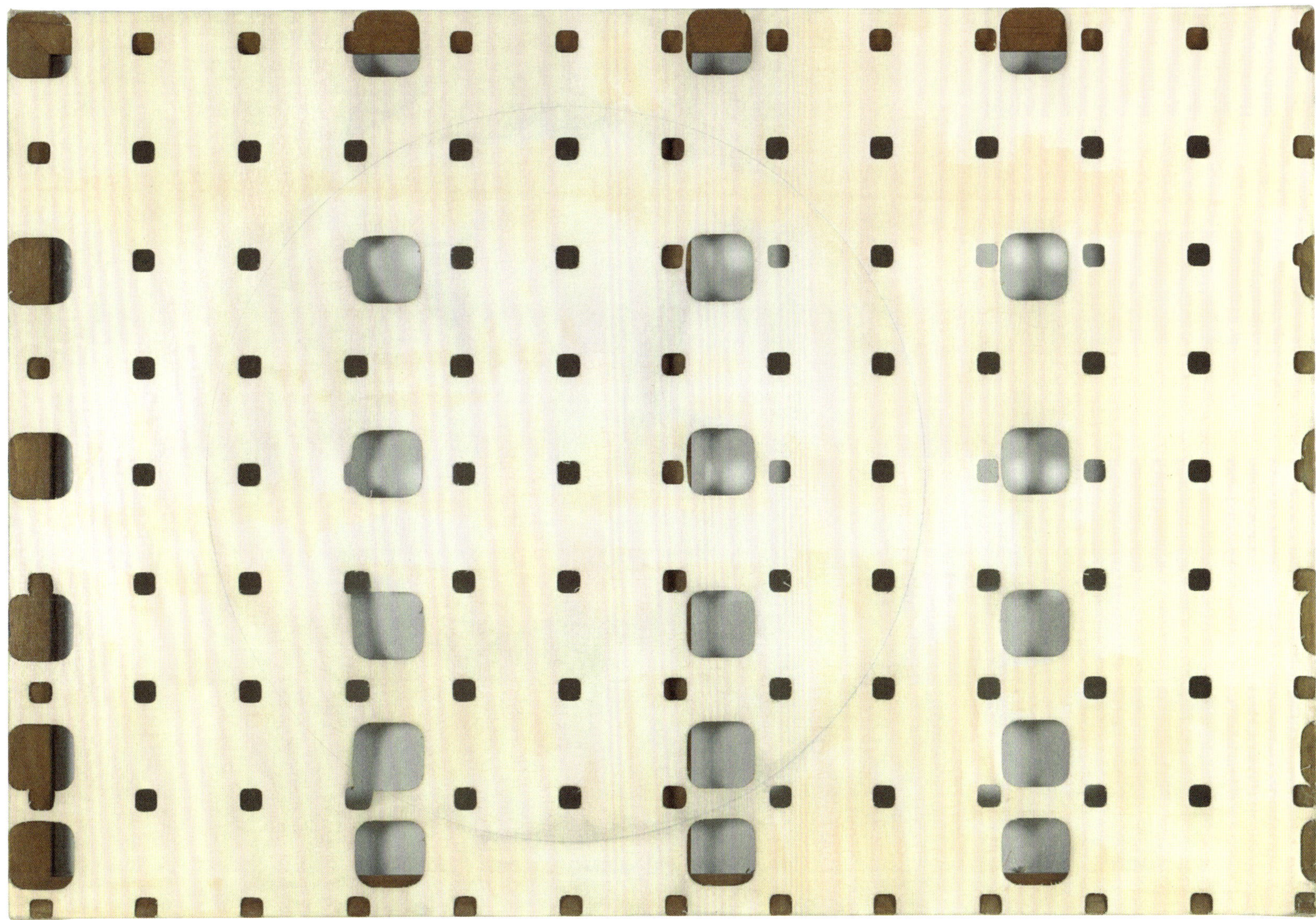

in disrupting the status quo, and there was a drastic evolution in her painting toward ever more critical positions. In 1968 she wrote:

> One concept of paint is its being matter in liquid state. Two painters who thought of it this way were Pollock and Lewis [*sic*], Moose's [Robert Morris's] current two painter heroes. Another concept of paint is its being matter in solid state. A painter who thinks of it this way is Lee Lozano, whose bowels function magnificently.[27]

Those sorts of bodily functions were not breached in Lozano's work (although all manner of sexual acts and penetrations were) or in Johns's cataloguing of negating gestures; but in 1978, Andy Warhol took up the challenge in his chastely titled Oxidation paintings (page 82). In this body of work, the physical (perhaps even psychological) abuse of painting on canvas was taken to an ultimate extreme, utilizing the universally recognized humiliation of pissing on something as the final injustice toward the practice. Though it is easy to read the dribbles and spatter of urine on the copper surfaces of these works as a joke on Pollock, as well as to find a certain abstract beauty in them, they remain deeply iconoclastic gestures that take the assaults described above to a categorical conclusion.

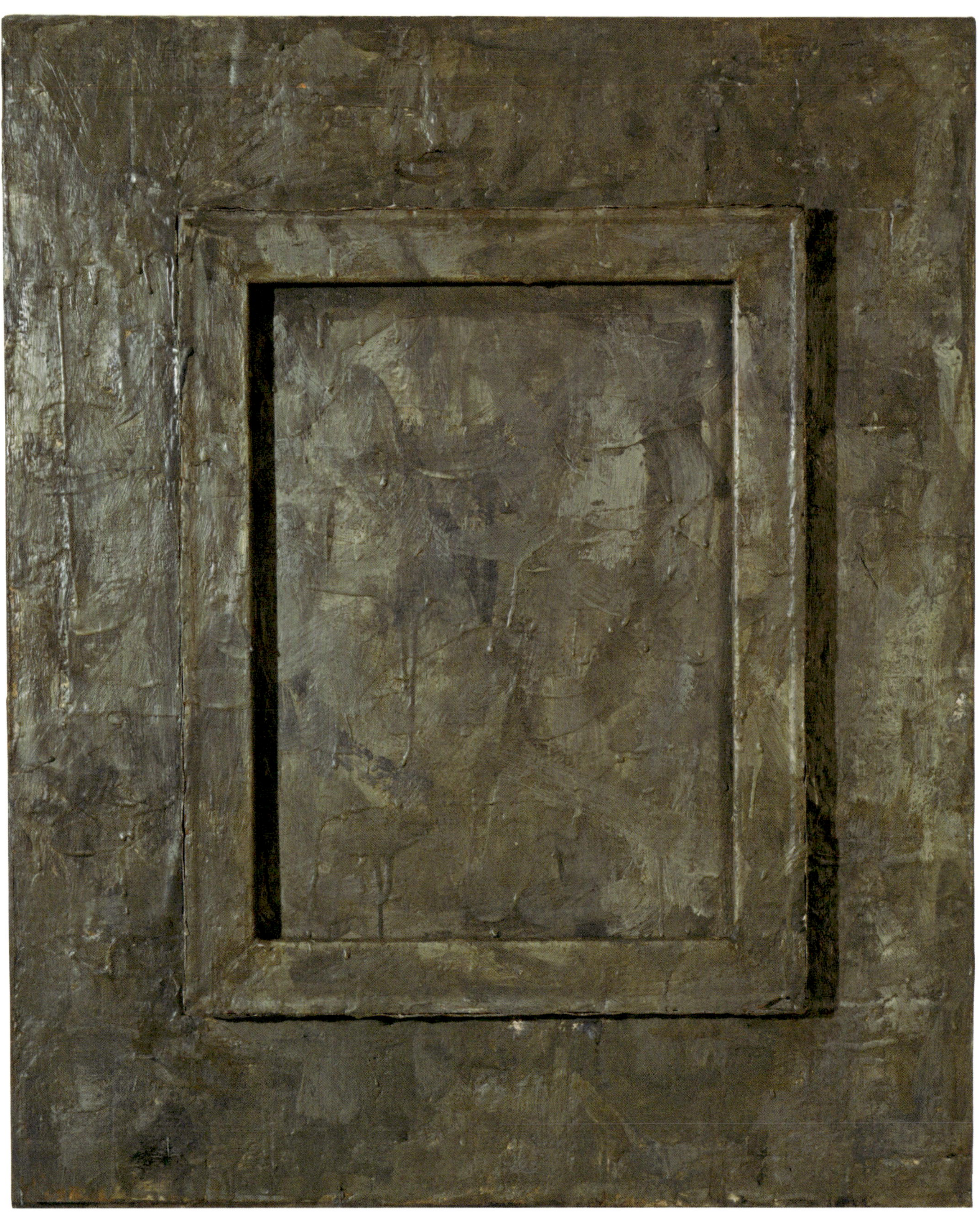

Iconoclasm

More cerebral, and less literal, refutations also attend to this lineage of critical painting. One well-trodden path involved what Johns called the "shunning statement" of turning a canvas around so that its conventional "front side" and, by extension, its subject and entire raison d'être were denied. Johns pursued this in *Canvas* (1956), which consists of a backward-facing canvas within a larger, more convention-ally oriented one. The entire composition is covered in a neutralizing yet extremely physi-cal crust of collaged newspaper and encaustic that elides the distinction between object and subject, or image and object, in much the same way that his targets or flags do. The viewer is plainly aware of looking at a handmade, rather painterly work, but is led to doubt that the entire story is being told because one suspects another painting, another answer, is being withheld.

The Italian artist Giulio Paolini was preoc-cupied for much of his career with phenom-enological investigations of painting, using the format of the wall-mounted rectangle to ques-tion ideas about image, structure, illusion, space, and gesture. In *Senza titolo* (Untitled; 1962) he placed three successively smaller stretched canvases inside one another and turned the presumably painted surface to the wall in a triple denial of the typical transaction between painting and viewer. The resulting work is exemplary of the raw realism that was a goal of the Arte Povera movement with which he was associated, but also reflects Paolini's more than forty-year rumination on what consti-tutes the experience of looking at painting—a focus that distinguished him from the more multimedia members of this group. Such quiz-zical objects are products of his position that painting is "a question without an answer."[28]

Roy Lichtenstein also dealt with the distinc-tions between different modes of seeing, between the facts one reads on the surface of a canvas and what is depicted in the image. In

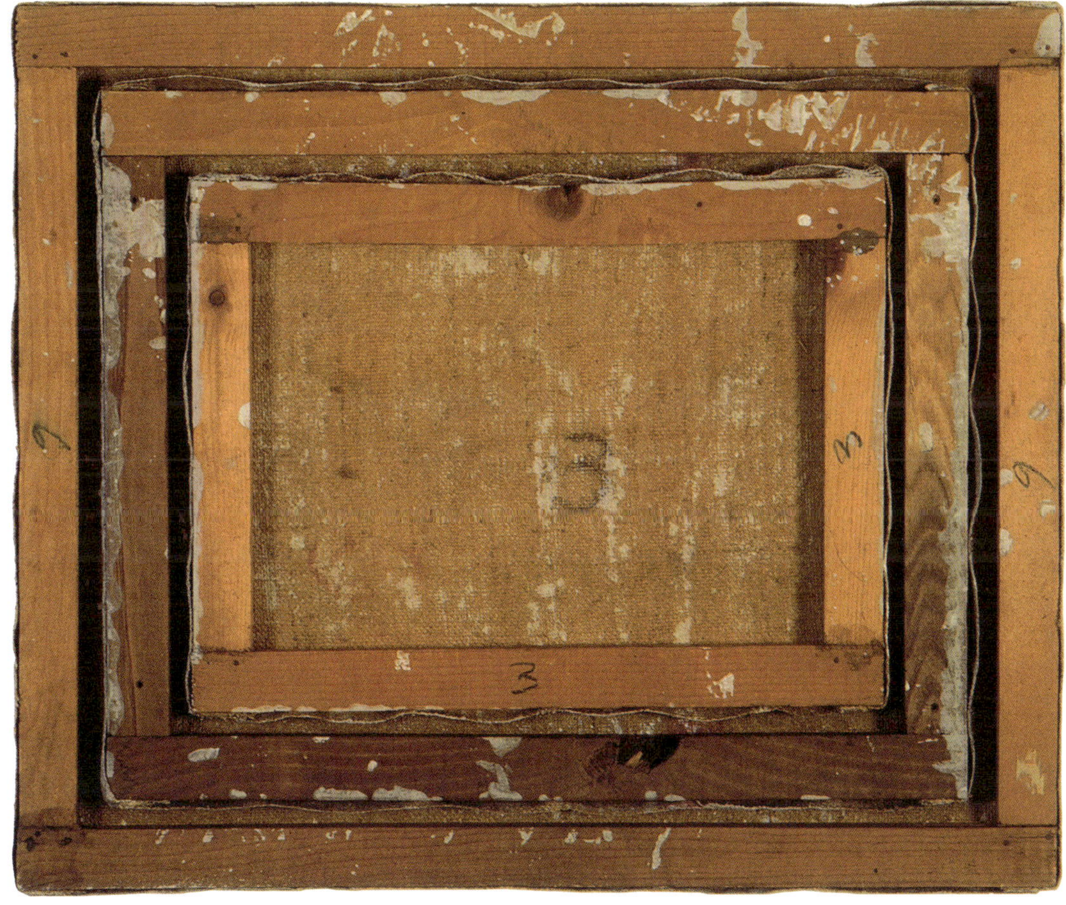

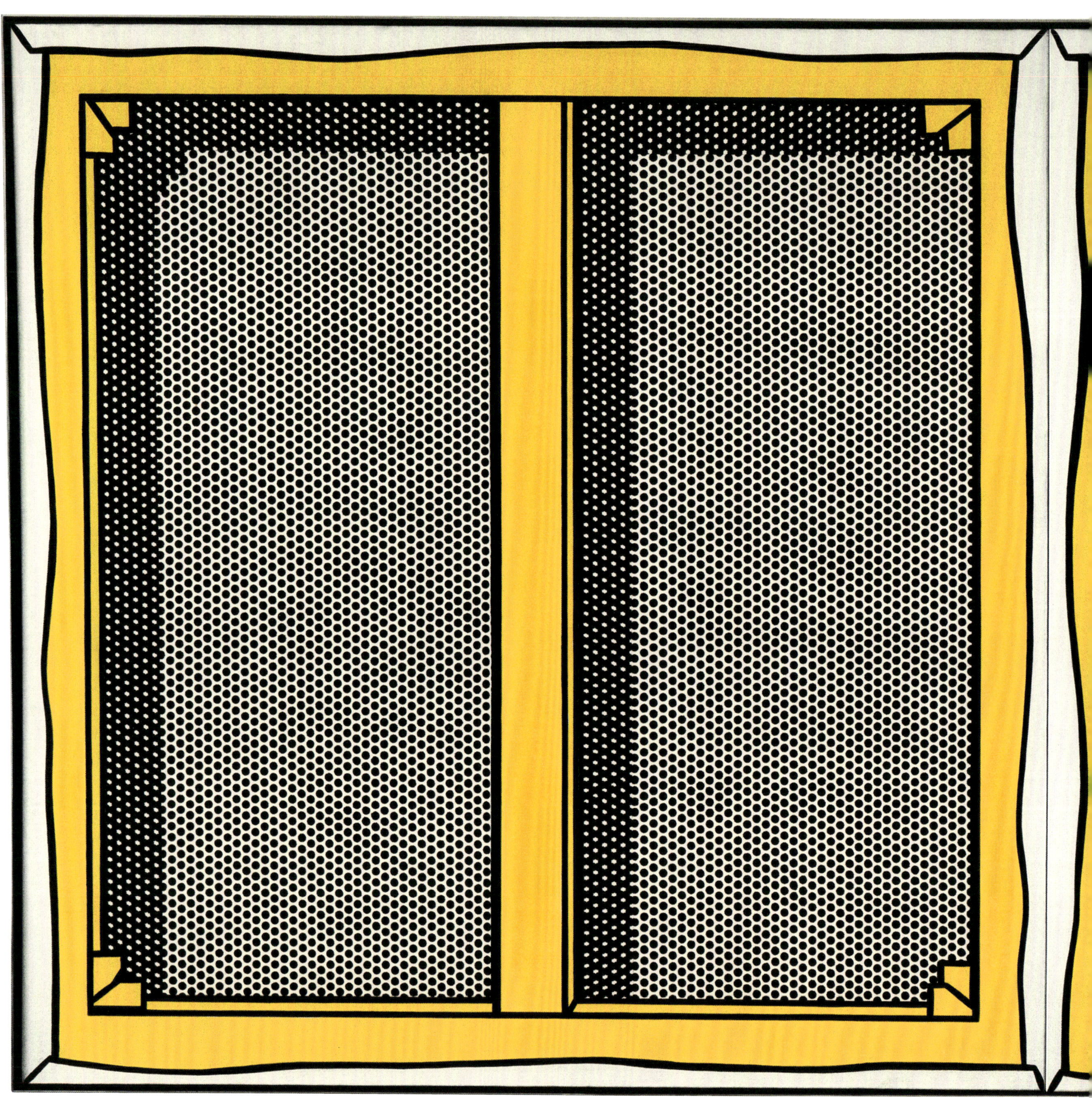

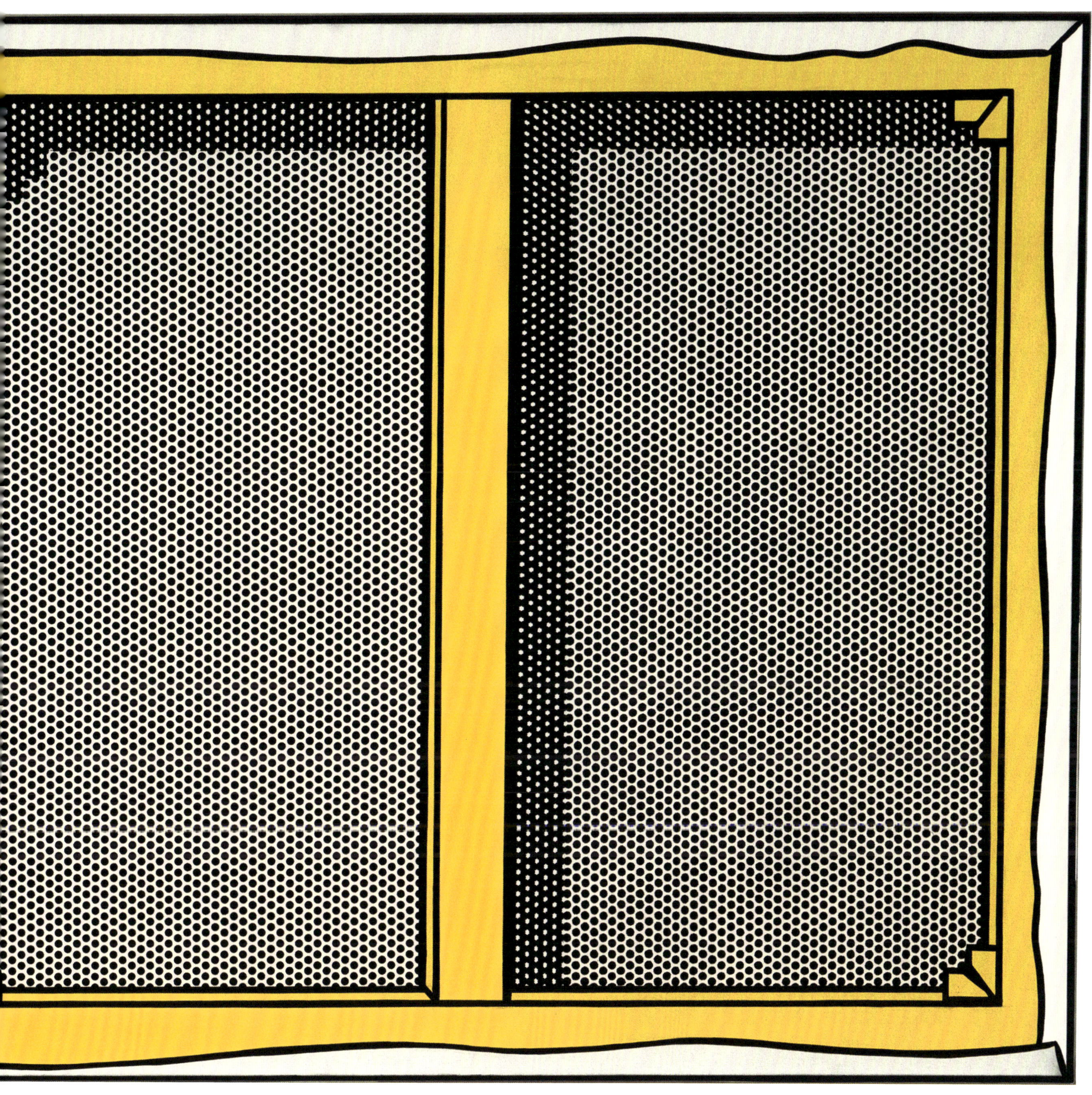

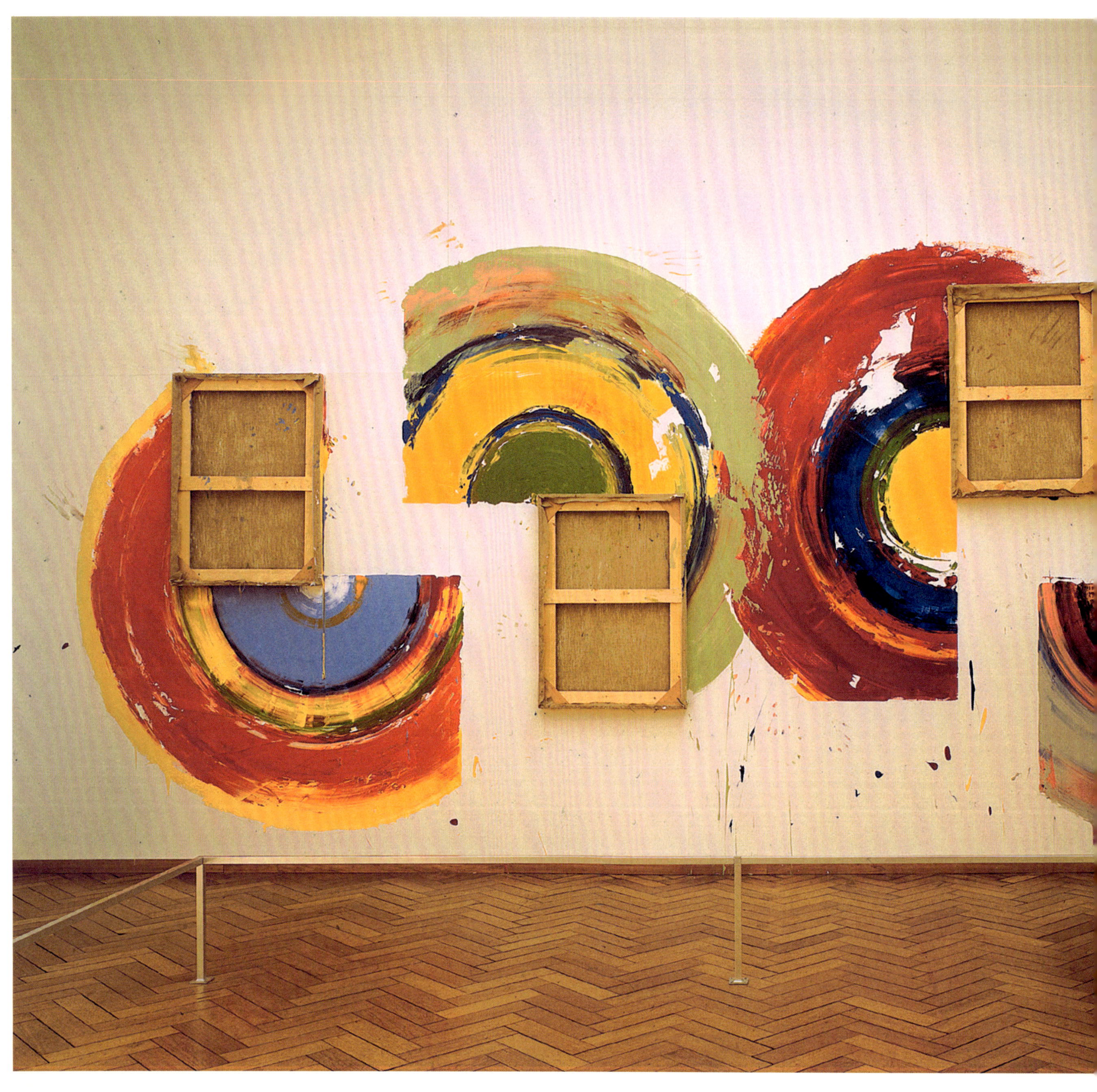

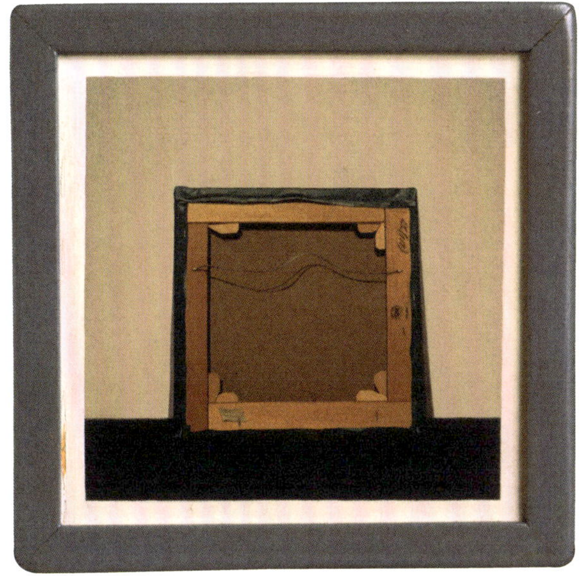

Stretcher Frame—Two Panels (1968; pages 36–37), he shares with Johns and Paolini the iconoclastic gesture of turning the canvas around, but unlike them, he renders it in an illusionistic way. The realism suggested by shadows and the faithful representation of irregular canvas edges and corner shims is complicated by Lichtenstein's signature benday-dot method, which recalls commercial printing techniques, especially those of cartoons. Such a subject would be found only in the province of an advanced, fine-art discourse, and yet the quotidian style of the work slyly suggests it could be fodder for the Sunday funny pages. This bridging of high and low through the language of commercial printing techniques is one of Lichtenstein's unique contributions to art, and is poignantly attempted in this smart body of work.

Richard Pettibone has made quotation and sly upbraiding of art-world conventions, machinations, and power structures a subject of his art since the early 1960s, and he is best known for making miniature reproductions of works by artists who dominated the critical discourse of the day. The reversed canvas approach was first evident in his work in *Jasper Johns, "Canvas," 1956* (1973), a reprisal of Johns's aforementioned *Canvas*, but reappeared later with even more bite in *Andy Warhol, "Flowers," 1964 (rear view)* (1974; above), from Pettibone's lesser-known series of photorealist paintings. Here, the nonpublic back rooms of museums and galleries become the ignominious stage on which star works such as those by Warhol are shown to be rather uncommanding commodities. Predating the related work by Louise Lawler by almost a decade, they are especially prescient because they are formatted to look like the photographs on which they were based, extending Pettibone's own vicious circle of "pictures of pictures."[29]

Equally balanced between the esoteric and the accessible are the installations that Richard Jackson began creating in 1970, in which canvases loaded with bright acrylic paints were turned to the wall and smeared across its surface (left). The resulting rainbowlike residue is both violently iconoclastic at its core, as the paint is physically removed from the support during the process, and surprisingly beautiful. Like Paolini, Jackson has preoccupied himself for more than forty years with the processes and conventions

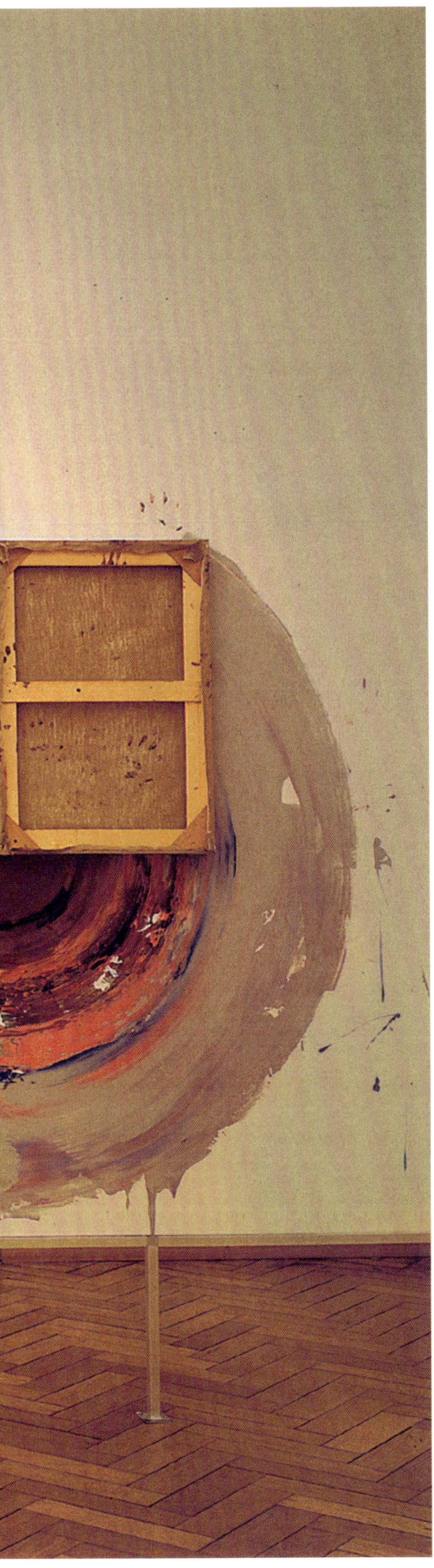

of painting, pushing both to often extreme limits. In speaking about these early experiments and how they have carried on throughout his work, Jackson has said: "It is my idea to try to expand painting, not just in size but to see how far it could be extended or pushed. I don't feel my work as a criticism of painting but an optimistic view of what it could be."[30]

An analogue to turning the front of the canvas away from the gaze of the viewer is the emptying out of the painting, leaving only the frame to mark out a field of activity or absence. Dan Flavin was a frequent adherent to this method. He famously adopted commercially available fluorescent lights as his preferred medium in 1961, first as appendages to painted rectangles and eventually as a stand-alone medium. The painterly derivation of this work carries forward in much of Flavin's later art, in which color, light, space, and depth are manipulated and communicated through the fluorescents. In works utilizing a closed rectangular format, such as *Untitled (to Bob and Pat Rohm)* (1969; page 40), the connections to painting are especially clear. Here, a square boundary in the form of fluorescent tubes marks off a territory within which color is restrained, intermingled, and manipulated, but without resorting to paint and canvas. It is perhaps also meaningful that in Flavin's work, containment within such structures is not absolute, and the colored light spills outside these limits, positing a porosity that is in opposition to the tightly bound traditions of painting.

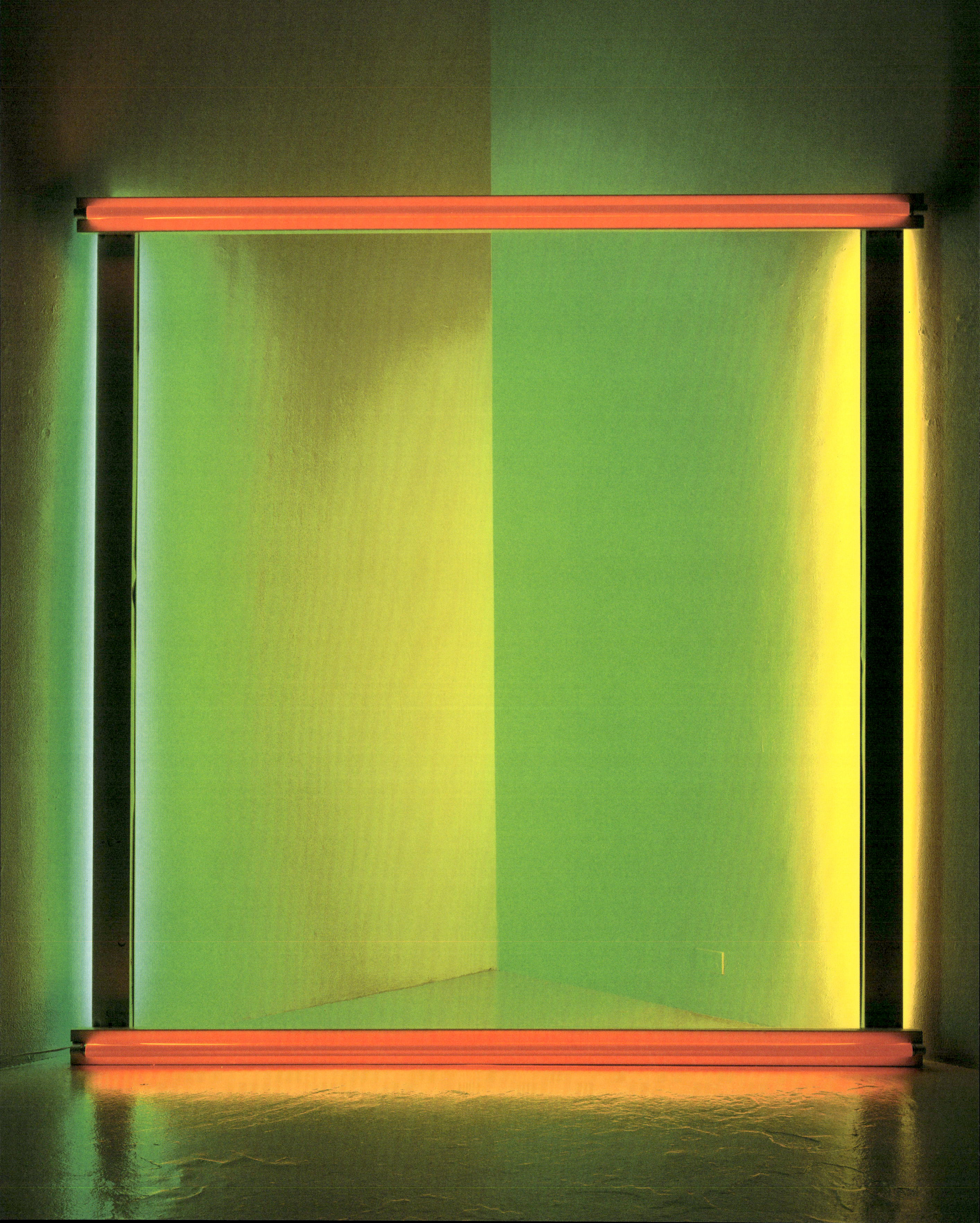

Critiques of Composition and Spontaneity

Abstract Expressionism was the institution against which many of the artists in *Target Practice* were rebelling, for not only was it exalted as an apotheosis of painterly freedom and innovation, but it required at its center a lone genius who was responsible for stirring up the fevered inspirations that took form on the canvas. Much of the art in *Target Practice* sets forth a different set of assumptions, including a treatment of paint and canvas as materials without any mystical properties and a conception of the artist as a cultural worker pursuing everyday truths rather than mythical visions. Douglas Crimp, writing about such critical practices during this period, noted that they "sought to contest the myths of high art, to declare art, like all other forms of endeavor, to be contingent upon the real, historical world. Moreover, this art sought to discredit the myth of man and the ideology of humanism which it supports. For indeed these are all notions that sustain the dominant bourgeois culture."[31] It may come as a surprise to some to hear so-called blue-chip artists like Johns and Lichtenstein described in such terms, but much of the art they were pursuing in the 1950s and 1960s had exactly these kinds of radical, even revolutionary concerns at their core. In particular, the rhetoric and increasing academicism of Abstract Expressionism was something begging to be knocked down. About this milieu, Johns has said: "In the 1950s there was a hangover where they [the Abstract Expressionists] were not producing private (pictures) but painting public pictures and refining statements. I am not interested in refinement."[32]

One of the cherished hallmarks of Abstract Expressionism is the notion of spontaneity, which if brought to bear on a canvas with élan, dashing brushwork, and an innate grasp of the composition as a whole would doubtless result in a masterpiece. Between the two of them, Johns and Rauschenberg systematically attacked the primacy of inspired composition and divine spontaneity in the mid-1950s to early 1960s. One of the most shocking affronts came in the two-stage effort of Rauschenberg's *Factum I* and *Factum II* (both 1957). The first followed Rauschenberg's "combine" method of composing a painting with all manner of material, including collaged printed matter and fabric as well as expressionistic slashes of paint whose resultant drips signify a lack of premeditation. That spontaneity, however, was mocked in the second work when those same brushstrokes were replicated, if not drip for drip, then close enough to expose such a way of working as just another stylistic painterly affectation. Johns's *Thermometer* (1959; page 42) enacted a similar parody, seeking to measure the "heat" of his high-keyed colors and jazzy brushwork by sticking a working thermometer in the center of the canvas. Stenciled numbers track the temperature but do not correlate with warm or cool colors as described in the predominant color theories of the day espoused by Josef Albers

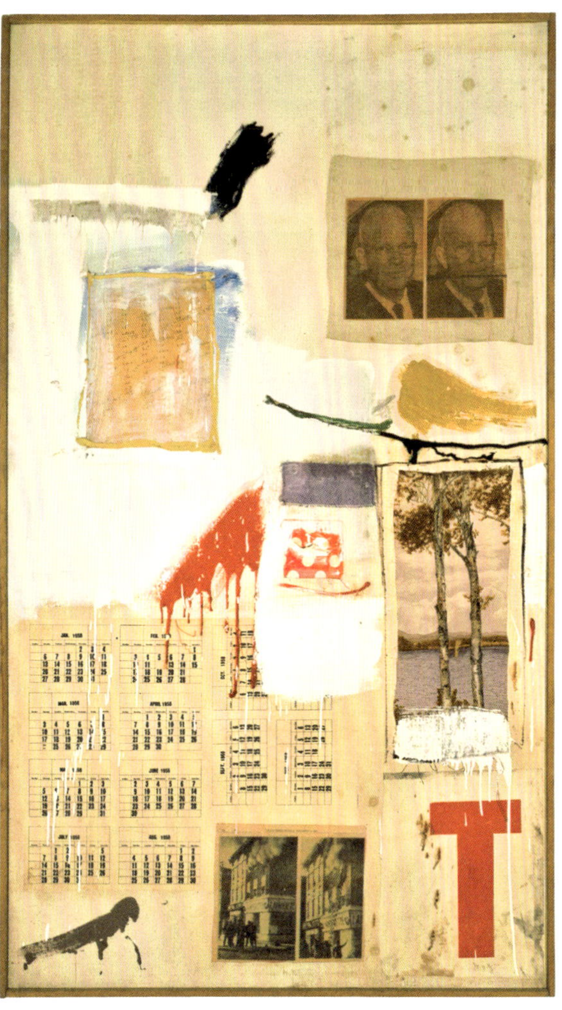

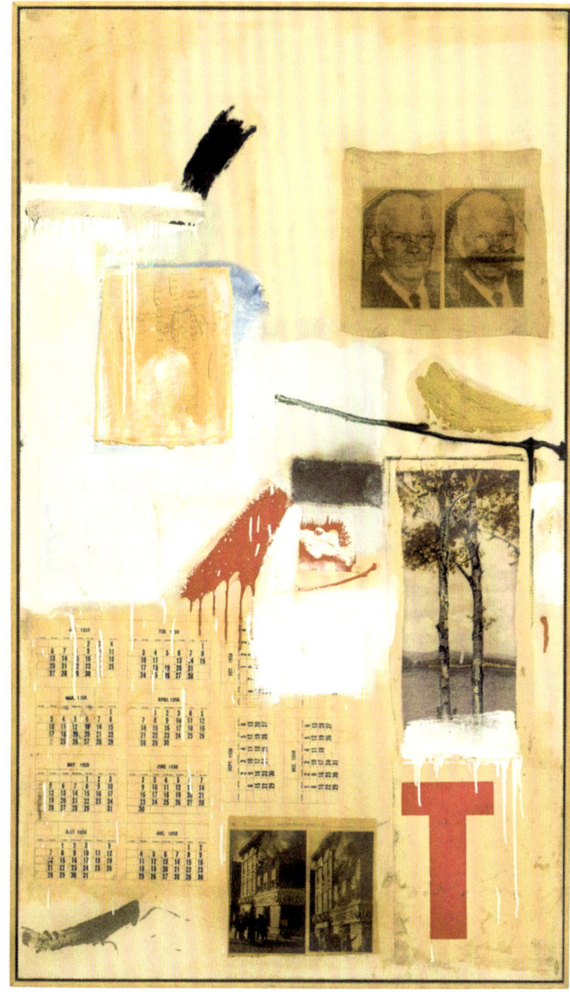

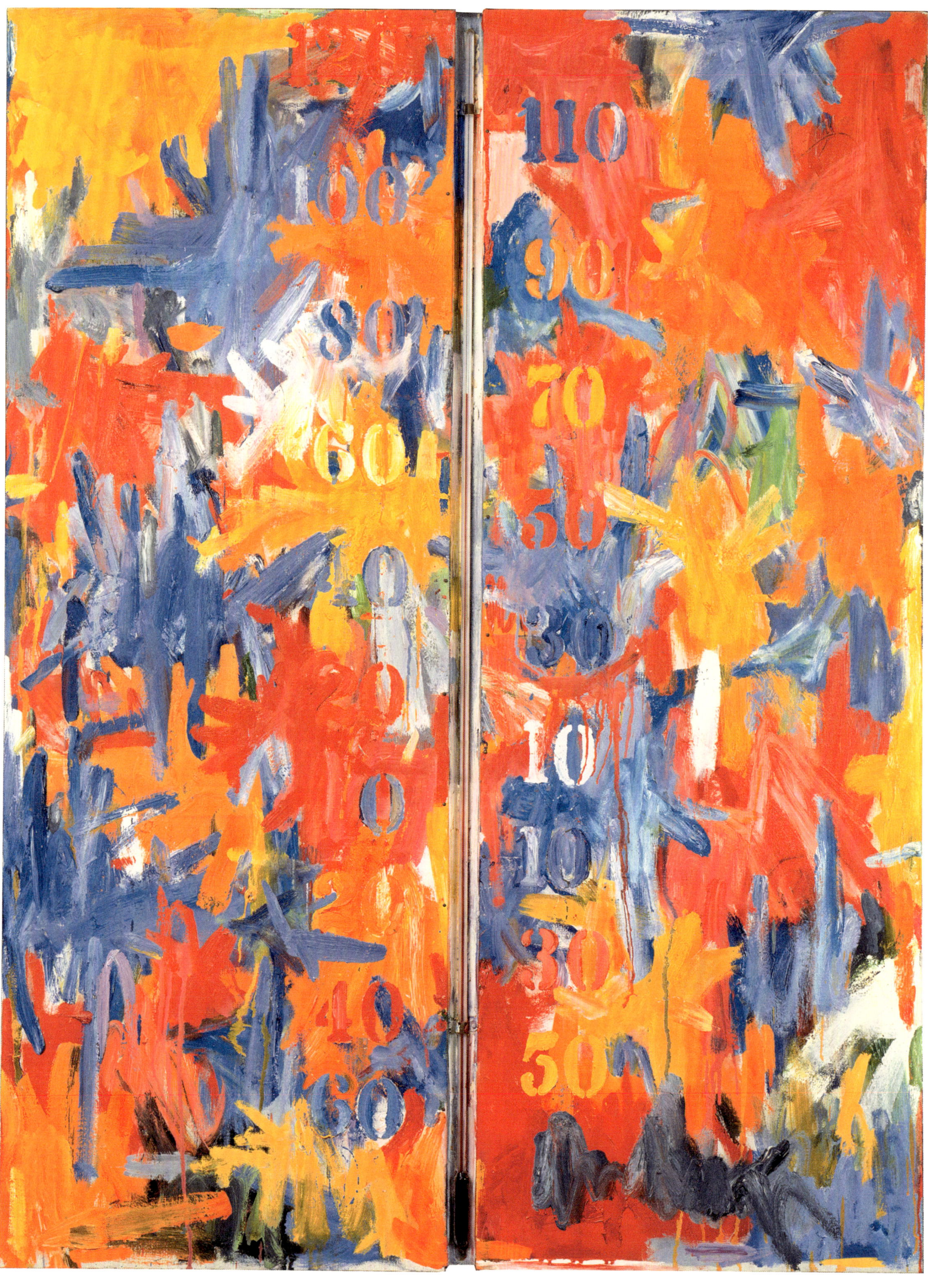

Left: Jasper Johns, *Thermometer*,
1959. Oil on canvas with thermometer.
Seattle Art Museum, Partial and promised gift of Bagley and Virginia Wright,
in honor of the museum's 50th year.

Right: Jasper Johns, *Thermometer*,
1960. Charcoal and pastel on paper.
Seattle Art Museum, Promised gift of
the Virginia and Bagley Wright Collection, in honor of the 75th Anniversary
of the Seattle Art Museum.

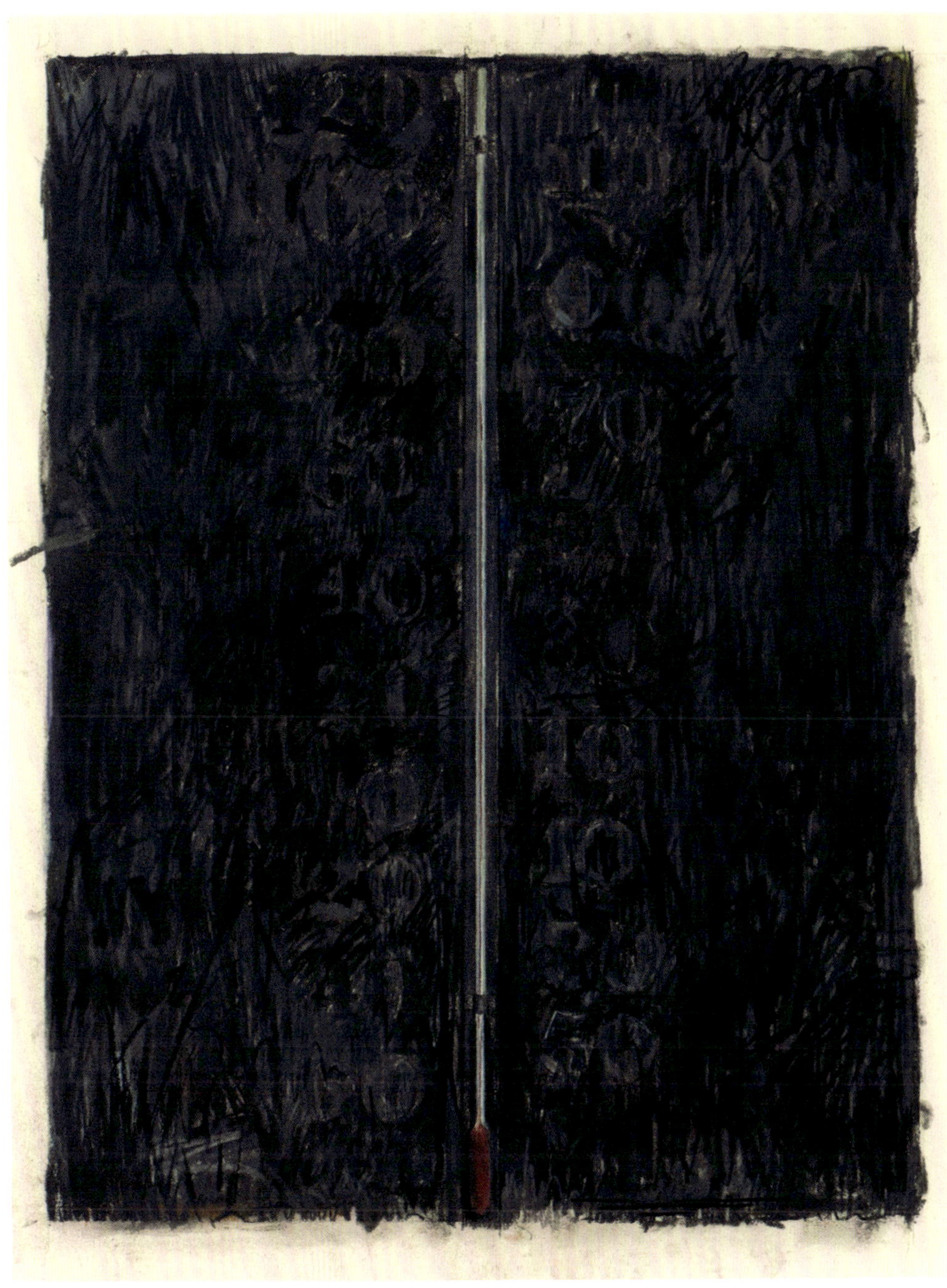

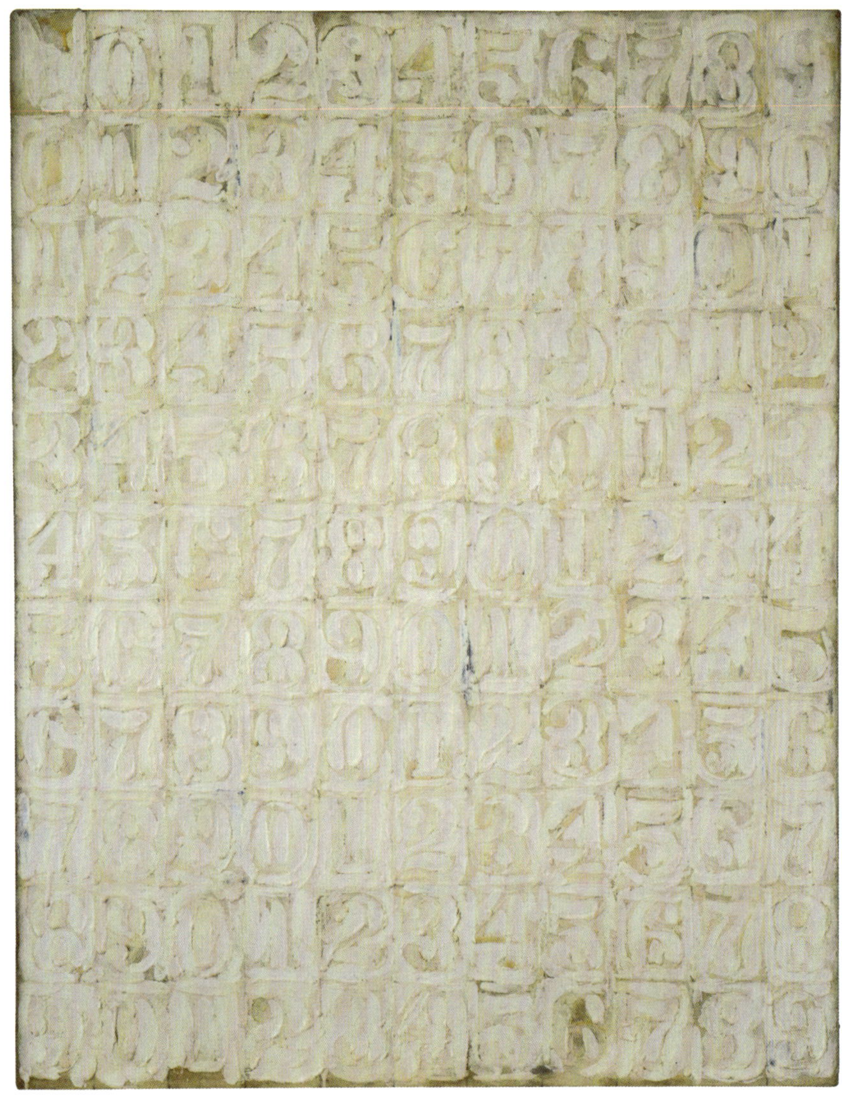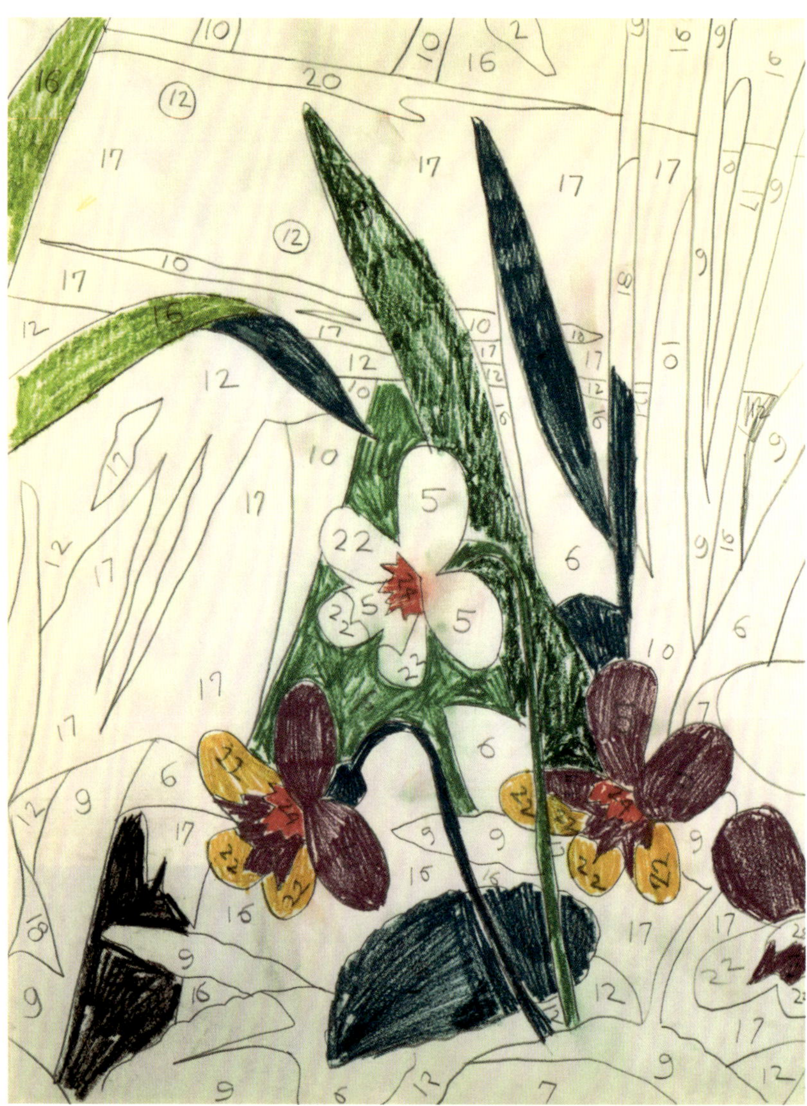

or Hans Hofmann. During this period, Johns followed another working method by which he would make a drawing of a painting done the previous year. For example, *Thermometer* (1960; page 43), echoing *Factum I* and *II*, goes against tried-and-true conventions of drawings as preparatory studies in that it effectively "copies" an already executed idea. The conception of drawings as copies, or at least reproductions, as if they were black-and-white illustrations in a printed medium, is bolstered by the fact that these subsequent drawings (and ones exist for many of Johns's exalted works from this time, including *False Start*, *Jubilee*, *Out the Window*, *Device Circle*, and others) are leeched of color, made in black, white, and gray, and closely copy the form and placement of otherwise seemingly spontaneously placed brushstrokes in the corresponding paintings.

Approaching from a different front, Johns's number paintings defraud the artistic aspirations of painterly composition with similar cutting precision. In works such as *White Numbers* (1958), he effectively takes all the guesswork out of issues of composition: where figures are to be placed or what sort of pictorial hierarchy will guide the viewer's eye. Instead, Johns divided the canvas into a grid and inserted a stenciled number in each resulting box, counting from 0 to 9 until the grid was filled out. The only oddity of these works is that the box in the upper left corner is always left blank, as it is in the similar alphabet works, where letters are used instead of numbers. Such a

Above left: Jasper Johns, *White Numbers*, 1958. Encaustic on canvas. Collection of Charles Simonyi, Seattle.

Above right: Andy Warhol, *Do It Yourself (Flowers)*, 1962. Colored crayon on paper, 24 x 18 in. (61 x 45.7 cm). Private collection. (catalogue only)

Opposite: Gerhard Richter, *Farbtafel*, 1966–78. Lacquer on canvas. The Museum of Contemporary Art, Los Angeles, Partial and promised gift of Blake Byrne.

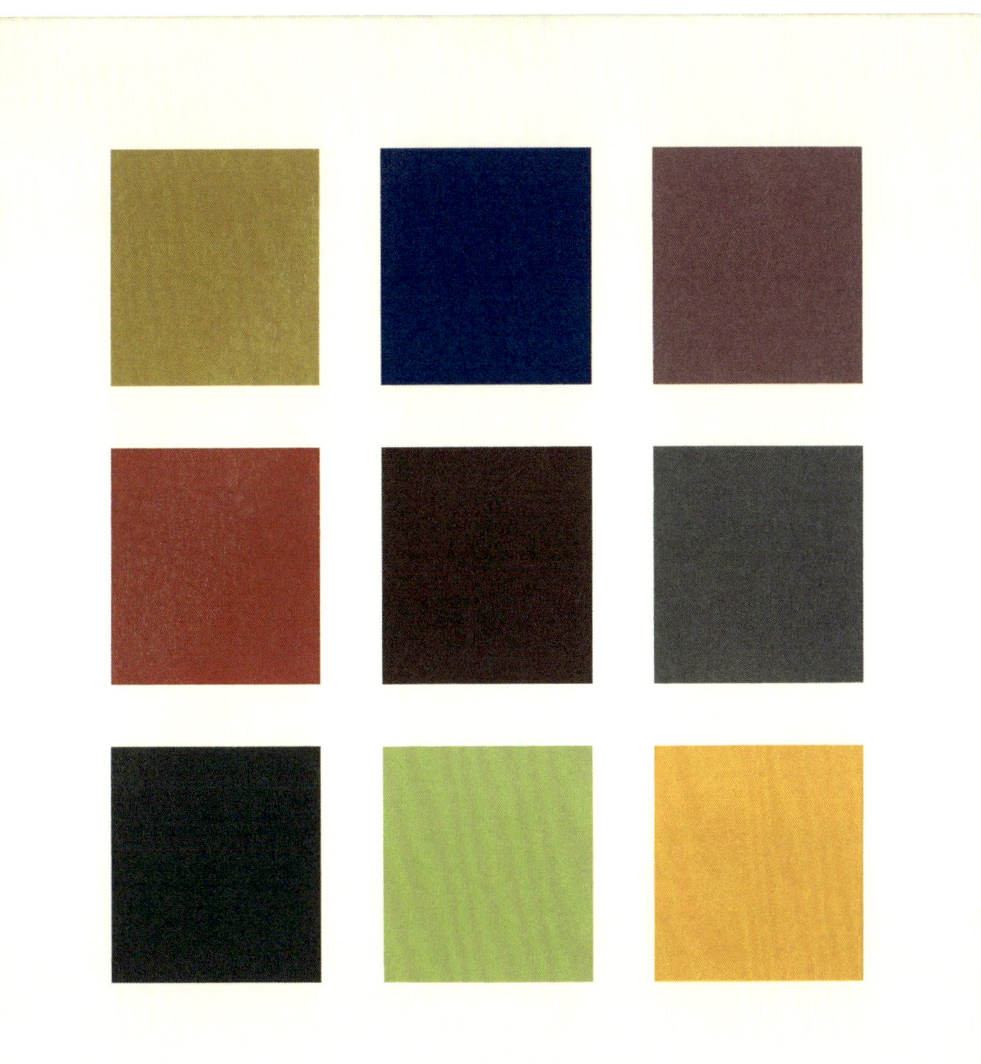

When any artistic procedure can be prescribed so as to "guarantee" a quality result, you can be assured that artists will rush to prove that theory wrong, and Johns's number works directly attack this way of thinking.

The related *Farbtafel*, or color chart, works that the German artist Gerhard Richter initiated in 1966 pursue a similar line of critique, adopting a grid and then filling in those standardized boxes with an array of reasonably pleasing colors. The paintings, with their clinical coolness and system-driven method, are analogously "algorithmic," opening up the possibility of literally innumerable permutations that might as well be left up to a computer to complete. Such a mocking disregard for the necessity of the artist to complete the painting also surfaces in the limited but searing body of work that Warhol titled *Do It Yourself.* Made in 1962 and comprising only five paintings and two drawings, the works are based on color-by-number sets made by the Venus Paradise company to accompany their line of colored pencils.[35] Reducing the act of painting to hobby craft, in which the artistic decisions of composition and even choice of color have already been taken care of by a corporate body, this series drags the tradition of painting to the brink of ridicule and extends Johns's number works in a humorous but no less critical way.

Other significant forays into this territory, where painting is assumed to be no more than a set of mutually accepted rules, include John Baldessari's series of text paintings from the late 1960s and much of the mockingly self-referential works of the Belgian artist Marcel Broodthaers. During this period, Baldessari engaged a commercial sign painter (another jab at fine art) to carefully letter his canvases with punning in-jokes about the academic and institutional expectations for art. In *Composing on a Canvas* (1967–68; page 46), for instance,

mechanistic process (although counterbalanced by the rich texture and subtle coloration of the encaustic) flies in the face of all prior preconceptions about painting and had huge implications for subsequent generations of artists, regardless of their chosen medium. The nihilistic reality of these works has been noted by Johns's younger colleague Robert Morris: "[A] way to describe it is as a self-enclosed and self-completing mechanism, or part of an a priori, spring-loaded algorithm or rule for sequences, which nullifies the freedom for certain aesthetic decisions."[33] Such drastic measures did not come about unprovoked, however. The ascendant cultural climate of the time produced many outlandish exclamations, among them art critic Clement Greenberg's prescriptions for modernist painting:

COMPOSING ON A CANVAS.

STUDY THE COMPOSITION OF PAINTINGS. ASK YOURSELF QUESTIONS WHEN STANDING IN FRONT OF A WELL COMPOSED PICTURE. WHAT FORMAT IS USED ? WHAT IS THE PROPORTION OF HEIGHT TO WIDTH ? WHAT IS THE CENTRAL OBJECT ? WHERE IS IT SITUATED ? HOW IS IT RELATED TO THE FORMAT ? WHAT ARE THE MAIN DIRECTIONAL FORCES ? THE MINOR ONES ? HOW ARE THE SHADES OF DARK AND LIGHT DISTRIBUTED ? WHERE ARE THE DARK SPOTS CONCENTRATED ? THE LIGHT SPOTS ? HOW ARE THE EDGES OF THE PICTURE DRAWN INTO THE PICTURE ITSELF ? ANSWER THESE QUESTIONS FOR YOURSELF WHILE LOOKING AT A FAIRLY UNCOM -
PLICATED PICTURE.

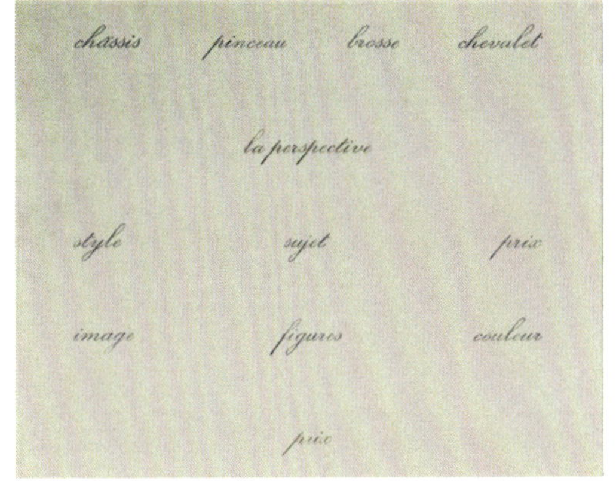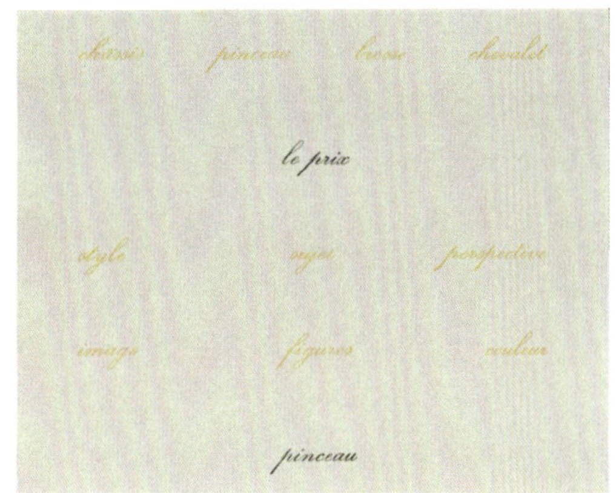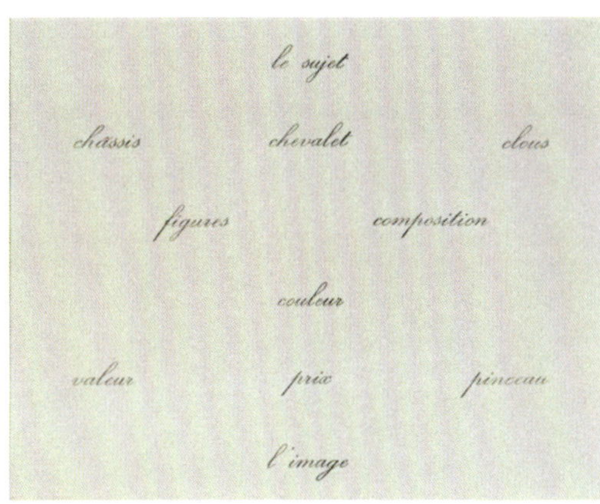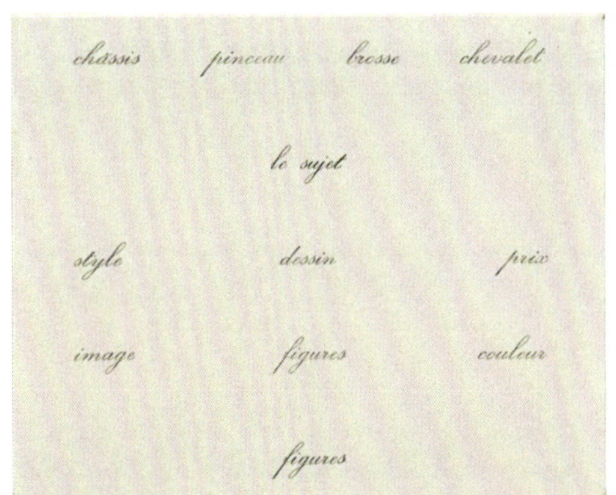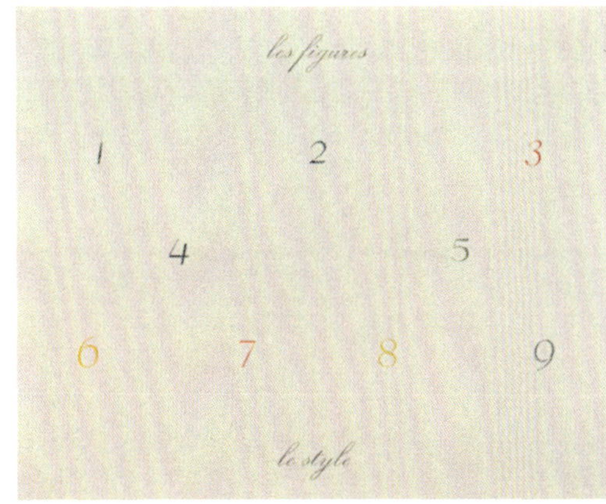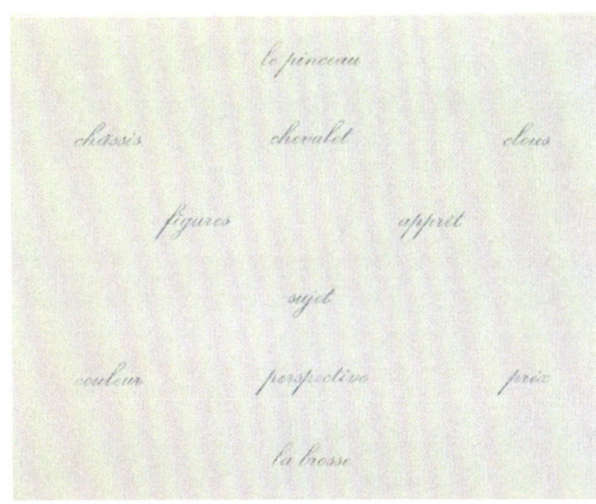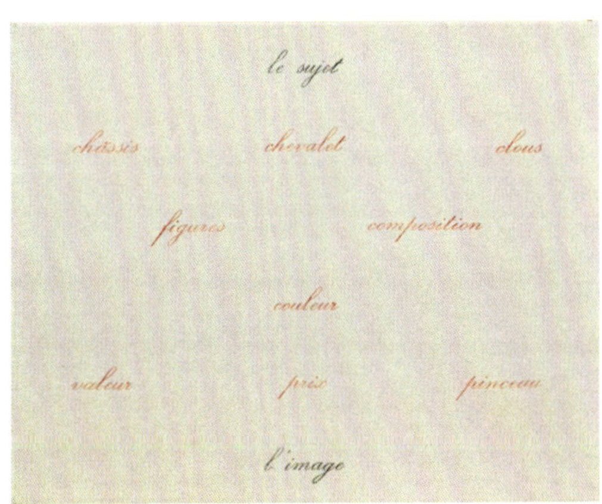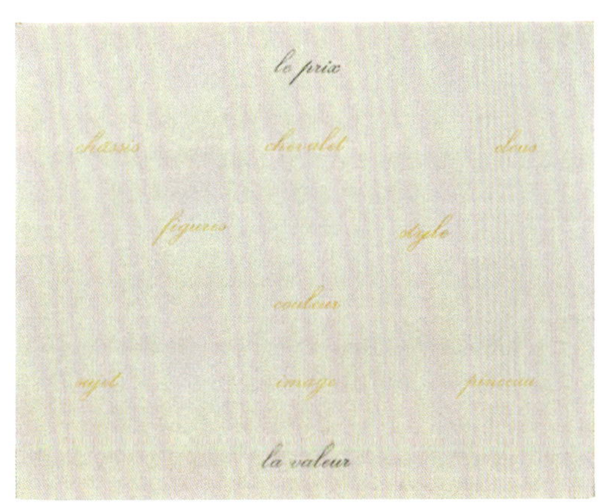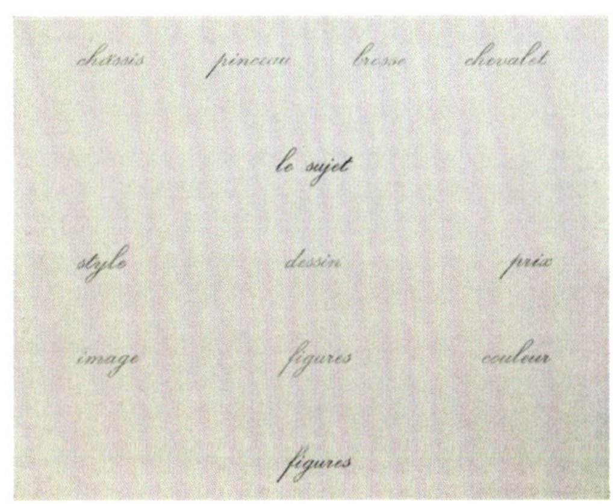

Left: John Baldessari, *Composing on a Canvas*, 1967–68. Acrylic on canvas. Museum of Contemporary Art San Diego, Gift of the artist.

Above: Marcel Broodthaers, *Paintings/Peintures (serie l'art et les mots)*, 1973. Oil on canvas. Tate: Purchased 1983.

he enumerates the pertinent questions that any self-respecting and earnest painter of the old school would ask him- or herself, adopting the voice of a tenured academician, or that might be found in a "how-to" guide for painting: What is the proportion of height to width? What is the central object? How are the shades of dark and light distributed? In *Paintings/Peintures (serie l'art et les mots)* (1973), Broodthaers takes this essentialism to another extreme, covering nine canvases with delicately scripted words (in French) that pertain to the essence of painting, whether in relation to composition, subject matter, materials, display, or even economics. These include: *le sujet, les figures, la peau, le style, l'image, la brosse,* and *le prix.*

Mel Bochner, much of whose work was concerned with similarly self-referential systems

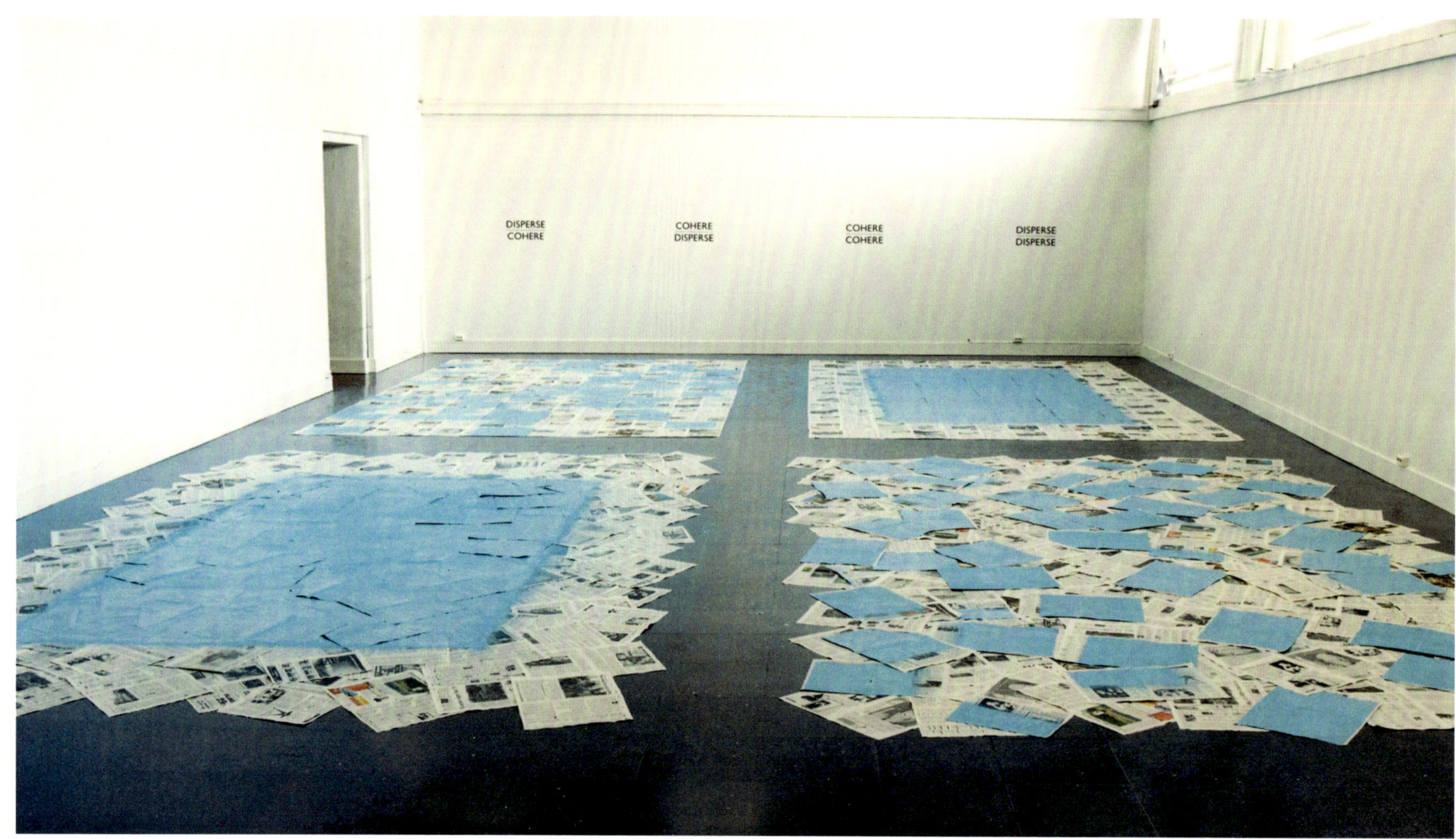

for measuring and declaring space as fact, primarily within the field of sculpture, turned his attention to painting as well and, in particular, fixed ideals of composition. In his room-size installation *Theory of Painting* (1969–70), he used both wall and floor to deconstruct basic tenets of painting, creating four rectangular fields on the ground with newspapers and blue spray paint. Two fields had straight, orderly edges, and two had ragged edges, while the spray paint that was applied to the newspapers either followed the logic of the external edge (or it could easily be the other way around) by remaining contained in a rectangle or was scattered irregularly within the field. Vinyl texts on the wall dryly explained the four permutations: Disperse/Cohere; Cohere/Disperse; Cohere/ Cohere; Disperse/Disperse. Here, Bochner participates in the debunking of academic prescriptions for painting in much the same way that Johns and others pursued it, including

making the requirement that the artist execute the work optional. But he also radically shifts the discussion into an environmental direction (taken up elsewhere in *Target Practice*), where the wall is no longer the only arena in which to act and where verticality is no longer presumed. The relationship of the medium to its support is also scrambled, which is not unrelated to ideas of figure and ground, but in this work, "ground" becomes extremely loaded and boldly literal. As Richard S. Field has noted about this piece, "'Ground' alludes not only to the canvas and the modernist enterprise's reductive focus on the shape and edge of the support, but to the philosophical basis for reason and argument, to the floor of the institutions that traffic in and consume works of art, to the tradition of the cubist collage and its ambiguous valorizing of everyday life and its detritus, and, finally, to the reabsorption of art into the background noise of continued cultural (and physical) entropy."[36]

Above: Mel Bochner, *Theory of Painting*, 1969–70. Newspaper, spray paint, and vinyl text. The Museum of Modern Art, New York, Committee on Painting and Sculpture Funds, 1997.

Right: George Maciunas, Photodocumentation of Shigeko Kubota's performance *Vagina Painting*, 1965. Gelatin silver print. The Gilbert and Lila Silverman Fluxus Collection, Detroit.

Page 50 left: Nam June Paik, *Zen for Head*, 1962. Film stills of his performance at the 1962 Neuste Festspiele, Wiesbaden. Courtesy of the Nam June Paik Art Center and Hessischer Rundfunk.

Pages 50 right and 51 left: Paul McCarthy, *Face Painting—Floor, White Line*, 1972. Production stills from 16mm film transferred to DVD. Courtesy of the artist and Hauser & Wirth, Zurich and London.

Page 51 right: Yayoi Kusama, *Self-Obliteration*, 1967. Stills from 16mm film transferred to DVD. Courtesy of the artist, Victoria Miro Gallery, Gagosian Gallery, Ota Fine Arts.

Shifting the Paradigm

A sense of painting succumbing to entropic forces is charted in several temporal, media-based works in the exhibition, in which bodies become intermediary surfaces or implements, and other professions with parallels to painting are evoked. As has been noted with regard to the Gutai artists in Japan, alternate methods for making a painting, including boxing with paint-soaked gloves, began to take hold in the 1950s, many of which were spiked with humiliating in-jokes. Kazuo Shiraga, for instance, famously made paintings using his feet (a much less dexterous and therefore artless method), and later, in 1965, Shigeko Kubota did a per-formance titled *Vagina Painting* that brought painting and menstruation, as well as sexual shock, together to mock the heroic gestures of the historically male-dominated tradition. With a brush attached to her underwear, she applied red paint to paper on the floor of a stage.[37] Her husband, Nam June Paik, had attempted something similar in his 1962 *Zen for Head* (page 50 left), in which he used his own head as a brush to make ink paintings, perhaps deriding the notion of ego in the creation of gestural abstractions by eliminating extraneous tools in order to join person and process indelibly. Likewise, in Brus's *Selbstbemalung* (Self-Painting) (1964; page 27), the white-painted head of the artist is

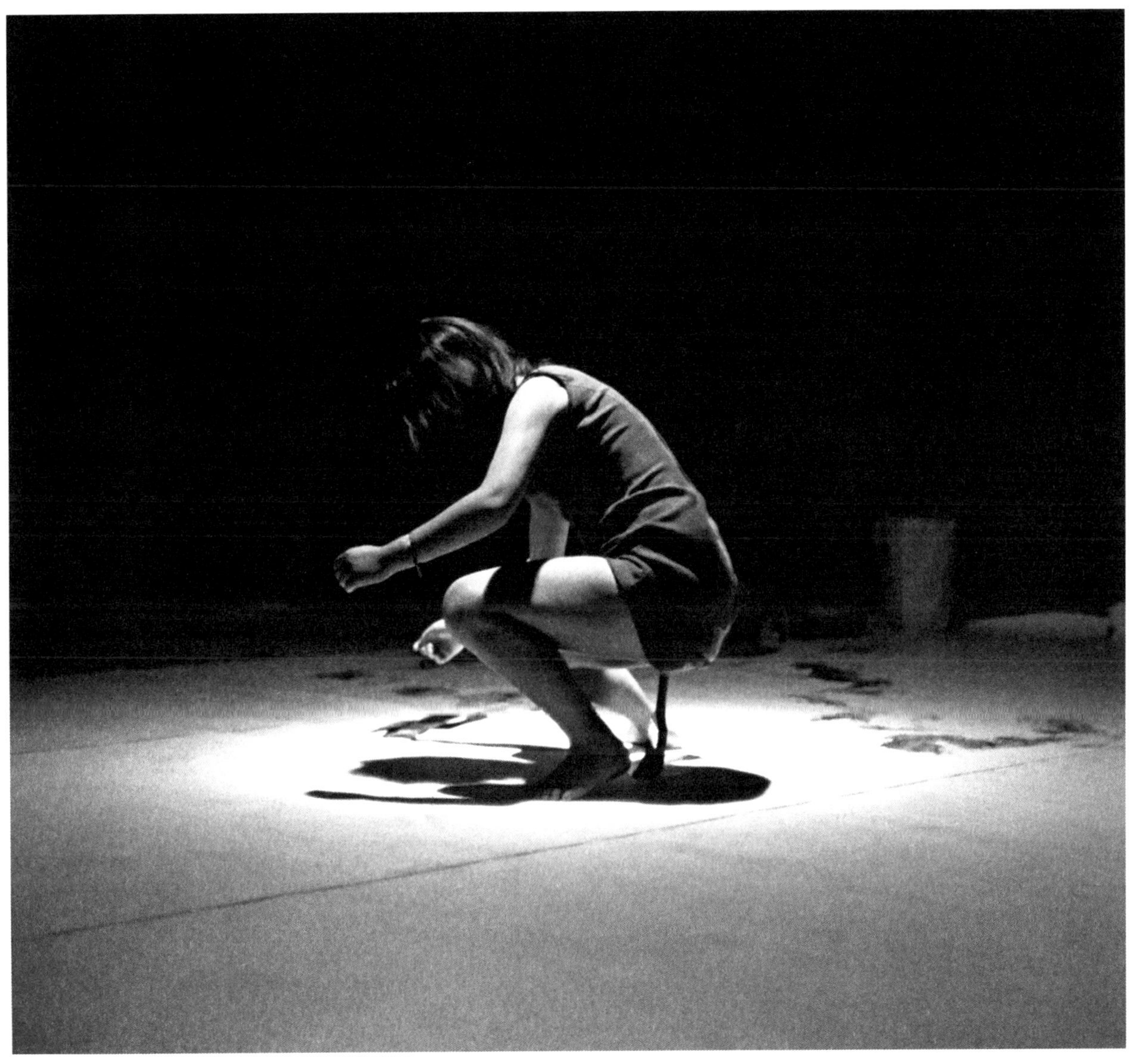

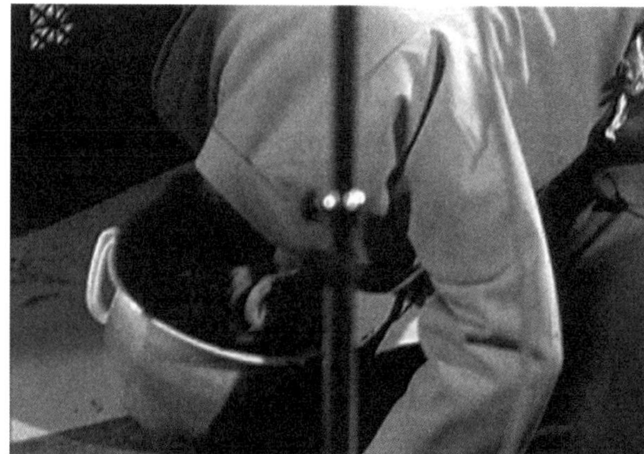

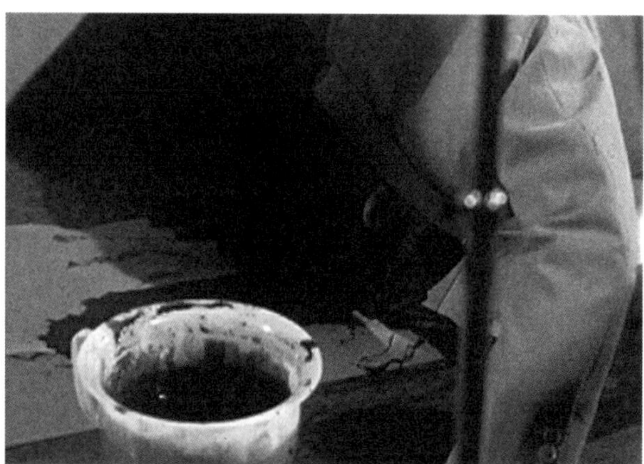

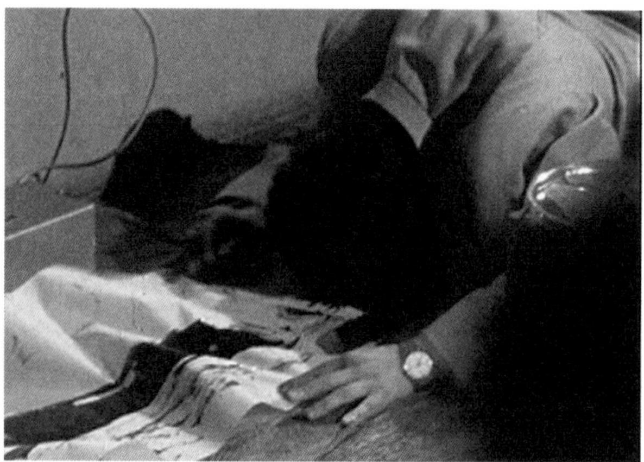

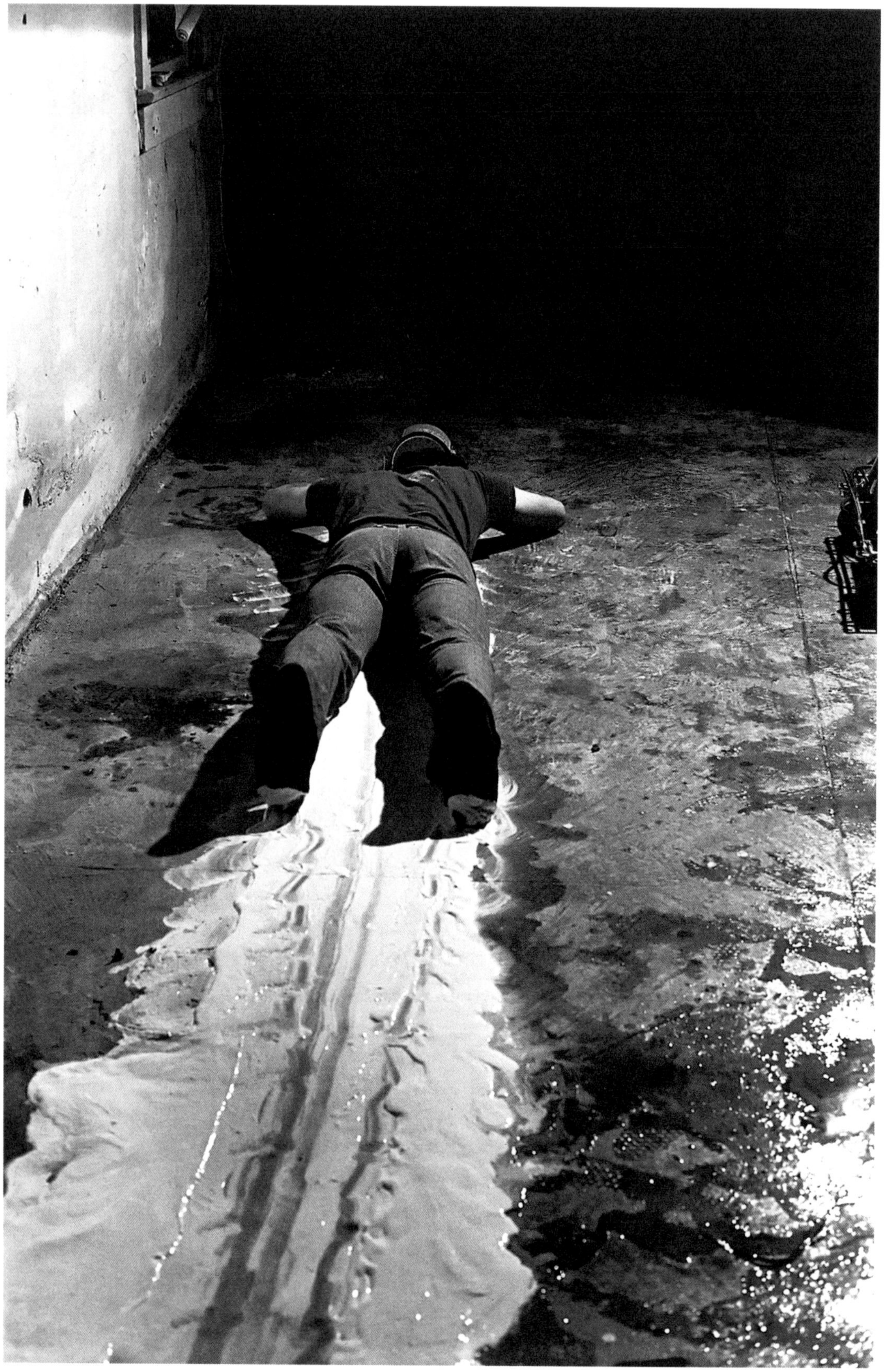

blurred with the painterly ground and becomes the support for a thick black line, merging actor and acted-upon. Continuing this legacy, Paul McCarthy would reimagine Paik's performance in 1972 in *Face Painting—Floor, White Line*, taking artlessness, a lack of refinement, and brute physical presence to an extreme. In this work, McCarthy is shown extending a broad white puddle of paint across a dirty studio floor, using his face to mop the viscous material from

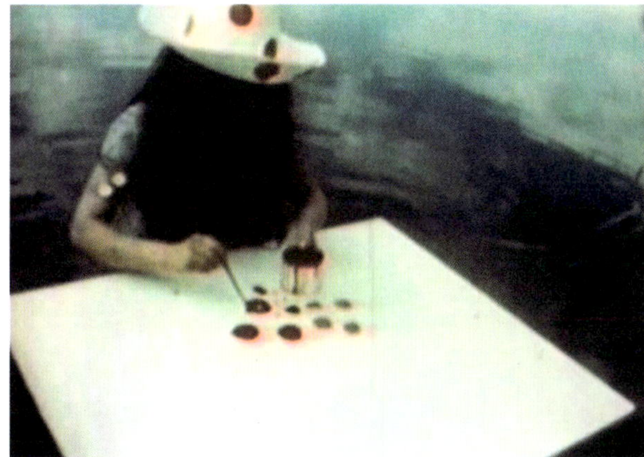

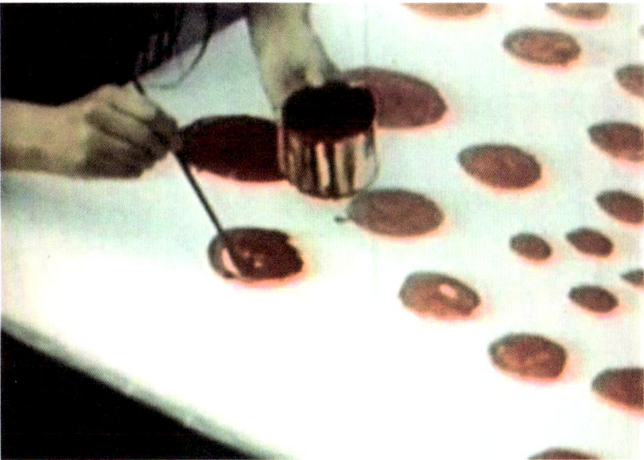

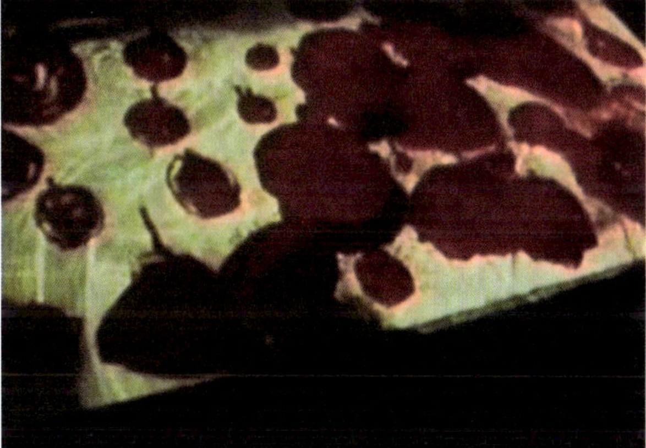

one side to another as his head pushes an over-turned can of paint.

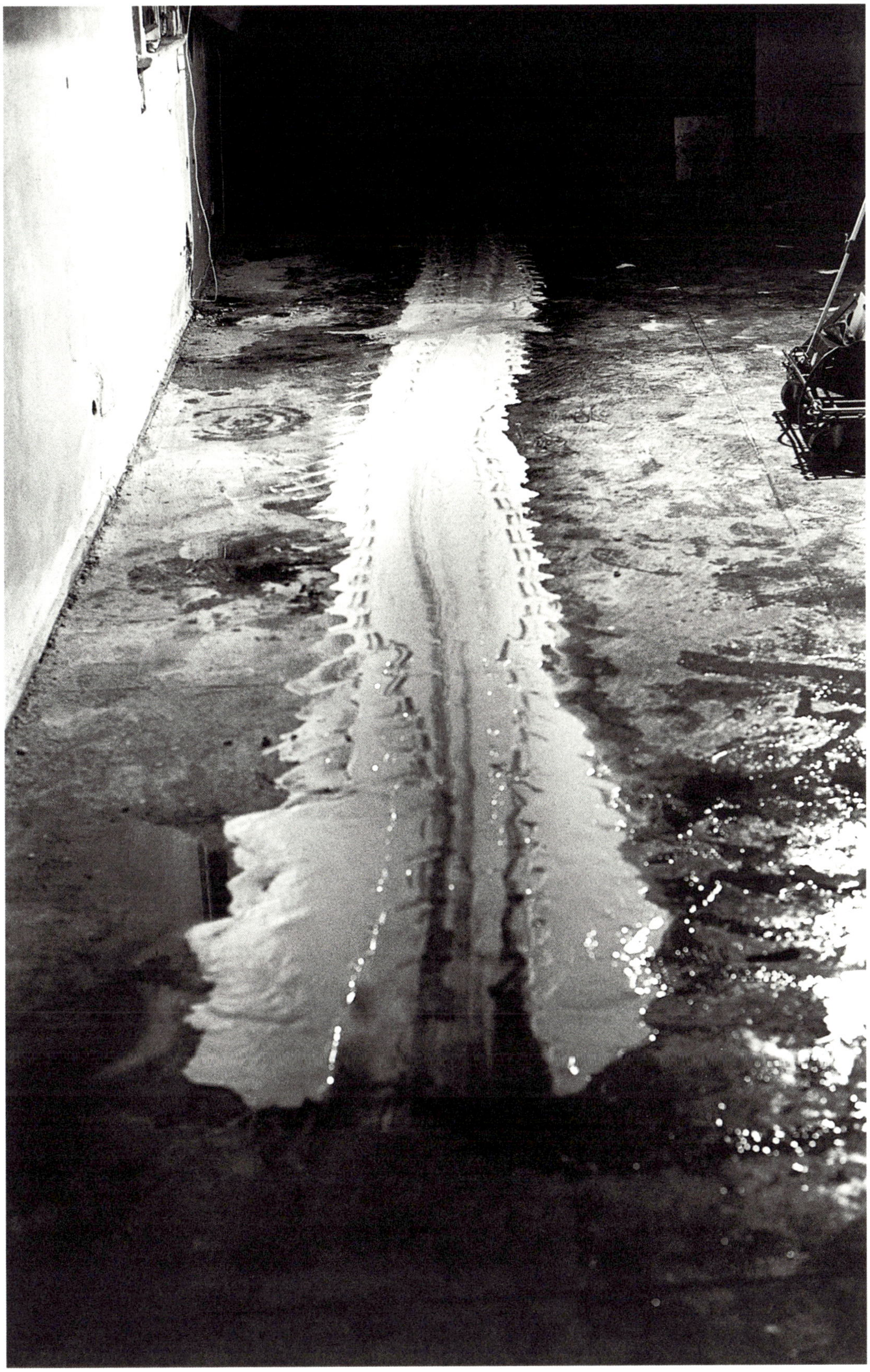

In Yayoi Kusama's *Self-Obliteration* film of 1967, the body is a surface on which painterly activity takes place, but the artist did not confine herself to a studio setting. Instead, seemingly the whole world belongs to her purview, and painting takes place all over. A park, a lake, the woods, and an urban loft space are all sites for action, while surfaces include a horse, a cat,

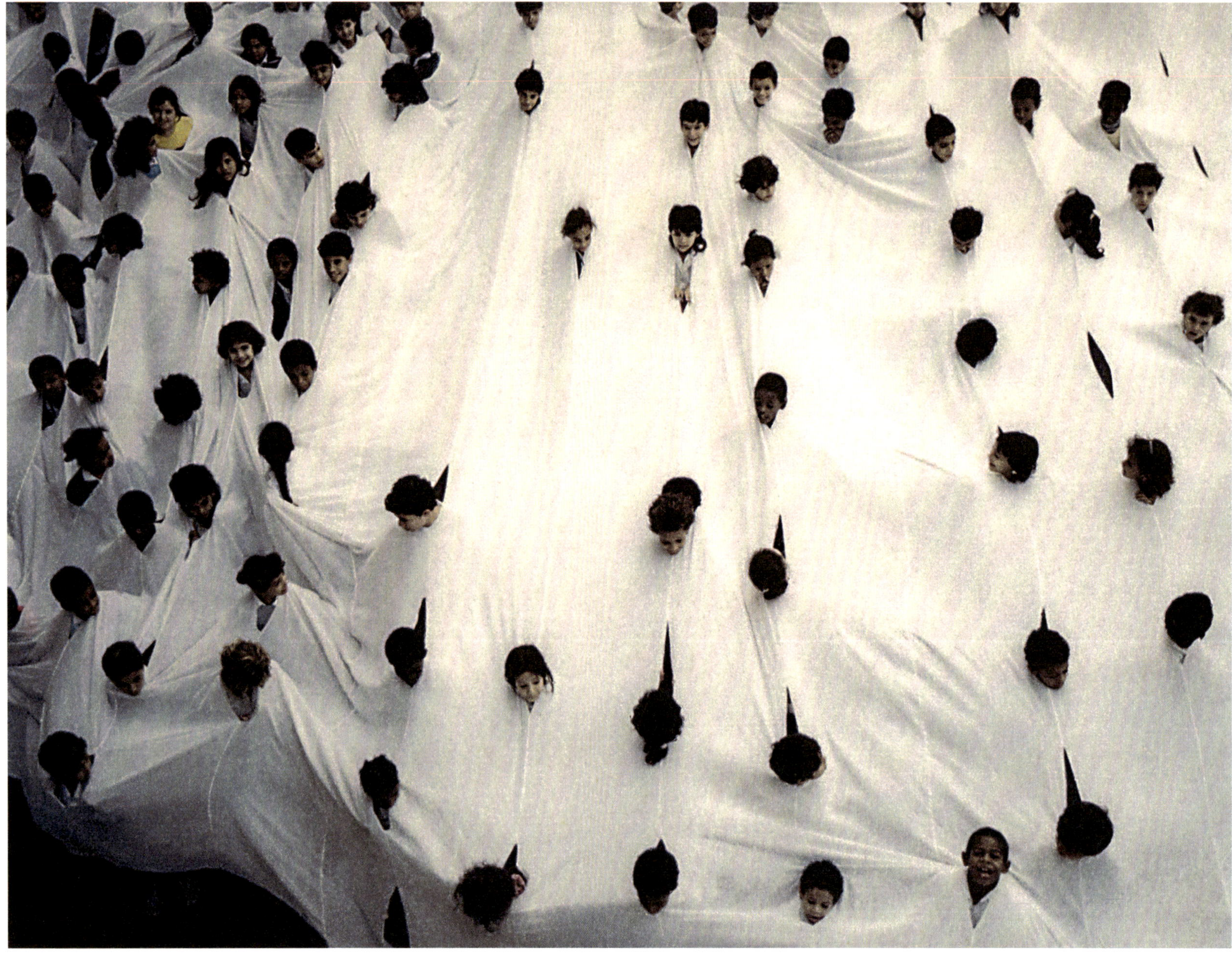

water, trees, and any willing semi-nude body. Her signature circular dots and gestures are likewise not tied down to a single time and place, and some of them, after they have been applied, migrate away in a bold expression of transitoriness that erodes any solidity and objecthood that painting may have had. One key moment shows her painting dots on a board in a pond, and as she submerges the board, the dots drift away on the water's surface. In Brazilian artist Lygia Pape's performance piece *Divisor* (Divider) (1968–91), the field of painting takes on almost universal scale and breadth. A thirty-by-thirty-meter sheet of white cloth is activated by throngs of people whose heads poke through regular openings cut in the fabric, extending the space found in Fontana's earlier gestures in both environmental and communal directions.

Painting takes another turn in two video works, equated with less noble professions than that of the sequestered genius putting brush to canvas. In Bruce Nauman's *Art Make-Up, Nos. 1–4* (1967–68), we see the artist pursuing something similar to Brus's *Selbstbemalung* by

Above: Lygia Pape, *Divisor*, 1968–91. Still from video projection. Projeto Lygia Pape Collection.

Right: Bruce Nauman, *Art Make-Up*, 1967–68. Stills from four 16mm films on video projected onto four walls: *No. 1, White*, 1967; *No. 2, Pink*, 1967–68; *No. 3, Green*, 1967–68; *No. 4, Black*, 1967–68. Electronic Arts Intermix, New York.

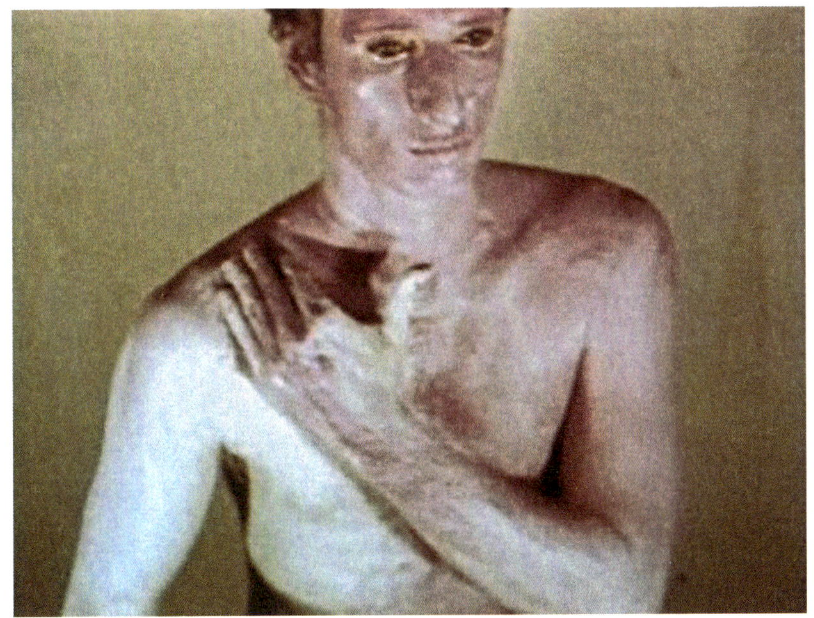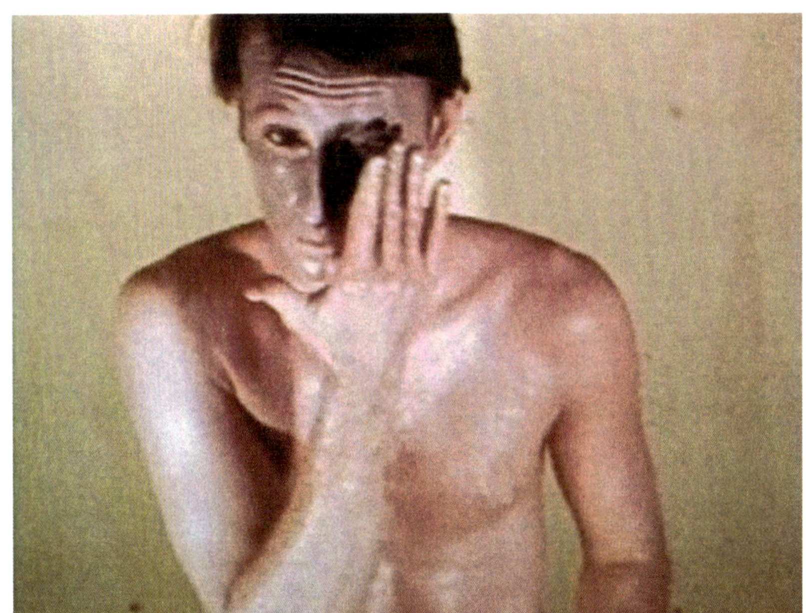
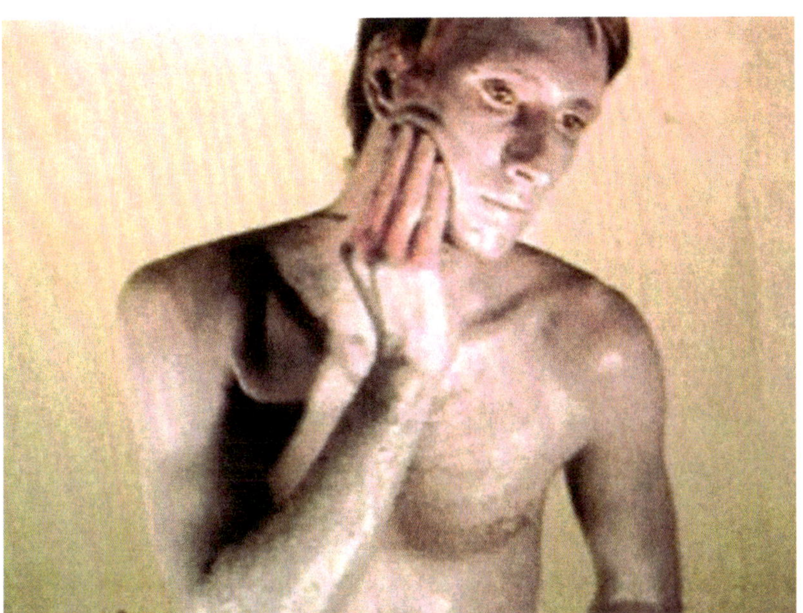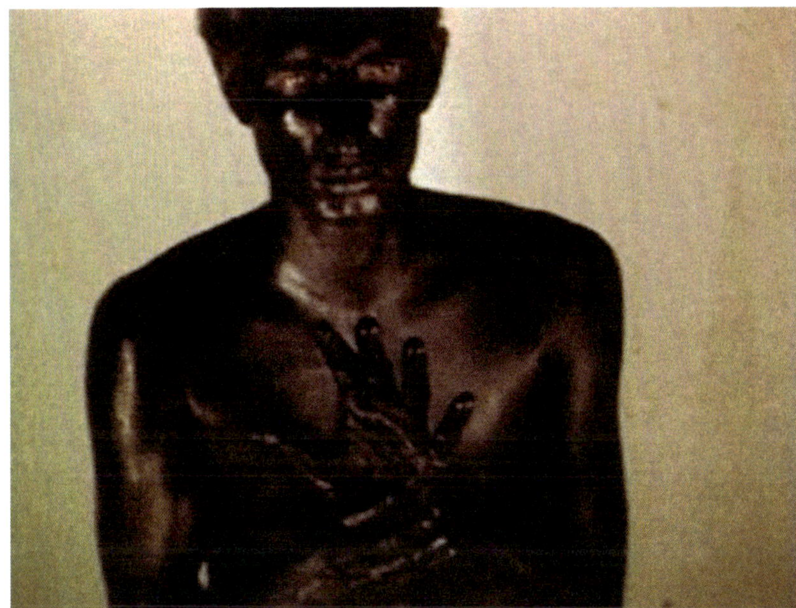

applying four different colored substances to his face and upper body. In so doing, Nauman turns himself into a monochrome (albeit four different ones). But the title of the work and his mirror-guided application of the medium bring the practice of painting in line with beauty rituals or the artifice of theater. Baldessari, in *Six Colorful Inside Jobs* (1977; page 54), aims in a different but no less humorous and deflating direction, conjuring the everyday house painter. In this thirty-five minute film, the six colors of the spectrum are paired with the days of the week, excluding Sunday (the day of rest), and a house painter proceeds to completely paint out the same room using each day's respective color.[38] As in the artist's aforementioned text painting, it is not necessary for Baldessari himself to do the physical work; more important is the way he promiscuously complicates distinctions between high and low. As the artist himself acknowledged, "I used to paint my father's rentals as a kid. There was a fine line between just painting a wall and Painting. Only by pointing out the differences, do I make a change from one to another."[39]

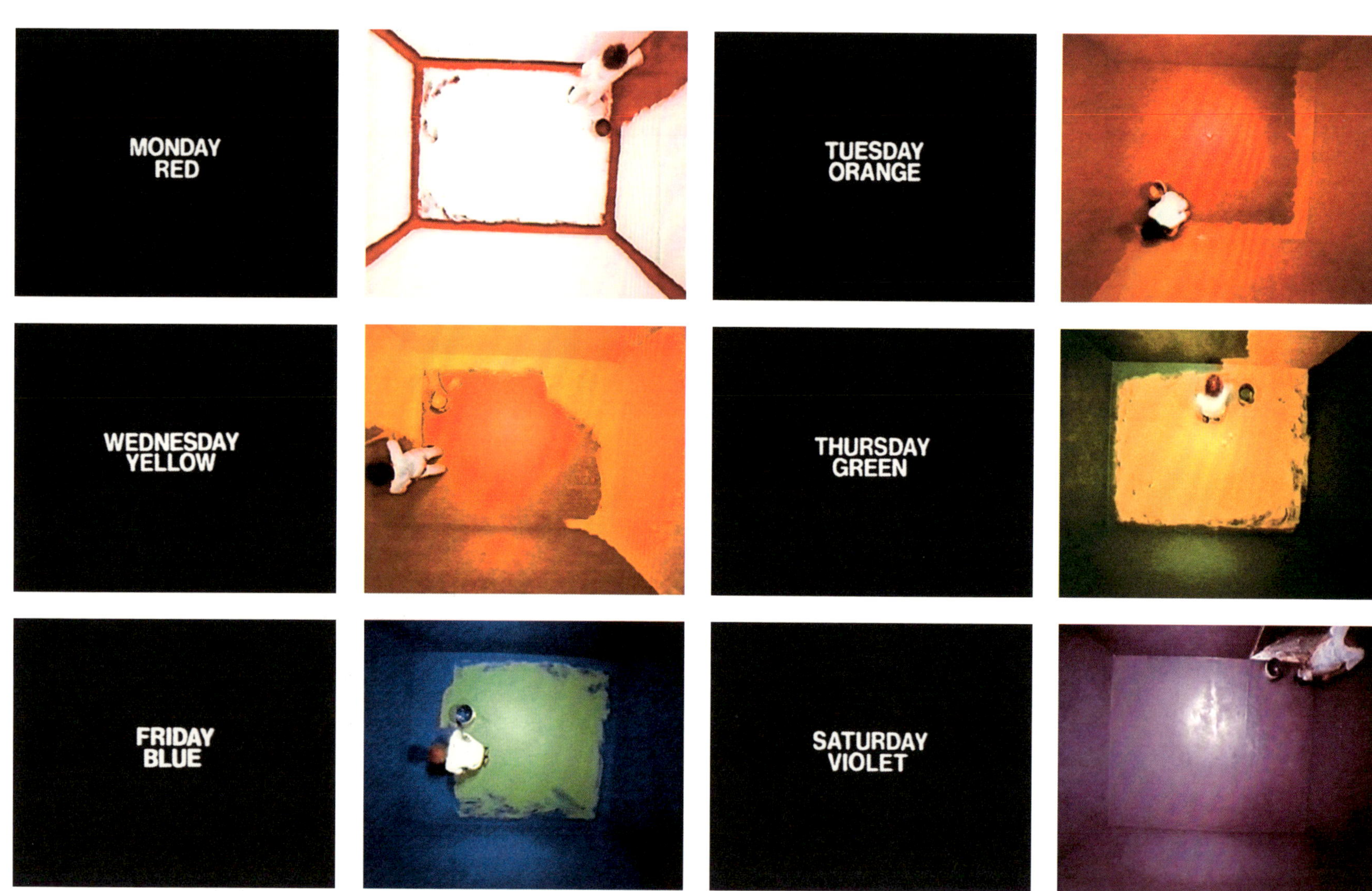
MONDAY
RED
TUESDAY
ORANGE
WEDNESDAY
YELLOW
THURSDAY
GREEN
FRIDAY
BLUE
SATURDAY
VIOLET

Mocking the Makeup of Painting

The same disruption of status that occurs when painting and Painting are put on an equal plane takes place in works in which the basic components—medium, support, gesture, composition, subject—are called out as everyday objects or ideas, rather than treated as sacred precepts. Rauschenberg's breakthrough combines were exemplary in this regard, loaded with scathing jokes and unflattering comparisons between hallowed painterly concepts and the detritus of the street. In a work such as *Untitled* (ca. 1954), one of his earliest combines, the surface is a virtual train wreck of all the constituent parts of a typical painting with its shards of wood, scraps of canvas, masking tape, and a smashed paint tube nailed in place as in a specimen box.

The artist's signature, a time-honored accoutrement of authorship, does not escape this rough treatment and is represented by a found scrap of paper glued to the top left corner on which is written the word "Bob."

In his combines, Rauschenberg found all manner of substitutes for "proper" painting materials, as evidenced in a classic later work such as *Octave* (1960; page 56). Here, paint is applied in many areas with a brush, but it is also unceremoniously squeezed out of a tube or merely evoked through the inclusion of a men's tie that looks like and functions within the composition as a brushstroke. Another sure innovation is the mysterious emanation of a long drip of black paint from a humble thumbtack. Canvas is certainly used,

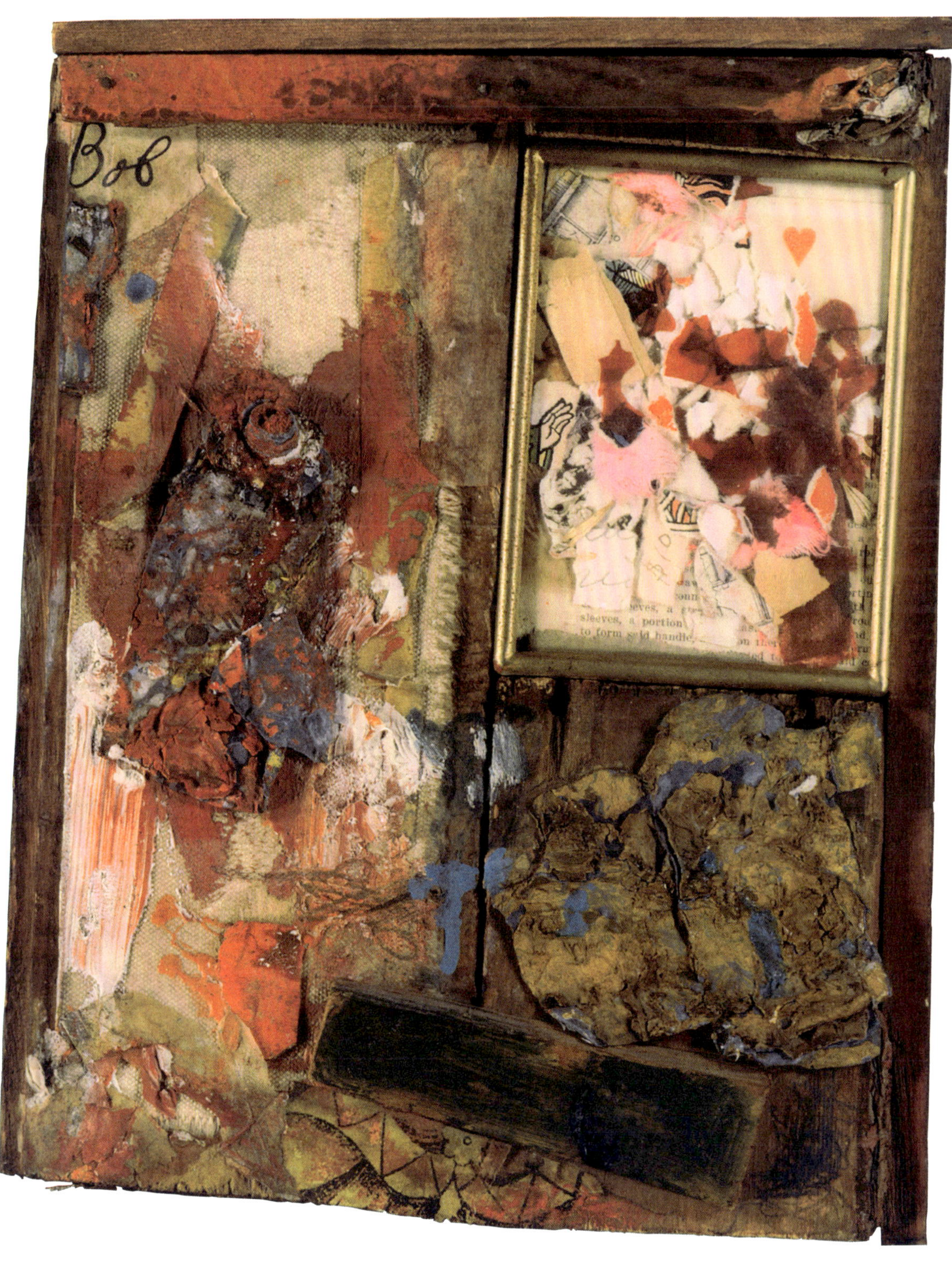

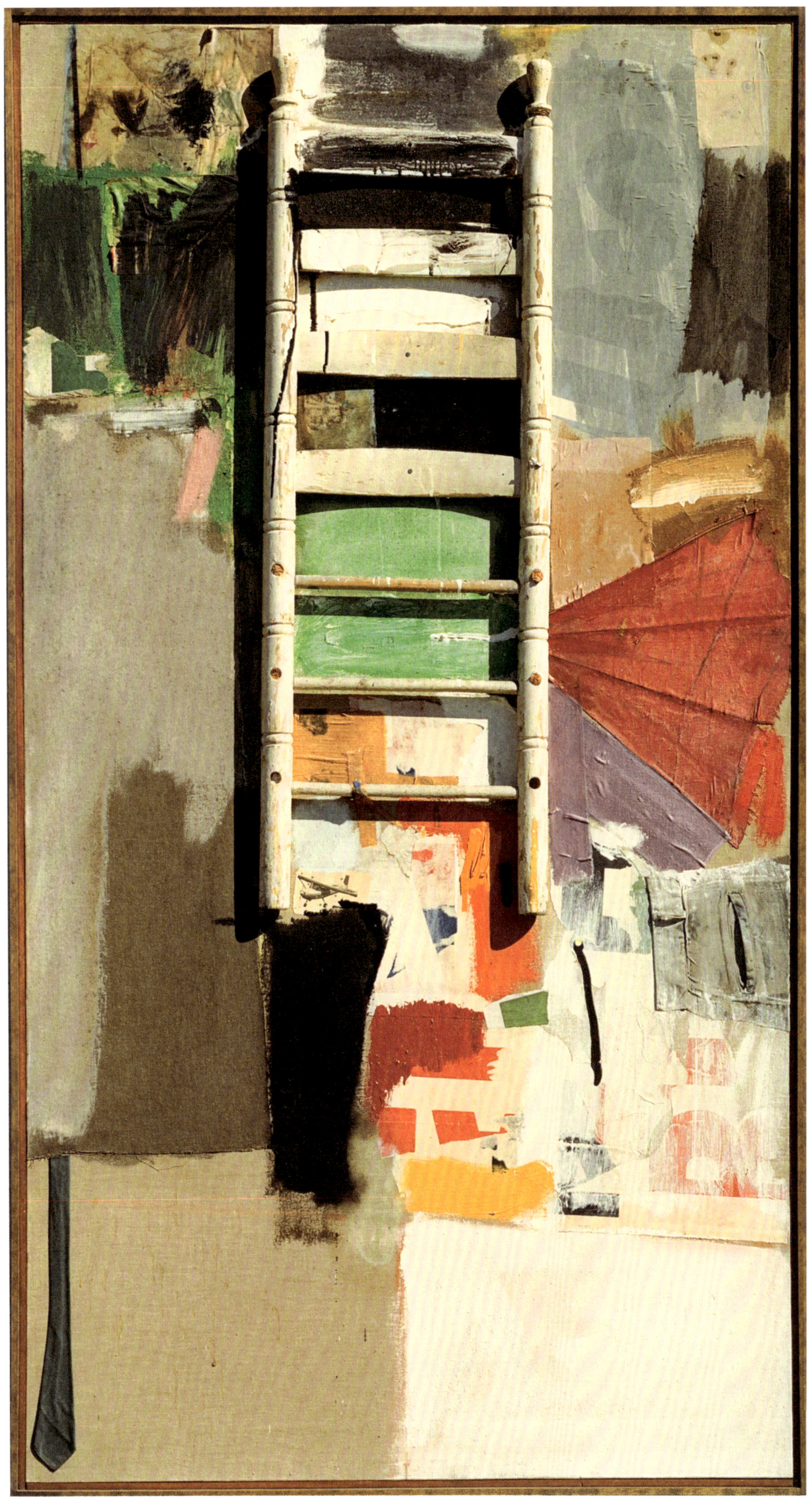

but other fabrics are also shown to be worthwhile supports, among them a broken umbrella, pink silk, part of a dress shirt (with size tag), and a section of trousers, back pocket and all. Instead of worrying over compositional structure or achieving geometric harmony, Rauschenberg relies on a found ladder-back from a chair to provide a readymade solution to that age-old problem of organization. Another highly influential aspect of the combines is their inclusion of printed materials taken from books, magazines, and newspapers, which, by virtue of their nature as reproductions that exist numerously in the world, challenge the idea of primacy. As Crimp has noted about the combines: "Notions of originality, authenticity, and presence, essential to the discourse of the museum, are undermined."[40]

Such was the goal as well of the Danish artist Asger Jorn, who openly challenged the idea of the original artwork in his "détournée" paintings, in which he overpainted found conventional canvases—landscapes, portraits, and the like—in disrespectful ways in order to give old forms new life. His *Détournement de paysage* (Détourned Landscape) (1959)—a bucolic landscape painting turned on its side to frame

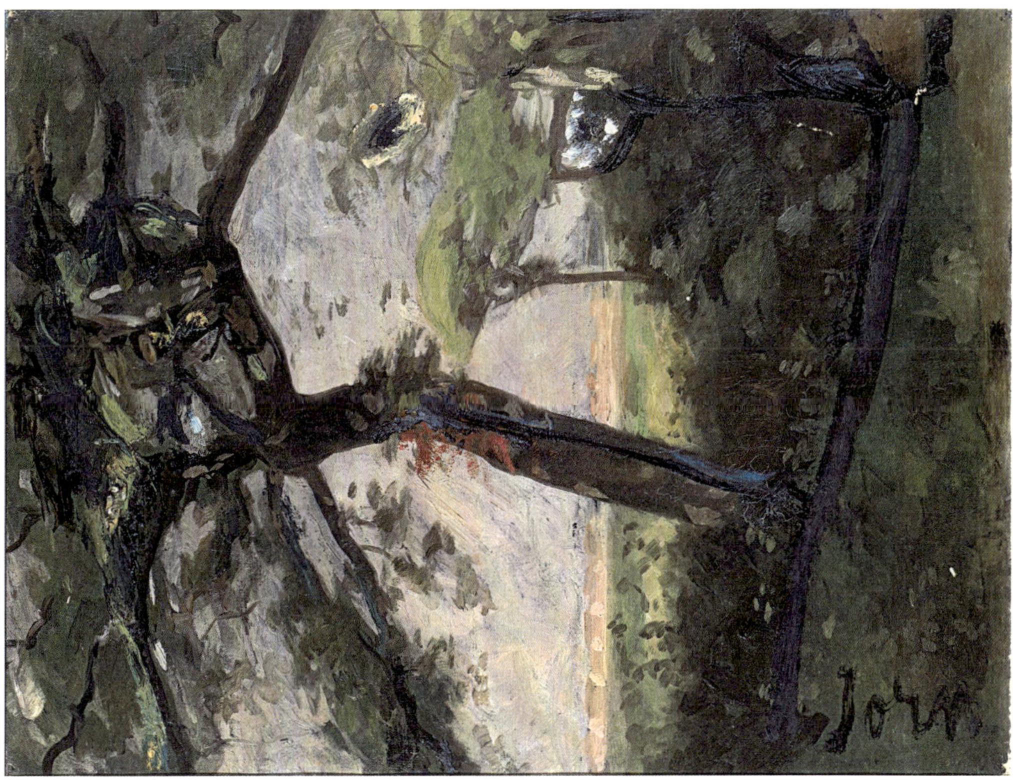

a newly painted face—is an excellent example of this, dating from the middle of his involvement with the radical Situationist International group in Paris, whose members, active throughout Europe between 1957 and 1972, strove to create disruptive "situations" for the viewer. The history, conventions, and status of painting were explicitly Jorn's target, as evidenced in his thoughts on this Situationist technique: "Détournement is a game born out of the capacity for devalorization. Only he who is able to devalorize can create new values. And only there where there is something to devalorize, that is, an already established value, can one engage in devalorization."[41] As the Situationists were prone to manifestos, Jorn wrote one on détournement that reveals its antiestablishment basis:

Be modern,
collectors, museums.
If you have old paintings,
do not despair.
Retain your memories
but détourn them
so that they correspond with your era.
Why reject the old
if one can modernize it
with a few strokes of the brush?
This casts a bit of contemporaneity
on your old culture.
Be up to date,
and distinguished
at the same time.
Painting is over.
You might as well finish it off.
Détourn.
Long live painting.[42]

The instructional nature of Jorn's project can be seen as the radicalized counterpoint to Greenberg's modernist prescriptions, and during this period artists on both sides of the Atlantic seemed to be preoccupied with the ossified rules of painting. The Canadian Iain Baxter, for instance, was very aware of the doctrinaire requirements that the art establishment placed on painting, and he found ways to ruffle the feathers of art authority figures. In his *Standards: 24* (1962; page 58), made during a period when he was entering works in juried competitions that had very strict

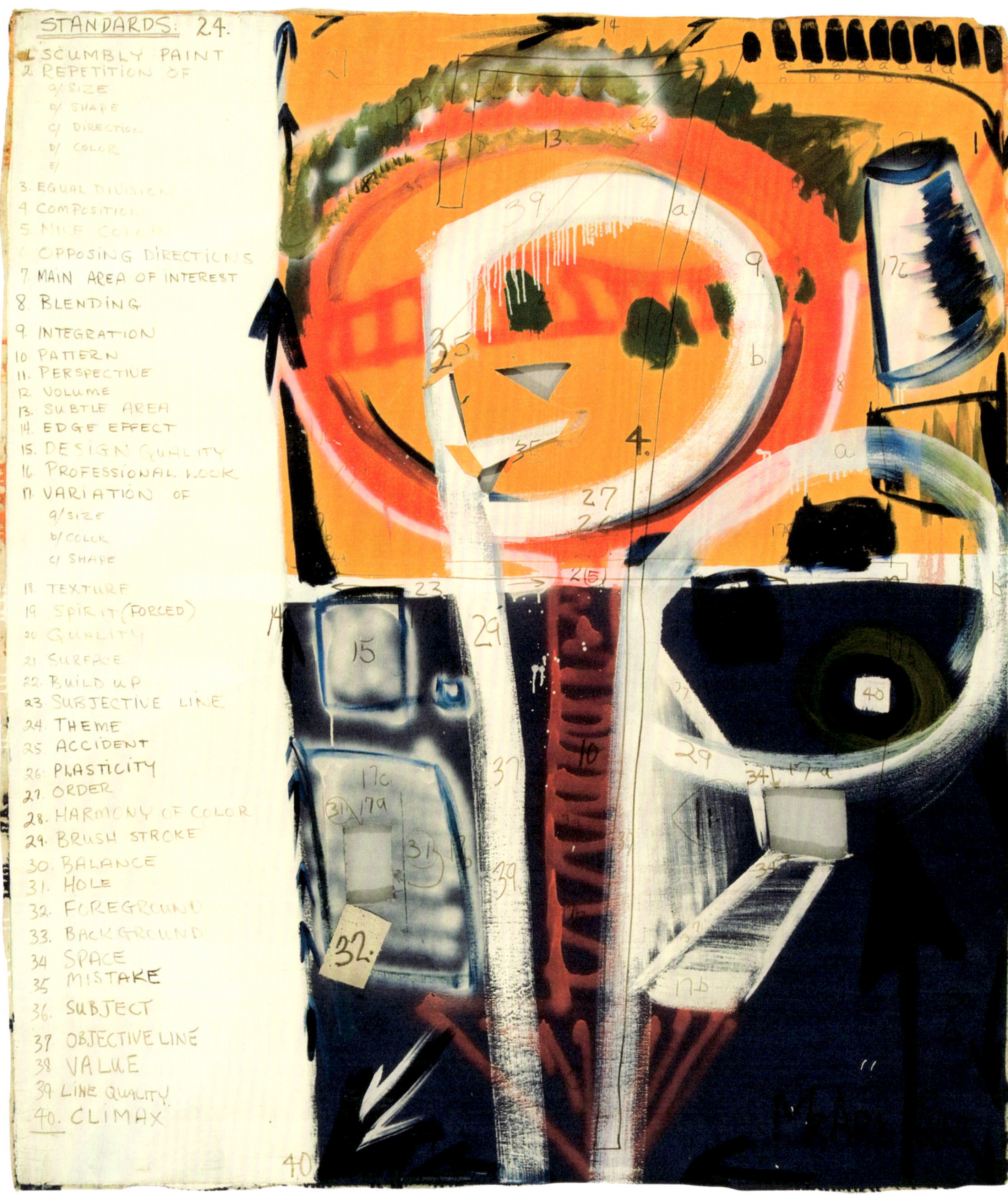

STANDARDS: 24.
1. SCUMBLY PAINT
2. REPETITION OF
a/ SIZE
b/ SHAPE
c/ DIRECTION
d/ COLOR
e/
3. EQUAL DIVISION
4. COMPOSITION
5. NICE COLOR
6. OPPOSING DIRECTIONS
7. MAIN AREA OF INTEREST
8. BLENDING
9. INTEGRATION
10. PATTERN
11. PERSPECTIVE
12. VOLUME
13. SUBTLE AREA
14. EDGE EFFECT
15. DESIGN QUALITY
16. PROFESSIONAL LOOK
17. VARIATION OF
a/ SIZE
b/ COLOR
c/ SHAPE
18. TEXTURE
19. SPIRIT (FORCED)
20. QUALITY
21. SURFACE
22. BUILD UP
23. SUBJECTIVE LINE
24. THEME
25. ACCIDENT
26. PLASTICITY
27. ORDER
28. HARMONY OF COLOR
29. BRUSH STROKE
30. BALANCE
31. HOLE
32. FOREGROUND
33. BACKGROUND
34. SPACE
35. MISTAKE
36. SUBJECT
37. OBJECTIVE LINE
38. VALUE
39. LINE QUALITY
40. CLIMAX

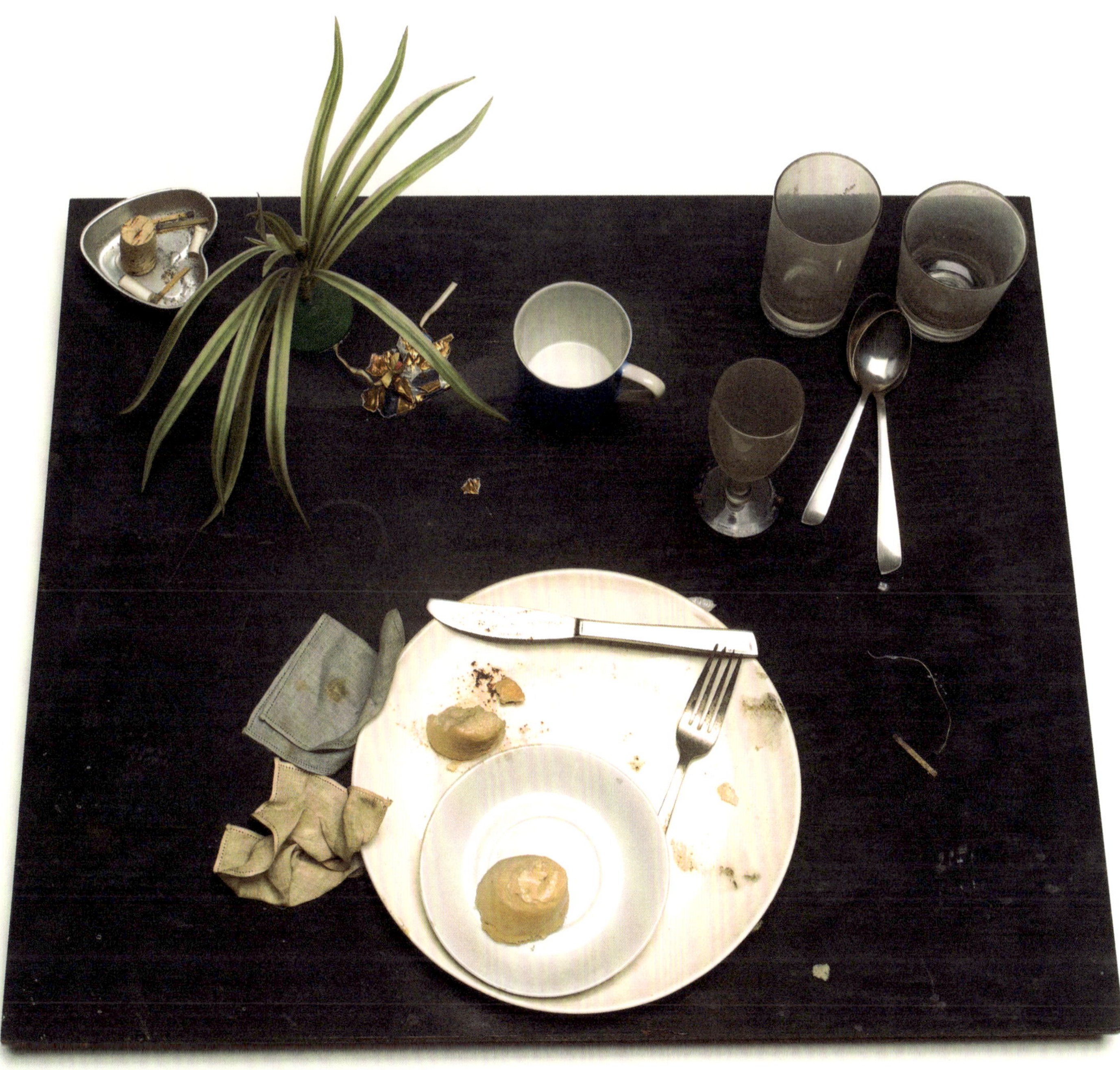

guidelines for acceptance, he enumerated all the necessary qualities to be found in the painting to make clear his nominal adherence to orthodoxy. Signed with the pseudonym Mr. Art Paint and featuring a numbered key, the painting carefully notes where the viewer can find such elements as subject, value, blending, pattern, edge effect, main area of interest, and finally climax. Fluxus artist Daniel Spoerri,

in his series of *Snare Pictures* begun in 1960, takes on the common procedures of picture making by affixing the residue of a meal (or other everyday activities) to a solid surface and then, in defiance of gravity, displaying it on the wall as painting. In *31 Variations on a Meal: Eaten by Bruce Conner* (1964), notions of chance and happenstance trump the considered deliberations of the traditional studio

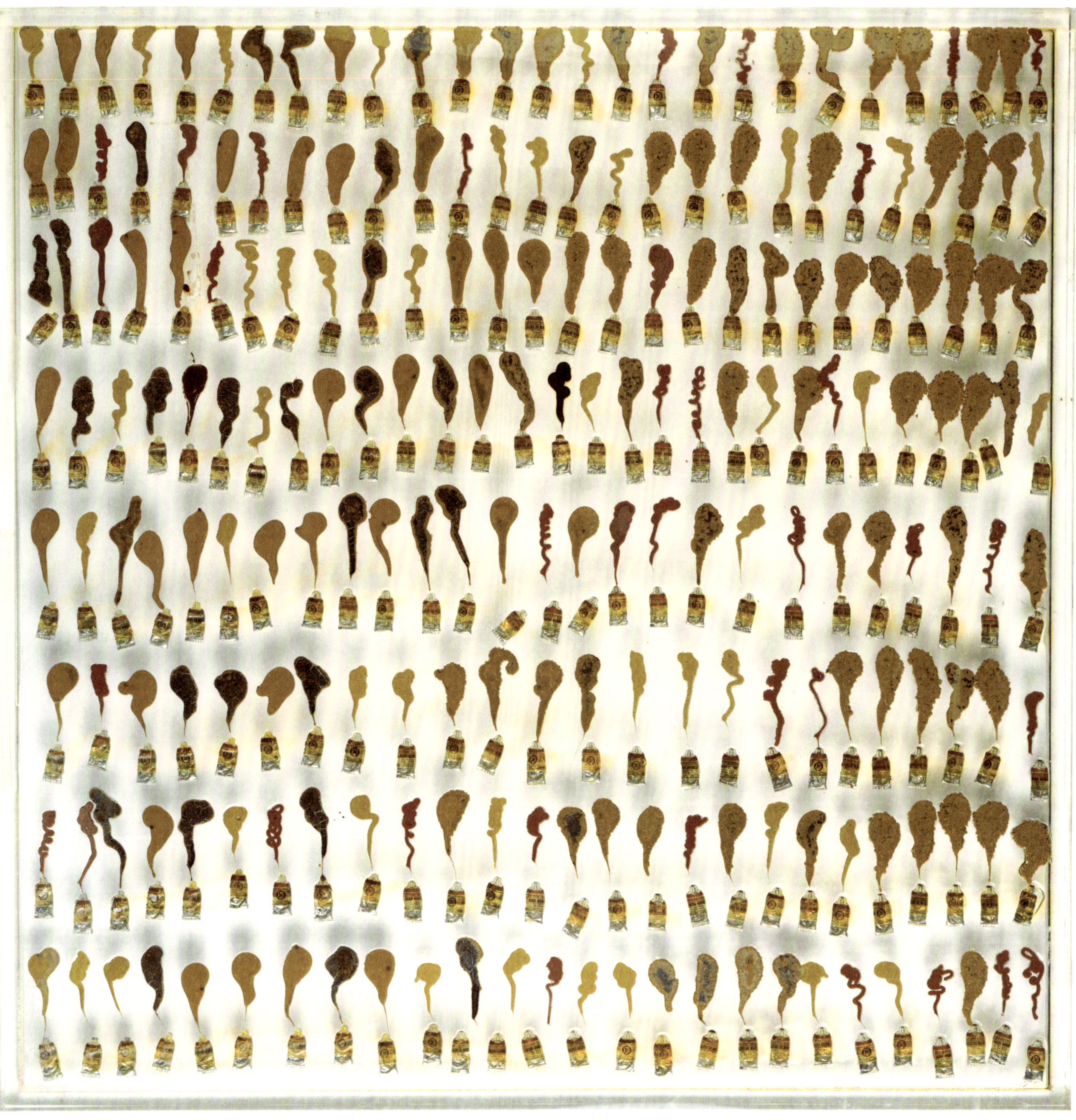

painter, and in fact the actions and movements of a person other than Spoerri himself—namely, fellow artist Conner—determined the ultimate arrangement of the objects.

Other ways of calling attention to the traditional components of painting were pursued by artists as diverse as Hélio Oiticica, Pape, Arman, and Pettibone. In his groundbreaking series of glass *Bólides*, the Brazilian Oiticica continued his systematic and highly motivated investigation of color by isolating different hues in glass bottles and jars, sometimes using materials drawn from the realm of fine arts, other times borrowing things more readily found in nature, fashion, or décor. In *B22*

and temporal dimension that could only be appreciated when released from the plane.'[43]

The French artist Arman used a different method to isolate color as object in his series of accumulated paint tubes. Freezing the gestural and spontaneous nature of Abstract Expressionism and its European equivalent Art Informel, and revealing the off-the-shelf, commercial nature of fine-art paints, *Ocher (Ochre)* (1967) proposes a hybridized art object—part sculpture, part painting—while alluding to time in a melancholic way. For in *Ocher (Ochre)*, the act of painting is positioned as a dead practice: the tubes and expelled paint are encased in clear acrylic the way fossils are

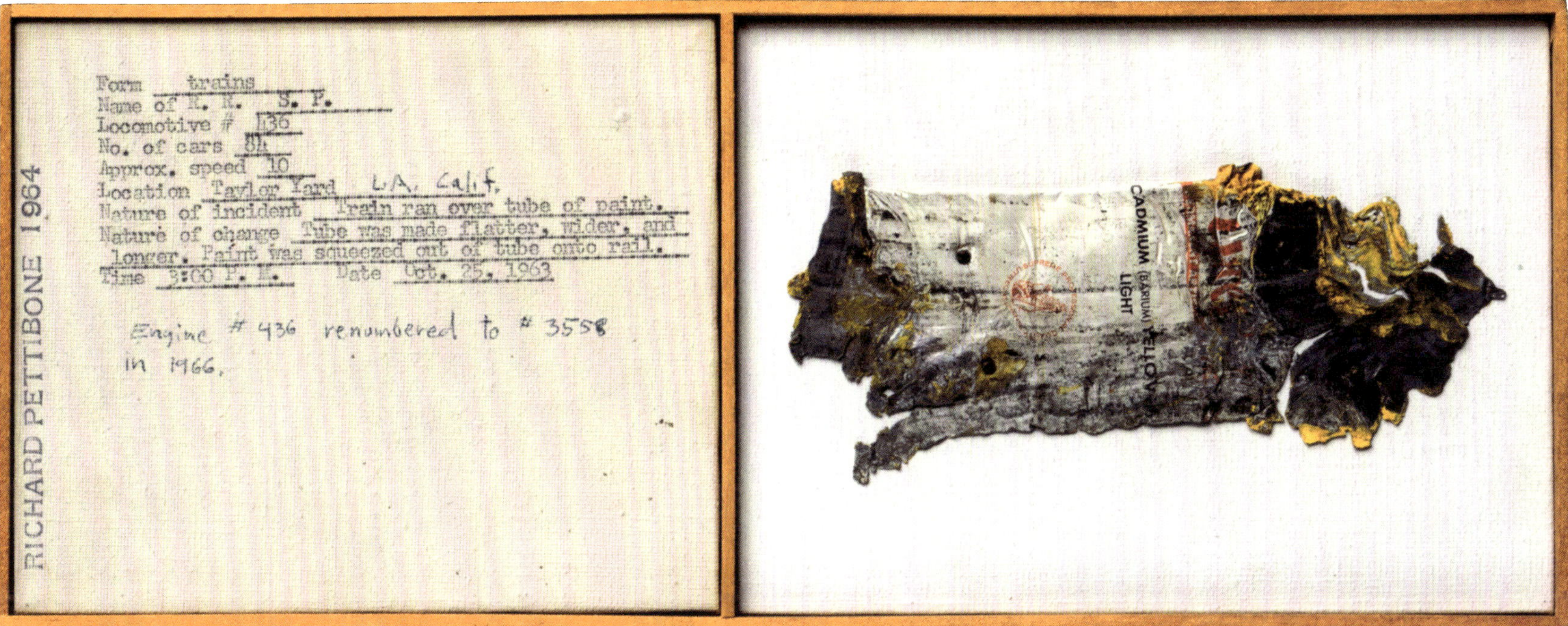

Bólide vidro 10 "Homenagem a Malevitch Gemini" 01 (B22 Glass Fireball 10 "Homage to Malevich Twin" 01) (1965; page 131), he stripped this exercise to its essence, placing two aftershave-lotion bottles filled with blue and yellow pigment side by side in a sculptural diptych. This work exemplifies the bold experimentalism with which Oiticica approached the conventions of painting. As Mari Carmen Ramírez has noted, Oiticica "considered color to be a fully autonomous system that had remained far too long subordinated to the pictorial support. As such, color had its own spatial

suspended in amber. A moment in time has been captured for study and reflection, but (as opposed to the openness in Oiticica's work) cannot be renewed. Pettibone orchestrated a related "death" in his *Untitled (Train ran over tube of paint, October 25, 1963)* (1964), which scientifically records in one panel the circumstances under which a locomotive smashed a tube of cadmium yellow paint. The "corpse" is pinned to a matching canvas like a butterfly specimen, the victim of a violently destructive act; but as the artist has pointed out, the work is also evidence of an outlandish way to "get the

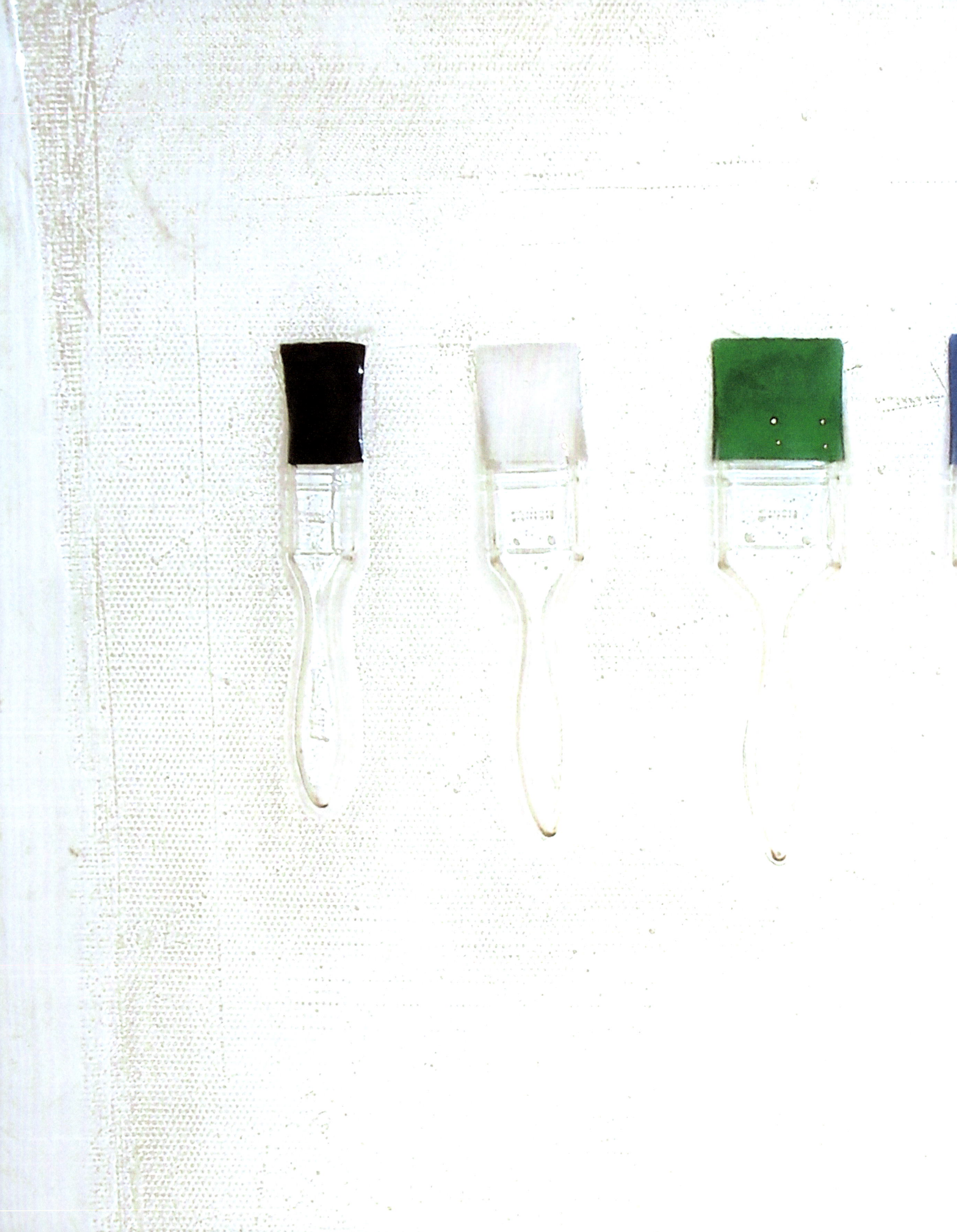

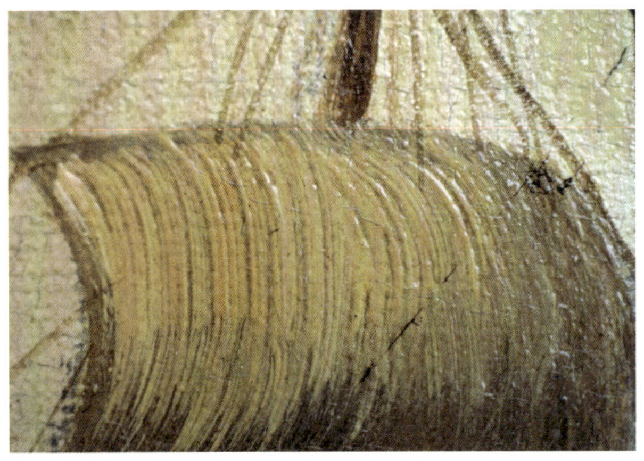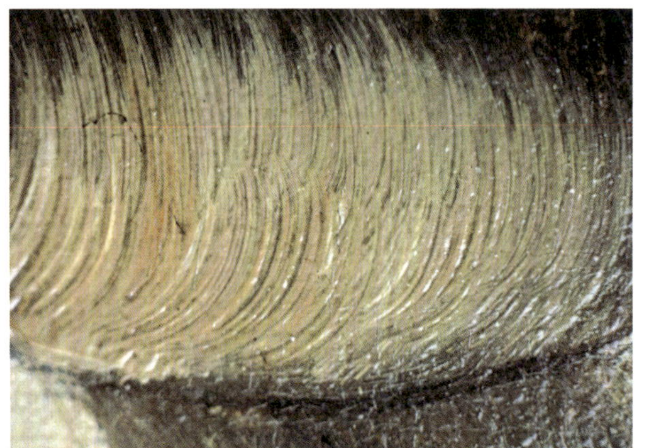

Pages 62–63: Iain Baxter, *Still Life with 6 Colours* (detail), 1965. Vacuum-formed plastic. Courtesy of the artist and Corkin Gallery, Toronto (since 2005 the artist has gone by the name IAIN BAXTER&).

Left: Marcel Broodthaers, *Tableau Bateau*, 1973. Stills from 80-slide projection. Collection of Pamela and Richard Kramlich.

Right: Joe Goode, *Torn Cloud Painting*, 1975. Oil on canvas. Portland Art Museum, Purchase: Funds provided by the Contemporary Art Council.

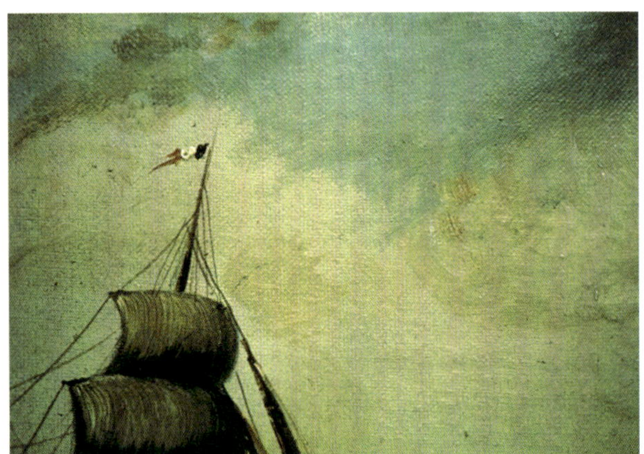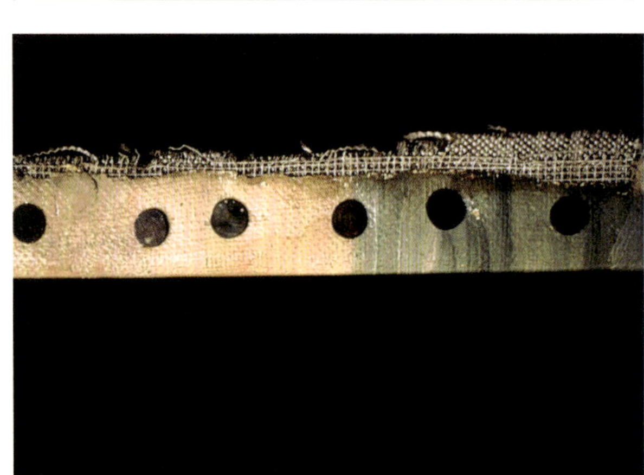

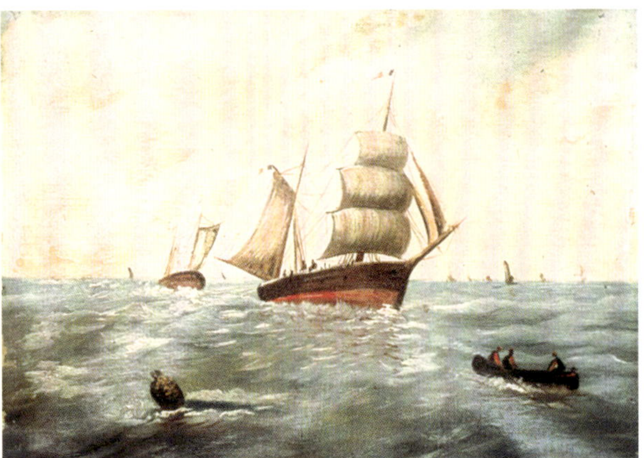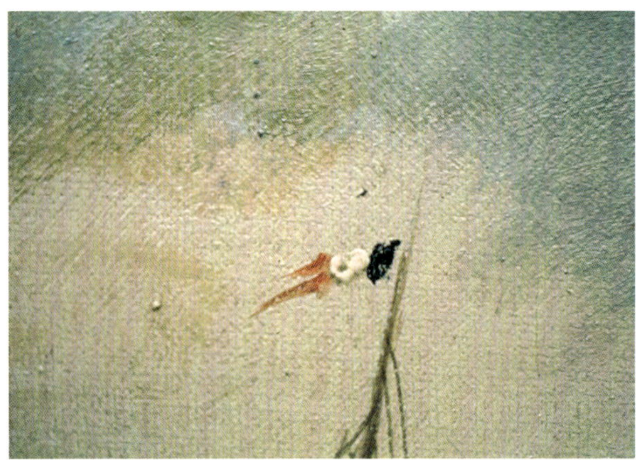

last little bit of paint out of the tube.'[44] A more elegiac feeling pertains to Baxter's *Still Life with 6 Colours* (1965; pages 62–63), in which six sizes of brushes, each with a different color applied to its tip, are pressed into vacuum-formed plastic as if preserving a trace of a bygone era. In this work and others in the series, in which cast-off materials such as plastic bottles are given the same treatment, Baxter puts forward a fairly bleak assessment of painting.

Other basic tenets of painting received equally cool and calculated revision during these years. In *Tableau Bateau* (Boat Picture) (1973), of which a few variations in differing media exist, Broodthaers scrutinized a generic nautical painting found in an antique store through eighty photographs that scroll through a sequence in a slide projector, picking apart the figures and objects in the picture as well as the prosaic painterly flourishes that coaxed it into

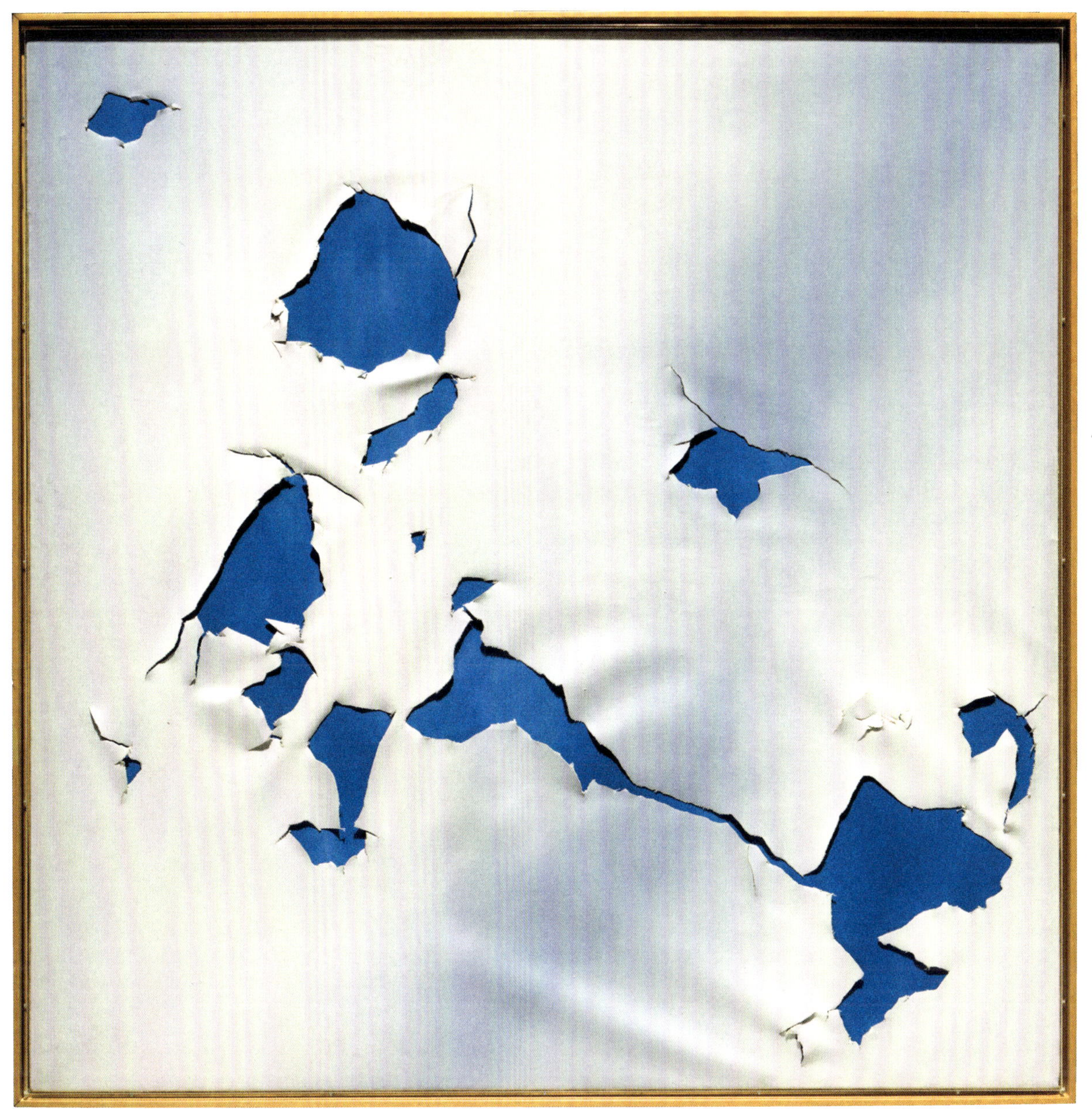

being. In a gesture betraying disappointment with painting's static nature, he reanimates the scene using jump cuts and strategic editing of the images, giving new life to the idea of a voyage at sea. Neil Jenney's *Paint and Painted* (1969; page 140) operates on a different track toward related ends, driving a wedge between the too easily conflated realities of the image and the process that created it. Overtly expressive brushwork laid on in horizontal striations that recall the works of Mark Rothko is held in check by the banality of what is depicted, namely, a can of paint and a prone but still loaded brush. Jenney further plays with conventions of signature and authorship by twisting the can so that "Paint by Pearl" reads as "Aint by Earl," a decidedly unheroic claiming of the work by default. Joe Goode has worked since the early 1960s toward a critical objectification of figure and ground, addressing real space and painterly space at the same time. In his series of *Torn Cloud Paintings*, he again forces viewers into a quandary about having it both ways. The escapism of believing in painterly illusion is simultaneously offered and revoked, and the artist maintains a fascinatingly frustrating middle ground.

Physical Deconstruction

If the works in *Target Practice* are any measure, one might say that between 1949 and 1978 painting was not killed off so much as tortured, and the protracted evisceration it suffered at the hands of artists in the name of renewing its possibilities is extraordinary. Tackling the physical parameters of the rectangular canvas support, artists pulled and stretched painting into new forms, inspiring mini movements such as Supports/Surfaces in France and experimentations all over the world. The support—typically canvas—and the surface—typically covered with paint—were the two essentialist poles around which many varied investigations took place. Richard Tuttle's influential paintings of the mid-1960s were one such exercise, dispens-ing with stretcher bars and rectangular formats in favor of irregular geometric shapes of un-stretched canvas pinned to the wall. Works such as *Untitled* (1967) got their coloration not with a brush but through staining in allover mono-chrome washes and further departed from tradi-tion in their eschewal of fixed orientation. In Brazil, Nelson Leirner took on the traditionally taut surface of the canvas in his *Homenagem a Fontana* (Homage to Fontana) series from 1967 with an immediately recognizable Pop solution: unzipping it as if it were a jacket. His mono-chrome canvases, coupled with their variously opened surfaces, made a witty riposte to Fon-tana's search for new realms beyond the picture plane. Coincidentally, in the United States, Karen Carson came upon the same solution

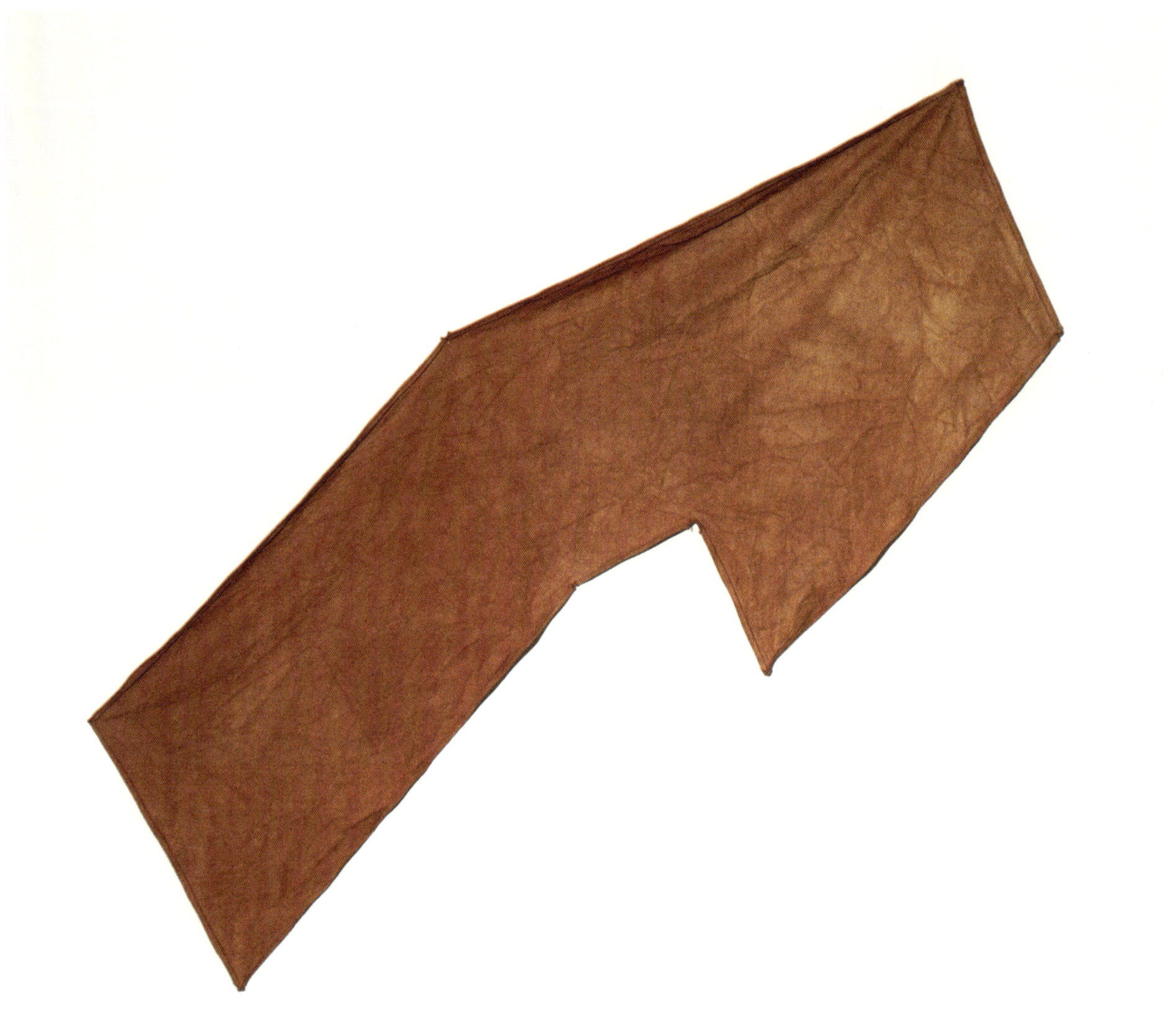

Below: Richard Tuttle, *Untitled*, 1967. Dyed canvas. Seattle Art Museum, Gift of Sidney and Anne Gerber.

Right: Karen Carson, *Untitled*, 1971. Textile, cotton duck, and industrial zippers. Los Angeles County Museum of Art, Purchased with funds provided by the Pasadena Art Alliance and the Rosamund Felsen Gallery.

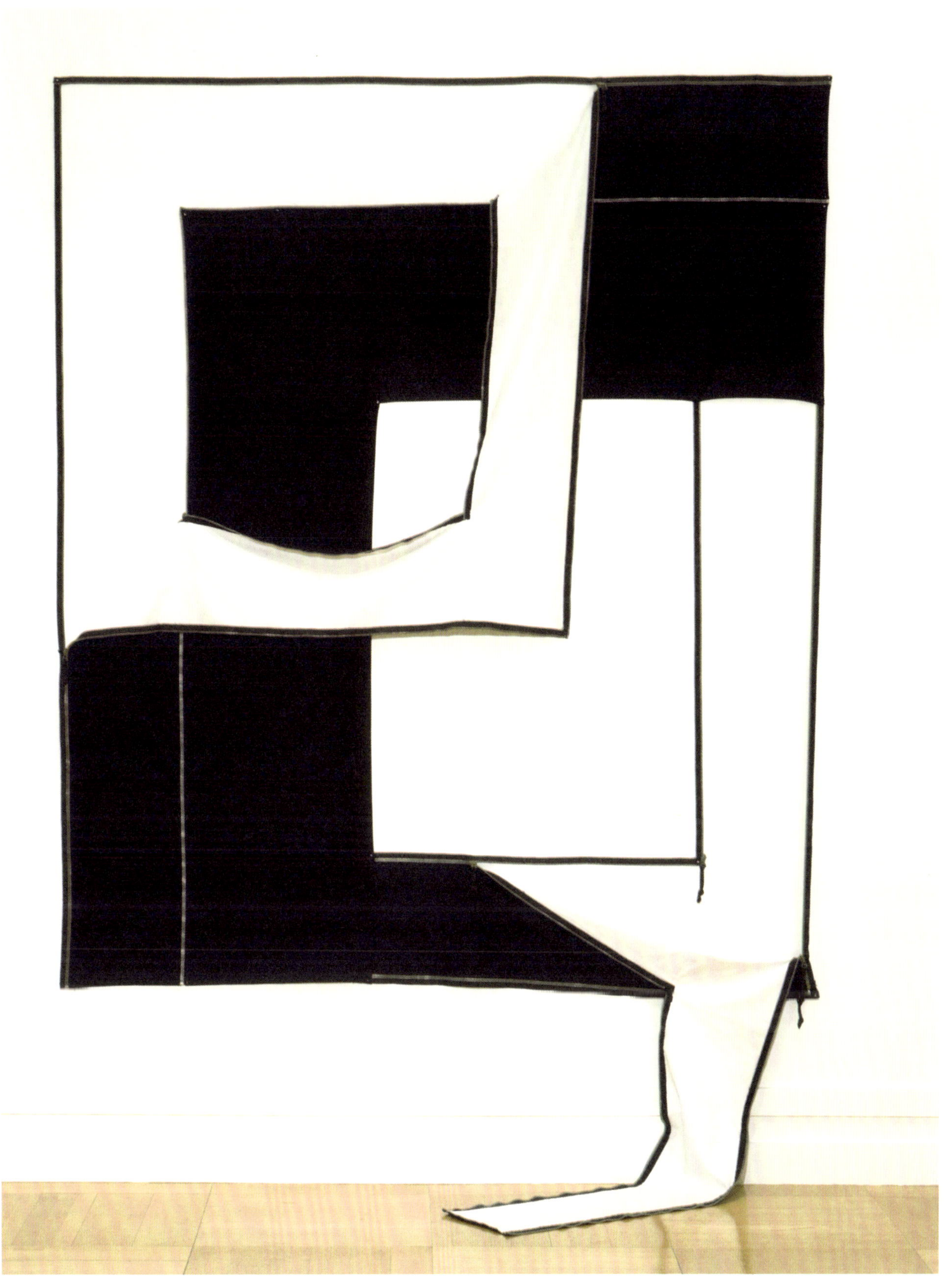

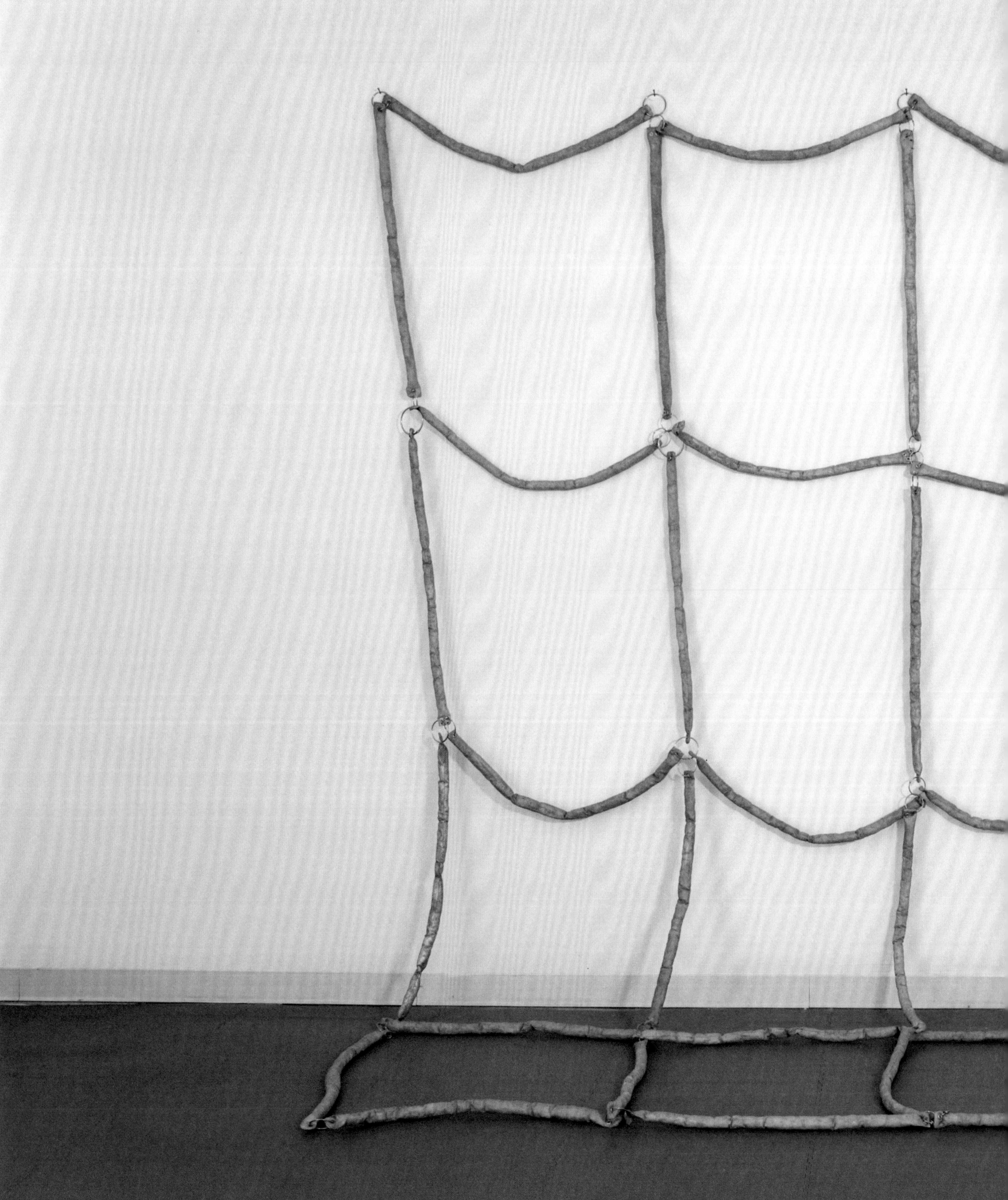

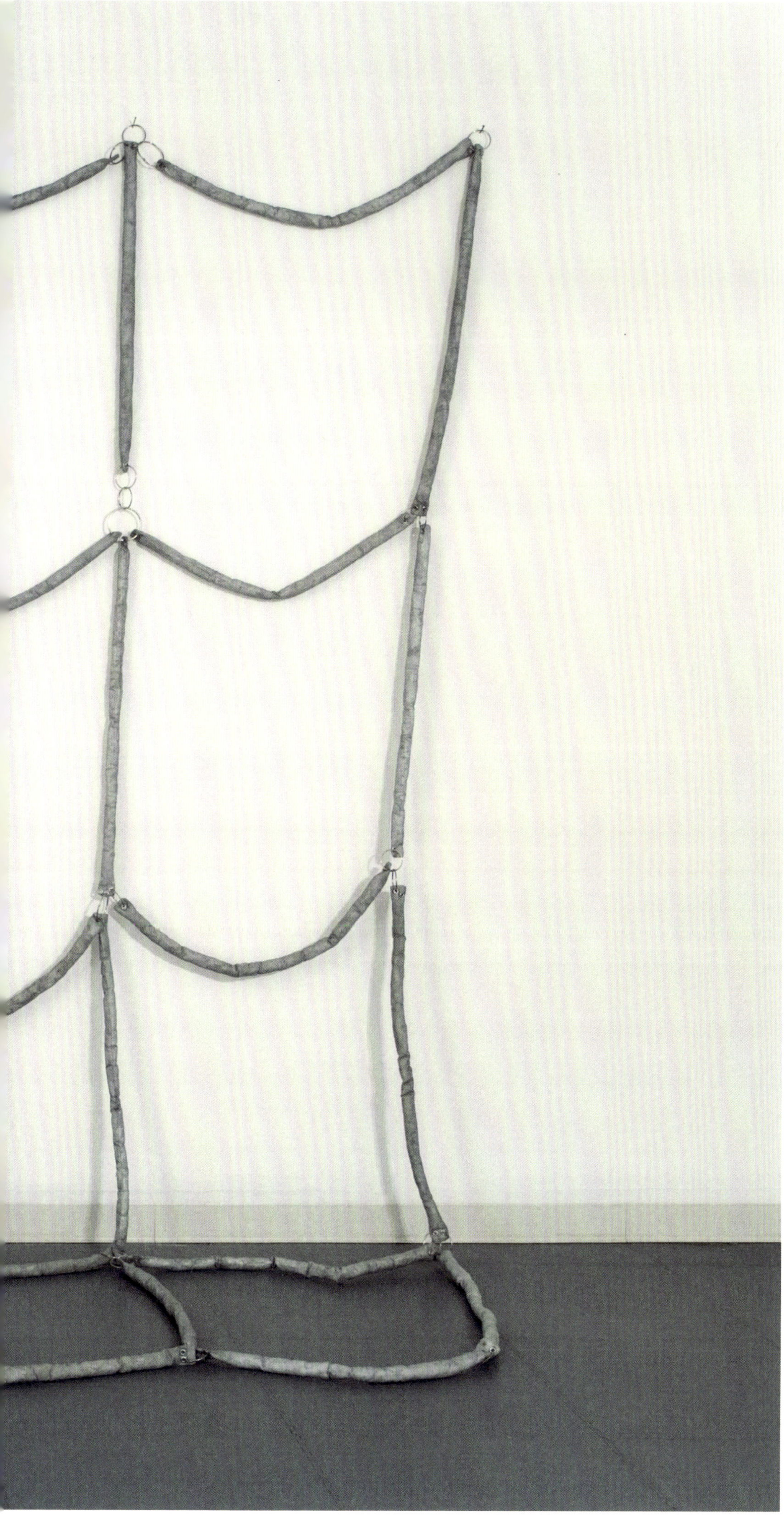

for undoing the hallowed ground of painting, although her unzipped canvases have a distinctly postminimalist feeling compared to the Pop-participatory aura of Leirner's. A piece such as Carson's *Untitled* (1971; page 67) also suggests a feminist critique, as working with fabric and zippers relates to the traditionally female and domestic sphere of sewing as opposed to the macho quest for truth of a studio practice.

A related sensibility can be found in Howardena Pindell's *Untitled* (1968–70; left), in which the rectangular field of taut canvas is again put into play. Here, the field is marked out by skeletal bars made from painted canvas that are stuffed with foam and connected by grommets to create a sagging grid that drapes onto the floor. Sam Gilliam likewise put paint and canvas through unlikely paces in his drooping, deconstructed forms. In *Bow Form Construction* (1968; page 139), for example, heroic notions of painting seem to be violently usurped in favor of shockingly everyday accumulations of paint, more studio drop cloth than exalted artifact, and, as such, refreshingly liberating. Lynda Benglis's garish knotted paintings from this period such as *Chi* (1973; below) and Alvin Loving's shredded tapestries of stained canvas such as *Untitled* (ca. 1970s; page 70) communicate a shared catharsis in the deconstruction of paint and its straight-laced support, opening the door to new possibilities.

By the late 1960s, painting had been pushed to the point where artists such as Benglis, in her poured paintings, questioned the very necessity

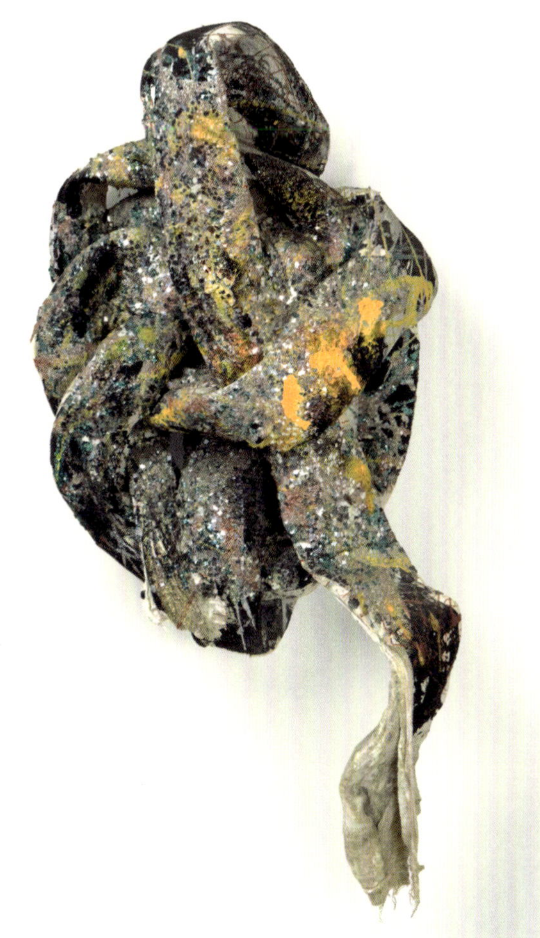

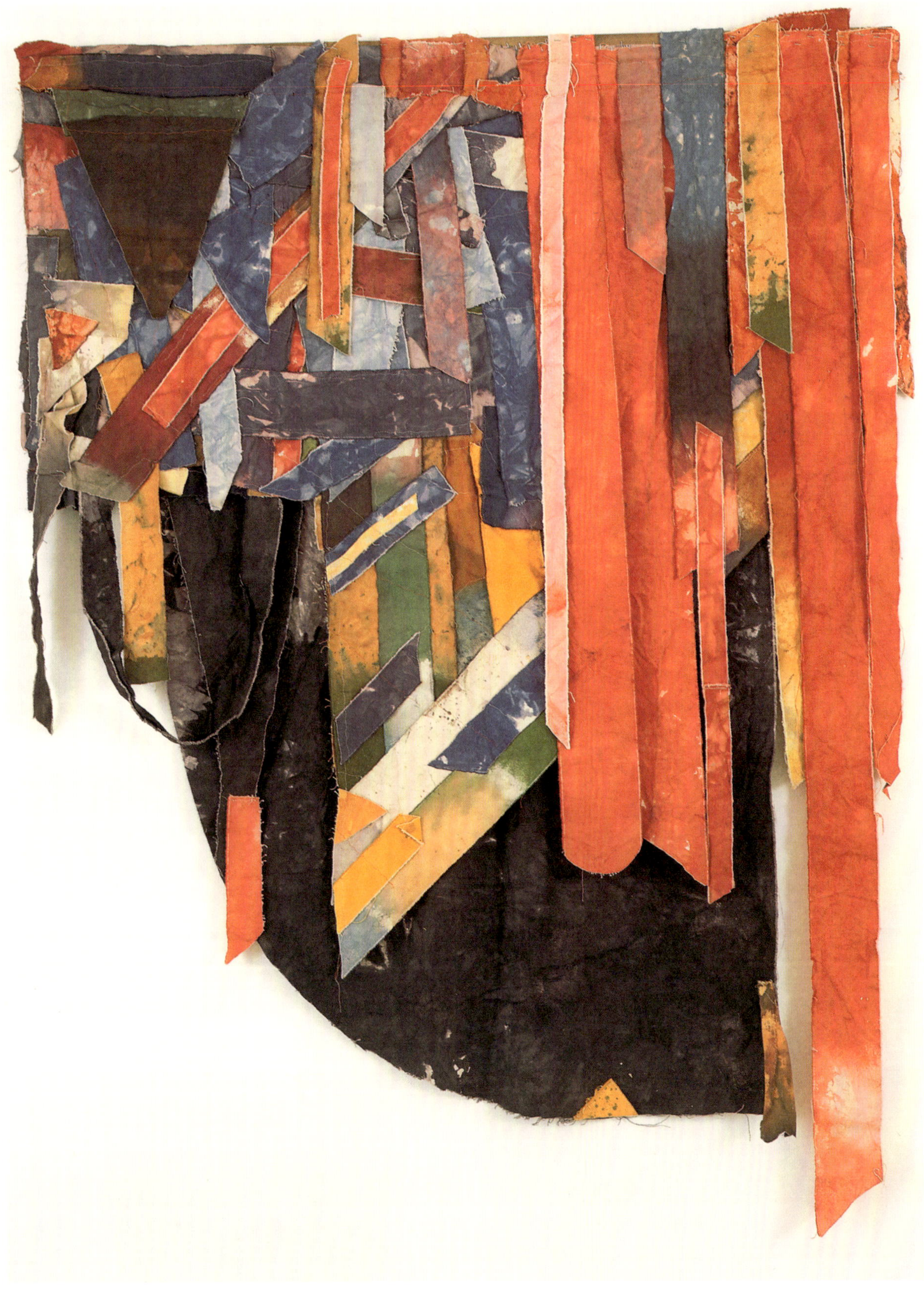

Pages 68–69: Howardena Pindell,
Untitled, 1968–70. Canvas, enamel,
grommets, and foam. Mott-Warsh
Collection, Flint, Michigan. Courtesy
of Sragow Gallery, New York.

Page 69: Lynda Benglis, *Chi*, 1973.
Aluminum screen, bunting, plaster,
silver paint, enamel, and sparkles.
Collection of James and Christina
Lockwood.

Left: Alvin Loving, *Untitled*, ca. 1970s.
Torn canvas. Guild Hall Museum,
East Hampton, New York, Gift of
Maddy and Larry Mohr, in memory
of Robert M. (Mac) Doty.

Right: Lynda Benglis, *Baby Planet*,
ca. 1969. Poured pigmented latex
paint. Courtesy of the artist and
Cheim & Read, New York.

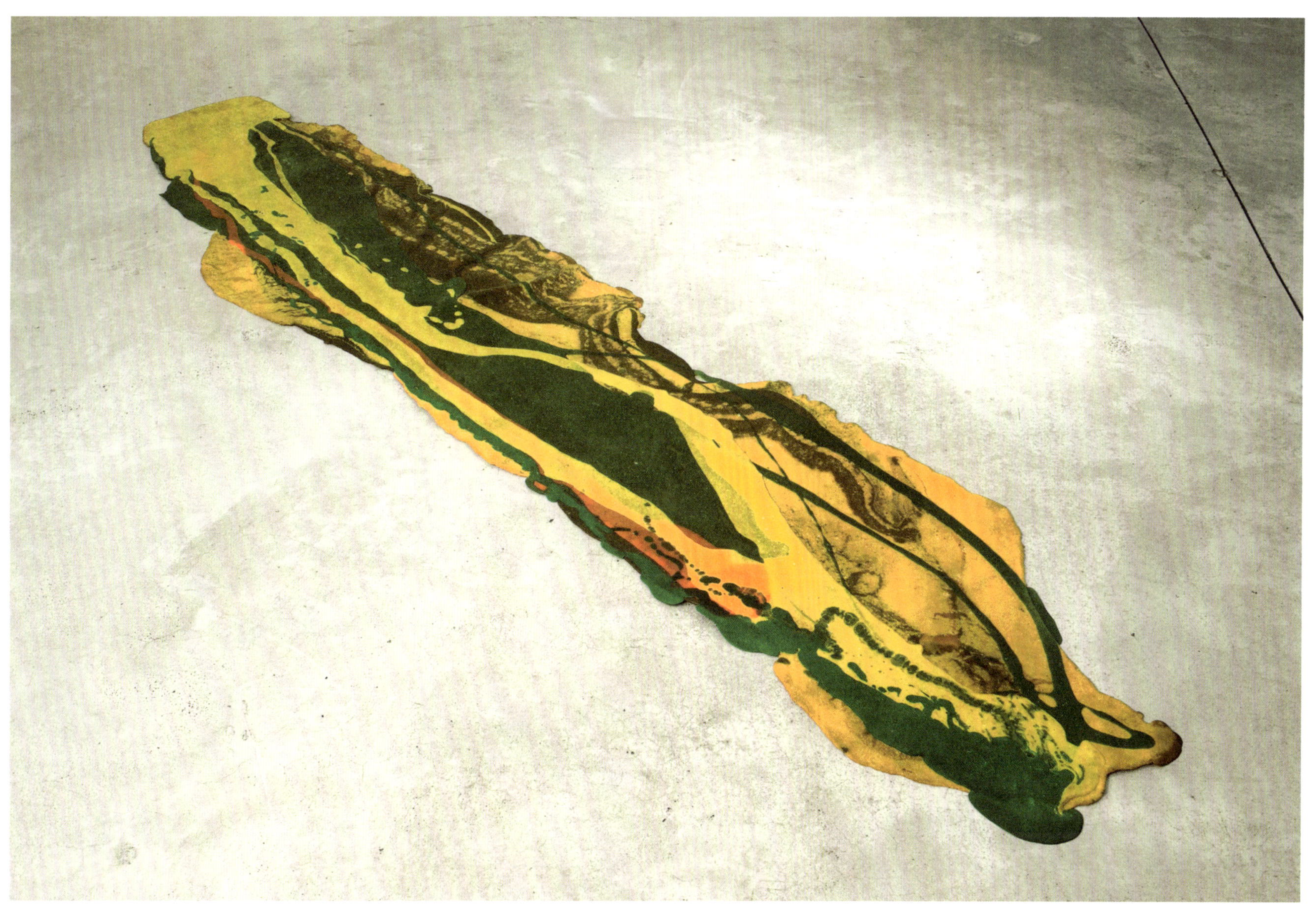

of canvas and deemed the wall itself extraneous. Looking at her *Baby Planet* (ca. 1969), a mass of latex paint poured directly on the ground, one is led to imagine an anti-institutional action where perhaps the heat was turned up to such a degree that a Pollock painting melted onto the floor. The artist's other works during this period pushed painting into three dimensions so that distinctions between it and sculpture became more and more difficult to identify. By the early 1970s, French artist Daniel Buren, whose work assumed increasingly hostile stances toward painting after he adopted stripes as his dominant motif in 1965 and 1966 (alongside partners in crime Olivier Mosset, Daniel Parmentier, and Niele Toroni, who briefly cohered in a mini movement dubbed BMPT), had also become dissatisfied with the static support on which painting was expected to exist. In *One Piece in Four Parts on 2 Parallel Walls* (March 1973, March 1976; pages 72–73), Buren allowed a rectangular patch of his printed striped canvas to disassemble and disperse, with three corners venturing outward to implicate the architecture of the museum or gallery in the completion of the painterly statement. Such dissipation both within and without the walls of the institution makes Buren's tightly focused practice crucial to appreciating the lengths to which the definitions of painting had been extended during these years.

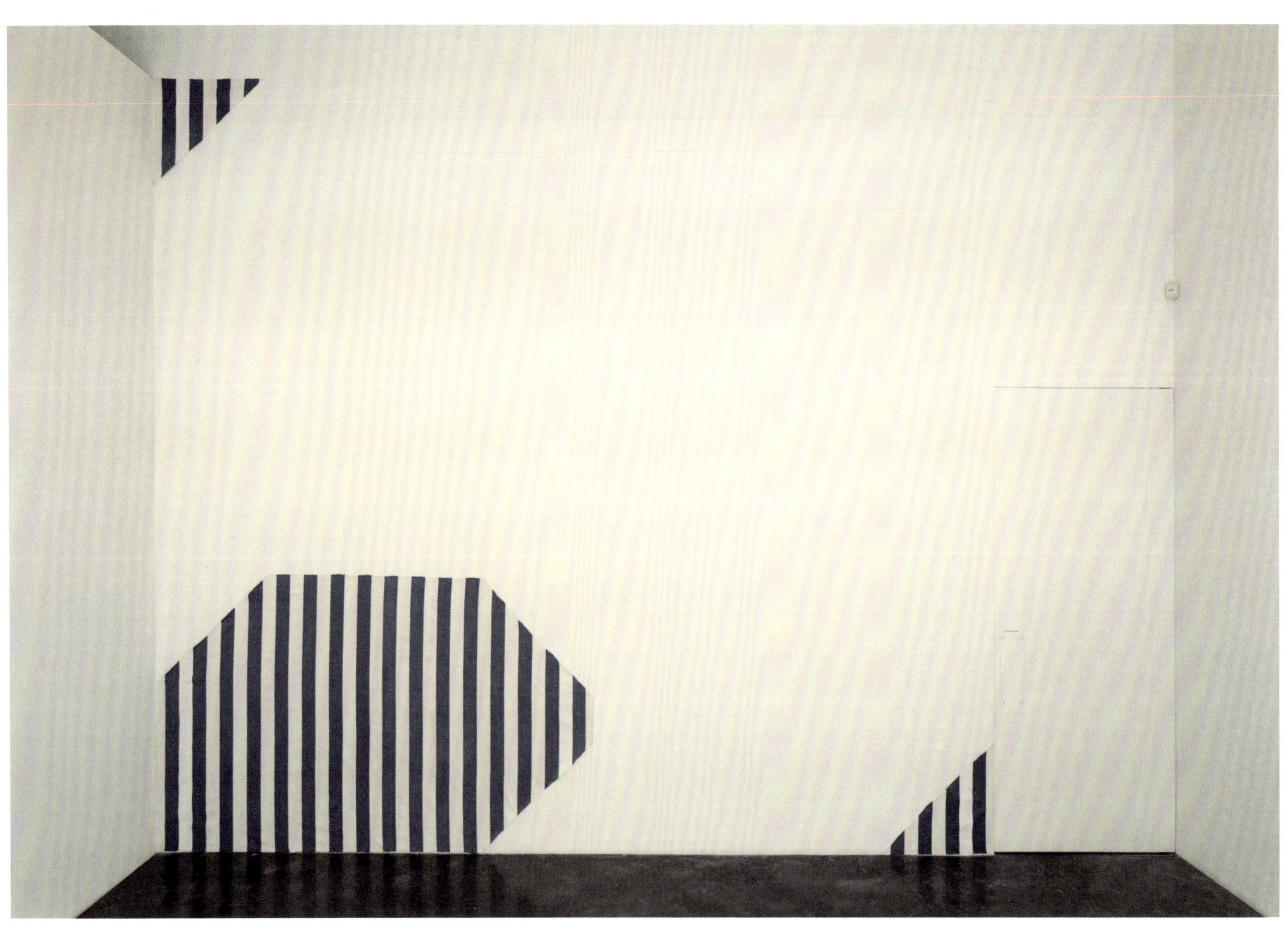

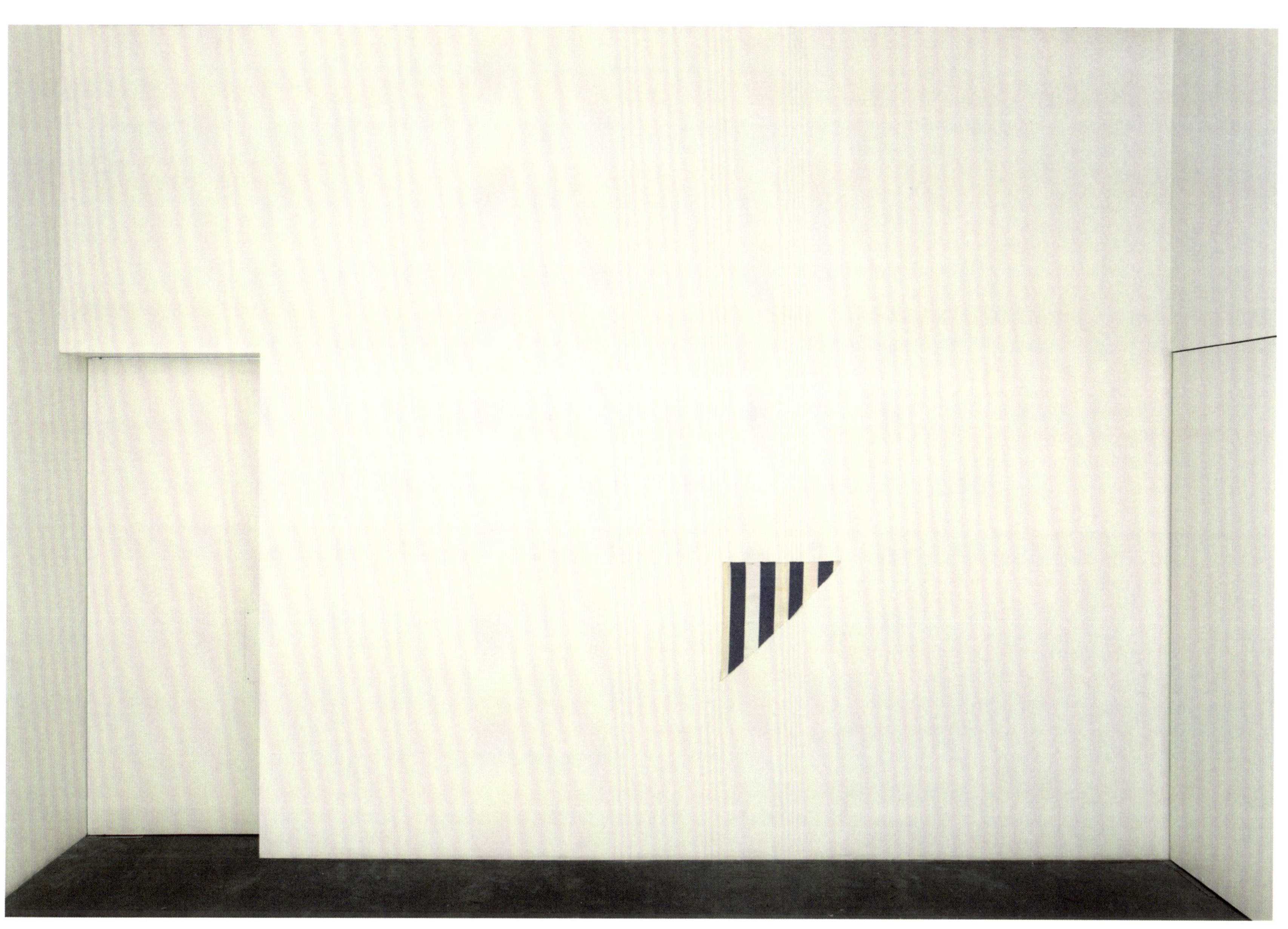

Environmental Disintegration

Buren's deployment of his striped motif disrupted cherished ideas of the painter at work in his or her studio crafting unique statements. In Buren's hands (or mind, as it were), painting had become a signifier, whereby the artist and the gesture are represented in the readymade material of striped awning canvas. This material could be seen on the one hand as egomaniacal in its signature status and in how all-encompassing it could theoretically become, and on the other as extremely selfless, for it could also be viewed as a very quiet, even banal intervention, whether in city streets or in museum spaces. This paradox is clearly exemplified in *Exposition d'une Exposition* (Exhibition of an Exhibition) (1972), his contribution to Documenta 5 that year, which consisted of light gray striped wallpaper that covered the walls of galleries housing bold signature paintings by artists such as Brice Marden and Jasper Johns. Here, Buren could be seen to be playing the deferential hand, allowing his "painting" to demurely recede into the background; yet at the same time his work also controls the discourse, claiming the infrastructure of the museum, including the artworks of other artists, as Buren's field of activity. Such a position acknowledges the deep (and not always adequately acknowledged) debt that the artwork owes to its institutional context, while also expanding the parameters of painting to an unparalleled degree.

The incredibly cogent march of innovation in the work of Oiticica mirrors many of the general contours of *Target Practice*. As he processed the legacy of geometric abstraction, he became increasingly aware of the phenomenological effects of color and both pictorial and physical space. In the dizzying progression from his *Spatial Reliefs* and *Bólides* to his ultimate unfolding of color, space, and form in the *Parangolés*, abstract painting became inexorably entangled for Oiticica with the celebratory aspects of life. Joyous and free movement, as manifested overtly in dancing but just as easily expressed in walking and being in the moment, became the structure on which his *Parangolés* defined their painterly terms—as colorful fabric constructs that need to be worn in order for their potential to be extracted. Taking the form of dresses, capes, and even flags, as in *P02 Parangolé bandeira 01* (P02 Parangolé Flag 01) (1964), they ushered painting off the gallery walls and out into the streets. As captured by filmmaker Ivan Cardoso in his film on Oiticica, *H.O.* (1979; pages 14–15), made the year before the artist's death, the *Parangolés* are action paintings taken to another extreme.

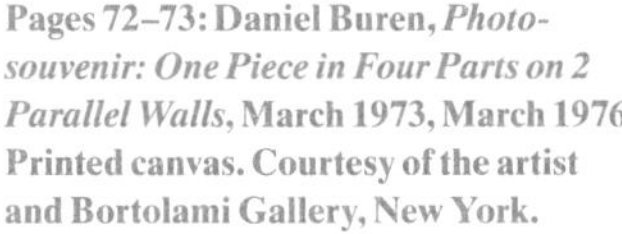

Pages 72–73: Daniel Buren, *Photo-souvenir: One Piece in Four Parts on 2 Parallel Walls*, March 1973, March 1976. Printed canvas. Courtesy of the artist and Bortolami Gallery, New York.

Below: Daniel Buren, *Photo-souvenir: Exposition d'une Exposition*, 1972. Printed wallpaper. Installation view at Documenta 5, Kassel, 1972, with work by Jasper Johns. Courtesy of the artist and Bortolami Gallery, New York.

Right: Hélio Oiticica, *P02 Parangolé bandeira 01*, 1964. Paint, canvas, tulle, plastic, and wooden pole, shown being performed by Miro de Mangueira during the exhibition *Opinião 65*, Museu de Arte Moderna, Rio de Janeiro, 1965. Cesar and Claudio Oiticica Collection.

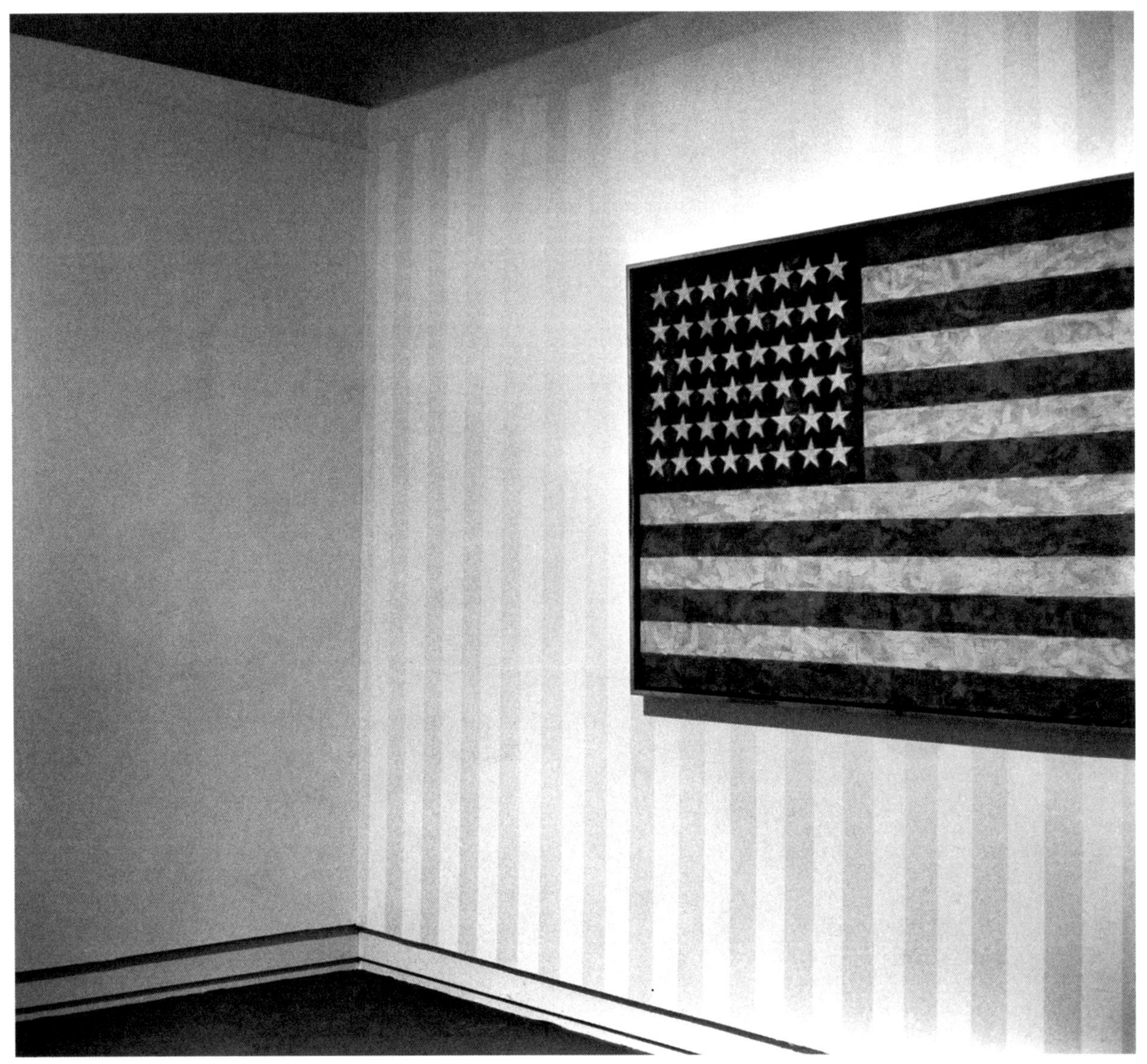

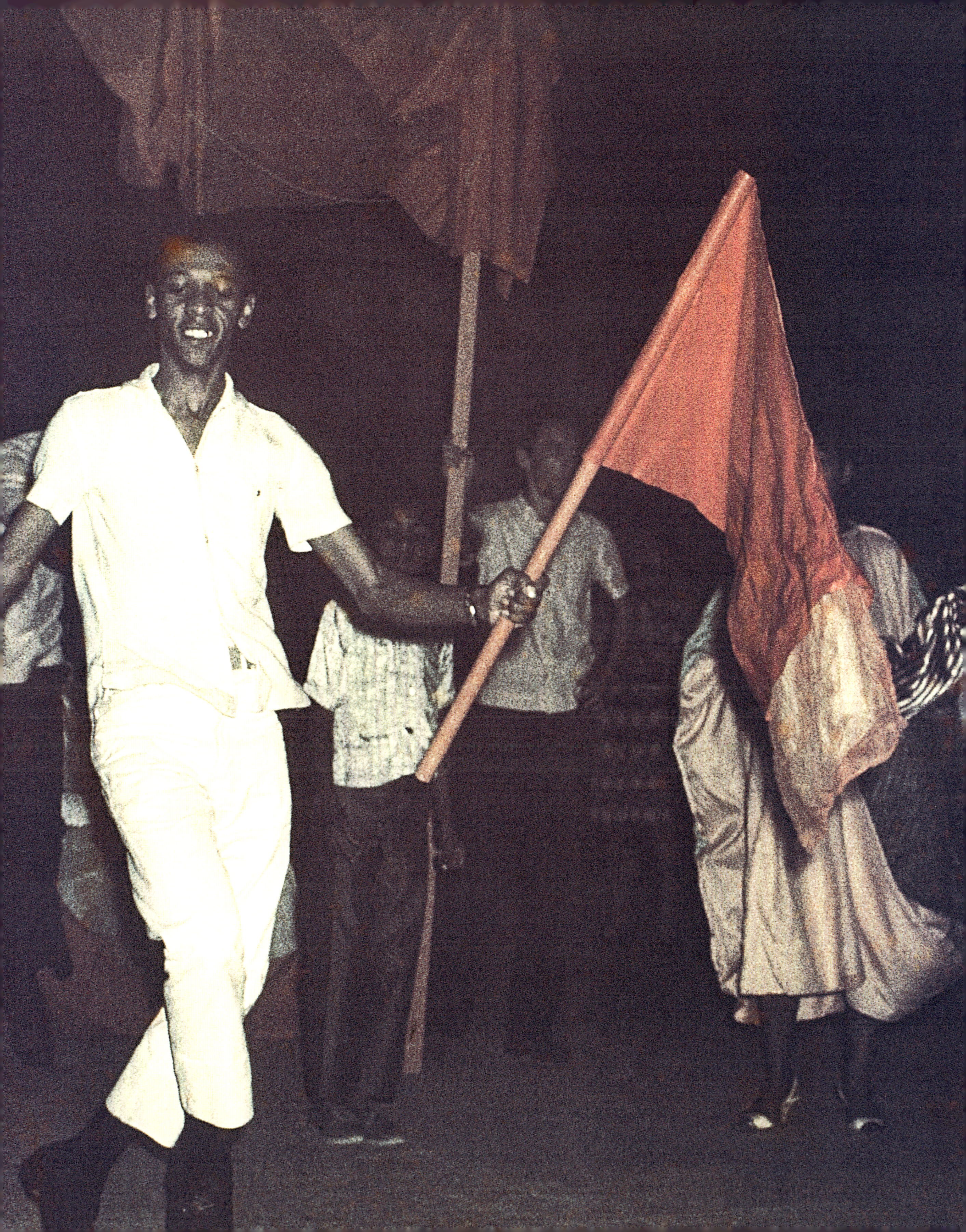

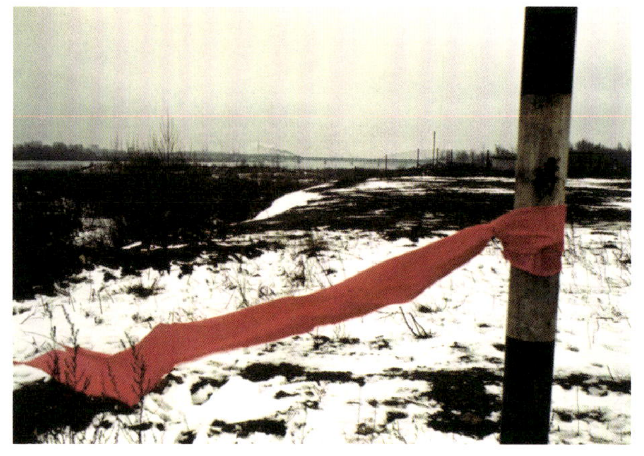

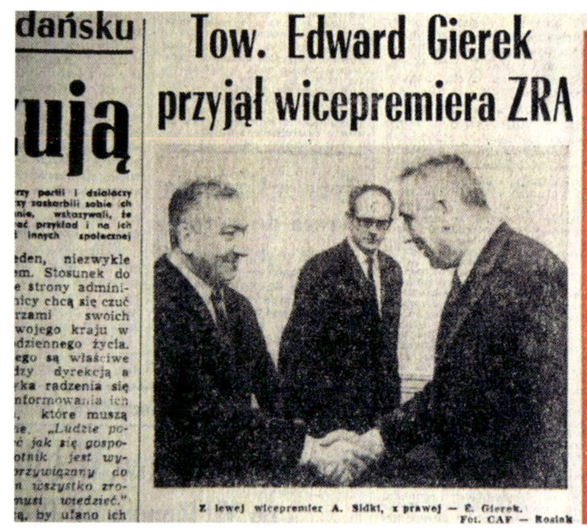
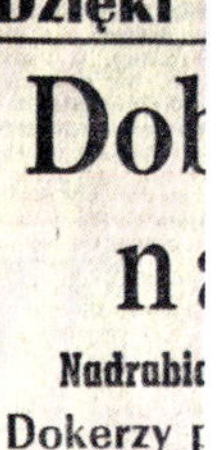

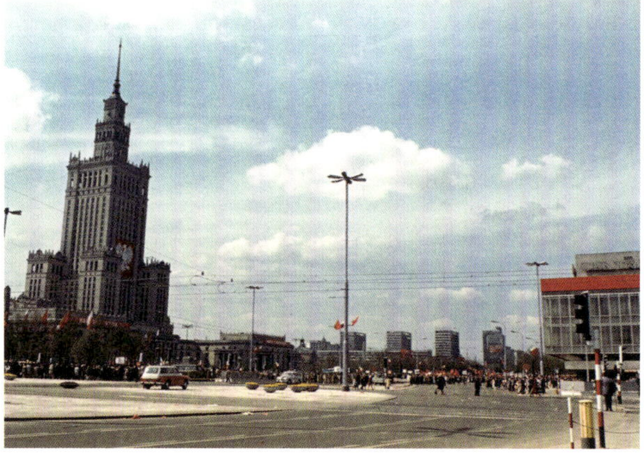

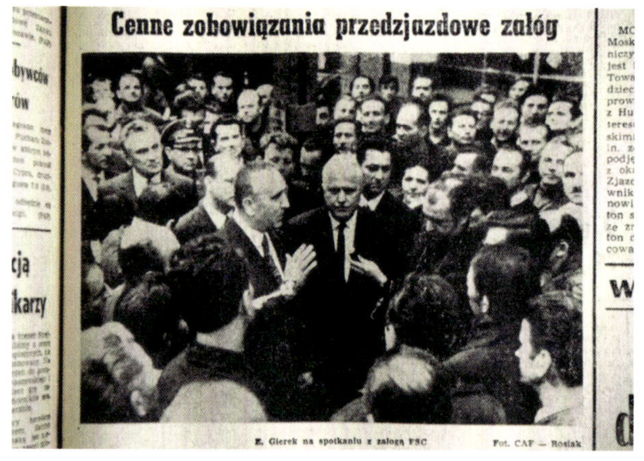

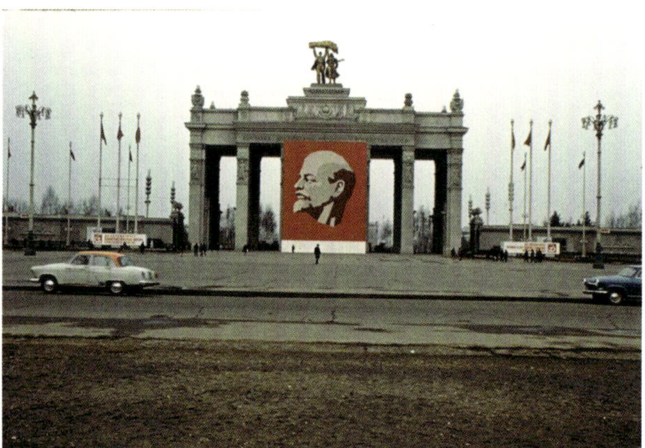

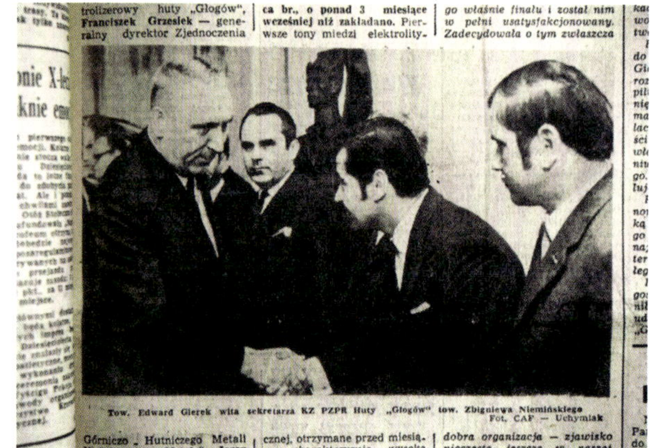

Left: KwieKulik (Przemyslaw Kwiek and Zofia Kulik), *Variants of Red* and *The Path of Edward Gierek*, 1971. Stills from slide show transferred to DVD. KwieKulik Collection.

Right: Edward Krasiński, *Intervention*, 1975/1981. Acrylic paint, collage, and blue tape. Courtesy of Anton Kern Gallery, New York.

On another continent and under different political conditions, the Polish duo KwieKulik (Przemyslaw Kwiek and Zofia Kulik) pursued projects that, like those of Buren and Oiticica, located painterly ideas and activity outside the museum and in the found landscape. In their slide show *Variants of Red* (1971), they created an archive of images from every conceivable social situation that featured a red object or detail. Thus a red ribbon on a fence, a red truck in the landscape, and the more loaded red banner with Lenin's face, for example, are collapsed together into a massive cataloguing that perhaps suggests that art is everywhere. On the other hand, because red is also the signature color of communism and, in the period and locale in which KwieKulik were practicing, an emblem of a totalitarian regime, it could also be seen as a menacing, inescapable fact of life. Like the open-ended projects

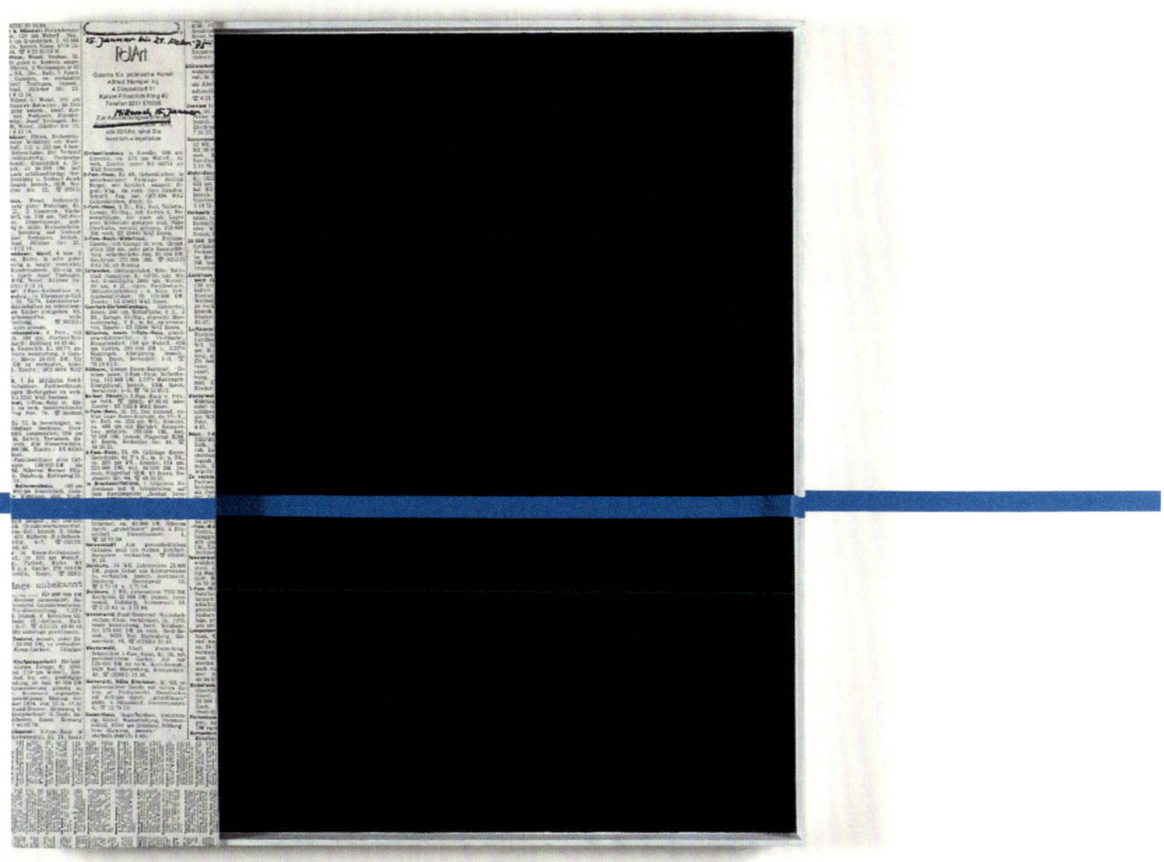

of Buren and Oiticica, this work attempted to track "possible configurations of everything with everything,"[45] offering the viewer a cavalcade of facts from which multiple conclusions could be drawn. *Variants of Red* is usually synchronized with a contemporaneous slide show titled *The Path of Edward Gierek* (1971), which compiles images of the eponymous Polish national leader at appearances all over the country. Less aesthetically obvious, it nevertheless proves the flexibility of the duo's accumulative and archival approach to art making. It is worth noting in this context the liberating yet apolitical adoption of the color blue at this same time by KwieKulik's countryman Edward Krasiński, whose use of blue tape extended outward from a traditional painterly context to cover and claim whatever walls or architectural features (even people) it encountered. Beginning in 1970, Krasiński's *Interventions* would originate in a black-and-white painting with some three-dimensional spatial effects from which and with which standard blue adhesive tape would illusionistically interact and then shoot beyond the frame of the support, leaving a trail of blue on every contiguous surface and object. A combination of Buren's democratic dispersion, Oiticica's spatial openness, and KwieKulik's everyday observations, Krasiński's blue tape achieved for painting a freedom and mutability it had never before enjoyed.

Last Rites

While painting continued to expand and mutate into new guises throughout the 1960s and into the 1970s, its most intellectual variant was guided by a self-criticality and self-awareness that kept it in constant dialogue with the past as well as with the strictures that had maintained order up to this point. The radicality of the more critical approaches to painting was evident only when tradition, or at least recognizable vestiges of the past, was part of its frame of reference. Hence the power of Buren's stripes or Benglis's messy puddles of paint. Distancing oneself as far as possible from painting while still remaining in opposition to its mores was thus a delicate and tenuous territory, but many artists, especially those engaged in conceptual art and what Lucy R. Lippard termed the "dematerialization of the art object," tiptoed to that precipice.[46]

Lawrence Weiner, for instance, is an artist who started out making paintings but eventually developed a text-based practice that relies on straightforward descriptions that stand in for more elaborately (and physically) executed objects. While his later work describes circumstances and phenomena that are primarily sculptural, many of his earliest text pieces were aimed at painting. In *An Amount of Paint Poured Directly Upon the Floor and Allowed to Dry [CAT #036]* (1968), for instance, the exhibitor can either enact this painterly order or simply include the words of its title on the wall or a sheet of paper to activate its agency. The result of the action is familiar enough and explained clearly enough so that merely envisioning it in one's mind (in any circumstance or location) satisfies the most basic conception of painting. Joseph Kosuth also approached the conventions of painting in a text-based way during this period, and in *'Title (Art As Idea As Idea)' ['PAINT-LESS']* (1968), he relied on the format of dictionary definitions to describe a state devoid of paint. Though the result is still an object in space, unlike the more ephemeral nature of Weiner's work, it suggests nevertheless a cerebral ending point for the practice of painting.

Lee Lozano, too, tried her hand at the evaporation of painting, writing out on graph paper in *No title (idea that cannot be drawn, Nov. 16, 1968)* (1968; page 81 top) the recipe for a painting using transparent paint that would presumably have so little visual effect that the

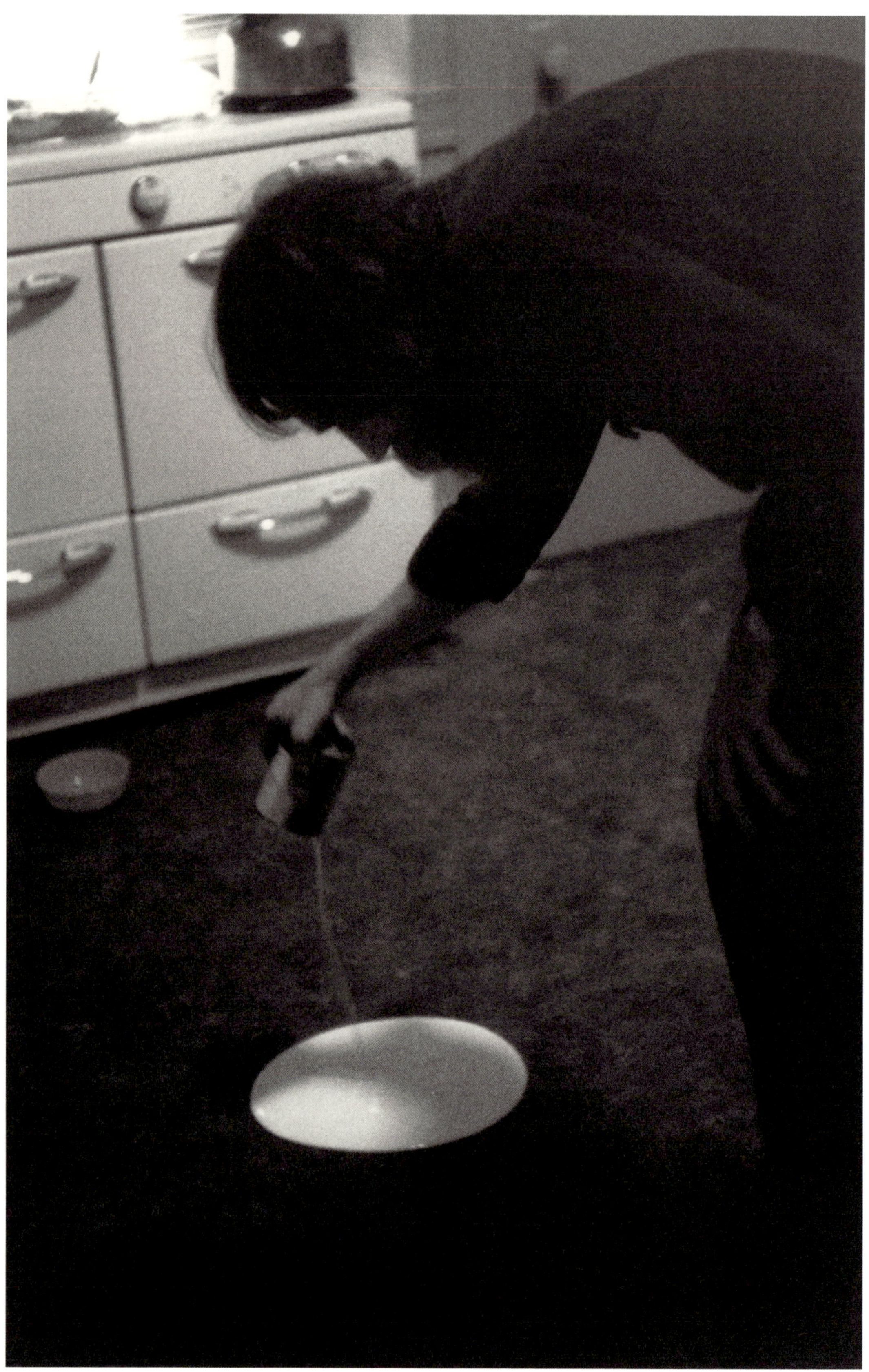

collection of dust on the painting might constitute the primary focus. As the title suggests, such a work defies description through schematic drawing. Iain and Ingrid Baxter, working together as N.E. Thing Co., while attending to all manner of phenomenological problems and issues in their work, did not exclude painting from their investigations, and in *Paint into Earth, Simon Fraser University, Vancouver, BC* (1966–68; page 80) they seem to have been rehearsing an early death for painting. Documented with a map and photographs, *Paint into Earth* shows a hole in the ground into which a can of paint was poured and left to dry, the location of the action recorded precisely on a map of Vancouver as if it were an archaeological site. Along similar lines, Oiticica, in a variant of his fecund *Bólide* series, set a can of paint on fire in *B38 Bólide Lata 01—Appropriação 02 "Consumitivo"* (B38 Fireball Can 01—Appropriation 02 "Combustible") (1966; page 81 bottom). Recorded in a small black-and-white photograph, as no other meaningful artifact was necessary to document the action, Oiticica's literal "ball of fire" let paint consume itself until it was fully extinguished. Across the various gestures discussed above, painting was tested, over and over, to the point that it was more or less left for dead.

UPON THE FLOOR AND ALLOWED TO DRY

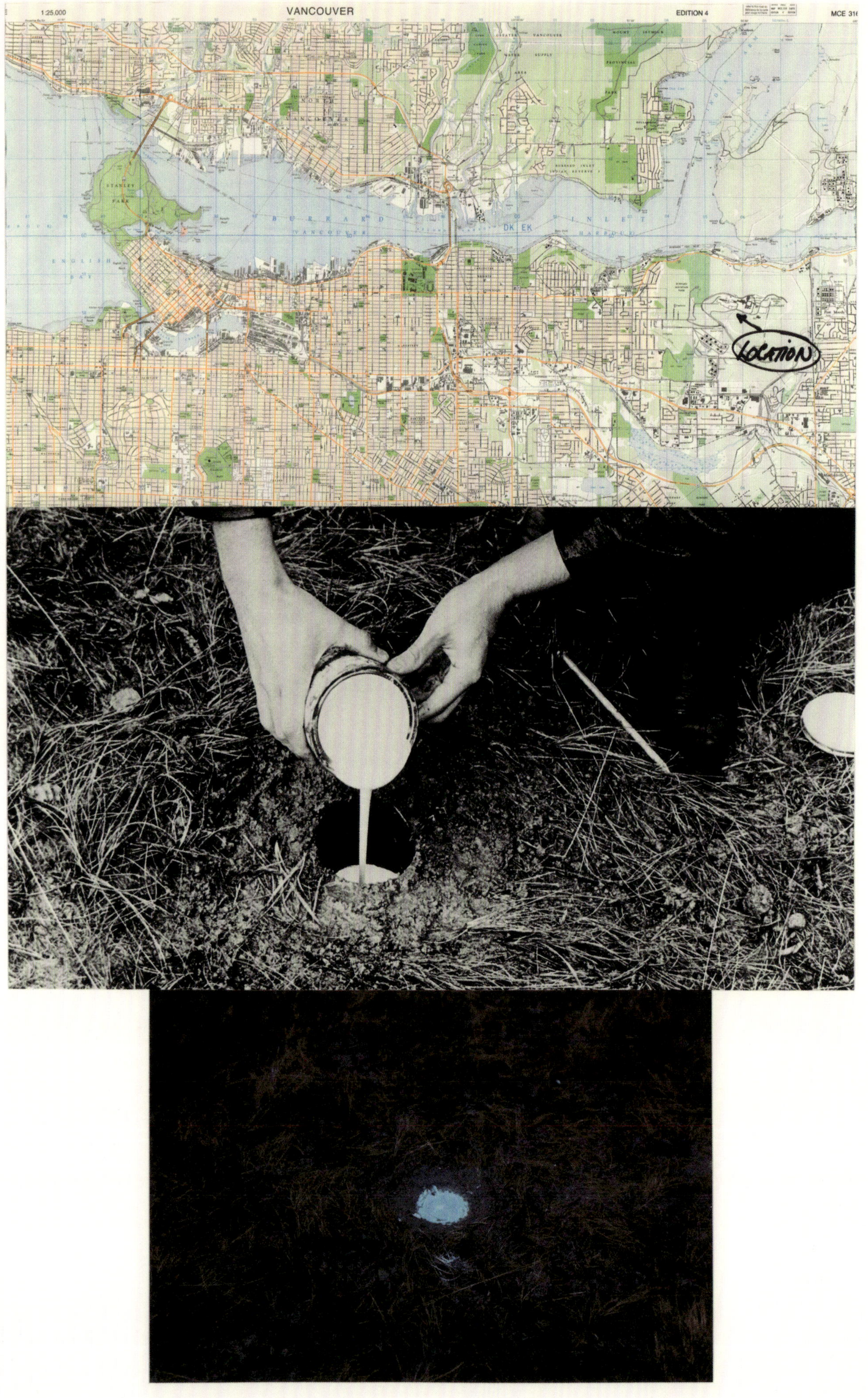

1:25,000
VANCOUVER
EDITION 4
MCE 31
LOCATION
STANLEY PARK
ENGLISH BAY
BURRARD INLET

Left: N.E. Thing Co., *Paint into Earth, Simon Fraser University, Vancouver, BC*, 1966–68. Gelatin silver print, chromogenic print, lithograph. Vancouver Art Gallery, Vancouver Art Gallery Acquisition Fund.

Top right: Lee Lozano, *No title (idea that cannot be drawn, Nov. 16, 1968)*, 1968. Ink and graphite on paper. Private collection, New York. Courtesy of Hauser & Wirth, Zurich and London.

Bottom right: Hélio Oiticica, *B38 Bólide Lata 01—Appropriação 02 "Consumitivo,"* 1966. Gelatin silver print. Cesar and Claudio Oiticica Collection.

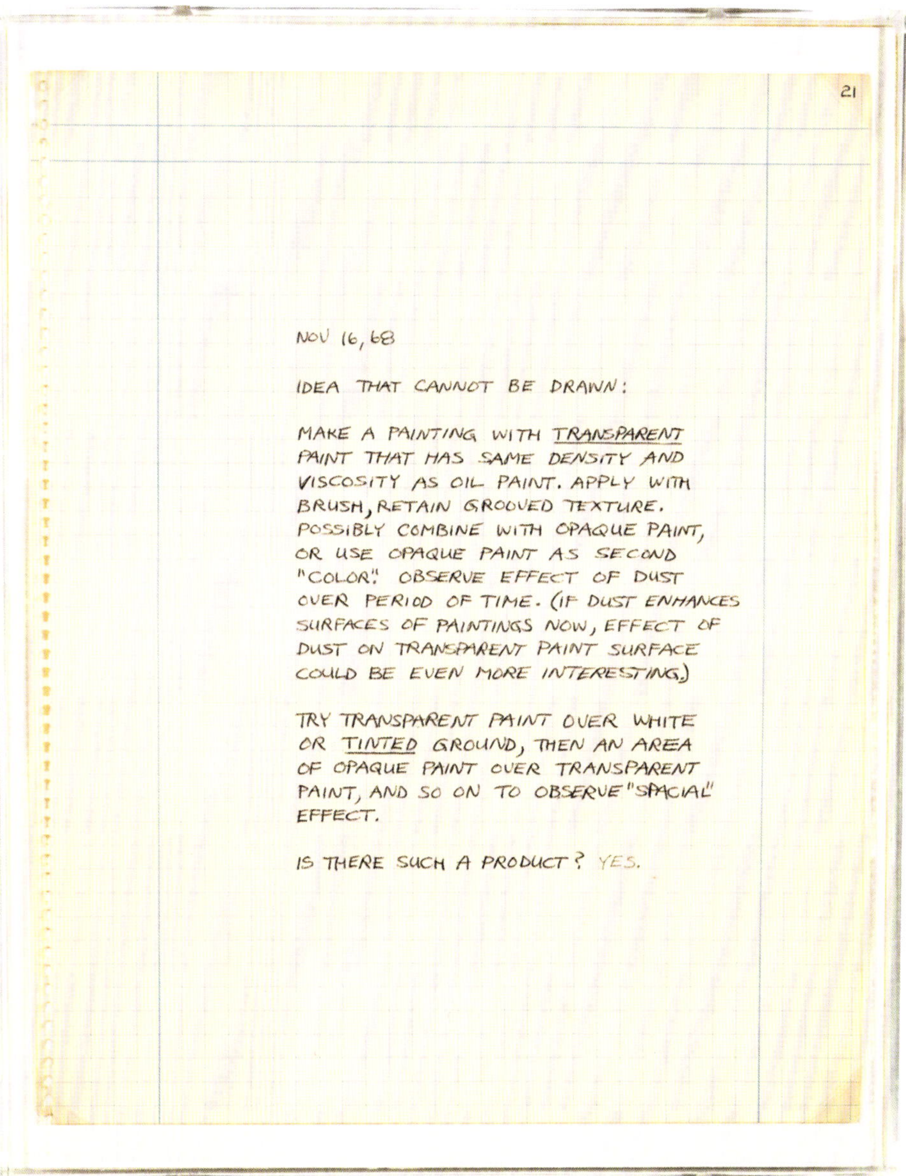

21

NOV 16, 68

IDEA THAT CANNOT BE DRAWN:

MAKE A PAINTING WITH TRANSPARENT
PAINT THAT HAS SAME DENSITY AND
VISCOSITY AS OIL PAINT. APPLY WITH
BRUSH, RETAIN GROOVED TEXTURE.
POSSIBLY COMBINE WITH OPAQUE PAINT,
OR USE OPAQUE PAINT AS SECOND
"COLOR." OBSERVE EFFECT OF DUST
OVER PERIOD OF TIME. (IF DUST ENHANCES
SURFACES OF PAINTINGS NOW, EFFECT OF
DUST ON TRANSPARENT PAINT SURFACE
COULD BE EVEN MORE INTERESTING.)

TRY TRANSPARENT PAINT OVER WHITE
OR TINTED GROUND, THEN AN AREA
OF OPAQUE PAINT OVER TRANSPARENT
PAINT, AND SO ON TO OBSERVE "SPACIAL"
EFFECT.

IS THERE SUCH A PRODUCT? YES.

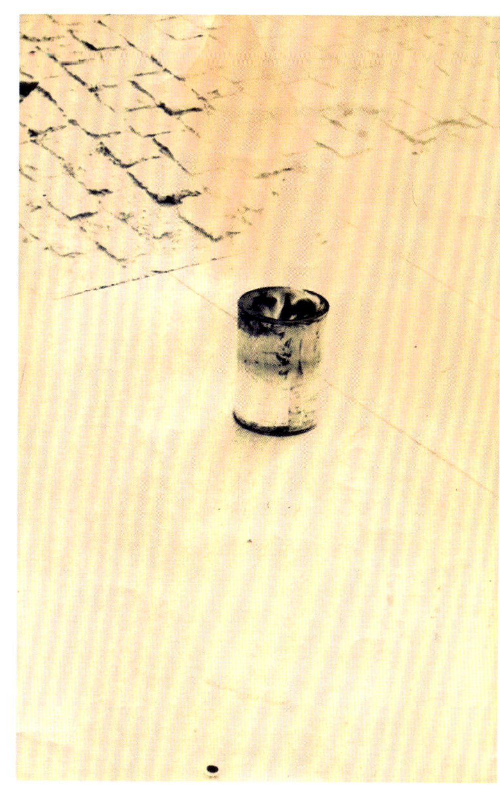

Conclusion

Of course, looking back over the years that followed this fertile period from 1949 to 1978, we can say with certainty that painting has not died; but the cuts, scrapes, and bruises it acquired during this intensive time were necessary wounds in the maturation of the medium and reminders of its mortality. Indeed, the end date of *Target Practice*—1978—coincides not only with Warhol's piss paintings (a rather ultimate symbol of painterly degradation) but also with the flowering in the late 1970s of a return to more conventional painterly values. The emergence of revived pictorial modes such as those explored by New Image Painting (concretized by the 1978 Whitney Museum of American Art exhibition of the same name and including artists such as Susan Rothenberg, Donald Sultan, and others), Transavanguardia (coined in a 1979 *Flash Art* article by Achille Bonito Oliva and heralded by Italian Neo-Expressionists such as Sandro Chia, Enzo Cucchi, Francesco Clemente, and others), Die Neue Wilden (the German variant whose exponents included A. R. Penck, Markus Lupertz, and Georg Baselitz, among others), and even painters such as Jack Goldstein and Troy Brauntauch from the "Pictures" group (inaugurated during the 1977 exhibition of the same name organized by Douglas Crimp at Artist's Space in New York) signaled a return from the abyss. The momentum of almost thirty years of intense introspection (and even longer if one considers all the important groundwork laid before Fontana punctured the surface) had begun to exert such a force on painting that a backlash was bound to occur. As early as 1981, when Crimp authored his influential essay "The End of Painting," he was already witnessing the beginnings of a rebound in the rhetoric that accompanied Barbara Rose's 1979 exhibition and book *American Painting: The Eighties*, in which she characterized the chain of events chronicled in the current exhibition as a period of "disorienting morality, social demoralization, and lack of conviction in all authority and tradition."[47] In the same publication, she went on to say, "Today, the essence of painting is being redefined not as a narrow, arid and reductive anti-illusionism, but as a rich, varied capacity to birth new images into an old world."[48] But for Crimp, the moment

was "reactionary," as evident in the reaffirmation of romantic approaches to painting to be found in shows such as *American Painting*, as well as others like the 1979 Whitney Biennial, the Royal Academy in London's *A New Spirit in Painting* (1981), and *Zeitgeist* at the Martin Gropius Bau, Berlin (1982). And yet, many of the artists included in *Target Practice* continued to hone particularly sharp, critical stances in their painting well past 1978 (Richter, Warhol, Johns, Paolini, Buren, Baldessari, and Jackson, among others), and newly emergent painters as

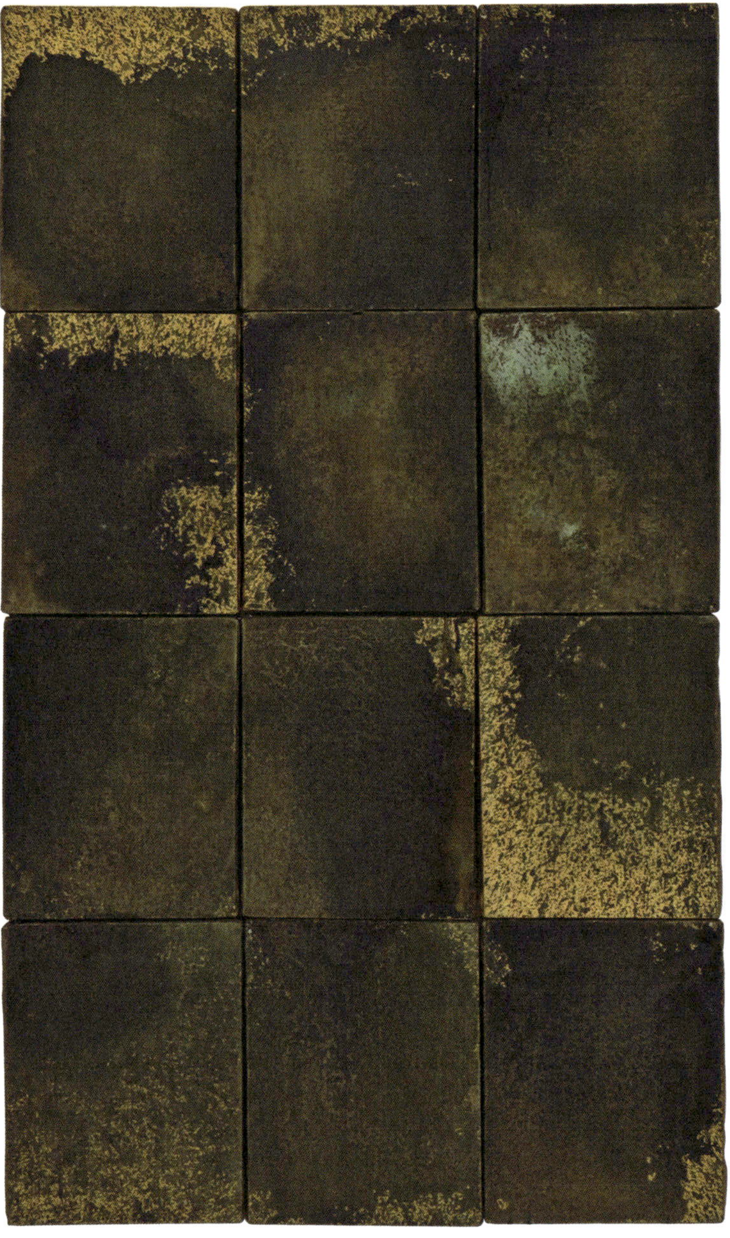

Below: Andy Warhol, *Oxidation Painting*, 1978. Mixed media on copper metallic paint on canvas. Collection of Merrill Wright.

varied as David Salle, Christopher Wool, and Martin Kippenberger certainly kept the practice on edge for many years, if not right up to the present.[49] The lessons learned from the artists in *Target Practice* continue to be relevant to many artists working today, proving that skepticism and doubt are not only necessary and healthy characteristics to maintain when pushing forward a tradition as weighty as painting but also signifiers of utmost respect and clarity. Painting in the late 1940s had reached a point where a corrective turn back toward the real world had become inescapable if the medium was to survive, and it took almost thirty years for this tough-love remedy to achieve its full effects.

Notes

1. It is interesting to note that another historical group exhibition, one to which this author owes a debt of influence, also took its beginning date as 1949. That exhibition, *Out of Actions: Between Performance and the Object, 1949–1979*, curated by Paul Schimmel at the Museum of Contemporary Art, Los Angeles, in 1998, included a 1949 Lucio Fontana *Buchi*, but was perhaps more grounded in Jackson Pollock's classic drip painting from 1949, *No. 1*, and concerned itself less with painting than with a broader examination of physical actions in art.

2. Quoted in Erika Billeter, "Lucio Fontana: Between Tradition and Avant-Garde," in *Lucio Fontana, 1899–1968: A Retrospective* (New York: Solomon R. Guggenheim Foundation, 1977), 19.

3. Lucio Fontana to Giampiero Giani, Albissola, November 2, 1949. The artists he mentions are likely those with whom he signed the "Secondo Manifesto dello Spazialismo" in 1948 (Gianni Dova, Beniamino Joppolo, Giorgio Kaisserlian, Milena Milani, and Antonio Tullier). In 1950 a third manifesto was drafted that included Joppolo, Milani, Giampiero Giani, Roberto Crippa, and Carlo Cardazzo. Enrico Crispolti, ed., *Fontana* (Milan: Charta, 1999), 143, 271–72.

4. Ibid., 32.

5. Alexandra Munroe, "Scream Against the Sky," in *Japanese Art after 1945: Scream Against the Sky* (New York: Abrams, 1994), 24.

6. Robert Morris, "Jasper Johns: The First Decade," in Jeffrey Weiss et al., *Jasper Johns: An Allegory of Painting, 1955–1965* (Washington, DC: National Gallery of Art, 2007), 213.

7. Ibid., 208.

8. Jeffrey Weiss, "Painting Bitten by a Man," in *Jasper Johns: An Allegory of Painting*, 16, 33.

9. Fairfield Porter, "Jasper Johns," *Art News*, January 1958, 20.

10. Leo Steinberg, "Jasper Johns: The First Seven Years of His Art" (1962), republished in *Other Criteria: Confrontations with Twentieth-Century Art* (New York: Oxford University Press, 1972), 51.

11. Jasper Johns, in a 1963 interview with Billy Klüver, stated: "The early paintings of mine seem to me to have been about, partly,…accuracy, and questioning whether there are such things…. It seems to me that the work I do now is…less concerned with accuracy—it's taken—since there didn't seem to be any such thing anyway, it was never achieved." In Kirk Varnedoe, ed., *Jasper Johns: Writings, Sketchbook Notes, Interviews* (New York: Museum of Modern Art, 1996), 85.

12. Weiss, "Painting Bitten by a Man," 17.

13. Recounted by his friend Jules Buisson. Unreferenced quote in Juri Steiner, "Night Flight: The Avant-Garde Urge Toward Action, Destruction, and Terror," in Stefan Zweifel, Juri Steiner, and Heinz Stahlhut, "*In Girum Imus Nocte et Consumimur Igni*"—*The Situationist International (1957–1972)* (Zurich: JRP/Ringier, 2006), 67–68.

14. Charles Baudelaire, "Mon coeur mis à nu" (1887), reprinted in ibid., 68.

15. Niki de Saint Phalle, in the film *[Niki de Saint Phalle Shooting a Tir]* (1962; color, sound, in English, 4:40 min.) (V 36 1962), Niki Charitable Art Foundation.

16. Ushio Shinohara, *The Avant-Garde Road* (Tokyo: Bijutsu Shuppansha, 1968), 10. Translated by Lyn Katsumoto.

17. Thomas Crow, "Rise and Fall: Theme and Idea in the Combines of Robert Rauschenberg," in Paul Schimmel et al., *Robert Rauschenberg: Combines* (Los Angeles: Museum of Contemporary Art, 2005), 248.

18. Charles Stuckey, "*Minutiae* and Rauschenberg's Combine Mode," in Schimmel, *Robert Rauschenberg: Combines*, 206.

19. Billeter, "Lucio Fontana," 13.

20. Attributed to Fontana's last interview in 1968 by Paul Schimmel in "Leap into the Void: Performance and the Object," in Paul Schimmel et al., *Out of Actions: Between Performance and the Object, 1949–1979* (Los Angeles: Museum of Contemporary Art, 1998), 22.

21. Philippe Vergne, "Otto Muehl," in Joan Rothfuss and Elizabeth Carpenter, eds., *Bits & Pieces Put Together to Present a Semblance of a Whole: Walker Art Center Collections* (Minneapolis: Walker Art Center, 2005), 408.

22. Ibid.

23. Dave Hickey, "Available Light," in Dave Hickey and Peter Plagens, *The Works of Edward Ruscha: Essays* (New York: Hudson Hills Press in association with the San Francisco Museum of Modern Art, 1982), 24.

24. Ibid.

25. Weiss, "Painting Bitten by a Man," 28.

26. Ibid., 23.

27. Lee Lozano, April 17, 1968. In Sabine Folie, "*Seek the Extremes…*": *Lee Lozano* (Nuremberg: Verlag für moderne Kunst, 2006), 76.

28. Giulio Paolini quoted in Douglas Fogle, "Giulio Paolini," in Rothfuss and Carpenter, *Bits & Pieces*, 448.

29. Richard Pettibone interviewed by Ian Berry, in Ian Berry and Michael Duncan, *Richard Pettibone: A Retrospective* (Saratoga Springs, NY: Tang Teaching Museum and Art Gallery at Skidmore College, 2005), 17.

30. Richard Jackson interviewed by Hans Ulrich Obrist, in *Richard Jackson: Deer Beer* (Cologne: Oktagon, 1998), 17.

31. Douglas Crimp, "The End of Painting," *October* 16 (Spring 1981): 75.

32. Jasper Johns interviewed by Jay Nash and James Holmstrand, "Zeroing In on Jasper Johns," *Literary Times* (Chicago), September 1964, 1, 9, 14; reprinted in Varnedoe, *Jasper Johns*, 105.

33. Morris, "Jasper Johns: The First Decade," 217.

34. Clement Greenberg, "Modernist Painting" (1960), in *Clement Greenberg: The Collected Essays and Criticism*, ed. John O'Brian, vol. 4, *Modernism with a Vengeance, 1957–1969* (Chicago: University of Chicago Press, 1993), 86.

35. Georg Frei and Neil Prinz, eds., *Warhol 01: The Andy Warhol Catalogue Raisonné—Paintings and Sculpture 1961–1963*, vol. 1 (New York: Phaidon, 2001), 193.

36. Richard S. Field, "Mel Bochner: Thought Made Visible," in *Mel Bochner: Thought Made Visible, 1966–1973* (New Haven: Yale University Art Gallery, 1995), 46.

37. Kristine Stiles, "Uncorrupted Joy: International Art Actions," in Schimmel et al., *Out of Actions*, 279.

38. Coosje van Bruggen, *John Baldessari* (New York: Rizzoli, 1990), 104.

39. Ibid., 105.

40. Douglas Crimp, "On the Museum's Ruins," *October* 13 (Summer 1980): 56.

41. Asger Jorn, "Peinture détournée," in *Vingt peintures modifiées par Asger Jorn* (Paris: Galerie Rive Gauche, 1959). Translated by Thomas Y. Levin.

42. Ibid.

43. Mari Carmen Ramírez, *Hélio Oiticica: The Body of Color* (Houston: Museum of Fine Arts, 2007), 20.

44. Berry and Duncan, *Richard Pettibone*, 15.

45. Brochure for the exhibition *Polish Socialist Conceptualism of the 70s*, curated by Lukasz Ronduda in collaboration with Barbara Piwowarska at Orchard Gallery, New York, 2007.

46. Lucy R. Lippard, ed., *Six Years: The Dematerialization of the Art Object from 1966 to 1972* (New York: Praeger, 1973).

47. Barbara Rose, *American Painting: The Eighties* (Buffalo, NY: Thorney-Sidney Press, 1979), unpaginated.

48. Ibid.

49. Gaylen Gerber, Sergej Jensen, Michael Krebber, Lucy McKenzie, Ivan Morley, Steven Parrino, Anselm Reyle, and Johannes Wohnseifer are just some of the myriad artists who inherited this mantle and have carried forth an interrogative ethic in painting.

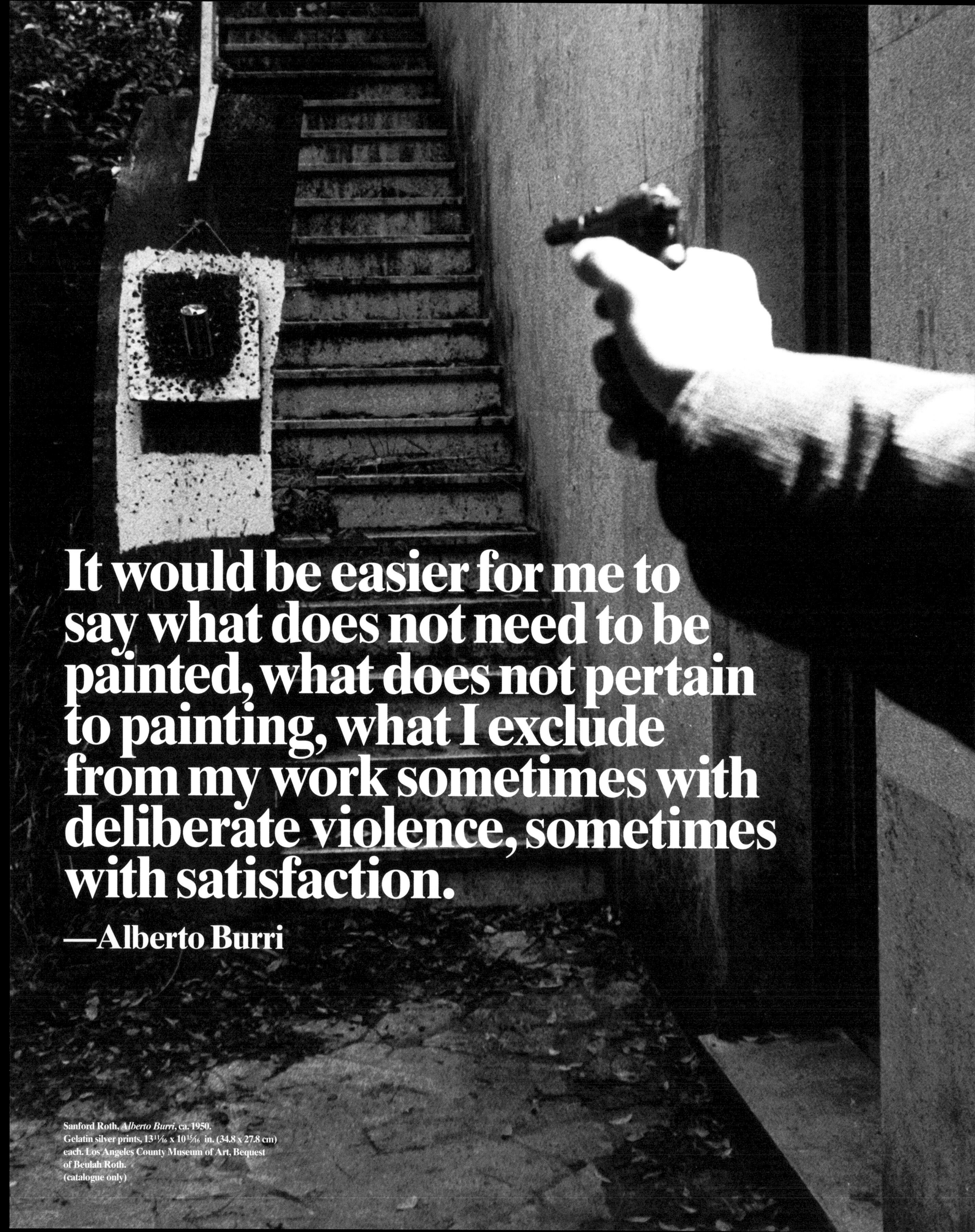

Sanford Roth, *Alberto Burri*, ca. 1950.
Gelatin silver prints, 13¹¹⁄₁₆ x 10¹⁵⁄₁₆ in. (34.8 x 27.8 cm)
each. Los Angeles County Museum of Art, Bequest
of Beulah Roth.
(catalogue only)

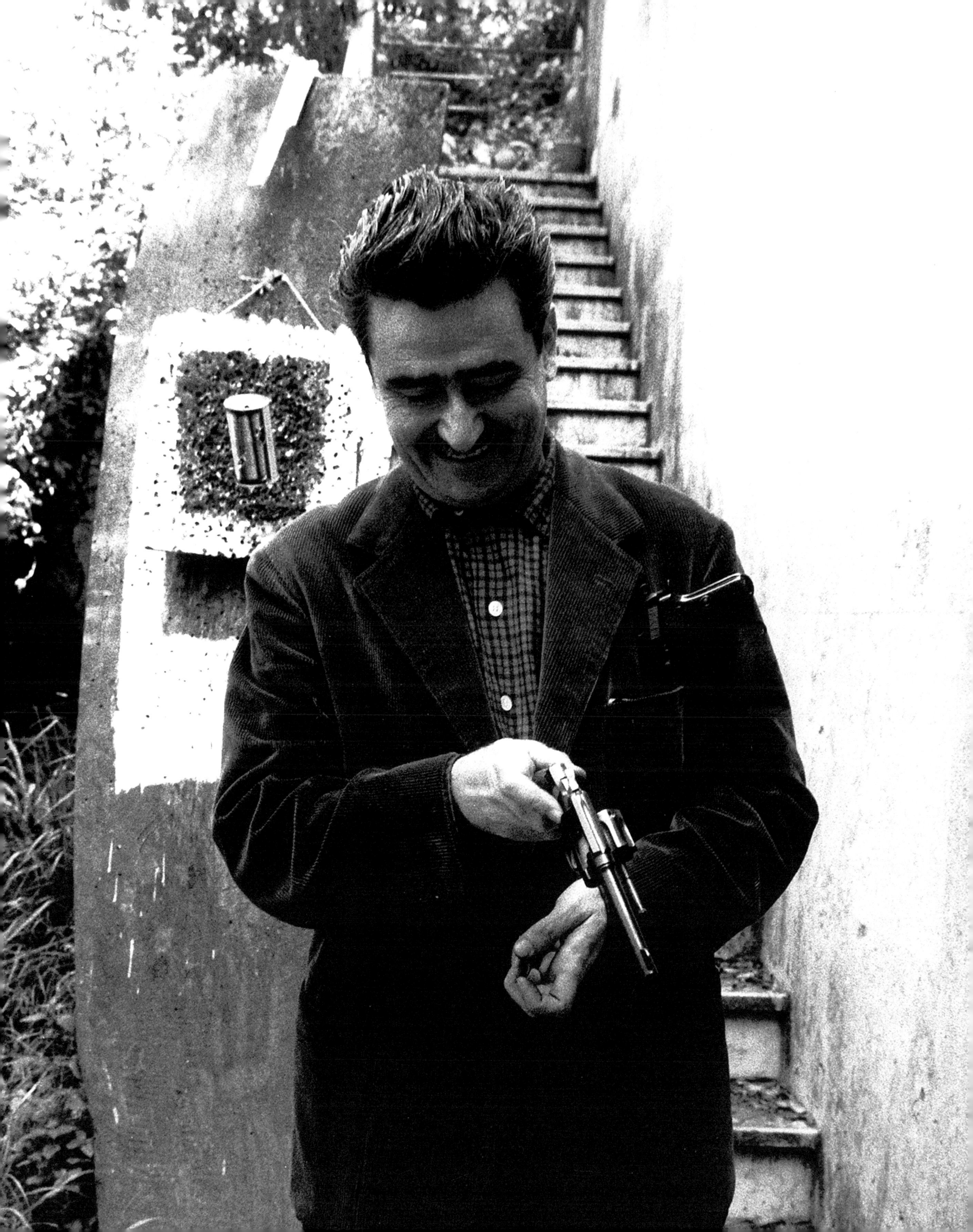

This Is Not a Painting
Space Exploration and Italian Art

Elizabeth Mangini

I did not make holes in order to wreck the picture. On the contrary,
I made holes in order to find something else.[1]

—Lucio Fontana

g:
nd Postwar

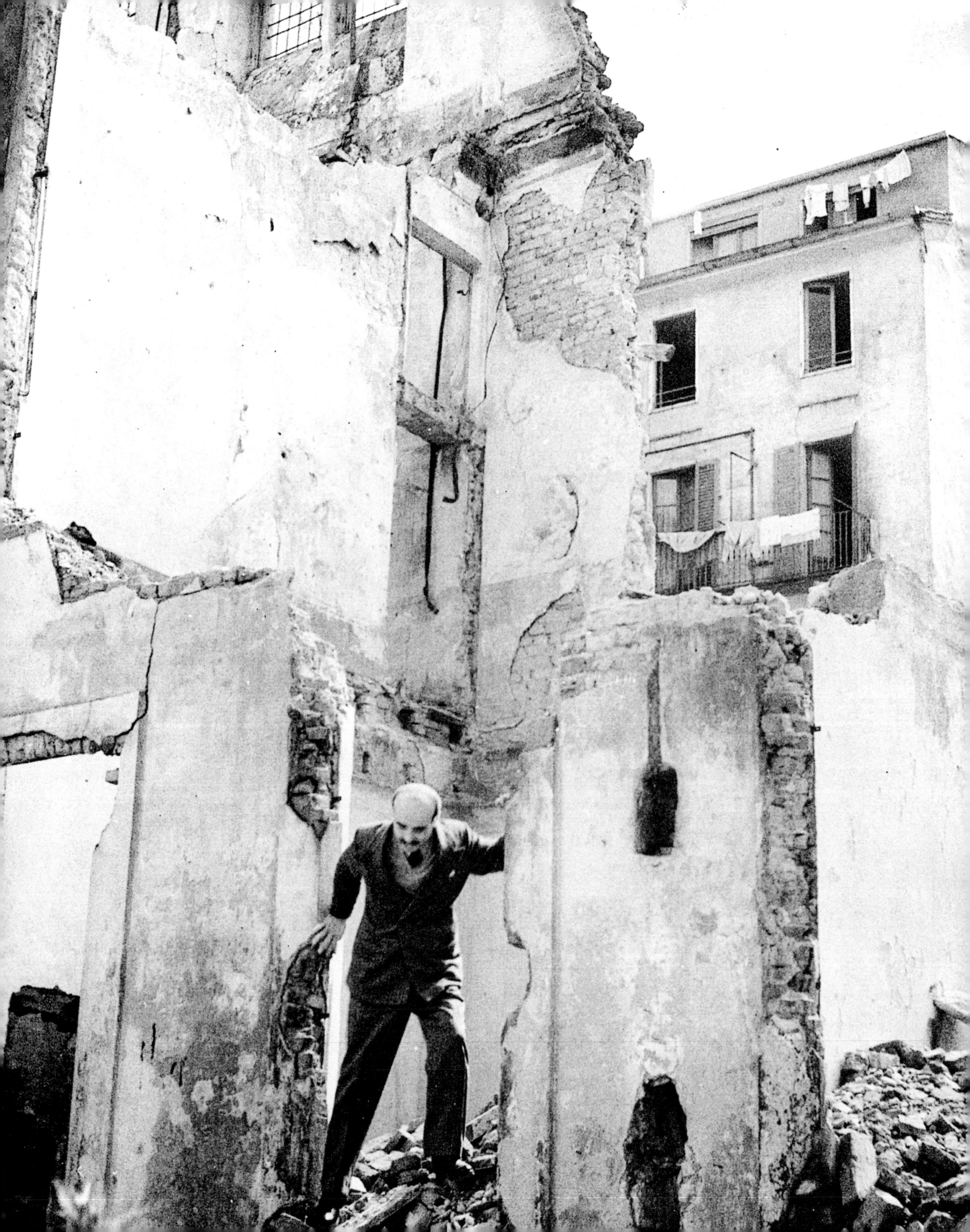

In the last interview recorded with Lucio Fontana, six weeks before his death in 1968, the artist claimed that the perforation of canvases that had made him both famous and infamous was not an act of desecration but instead the product of a desire to reach beyond the boundaries of the flat picture plane in order "to find something else."[1] These "paintings," made during the 1940s–60s, had a profound influence on later artists in Italy and across Europe, including Fontana's student Piero Manzoni, the Italian *décollagiste* Mimmo Rotella, and Nouveaux Réalistes such as Niki de Saint Phalle and Yves Klein, all of whose practices might be said to partake of a destructive interpretation of the elder artist's gesture. For contemporary viewers and scholars of Fontana's still-compelling *Concetti spaziali* (Spatial Concepts), questions remain as to how to reconcile his influence on later generations and the visceral reactions we have to these seemingly violated canvases with the artist's own understanding of these works. To answer that, we must consider what that "something else" was that Fontana hoped to find, and how his and others' impulses to spatialize painting can be contextualized within the aesthetic debates taking place in postwar Italy.

The most common interpretations usually set the artist against the backdrop of the contest between realism and abstraction that emerged as Italian artists tried to relearn the lessons of early twentieth-century modernism, which had been at least partially eclipsed during the years of Fascism and World War II.[2] In the period immediately after the war—the late 1940s and early 1950s—painting in Italy was intensely political, with artists organizing, reorganizing, and publishing manifestos that spelled out each group's ideas about the role of art in a postwar context.[3] Indeed, at least twenty-two Italian artists' manifestos were published between 1945 and 1960, with the debate tending to fall along political lines.[4] The Communist Party, for example, strongly encouraged the continuation of a socially oriented realism, while others on the left, including the association of artists known as Forma, championed the purity of abstraction as an antidote to the propagandistic realism of Fascism.[5] Even if these groups' formal approaches seemed at times diametrically opposed—realism versus abstraction—

they shared the same basic supposition that painting is connected to political commitment.

Although these nationalistic efforts to define an "Italian art" at mid-century help contextualize the relationship between art and the sociopolitical challenges of rebuilding that fractured country, they provide only a partial framework for interpreting the work of Fontana, an older artist who had spent most of the war years abroad in his native Argentina, where he was part of a vanguard modernist art scene.[6] His works should also be understood as part of a wider, vibrant intellectual culture in postwar Milan, one in which the traditional realism/ abstraction debate was superceded by an interest in a new kind of realism: a spatial and material realism that sought to link the time and space of the art object with the time and space of human experience. In contemporary Milanese intellectual circles, philosophers espousing phenomenology and existentialism promoted the idea of consciousness as being rooted in first-person experiences and perceptions of things in the world. Looking at Fontana's *Concetti spaziali* alongside the emergence of these theories of perception in Milan reveals the basis on which his innovations became so important for subsequent generations of Italian and other European artists.

In Rome, Fontana's contemporary Alberto Burri was making works out of torn and scorched burlap sacks or burned plastic that are often read as performances of, or responses to, the violence of the war years. Yet some scholars have argued that his art should be seen in a more nuanced light, as enacting a balance between destruction and construction, between damaging and mending.[7] As such, Burri, like Fontana, was also traversing a path that evaded the nationalist debates in postwar Italy. His works engaged a phenomenological experience of materials that would prove indispensable for later movements such as Arte Povera, which emerged toward the end of the 1960s.

While the critical developments of the 1950s give us insights into the work of Fontana and Burri, they can also hinder our understanding of it. In 1952, in his book *Un art autre,* the French artist Michel Tapié introduced the broad category of Art Informel (Arte Informale in Italian). The term, which was later applied to the works of both Fontana and Burri, quickly became a catch-all for improvisational, abstract, and gestural practices that were seen as rejecting the traditions of Western painting and emphasizing the subjectivity of the individual creator. This tendency included artists as diverse as Tapié, Jean Dubuffet, and some of the Nouveaux Réalistes in France; the German artist Wols [Alfred Otto Wolfgang Schulze]; Abstract Expressionists such as Jackson Pollock and Willem de Kooning in the United States; the Italian Emilio Vedova; and even some kinetic artists such as Gianni Colombo and his colleagues in Gruppo T, all of whose works were considered to be responding to the crises of the individual in society.[8] As distinct as the artists were who were included under this umbrella, Arte Informale still reads too much as a style—as a school or a mode of making paintings that are primarily flat rectangular planes to be hung on the wall.[9] Although some critics lumped Fontana and Burri in with Informale, I argue that they in fact opposed these mid-century paradigms by resisting the notion of a cohesive "style" at the very moment when critics were attempting to pin down national and international trends with terms such as Informale/Informel. Moreover, through an adulteration of the tactics of the historical avant-garde of the first half of the century, namely the use of monochrome in combination with self-conscious gesture, and through Fontana's incorporation of three-dimensional space, they circumvented stylistic discussions and eschewed the separation of media in favor of a more relevant, if messy, synthesis of experience.[10] Such projects extended beyond painting and opened up a free space in which to make art, one in which materials and presences, as opposed to "pictures," were foregrounded.[11] These artists modeled new ways of considering the work of art in an expanded field of contingencies for younger artists such as Manzoni, Klein, Saint Phalle, the kinetic artists of Gruppo T, and the sculptural and conceptual practitioners of Arte Povera.

In 1947, only a few months after returning to Italy from Buenos Aires to find his studio and its contents destroyed by Allied bombings, Fontana published the first of numerous manifestos on Spazialismo (Spatialism), outlining a new direction in art that superceded the realism/abstraction debate by arguing for a new mode of working that took a more phenomenological approach to realism, such that it could encompass abstraction as well. The "Primo manifesto dello Spazialismo"—signed by Fontana, Benjamino Joppolo, Giorgio Kaisserlian, and Milena Milani—distinguished between gestures and materials, claiming that art is made primarily through creative acts that endure as milestones of human experience and that materials are secondary and, by nature, ephemeral.[12] Anticipating, perhaps, the arguments over style that would come with Arte Informale several years later, these artists pursued a diverse range of abstract practices that did not conform to strict rationales or traditional media. They did not assign specific political tasks to their work, nor did they operate under a formal ideology or system of representation. Instead, they created objects and environments that aimed to communicate phenomenological experiences of reality. This is not to say that these works had no political aspects, however. On the contrary, the politics of such art came in the repositioning of the perceiving subject at the center of the work of art, in suggesting an empowered viewer in communication with the artist through the object or environment. It was at this time that Fontana, who was trained as a sculptor and ceramist, began to make spatial environments (*Ambienti spaziali*) that used light and three-dimensional space to engage the viewer in an aesthetic experience, a practice he would continue throughout the 1950s and 1960s.

In 1948 Fontana issued a "technical manifesto" of Spatialism ("Manifesto tecnico dello spazialismo"), which refined his earlier ideas and directly addressed the realism/abstraction divide by proposing a third way. Here the artist wrote that representation in twentieth-century art was so divorced from the technological necessities of art that it "would be a farce" to continue to make work in this way. He further suggested that abstraction, as it had been pursued through the deformation of representational forms, "does not correspond to the needs of contemporary man." As an alternative, he laid out a prescription for an art existing in both time and space—in all four dimensions of human experience.[13] A year later, the artist began work on his first perforated canvases, the *Buchi* (Holes), which, following the principles of Spatialism, could be considered both abstract, with their near-monochromatic surfaces, and

Right: Installation view of Lucio Fontana's *Spatial Light-Structure in Neon* for the 9th Milan Triennial, Palazzo dell'Arte, 1951. Courtesy of the Fondazione La Triennale di Milano. (catalogue only)

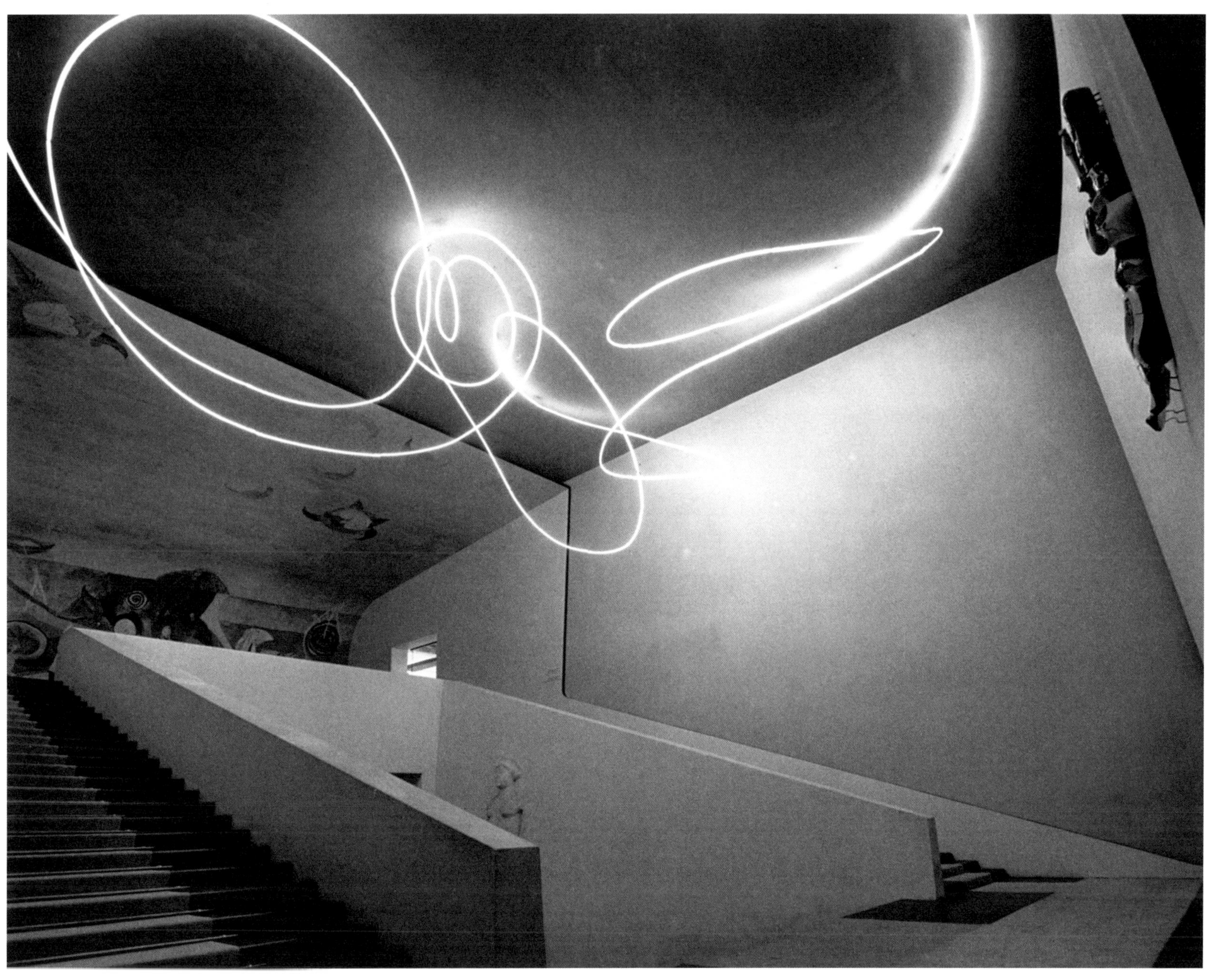

realistic, in their deployment of materials and overtures to three-dimensionality. These canvases, which he would continue to make for the balance of his career, both eschewed illusionism in favor of perceptual reality and exceeded the flat planes of the most austere abstract paintings through theatrical framing, gritty collage, and the laceration of the canvas. In some examples, mirrors and lights placed behind, or in front of, the canvases suggested the fourth dimension by incorporating the movement of the viewer in front of and around the object into the experience of the work. Most important, by breaking the finite plane of the canvas, these works proposed that the time and space of the art object existed on the same perceptual horizon as the time and space of human experience.

Although Fontana had previously used the term *scultura spaziale* (spatial sculpture) to describe some of his objects, with the *Buchi* he dropped the medium specificity and insisted,

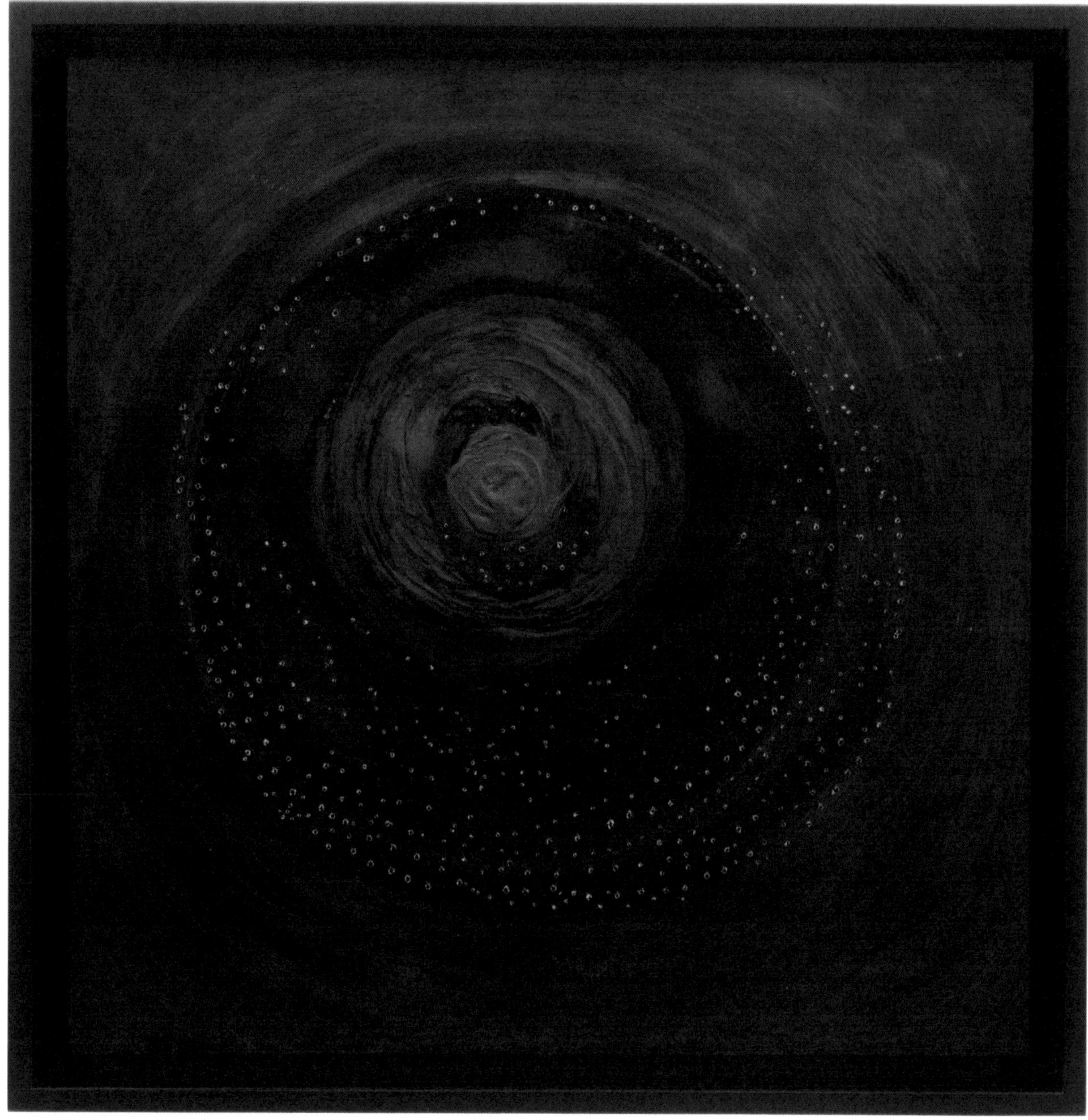

as he would for many years, that these new works were no longer subject to the limitations of traditional media.[14] For the artist, they were neither paintings nor sculptures, but tools for conceptualizing space. *Concetto spaziale (C.49B2)* (Spatial Concept [C.49B2]) (1949; page 20), exemplifies these earliest experiments with perforated canvas. Made of paper mounted to canvas, it records the artist's seemingly scattershot penetrating gestures, ones that in their violation of the pure white monochrome might call up the image of Fontana clambering

through the disarray of his wrecked studio only two years earlier (page 88). Living amidst the desecration of once solid structures, could one avoid making work that was about destruction too? Yet a closer look reveals that the artist's actions were not aimed solely at despoiling the unbroken surface of the picture plane. Distinct shapes emerge within the frame: a circle at the center right, and a triangle or parabolic shape at the upper left that appears to orbit the circle. These were not random stabs made in a fit of rage against the canvas or against the traditions of painting, as the attempted association with Informale might suggest, but deliberate marks made of actual space instead of pigment. Still, for all the familiar geometric shapes we may locate, the work does not yield an image in the traditional sense. The effect of the holes is to break the plane of representational space, effectively nullifying its illusionistic pretense and opening up an experience of the object qua object in the time and space shared by the viewer.[15] Most important, Fontana's holes record a temporally executed gesture, an act of which the cut is a palpable trace in three dimensions. The brutality we might perceive today, and indeed argue for in the context of the present exhibition, exists perhaps in the way the holes close off illusionism, resisting one of painting's traditional functions, if only to open it up again to new possibilities. Aggression, should we seek it, is located less in the holes' physical desecration of the canvas than in the radical reconfiguration of the role of both artist and viewer in relation to the object.

In order to fully appreciate the significance of Fontana's linking of the work of art with the contingencies of the viewer's time and space, one must recognize that much of what was happening in postwar Italian aesthetics was in reaction to the writings of Benedetto Croce, whose views on artistic autonomy had dominated the Italian context for the first half of the century. In his 1901 treatise *Aesthetic,* Croce had argued for an "ideal" art that was separate from the concerns of everyday life: that is, for him, the work of art was autonomous, complete unto itself.[16] Fontana's art, which was contingent on the presence of the viewer, would have been antithetical to Croce's views. Gillo Dorfles, the prominent Italian critic and painter, attempted in 1953 to take stock of the state of Italian aesthetics after Croce's death the previous year.[17] He identified philosopher Antonio Banfi's approach to the arts, which took into account the physical and contextual realities of artistic practice, as an important counterposition to Croce. Banfi's example was especially significant because it gave rise to an Italian school of phenomenology in Milan, where Enzo Paci emerged in the postwar years as a main theoretician of an "existential phenomenology."[18] These ideas also spread to the nearby University of Turin, where Luigi

Pareyson posited the reception of the artwork by an active viewer/participant as central to its formation of meaning. His theory of "formativity" was an important influence on students such as Umberto Eco and Gianni Vattimo, who both continued Pareyson's interest in the aesthetics of reception.[19] Both schools of thought provided fertile alternatives to the debates about postwar painting by reinserting the artwork into the fabric of everyday life and human experience, a shift that altered the character of the art produced in Italy at this time.[20]

In their introduction to Paci's influential 1963 book *The Function of the Sciences and the Meaning of Man,* translators Paul Piccone and James E. Hansen argue that, for Paci, the broader social crises facing postwar Italy were a result of the alienation of the individual—the perceiving subject—by a scientific approach to the phenomenological world: Trapped within a self-contained system where means and ends become indistinguishable, this pseudorationalism camouflaged as "scientific neutrality" is divorced from the creating subject who originally constitutes it, and it becomes another tool for the manipulation and oppression of man.[21]

By restoring the subject to the center of his analysis of perceptual experiences, Paci wedded phenomenology to Marxism, since he believed that the subject's alienation from the original *telos* was at the root of many of the social problems facing a rapidly industrializing Italian society. For Paci—writing from the standpoint that there is an innate purpose to human life— postwar industry, rampant capitalism, and the cool objectivity of science had distanced man from accessing this understanding of his own being. For mid-century artists like Fontana, who aimed to create experiences rather than consumable objects, such views of phenomenology offered a way of connecting art and life by thinking about objects and forms as tools for the affirmation of subjectivity. Such subjectivity had been and continued to be jeopardized in the nationalist, sectarian atmosphere surrounding postwar politics and painting, and was, just as detrimentally, hyperbolized by Arte Informale. The material and spatial presence of Fontana's early *Concetti spaziali* made the artist's gestures perceptible and allowed viewers to understand that the work did not transcend everyday experiences so much as it embodied them.

Burri's works also typify a physical experience of materials and presence that was incompatible with Croce's notion of artistic autonomy. Burri was a signatory to the 1951 "Manifesto del Gruppo Origine," which aimed to reassert abstraction while avoiding all decoration and allusion to formalism. Instead, the artists of this group, founded in Rome in 1950, proposed an art that, while initially two-dimensional, emphasized the concrete and humble materials of its construction.[22] In Burri's early canvases, a reconsideration of nonfigurative abstraction can be seen in the use of "low" materials such as burlap and cardboard, which were read as being

that reemphasizes the physical presence of the materials. Here, instead of opening the canvas to the space beyond/behind it as Fontana did, Burri suggests the destruction of the picture plane, but then reconstitutes and reinforces its materiality by stitching it back together, again creating a tenuous balance between the two extremes. Inasmuch as a work such as *Sacco* (Sack) (1955) can be seen as a collage of disparate elements, Burri contrasts areas that have been violated with ones that have been carefully restored in order to create an oppositional equilibrium that asserts the physical presence of the object in the real time and space of the viewer.

Below left: Alberto Burri in his studio, 1954. Photograph by Josephine Powell. Collection of KOC University, Istanbul. (catalogue only)

Below right: Alberto Burri, *Combustione plastica*, 1964. Polyvinyl chloride calcinated on a plate of aluminum, 59¼ x 98¾ in. (150.5 x 250.8 cm). Musée d'Art Moderne, Centre Georges Pompidou, Paris. (catalogue only)

Opposite: Alberto Burri, *Sacco*, 1955. Burlap, cardboard, muslin, and paint. Seattle Art Museum, Gift of Hester Diamond in memory of Alberto Burri, 95.134.

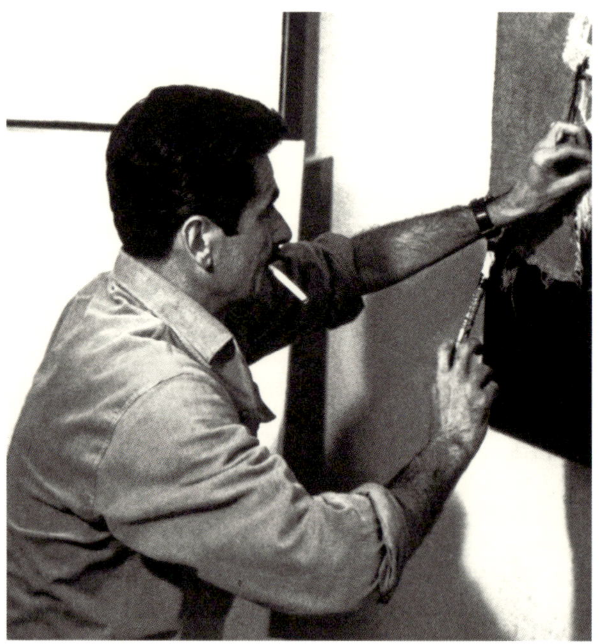

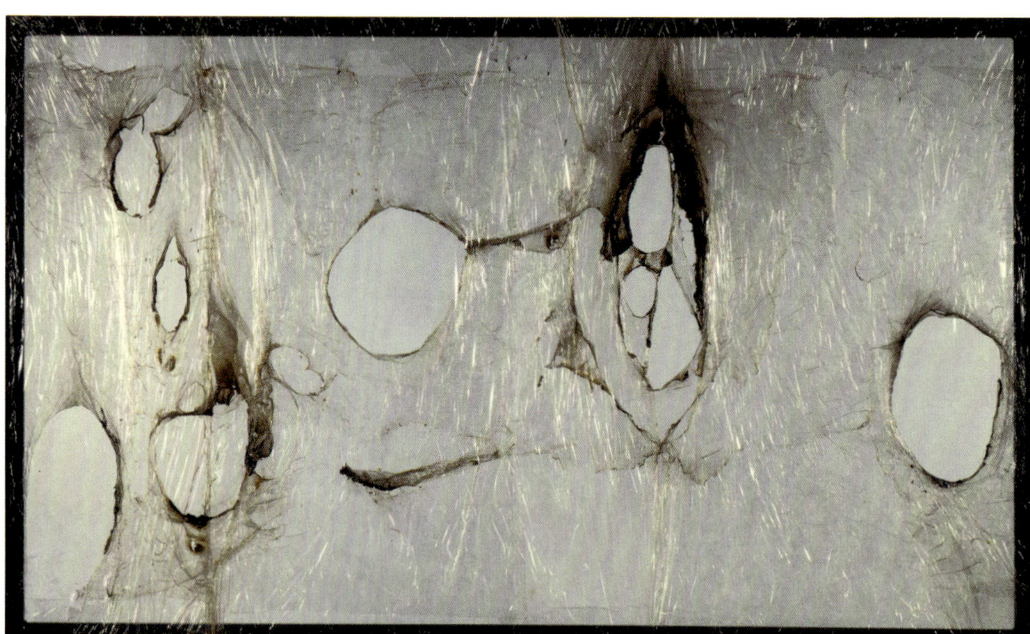

antidecorative.[23] For the artist, these works may have foregrounded the materials themselves, but it was the way in which he acted upon them that first endeared him to the critics of Informale. On the one hand, there is the tearing and ripping of the burlap sack, the kind of quick "expressive" gesture understood in the context of Informale as being liberating for the postwar individual. Yet there is also the slow, deliberate action of sewing the pieces back together.[24] Like Fontana's deliberate punctures, Burri's suturing of the canvas opposes the seemingly uncontrolled gestures of Informale. Moreover, this reconstruction dissolves distinctions between foreground and background, creating a tension

Throughout the 1950s, Burri expanded his practice to include new materials such as wood, metal, and plastic and began using fire as a formative "tool." His works were acknowledged by the French critic Pierre Restany as having influenced his conception of Nouveau Réalisme, a movement he identified and introduced in an exhibition at Milan's Galleria Apollinaire in 1960.[25] Many of the artists who cosigned Restany's founding declaration later that year—including Arman, Klein, Daniel Spoerri, Jean Tinguely, and *décollagistes* Jacques Villeglé and Raymond Hains—pursued a kind of urban realism that often incorporated the detritus of everyday experiences

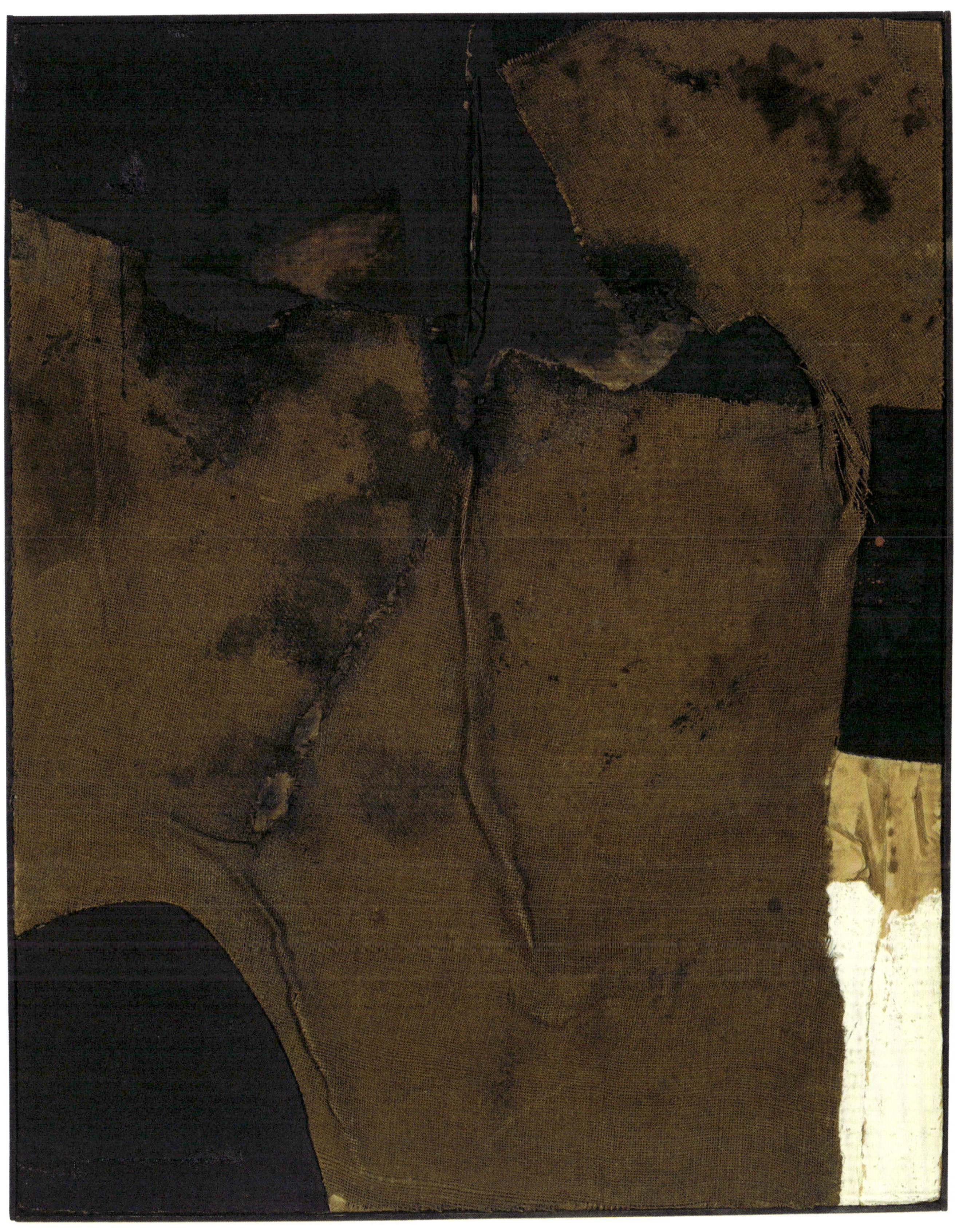

into their works. Saint Phalle and Rotella would join the movement in 1961 in Paris, but Italy remained an important touchstone of Nouveau Réalisme and was the site of a tenth-anniversary festival in the 1970s. These artists' interests in connecting art and everyday life certainly relied on the examples of prewar avant-garde efforts, including Dada's rejection of style and the subversive tactics of the Situationists, but they also built upon Fontana's and Burri's forays into phenomenological space and their fore-grounding of material presences.

Fontana purchased one of Burri's sliced and sutured works in 1952, and during this same decade he continued his own exploration of *Concetti spaziali* using a wide variety of materials, from canvas, bronze, and ceramics to neon, environments, and even television. Some critics and scholars have linked Fontana's interests in space to the contemporaneous explorations of outer space during the cold-war years, and indeed one must consider this context as part of a widening experience and concep-tualization of the phenomenological world.[26]

Left: Lucio Fontana, *Concetto spaziale*, 1958. Graffiti, cuts, and dye on paper mounted to canvas. Fondazione Lucio Fontana, Milan.

Right: Lucio Fontana, *Concetto spaziale—Attesa*, 1964–65. Tempera on canvas, lacquered wood, 58¾ x 46 x 2 ⅜ in. (149.2 x 116.8 x 6cm). Walker Art Center, Minneapolis, T. B. Walker Acquisition Fund, 1998. (catalogue only)

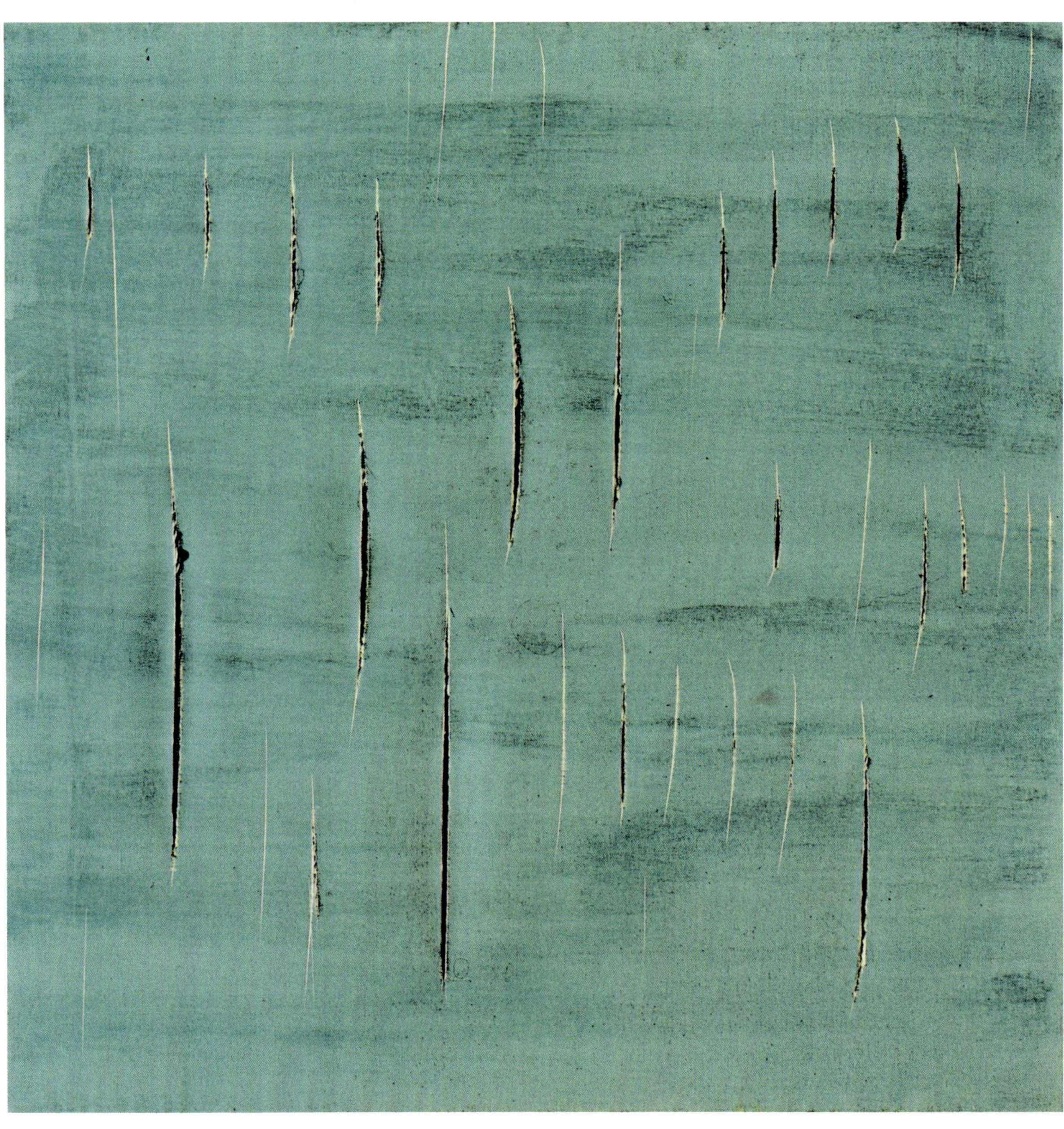

Works similar to *Concetto spaziale* (1952; page 92) that seem to display almost galactic forms have even been directly compared to photographs of the surface of the moon. However, in terms of the artist's local context and the importance of his oeuvre for later generations, the focus on outer space is less constructive than an investigation of phenomenological space. Indeed, by the late 1950s, when space exploration was reaching its peak, Fontana backed off such suggestive works and began a new series of even more restrained monochrome canvases.

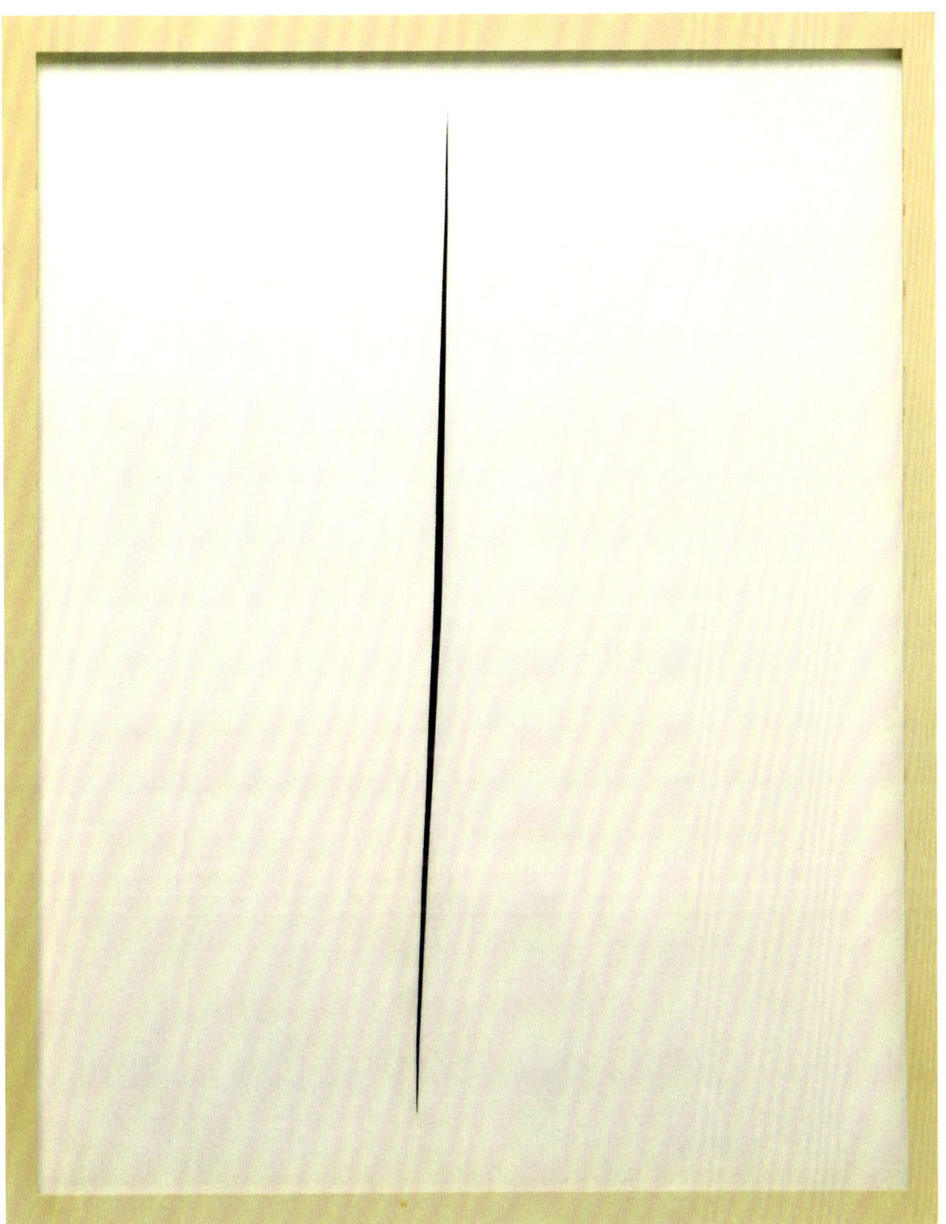

In 1958 Fontana created his first of the so-called *Tagli* (Cuts), using a box knife to make vertical tears in canvas surfaces.[27] The works in this series, produced from 1958 to 1964, are all titled *Concetto spaziale/attesa* (Spatial Concept/Expectation). Early examples, such as one from 1958, display numerous vertical cuts across the surface. Here, slashes of varying depths show the artist appearing at times tentative and probing, and at other times sure of his actions. In such early works the cuts cluster together—a field of gashes mark the plane—as if Fontana was searching for something through these encounters. In later examples, as in one from 1964–65, a single slit interrupts the canvas. A photograph of the artist in his studio (page 98) reveals the challenge he faced in confronting these inviolate canvases. Although his actions were likely conditioned to some extent by the photographer's presence, we can see a drama unfolding as Fontana approaches the work. Standing with knife in hand at a remove from the stark monochrome surface, he seems to pause in anticipation, in expectation perhaps, of the gesture that will irrevocably alter the surface. Like the slow, deliberate action of Burri as he sutures torn burlap, Fontana appears aware of the gravity of the act. The result communicates neither violence nor anger, but careful acceptance of the need to sacrifice the idea of the inviolate whole. With the first breach of the surface, the first millimeter of the knife's penetration, the transcendent monochrome is thrust into conversation with the space around it—a chaotic, phenomenological horizon that it shares with the artist and the viewer. Reflecting on the *Tagli* in 1968, Fontana argued that in making these lacerations, he understood art's revolutionary potential as essentially conceptual: "In art the revolution is social and not just visual. It is a revolution in thought."[28]

Was this conceptual revolution that thing Fontana was searching for when he breached the canvas? Certainly, both he and Burri, in their investigations of subjectivity via gesture and their redress to historically avant-gardist propositions such as the monochrome, opened a new field of possibilities for the artists who came after them. Manzoni and Klein separately took up the project of the monochrome with a particular vengeance, and each hyperbolized—and even mocked—gesture and the

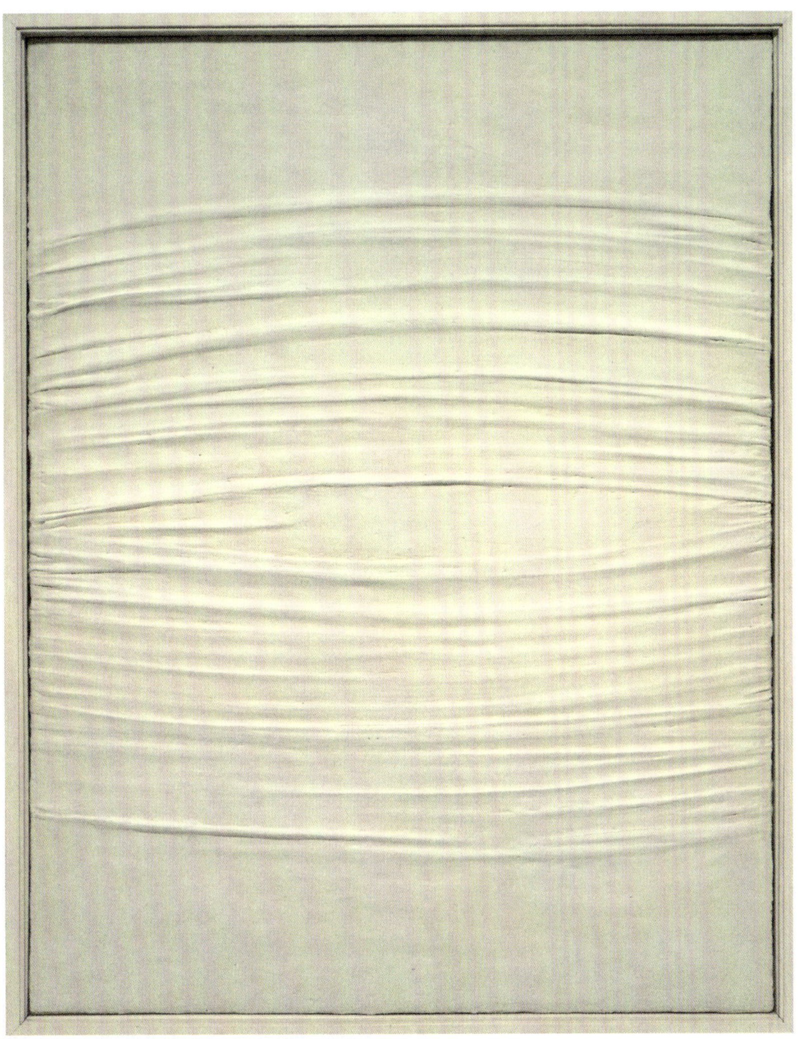

constituent materials. These are two facets of a single project that built upon Fontana's use of the monochrome to position his works as conceptual objects whose meaning relied on a making subject and a perceiving subject.

Simultaneously, in France, Klein had embarked on what he called his monochrome adventure, notably presenting an exhibition of nearly identical blue canvases at the Galleria Apollinaire in Milan in 1957.[30] He wrote that this foregrounding of color aided him in creating perceptible artistic states: "I devoted myself to the 'refinement' of space, which is my ultimate way of treating color. It is no longer a question of seeing color, but rather of 'perceiving' it."[31] Klein's use of his patented shade of blue in these monochromes was also one of the ways he confronted the marketing of the artist's subjectivity. At other times he took artistic gesture to extremes, as evidenced in his fire paintings (pages 152–153). For Klein, who called himself "the painter of space," these actions were as important, if not more important, than the "paintings" themselves, and they were documented meticulously. Destruction may have been literalized in works such as the fire paintings, but here, too, the real transformation lay in the relationship between the work and the viewer on the level of perception.

In these younger artists' works, Fontana's and Burri's investigations of avant-garde tropes approached a new conceptual revolution, which was perhaps the most "violent" legacy of their art: an iconoclasm that, even though it may have been aimed at destabilizing the authenticity of the gesture, had the effect of empowering the viewer, whose phenomenological relationship with the work of art became essential to its meaning. It was not until the mid-1960s, with the ascendance of Arte Povera, that painting in Italy truly yielded to object-based practices. Works such as Michelangelo Pistoletto's early mirror paintings (page 100), which literalize the viewer's involvement by reflecting his or her image in the surface, provided yet another bridge between the investigations into subjectivity.[32] Indeed, the new generation's direct address to the viewer as a perceivable participant in the work of art would have been impossible without Fontana's early navigations of that perceptible "something else" beyond the painting's surface.

notions of authenticity ascribed to it.[29] Manzoni pursued a series of "paintings" that explored not just a single color but the *absence* of color in various materials. On the one hand, these *Achromes*, as he called them, were, like Duchamp's notorious objects of the early twentieth century, "readymade" works that eclipsed the artist's role; on the other hand, they made the artist's persona the essential nucleus around which the work revolved. Manzoni challenged the idea, espoused by Arte Informale, that an artwork is something that comes from within the artist with these *Achromes* and with his infamous *Merda d'artista* (Artist's Shit) (1961), editioned tin cans filled with his excremental emissions. Indeed, because such works purport to offer the viewer conceptual or physical traces of the artist himself, both series have been accepted as art, regardless of the worth of their

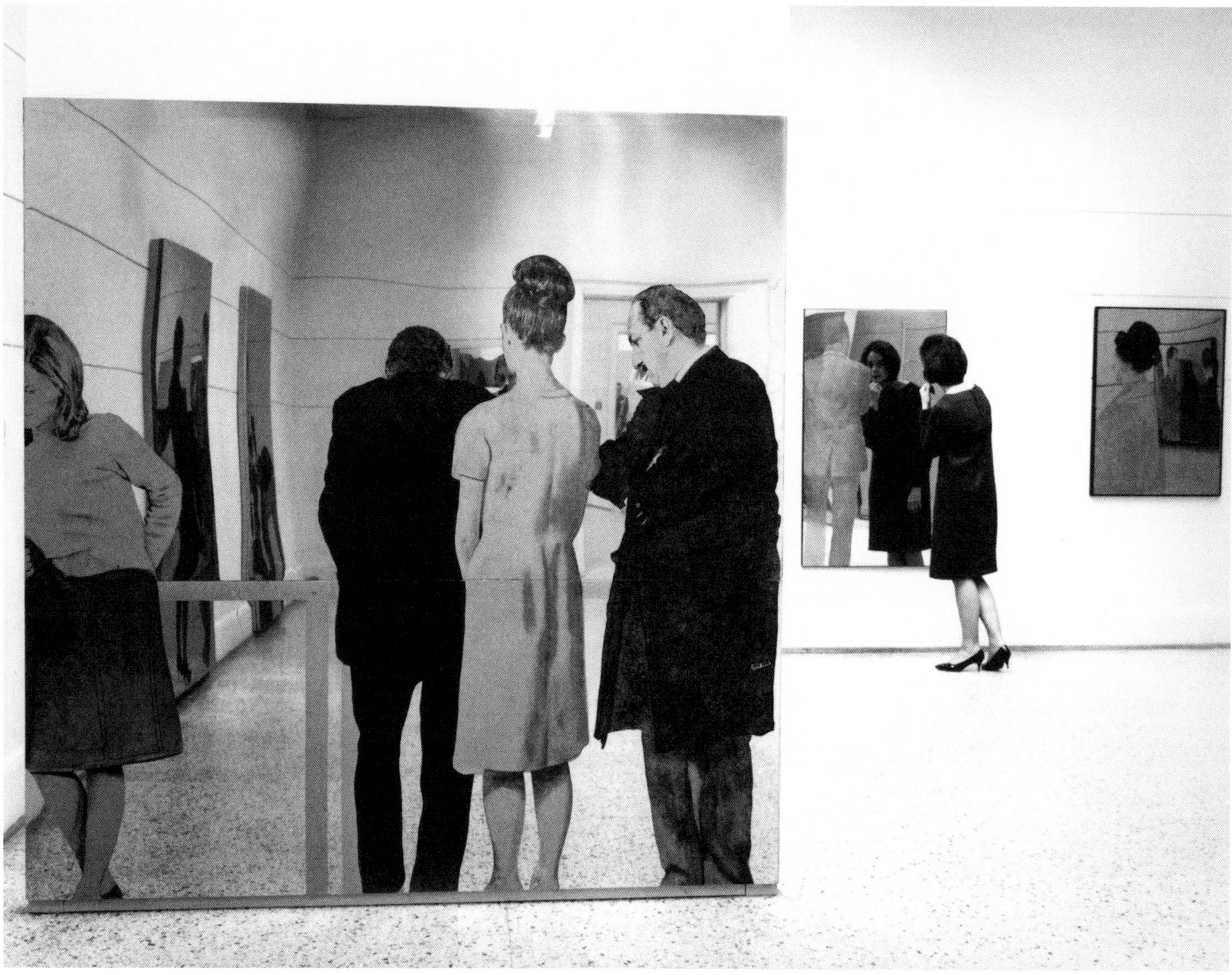

Notes

1. Tommaso Trini, "The Last Interview Given by Fontana" [July 19, 1968], *Studio International* 184, no. 949 (November 1972): 164. In this conversation with Trini, Fontana discusses the importance of the "hole" as a conceptual leap outside of the limitations of the picture frame and one's own understanding of art.

2. As many critics and scholars have noted, Italy did not have the extreme learning curve that Germany experienced in these years because the Fascist regime had been much more lenient when it came to artistic expression. Marcia Vetrocq provides an excellent account of the early postwar situation in Italy, especially the debate surrounding European versus American influences and the preservation of an "authentic" national style. See Marcia Vetrocq, "National Style and the Agenda for Abstract Painting in Post-War Italy," *Art History* 12, no. 4 (December 1989): 448–71.

3. It was a debate that had started in the early twentieth century and gained a particular urgency after World War II, when the nationalist rhetoric of Mussolini and Marinetti had clearly failed to restore Italian culture to its previously elevated status. For a longer discussion of this background, see ibid., 448–49.

4. Excerpts and full texts of most of these manifestos, with translations by Stephen Sartarelli, are reprinted in Germano Celant, ed., *The Italian Meta-morphosis, 1943–1968* (New York: Guggenheim Museum; Rome: Progetti Museali Editore, 1994), 708–25. Because there was significant crossover among the different groupings and regroupings, strict divisions are nearly impossible and beyond the scope of this study. Vetrocq provides an excellent discussion of these years, but does not discuss Fontana and Spatialism in relation to these debates.

5. The sectarian nature of this cultural sphere can be closely tied to the fractured state of the nation, which had to recover from both the world war and a civil war between the Nazi-backed Fascist remnants in and around Milan (Mussolini's *Republicca di Salò*) and the widespread partisan (*partigiani*) Resistance. It was this civil struggle that defined the final years of World War II as the Allied troops slowly made their way north along the peninsula. For a general history, see Paul Ginsborg, *A History of Contemporary Italy: Society and Politics, 1943–1988* (London: Penguin, 1990; repr., New York: Palgrave Macmillan, 2003). For connections to art of the era, see Mario De Micheli, "Realism and the Post-War Debate," trans. John Mitchell, in Emily Braun, ed., *Italian Art in the 20th Century: Painting and Sculpture, 1900–1988* (London: Royal Academy of Arts; Munich: Prestel, 1989), 282.

6. Fontana was born in Rosario, Argentina, to Italian parents; went to Italy at the age of six to attend school; and traveled back and forth intermittently between 1921 and 1940, when he settled in Buenos Aires for seven years. He

Left: Installation view of the exhibition *Michelangelo Pistoletto: A Reflected World*, Walker Art Center, Minneapolis, April 4–May 8, 1966. (catalogue only)

returned to Milan in 1947, where he spent the rest of his life.

7. In a recent essay Jaimey Hamilton argues that Burri's works must be seen in the context of the war, during which he served as a doctor in the Italian army. He was captured and spent four years in a POW camp in Texas, where he began using burlap sacks as substrates for paintings. However, Hamilton ultimately posits that Burri's later action of tearing and stitching was related more to his exposure to Informale in Rome after his return from the camp and that it enacts a suturing of the wounds of modernist painting, which was seen to be in crisis. See Jaimey Hamilton, "Making Art Matter: Alberto Burri's *Sacchi*," *October* 124 (Spring 2008): 31–52.

8. Yve-Alain Bois argues that the designation Informel (as it is used in French) presumes a kind of movement or "ism" that wrongly eclipses the real import of the abstraction practiced by artists such as Wols, Dubuffet, and Jean Fautrier. Instead, he counters that Georges Bataille's term *informe* (formless) suggests an engagement with base materialism and other Surrealist tendencies that continues an important aspect of avant-garde activity in the postwar period. See Yve-Alain Bois, "No…to Informel," in Yve-Alain Bois and Rosalind Krauss, *Formless: A User's Guide*, 138–43 (New York: Zone, 1997).

9. This presented problems for the reception of these works, then as now. In 1961 the philosopher Enzo Paci noticed that works such as those by Fontana and Burri seemed to share the contemporary interest in phenomenology. However, he maintained that they did not go far enough into the realm of reality and as works of art to be hung on a wall, they remained alienated from the rest of life. See Enzo Paci, "Fenomenologia e Informale," *Il Verri*, no. 3 (June 1961): 159–60.

10. For a discussion of Fontana's early works and the genesis of the Informal artists, see Maurizio Calvesi, "Informel and Abstraction in Italian Art of the Fifties," trans. Meg Shore, in Braun, *Italian Art in the 20th Century*, 289–99. For more on the Italian commitment to the idea of synthesis among the arts as it evolved after the Fascist period, see also Romy Golan, "Italy and the Concept of the 'Synthesis of the Arts,'" in *Architecture + Art: New Visions, New Strategies*, ed. Eeva-Liisa Pelkonen and Esa Laaksonen (Helsinki: Alvar Aalto Academy, 2007).

11. See the interview with Lucio Fontana in Carla Lonzi, *Autoritratto* (Bari: De Donato, 1969), 94–96.

12. Fontana had previously contributed to but did not sign the 1946 "White Manifesto" ("Manifesto Blanco") with a group of artists in Argentina, where he was a cofounder of the Academia Altamira in Buenos Aires. The 1947 manifesto was the first to introduce the concept of Spatialism, which would dominate the last two decades of the artist's career, and marked a major shift in his production. See Fontana et al., "Primo manifesto dello Spazialismo (Milan, May 1947)," in Celant, *The Italian Metamorphosis*, 713.

13. See reprints in English in Celant, *The Italian Metamorphosis*, 710–15.

14. See Trini, "Last Interview."

15. Some have argued that this expansion into space echoed the actions of artists such as Pollock and de Kooning across the Atlantic. Others suggest that Arte Informale in Italy was seen as coming from a European tradition of abstraction. For diverse perspectives on the reception of Informal art in Italy, see Enrico Crispolti, ed., "Breve antologia di poetica," *Il Verri*, no. 3 (June 1961): 128–40. These collected statements include one each by Pollock, Clement Greenberg, and Harold Rosenberg.

16. Benedetto Croce, *Aesthetic* (1901), trans. Douglas Ainslie (Boston: Nonpareil, 1978). For a brief analysis of the impact of Croce's theories, see Frederic S. Simoni, "Benedetto Croce: A Case of International Misunderstanding," *Journal of Aesthetics and Art Criticism* 11, no. 1 (September 1952): 7–14

17. Dorfles argued that after the war "Italian philosophical thinking sought to regain the time lost, and so appeared more explicit in its disagreement and in its criticism, which turned against the aesthetic dictatorship of Croce." However, he noted that Croce was still an important figure, well respected for his ability to stand up to Fascism, and it was not until after his death that a real change could be maintained. See Gillo Dorfles, "New Currents in Italian Aesthetics," *Journal of Aesthetics and Art Criticism* 12, no. 2 (December 1953): 184.

18. Paci started the journal *Autaut*, which became the primary vehicle for the dissemination of phenomenology in Italy. It was a publication in which writers opposed to Croce's idealism shared ideas about their understanding of art as a form of communication and, therefore, connected to everyday life. *Autaut* began publication in 1952. The title, roughly translated, means "ultimatum."

19. Eco, especially, wrote prolifically about art and culture in the late 1950s and 1960s, and his 1962 book *Opera Aperta* (*The Open Work*) posited that the work of art was a field of information that had to be engaged with and navigated by an active viewer or reader. Umberto Eco, *The Open Work*, trans. Anna Cancogni (Cambridge, MA: Harvard University Press, 1989). Originally published as *Opera Aperta* (Milan: Fabbri, 1962).

20. For more on Paci's phenomenology, see Giovanna Borradori, "'Weak Thought' and Postmodernism: The Italian Departure from Deconstruction," *Social Text*, no. 18 (Winter 1987–88): 42.

21. Paul Piccone and James E. Hansen, "Introduction" to Enzo Paci, *The Function of the Sciences and the Meaning of Man*, trans. Piccone and Hansen (Evanston, IL: Northwestern University Press, 1972), xxi. Originally published in Italian as *Funzione delle Scienze e Significato dell'Uomo* (Milan: Il Saggiatore, 1963). Page citations are to the English edition.

22. See Giuseppe Capogrossi, Mario Ballocco, Ettore Colla, and Alberto Burri, "Manifesto del Gruppo Origine," in Celant, *The Italian Metamorphosis*, 714.

23. Some have suggested that the use of burlap sacks is a direct reference to the war years the artist spent as a POW in Texas and also to the food aid provided to Italy by the Marshall Plan. Hamilton argues that Burri may simply have begun using these substrates at the Texas camp for no other reason than that they were readily available. See Hamilton, "Making Art Matter," 31–52.

24. Carolyn Christov-Bakargiev interprets Burri's sewing action as asserting the importance of the surface; see her essay "Alberto Burri: The Surface at Risk," in *Burri: 1915–1995 Retrospektive*, ed. Carolyn Christov-Bakargiev and Maria Grazia Tolomeo, 79–94 (Milan: Electa, 1997).

25. Federica Pirani, "Interview with Pierre Restany," in Christov-Bakargiev and Tolomeo, *Burri: Retrospektive*, 137.

26. See especially Sarah Whitfield, "Handling Space," in *Lucio Fontana* (London: Hayward Gallery; Berkeley: University of California Press, 1999), 11–51.

27. Anthony White points out that the *Tagli* were made after a lukewarm response to the collagelike *Buchi* at the 1958 Venice Biennale. He argues that these were also made after Fontana saw Yves Klein's blue monochromes in Milan in 1957 (Fontana bought one of Klein's works from the show) and Jackson Pollock's work in Rome and Venice, and that the artist may have felt the need to pursue an even more radical gesture and readoption of the monochrome. See Anthony White, "Industrial Painting's Utopias: Lucio Fontana's *Expectations*," *October* 124 (Spring 2008): 98–124.

28. See Trini, "Last Interview," 164.

29. See Benjamin H. D. Buchloh, "Primary Colors for the Second Time: A Paradigm of Repetition of the Neo-Avant-Garde," *October* 37 (Summer 1986): 41–52. Buchloh argues that the specific conditions of the post-WWII period make the process of repetition and thus recuperation a necessary and authentic mode of production. The meaning, he says, can be found in those very acts of copying that the German literary critic Peter Bürger and others see as falsifying the work of neo-avant-garde artists such as Manzoni and Klein. For Buchloh, the postwar period offers another chance to continue the project of the historical avant-garde, but by working within the paradigms set forth by the earlier artists, these younger proponents of the monochrome were better poised to transgress the institutions of art.

30. This shade of blue is known by the name under which the artist retained an exclusive patent, IKB, or International Klein Blue.

31. The emphatic quotation marks are Klein's. See Yves Klein, "My Position in the Battle between Color and Line" [1958], in *Overcoming the Problematics of Art: The Writings of Yves Klein*, trans. Klaus Ottmann (Putnam, CT: Spring Publications, 2007), 20–21.

32. Later generations, including the Arte Povera artists, would have encountered Fontana not just as an elder but also in exhibitions held at the same spaces in which they exhibited. See, for example, Enrico Crispolti, ed., *Fontana* (Milan: Charta, 1959). Further, it should be noted that Umberto Eco, a student of the other major phenomenologist in Italy, Luigi Pareyson, was a champion of the works of artists such as those in Gruppo T and the related Gruppo N, as evidenced by his exhibition catalogue essay "Arte Programmata" ("Programmed Art"). See Umberto Eco, *La definizione dell' arte* (Milan: Bompiani, 1983), 231–36.

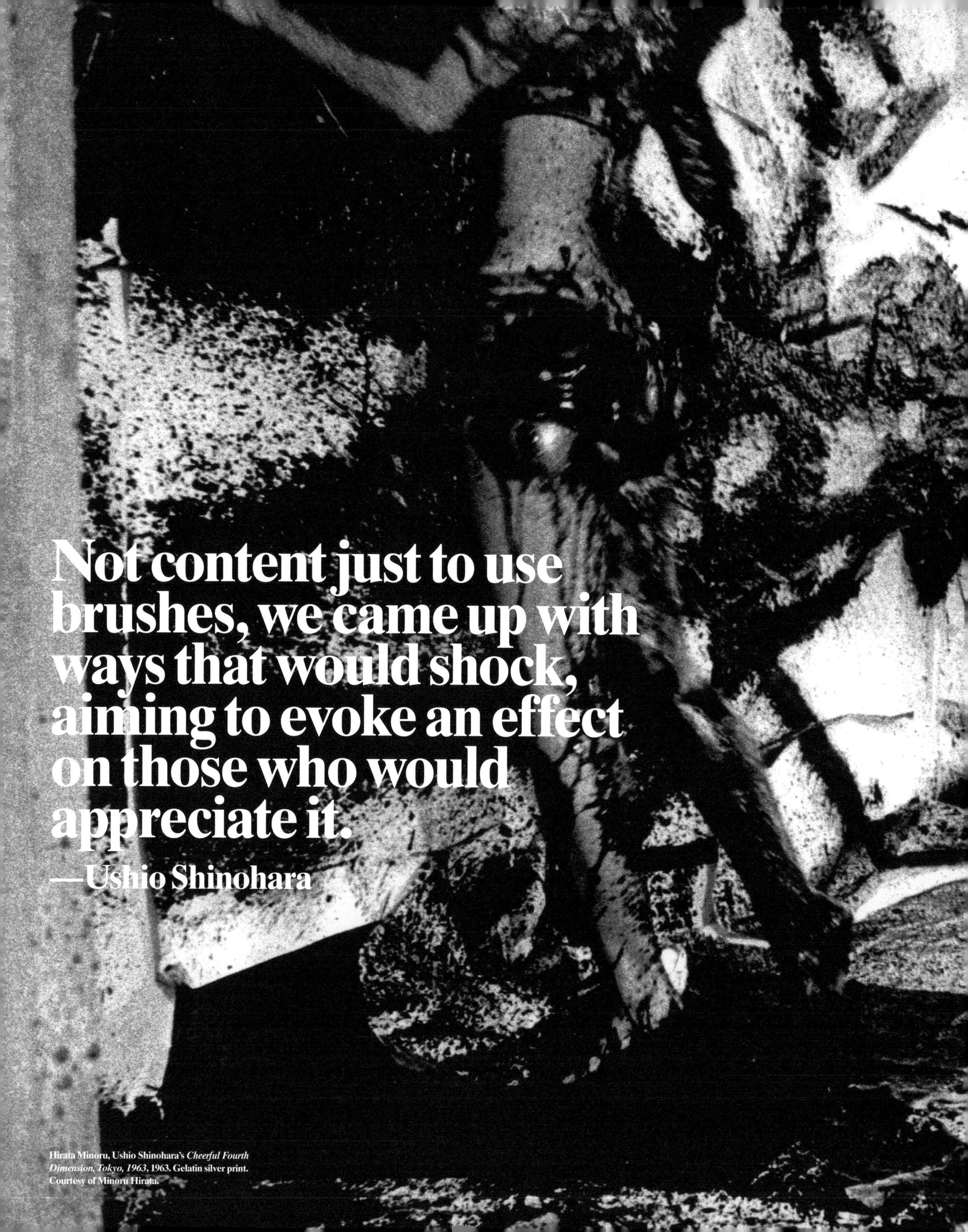

Hirata Minoru, Ushio Shinohara's *Cheerful Fourth Dimension, Tokyo, 1963*, 1963. Gelatin silver print. Courtesy of Minoru Hirata.

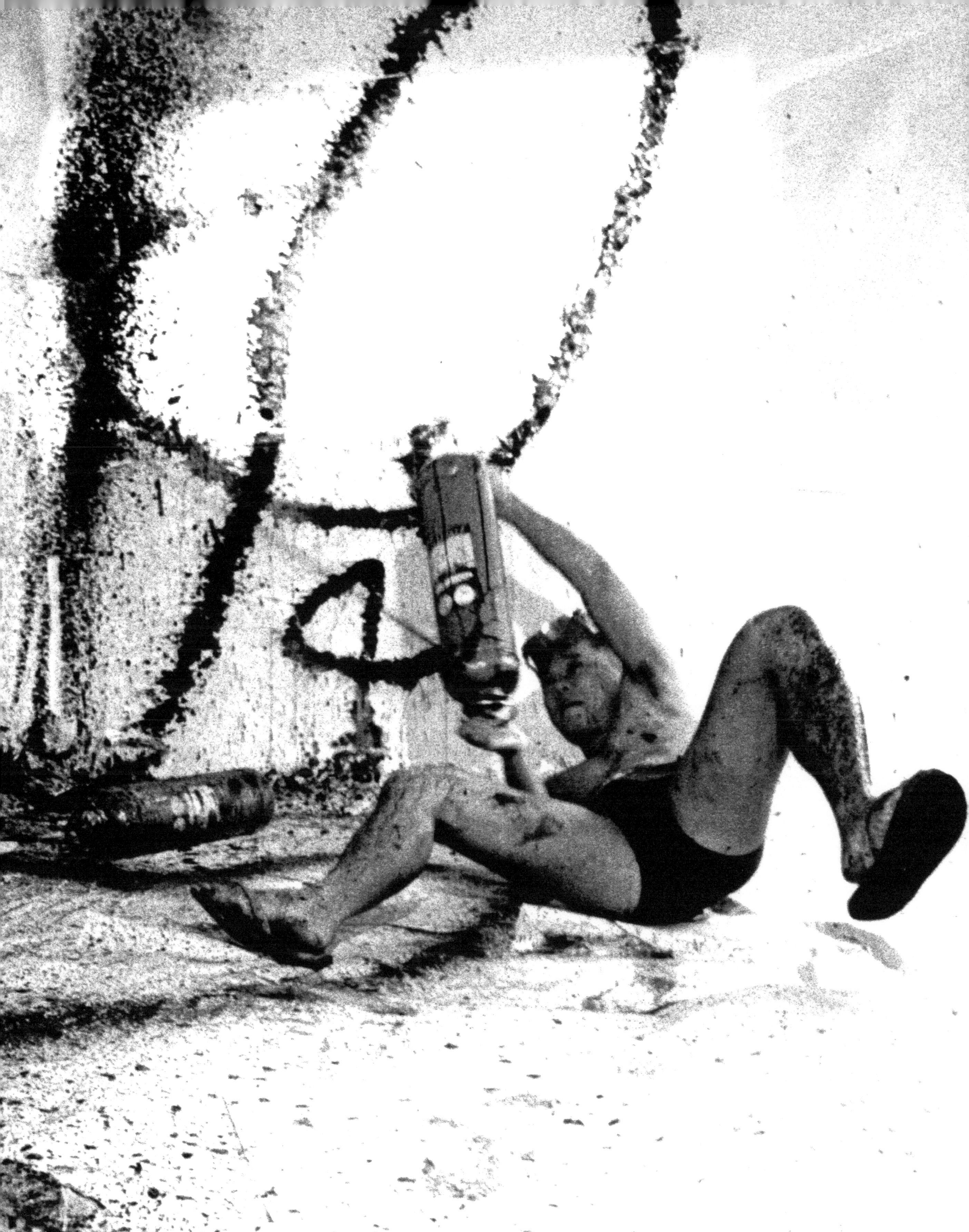

Breaking Through

Shōzō Shimamoto and the Aesthetic of *Dakai*

Mika Yoshitake

The thrill and excitement that destruction invokes is common to us all. We experience this everywhere in our daily lives. Even though destruction itself may be the opposite of creation, in this age, the boundary between the two no longer exists…. Despite our refusal to empathize with destruction, we must consider it as a constructive site in order to move forward.[1]

—Shōzō Shimamoto

nd the

Screams were heard as the artist Shōzō Shimamoto, dressed in black, used a wooden stick to repeatedly strike a luminous white tube from which thousands of ping-pong balls descended onto the stage in a bouncing whirlwind speeding uncontrollably toward the audience. As the artist continued to strike, a glittering cloud of silver confetti showered down on the stage in a gleaming ray of light, and just as the lights dimmed, Shimamoto disappeared into a thin sliver of darkness. Such a demonstration of the sheer vitality of form through the force of obliteration was unprecedented at the time, when abstraction and disfiguration were entrenched in art, especially the field of painting. For what was left here was pure imagination, the residual sound of balls bouncing without a trace of the artist or objects in sight. Performed at the *Gutai Art on Stage* exhibition in the summer of 1957, at the Ohara Kaikan Hall in Osaka, *Material Destruction* would be the culmination of the aesthetic strategies, including piercing, puncturing, exploding, and smashing, that formed the basis of Shimamoto's artistic labor. At the core of this labor is an interest in destruction as suggested by the artist's unusual use of the term *dakai*, derived from the Japanese title for this work, *Buttai no dakai* (物体の打壊), which literally means "to destroy an object by striking." Instead of using the standard Chinese characters for *dakai* (打開, a breakthrough), he replaced the second character *kai* (開, to open) with *kai* (壊, to destroy) to cast destruction "as a constructive site," a productive consideration of form through rupture. A material, physical, and ideological "breakthrough" in its own right, this performance was one of many that showcased the members of Gutai Bijutsu Kyōkai (Gutai Art Association), establishing them as a full-fledged avant-garde and eventually bringing them worldwide recognition.

Up until the mid-1950s, the Japanese art world had been dominated by two independent factions of the modern art establishment of *yōga* (Western-style painting). The first comprised artists associated with reportage painting, including Yamashita Kikuji, Ikeda Tatsuo, and Nakamura Hiroshi, whose works documented the urban wasteland of Japan in the aftermath of defeat as well as the detritus produced by the rise of mass capitalism during the decade following the country's economic recovery after World War II. The other major faction consisted of artists such as Okamoto Taro, Fukuzawa Ichirō, and Abe Nobuya, who continued to experiment with prewar avant-garde strategies of abstraction derived from discourses on duality and objective chance, central to the French Surrealists, as a means to create a "violent assault on the complacency of mundane consciousness."[2] After the suppressive war years, during which time the military government commissioned artists to make war paintings, Japanese artists were now confronting the failings of their country and the consequences of imperialism and nationalism without succumbing to previous didactic or apolitically abstract forms of representation.

In November 1956, the *World Art Today* exhibition in Tokyo presented the paintings of the Art Informel artists, including Jean Dubuffet, Jean Fautrier, and Wols [Alfred Otto Wolfgang Schulze], as well as Lucio Fontana and other Italian Spazialismo artists, and members of CoBrA, a group founded by artists from Copenhagen, Brussels, and Amsterdam. *World Art Today* had a profound effect on the modern Japanese art world. When the French Art Informel critic and entrepreneur Michel Tapié arrived in Japan (together with artist Georges Mathieu, who famously demonstrated "action painting" dressed in a kimono at the Daimaru department store in Osaka), he met Yoshihara Jirō, the leader of the Gutai Art Association, and the two men established an international parity between their respective national movements.[3] Art Informel's entrance into Japan, known as the "Informel shock," profoundly influenced questions surrounding artistic expression by introducing a form of abstraction that emphasized the crises of humanity and postwar social reality through an anthropomorphic, tactile materiality that resembled body and flesh. Although photography would perform a central role in recording the traces of Japan's atomic devastation, Informel evoked this devastation viscerally and brought about a transformation of the modern art establishment, resulting in a merging of Informel aesthetics and the mainstream (*yōga*), which was now simply referred to as contemporary painting (*gendai kaiga*). Although this new mainstream form of *gendai kaiga* served as the backdrop against which

Right: Shōzō Shimamoto, *Material Destruction*, from the exhibition *Gutai Art on Stage*, Osaka, May 29–July 17, 1957. (catalogue only)

the advanced art practices in the 1960s were staged, it also became the mainstay of commercial galleries, such as those that promoted works to the 1966 exhibition *New Japanese Painting and Sculpture* at the Museum of Modern Art, New York. More significantly, however, this climate of international artistic exchange collided with the heightened cultural and political influence of the United States within Japan during the 1950s, a situation that forced artists to rethink the entirety of their practice beyond the trope of painting.

Gutai was one of the most important groups to emerge from 1950s Japan, enlivening the field of painting into an experimental genre through a creative engagement with everyday materials. The term *Gutai* (literally, "concrete" or "embodiment") was coined by Shimamoto, who imbued it with a tactile conceptualization of art.[4] The group, formed by Yoshihara in 1954 and based in Ashiya City (near Kobe, along Osaka Bay), engaged in a wide range of artistic activities, including painting, performance, site-specific installations, mail art, and

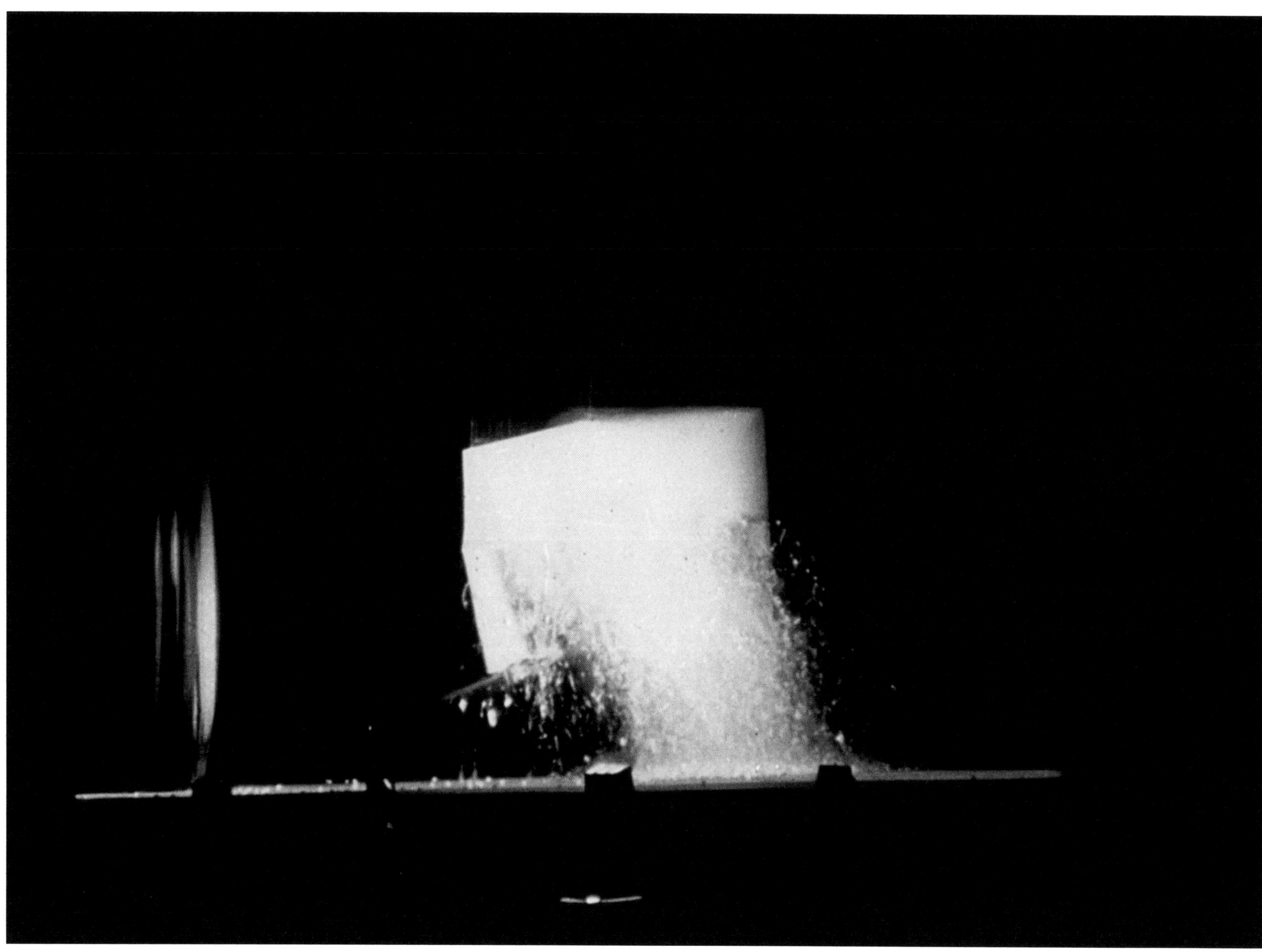

other forms of interactive art. In the "Gutai Manifesto" (1956), Yoshihara proposed an active engagement between the human spirit and materials, and the rediscovery of beauty in sites of ruin and decay. From 1955 to 1960, the Gutai group organized a range of outdoor performances, beginning with the *Experimental Outdoor Exhibition of Modern Art to Challenge the Mid-Summer Sun* (1955), which took place in a pine forest in Ashiya Park. Here, Kazuo Shiraga assembled long wooden poles into a conical shape and then swung at it with an axe, leaving gashes for viewers to see as they entered and looked up at the glistening sun. Motonaga Sadamasa made full use of the outdoor environment when he hung plastic tubes filled with colored water from tree branches, creating an allover installation in which the sun cast various shades of light through the colored droplets.

Gutai was highly influential to the American artist Allan Kaprow, who cited the group as a precursor to his Happenings in the 1960s. For the Gutai artists, as for Kaprow, the temporal process, both in the act of making/performing and the act of viewing/participating, was integral to the work. For example, in *Work: Bell* (1955), Tanaka Atsuko experimented with the directionality of sound by connecting multiple ringers wired throughout different floors of a building so that one could experience varied sonic proximities depending on one's position in space. In her most famous piece, *Electric Dress* (1956), she wore an elaborate costume made of colored lightbulbs and spun around onstage while the lights flickered in the darkness, recalling the neon ads that had begun to illuminate the urban landscape. Tanaka's idea of allowing the materials to dictate her work revealed a playful response to the weight of personal expressivity that dominated Abstract Expressionism and Art Informel in the West.[5] Yoshihara's ties with Tapié and Gutai's collaborations with Informel would eventually lead the group, particularly Shiraga, Tanaka, and Saburō Murakami, to focus predominantly on painting in the 1960s. However, Gutai's legacy remains as one of Japan's foremost hotbeds of experimentation with materials and site. During the early years of postwar economic reconstruction, the group's sensitivity to the quotidian environment reinvigorated art with the spirit of the everyday and pushed the two-dimensional limits of painting's representational conventions.

While the Gutai artists have been acknowledged internationally as the progenitors of the experimental avant-garde in Japan, my aim here is to further situate their work, and that of others who followed, within a narrative that focuses on the aesthetics of destruction as a central condition linking Japan's postwar art practices. By destruction, I refer to the geopolitical and psychosocial forces that particularize the Japanese avant-garde: first, the historical imprint of atomic destruction as a referent of Japan's loss and trauma during the war; and second, destruction as a sacrificial model whereby loss is the precondition for the work's existence. For example, Gutai's action-based works from the 1950s explored the performer's body as a site of destruction that violently embodied the visceral effects of war and the complexities of cultural continuity. Whether through wrestling with the earth's mud with one's entire body (Shiraga's *Challenging Mud*, 1955), painting with one's bare feet on boar's hide soaked with fresh red paint (Shiraga's

Wild Boar Hunting, 1963), crashing through large screens of paper (Murakami's *At One Moment Opening Six Holes*, 1955; page 115), or smashing paint-filled bottles against the canvas (Shimamoto's *Untitled*, 1956; page 116), Gutai artists sought to create a cathartic fusion of artist and materials. This essay focuses primarily on the work of Shimamoto as a case study of this methodological operation. By the 1960s, these strategies were carried over by the next generation, as evident in Neo-Dadaism Organizer's allover installations of industrial waste and subsequent destruction of works by fire, Hi Red Center's absurdist spectacles of dropping objects from a rooftop to the pavement below, and the event scores of Tokyo Fluxus, which destroyed the autonomy of the object through the activation of viewer participation. In contrast to the often liberatory and expressive theatricality of these prior groups, by the early 1970s groups such as Mono-ha and Bikyōtō aimed beyond the recuperation of objects and would radically subvert these practices through a language of self-negation, loss, and failure specific to the local historical moment; the renowned writer Yukio Mishima's ritual suicide in 1970 marked the apex of self-destruction.[6]

Erasure

The act of expression is related to thought, and the clarification of the self. The act of erasure is predicated on something that ought to be erased, but when we confront the surface that is opposite to us, it is predicated on the sense of our own presence.[7] —*Tashiro Yukitoshi*

Various experiments define Gutai, including the creative selection of tools such as abaci, vibrators, watering cans, electric bulbs, glass bottles, mechanical cars, bicycles, cannons, water, smoke, and the like as alternatives to the brush. For example, Kanayama Akira used a remote control that would dictate the path of his pigments, which were attached to mechanical cars. Without the artist's hand ever touching the canvas, many of Gutai's works followed both the chance operations inherent in automatism and the tactics of "deskilling," which disabled mastery over one's work by giving absolute agency to the effects of the raw tools themselves. The thread that distinguishes Shimamoto's work is his engagement with the idea of erasure. That is, his tools aimed toward a specific strategy centered on destruction as a productive form of loss, one that would challenge standard conventions of form and its relationship to the subject.

Shimamoto had studied literature at Kansei Gakuin University in Osaka, from which he graduated in 1953; while still a student, he had been introduced to Yoshihara through a faculty member at the university. The first works that he brought to Yoshihara's studio, in 1948, several years before the 1955 formation of Gutai, were two objects made of cement, each measuring 30 centimeters in diameter, with two exposed razor blades that touched at right angles, inciting a "teeth grinding" reaction.[8] Shimamoto evoked

space of the viewer physically (via the exposed blades) and literally (via the demarcation of direction). *Work* (ca. 1950) depicts the jagged lines of the razor blades in an abstract form, and yet fails to elicit the visceral response that the raw object itself provokes in our nerves.

In his efforts to transgress figuration, Shimamoto embarked on a series of works in about 1950 in which he continued to experiment with the gestural immediacy of drawing. Because the artist could not afford to purchase canvas, he instead glued together layers of weathered newspaper with starch and wiped the surface with quick, broad strokes of white industrial paint. He then began to scratch the

Below left: Shōzō Shimamoto, *Work*, ca. 1950. Oil on wood, 28½ x 24 in. (72.5 x 61 cm). Ashiya City Museum of Art & History. (catalogue only)

Below right: Shōzō Shimamoto, *An Arrow*, 1952. Graphite on paper, 6¾ x 4⅜ in. (17 x 11 cm). Ashiya City Museum of Art & History. (catalogue only)

Opposite: Shōzō Shimamoto, *Untitled*, 1950. Oil on newspaper intentionally pierced by the artist. The Rachofsky Collection.

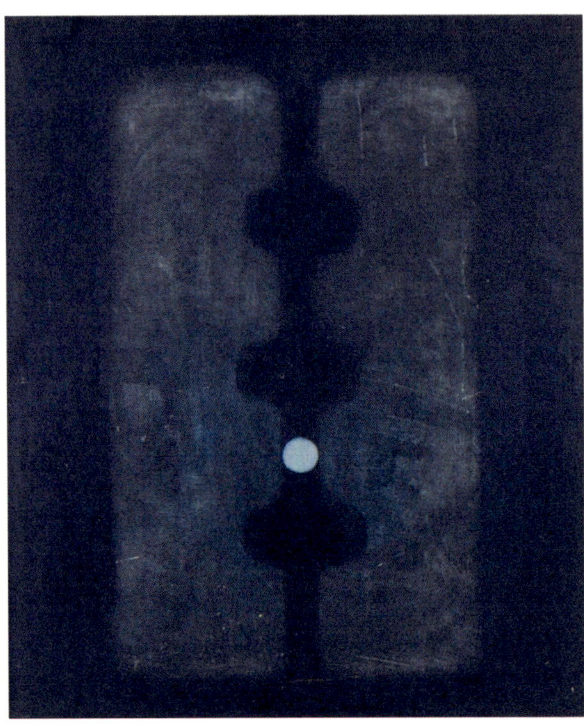

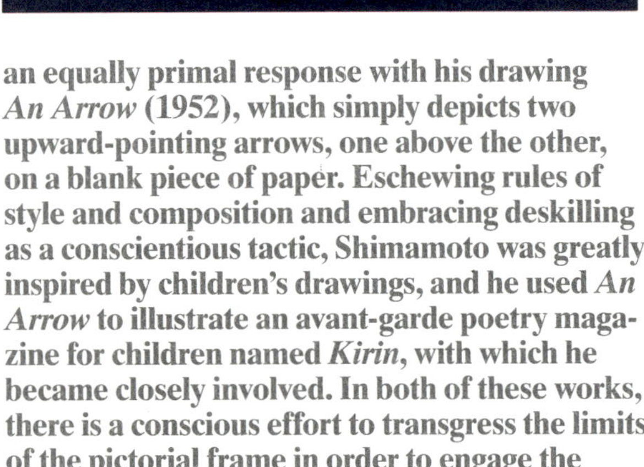

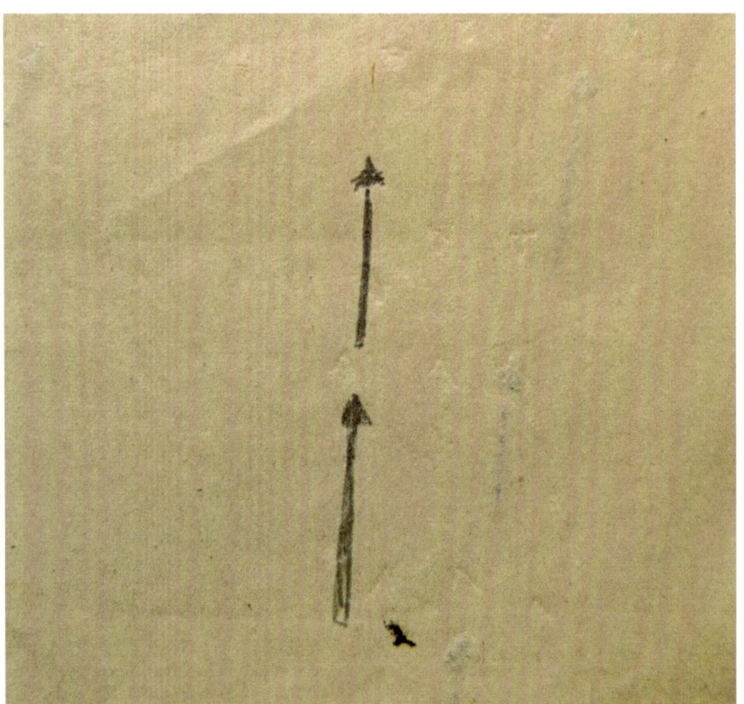

an equally primal response with his drawing *An Arrow* (1952), which simply depicts two upward-pointing arrows, one above the other, on a blank piece of paper. Eschewing rules of style and composition and embracing deskilling as a conscientious tactic, Shimamoto was greatly inspired by children's drawings, and he used *An Arrow* to illustrate an avant-garde poetry magazine for children named *Kirin*, with which he became closely involved. In both of these works, there is a conscious effort to transgress the limits of the pictorial frame in order to engage the

surface with a pencil in four large circular patterns. As he drew, his pencil accidentally ripped through the still-wet layers, puncturing the surface and exposing the printing underneath. This unexpected effect was precisely the type of encounter that Shimamoto had welcomed the previous year when he used simple gestures to transcend the boundaries of the frame. Only now, these allover rips and gouges did not simply transcend the verticality of the frame (as in *An Arrow*), the planar flatbed of painterly illusionism, and

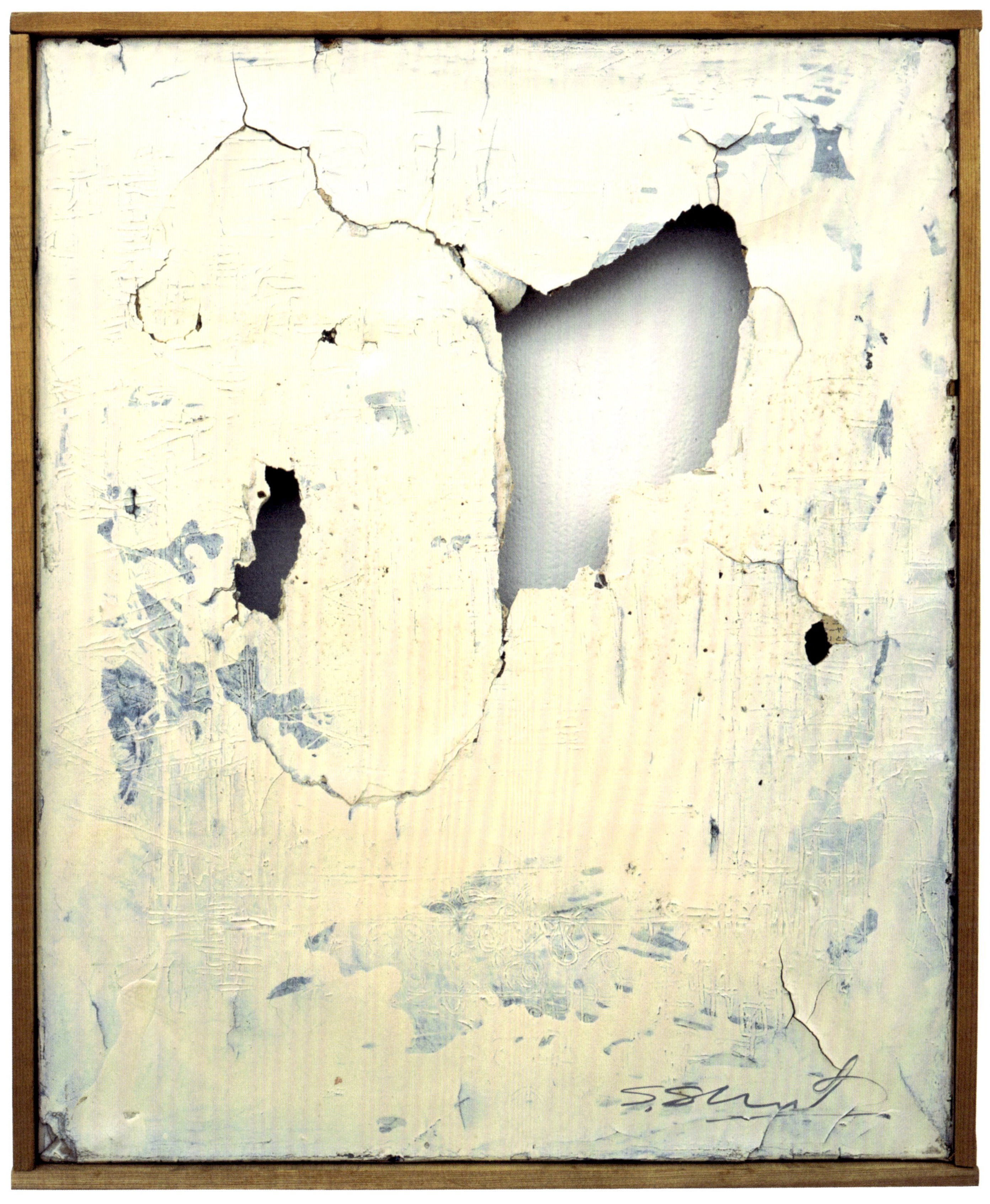

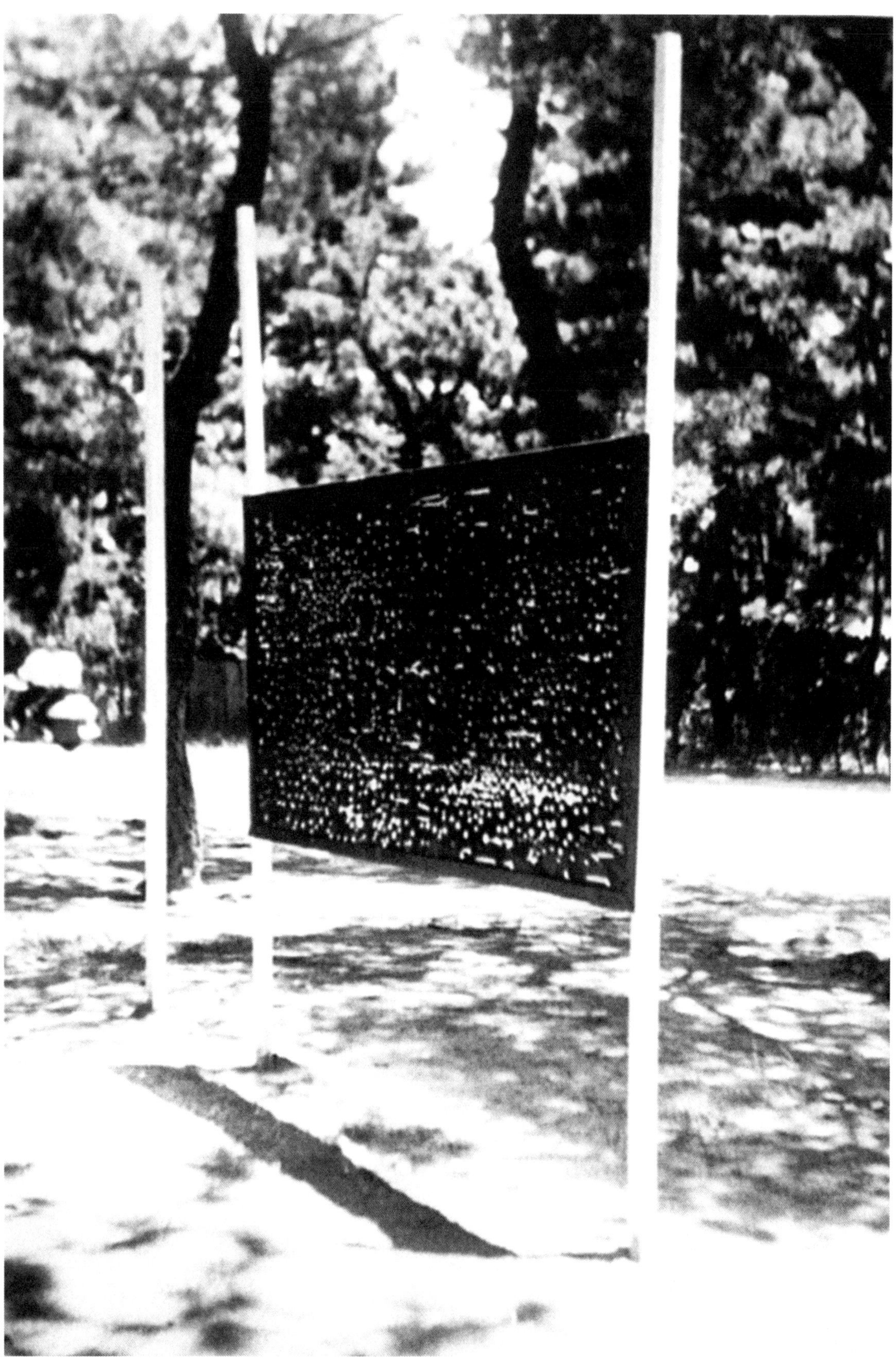

compositional form, they *eradicated* them. For Shimamoto, however, this eradication was not so much a formal investment as it was a way to engage a primordial layer of painting that would trigger a corporeal response in the viewer, stemming directly from the textural materiality of the punctured surface. The holes incite a physical rupturing of the body's senses, almost as if a surgeon's blade had pierced through flesh, leaving the dry skin tucked inside the edges.

At the third *Modern Art Exhibition*, at the Tokyo Metropolitan Art Museum in 1953, Shimamoto exhibited two large-scale pieces, *Work (Ifu)* (1952) and *Work (Mama)* (1953), each more than 5 feet high and 4 feet wide.[9]

stark contrast to Yoshihara's dramatic yellow streaks on black canvas in *Work*, also from 1953. Shimamoto would repeat these gestures over and over again in hundreds of newspaper works, and he continued to experiment further by expanding the cuts into full-fledged holes.

In the *Experimental Outdoor Exhibition of Modern Art to Challenge the Mid-Summer Sun*, Shimamoto pierced thousands of holes in a large billboard-size sheet of zinc-coated iron framed by two wooden posts on either side. Speed is the defining factor of *An Object Instantly Opened with Holes* (*Totan ni ana wo aketa mono*, 1955), as details of the work reveal the gnarled edges of metal hanging from the shot-through

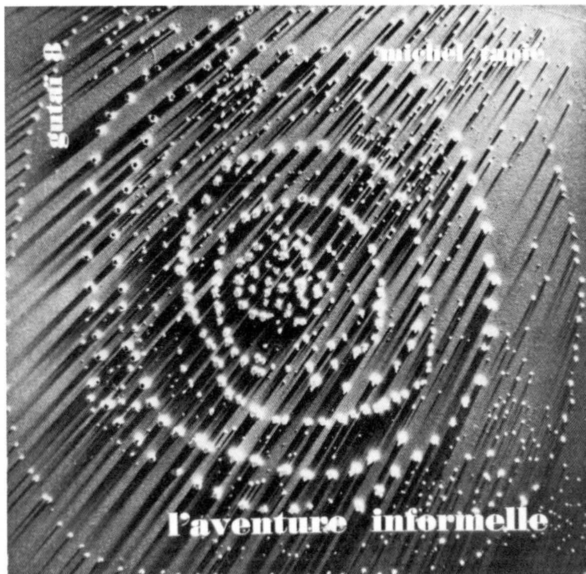

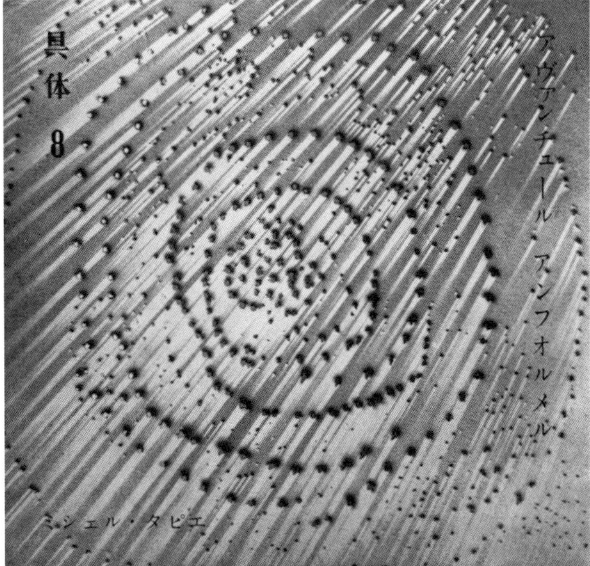

Consisting of black industrial paint on newspaper layered with stenciled wax paper, the works look as though made by fingernails scraping wildly across a blackboard. Some of the lines are composed of white dots that perforate the surface, leaving waxy raised areas that look like dried scar tissue. The sensory reaction is signaled further by the subtitles, *Ifu* (Awe-Inspiring Fear) and *Mama* (Mother), which mediate the material and symbolic elements at play. Particularly in the context of the rapid postwar economic reconstruction, these graffiti-like marks not only inscribe a fear of anonymity and the unknown but also confront the fear of forgetting. The nervous yet delicate fragility of the lines in Shimamoto's work lies in

holes. In a departure from his previous engagement with scratched surfaces, Shimamoto in this large-scale work captures an even greater bodily relationship through violent speed across space. There is thus a psychosocial element of violence enacted upon the unity of the frame, the temporal mark of an event, and a sharp intervention into the harmonious unity of one's presence. Formally, this destructive impulse is morphologically similar to the early punctured canvases of Fontana. His holes, often illuminated from behind as "spatial spectacles,"[10] caught the attention of Yoshihara, who featured the Argentine-Italian artist's work on the cover of *Gutai*, no. 8 (1957), a special issue on "l'aventure informelle." Fontana's practice is central to

Left: Cy Twombly, *Panorama*, 1959.
House paint and crayon on canvas,
101 x 233 in. (256.5 x 591.8 cm).
Courtesy of Thomas Amman, Zurich.
(catalogue only)

Right: Saburō Murakami, *At One
Moment Opening Six Holes*, 1955.
Gelatin silver print. Ashiya City
Museum of Art & History.

Page 116: Shōzō Shimamoto, *Untitled*,
1956, made at the *Second Gutai Art
Exhibition*, Tokyo, October 1956.
Ashiya City Museum of Art & History.
(catalogue only)

Page 117: Shōzō Shimamoto, *Work
(Created by a Cannon)*, 1956, shown
at the *Outdoor Gutai Art Exhibition*.
Ashiya Park, July 27–August 25, 1956.
Ashiya City Museum of Art & History.
(catalogue only)

the discourse on the objectness of painting, in which the holes produce a new order that the artist himself described as "the beginning of a sculpture in space."[11] For his part, Shimamoto was concerned more with the process—the temporality of the physical interaction and the transience of material decay—which takes precedence over the object itself.[12] With regard to the effects of temporality and transience, a closer reference can perhaps be found in the work of the American artist Cy Twombly, with its defiance of compositional form achieved by the allover dispersal of scratches and graphic fragments, as in *Panorama* (1959).

Twombly's practice is peculiar within the field of Abstract Expressionism in the United States, as his drawings do not lend themselves simply to a discourse on the authenticity of expression or spontaneity of action as exemplified in the work of Jackson Pollock but rather address the operations of effacement upon painting's sanctified visual plane. Using the language of the graffitist's mark, Rosalind Krauss has described the experience of the trace in Twombly's art as a form of violence not only upon the unity of painting's contained form but also upon a singular authorial presence:

> The violence that Twombly read in the traces left to mark the path of so many sprays of liquid thrown by Pollock from the end of stick or brush, the violence that he therefore "completed"—to invoke Harold Bloom's notion of the strong misreading—as graffiti, invested Pollock's traces with a form. For the formal character of the graffito is that of a violation, the trespass onto a space that is not the graffitist's own, the desecration of a field originally consecrated to another purpose, the effacement of that purpose through the act of dirtying, smearing, scarring, jabbing.[13]

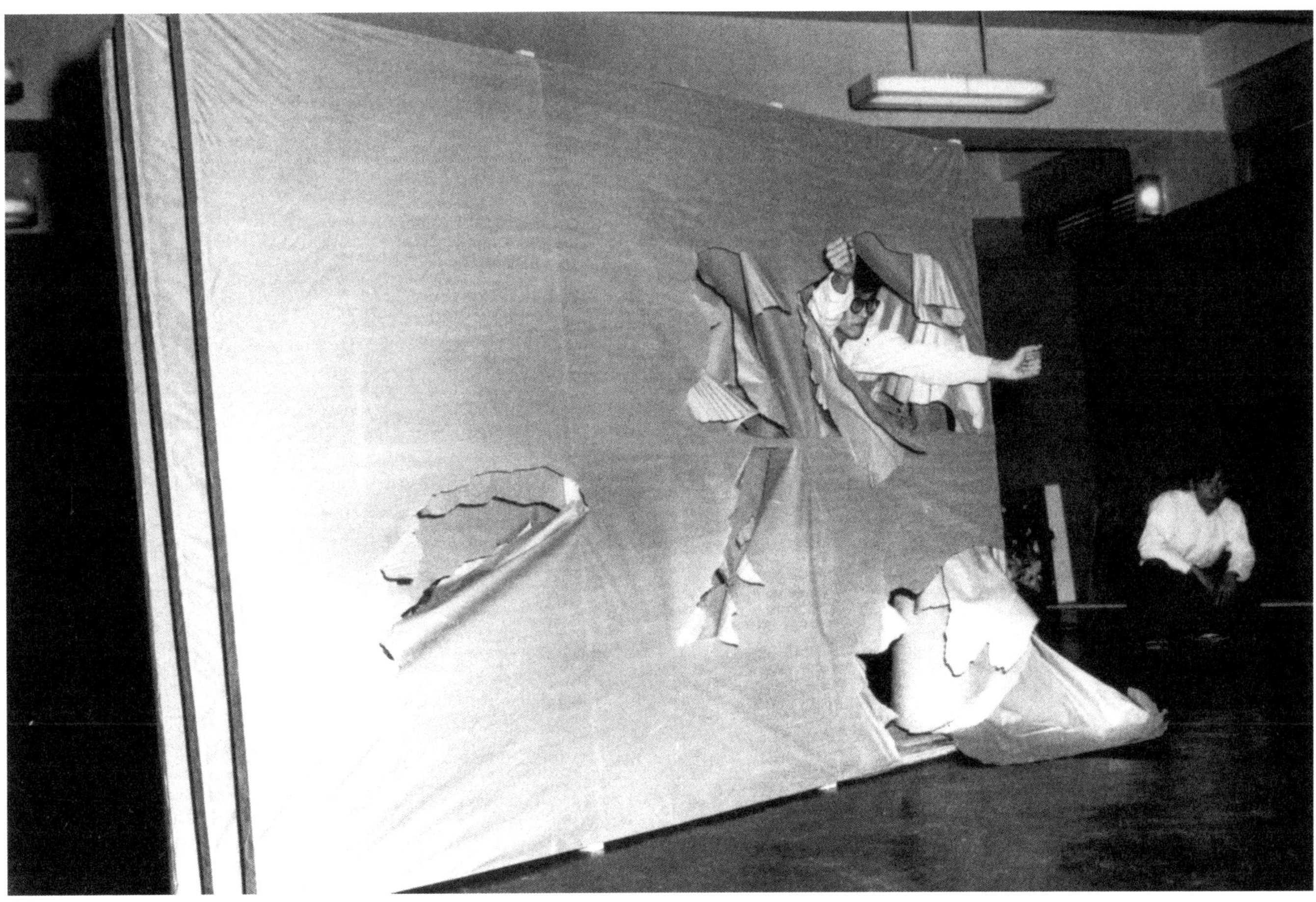

In her discussion, Krauss cites Jacques Derrida's *différance* to describe both the disjunction of time in Twombly's work (the temporal fragment of the graffitist's mark in the past and the viewer's later encounter with it in the present) and, by association, the condition of multiplicity that constitutes the work's presence. Whereas Twombly effaces the singularity of the trace through the operations of debasement and desublimation as latent forces that underlie Pollock's practice, Shimamoto introduces a third element, in addition to the divisibility of temporality and subjectivity, and that is total rupture.

The dispersion of singularity was something that the Gutai group had already adopted as a defining concept for their journals and exhibition posters. This element is captured in the shotlike holes that reveal individual letters of the group's name on the red cover of the second issue of the journal *Gutai*, in 1955, which was the first full-fledged feature on the group's experimental actions. Fragmentation was also featured the next year in issue 4, in which the two Japanese characters of the group's name, *Gu* on the recto and *tai* on a triangular flap on the verso, were revealed as one flipped through the first pages of the journal, as well as in Shimamoto's poster design for the *First Gutai Art Exhibition,* which included a rectangular flap that opens like a door. The hole as a device for enacting progress was central to Murakami's performances in which he thrust his fist through layers of large Japanese paper screens, as in *At One Moment Opening Six Holes* (1955). It was also a source for creative imagination in his work *Every Possible Landscape* (1956; page 122), which consisted of an empty rectangular frame hanging from a tree in Ashiya Park. In the designs and individual works of Gutai artists the hole is shown to be a springboard for transformation and a reflection of a constant desire for regeneration. In Shimamoto's experimentations between 1956 and 1961, there is a turn from the optical (allover incisions) to the corporeal, and the desire for change is rejuvenated through an obsessive, more violent engagement with destruction.

Surplus of Action

What is a gesture? Something like the surplus of an action.[14] —*Roland Barthes*

By 1955 Shimamoto had begun to experiment with a device far removed from the directness of the hand, namely, a handmade cannon filled with industrial paint and fueled by acetylene gas. Shimamoto blasted his first cannon in 1955, and the resulting *Work* indicates the explosive impact of the paint upon hitting the cloth, with its crumpled surface and thick blasts of black and red splashes, yellow paint cracks, and glass shards. Documentations of his performance at the *Outdoor Gutai Art Exhibition* (July 27–August 5, 1956) in Ashiya Park show that these works were massive in scale. In *Work (Created by a Cannon)* (1956; far right), the blasts are stained upon a four-by-four-meter piece of red vinyl. Considering the speed and immediacy of the process, the work's artistic labor resides in the utter consumption of materials and ultimately the subsumption of the artist. The artist is no longer really there, existing more as a ghost, dwarfed within the lavish smoke and scale of the work. Although the cannon functions symbolically as a virile source of machismo and self-indulgent prowess that links the work to that of Pollock, de Kooning, and even Dubuffet, here the weapon overpowers the artist himself, who is unable to control the massive swirl of blazing debris. Rather than being an "expression" (of the illusion) of an ego, the work acts as a violent cape that seeks to devour the viewing subject that stands before it, and in particular Shimamoto, for whom this work offers the conditions for perceiving anew, beyond preconceived limits of the self, and of being overcome by the surplus of this new experience. As he noted, "What is most gratifying about producing artworks is the discovery of a self that we never even knew."[15]

This consumption is further pronounced in *Untitled* (1956; right). To make the work, Shimamoto filled hundreds of glass bottles with seeds, fruit skins, hair, ash, paper, sand, cigarette butts, and dead insects mixed with synthetic paint and then smashed them onto a large stone that lay on top of an unstretched cloth positioned either directly on the floor or draped along the wall.[16] The impact of the paint and materials hitting the stone resulted in a spherically shaped splash that bleeds out from

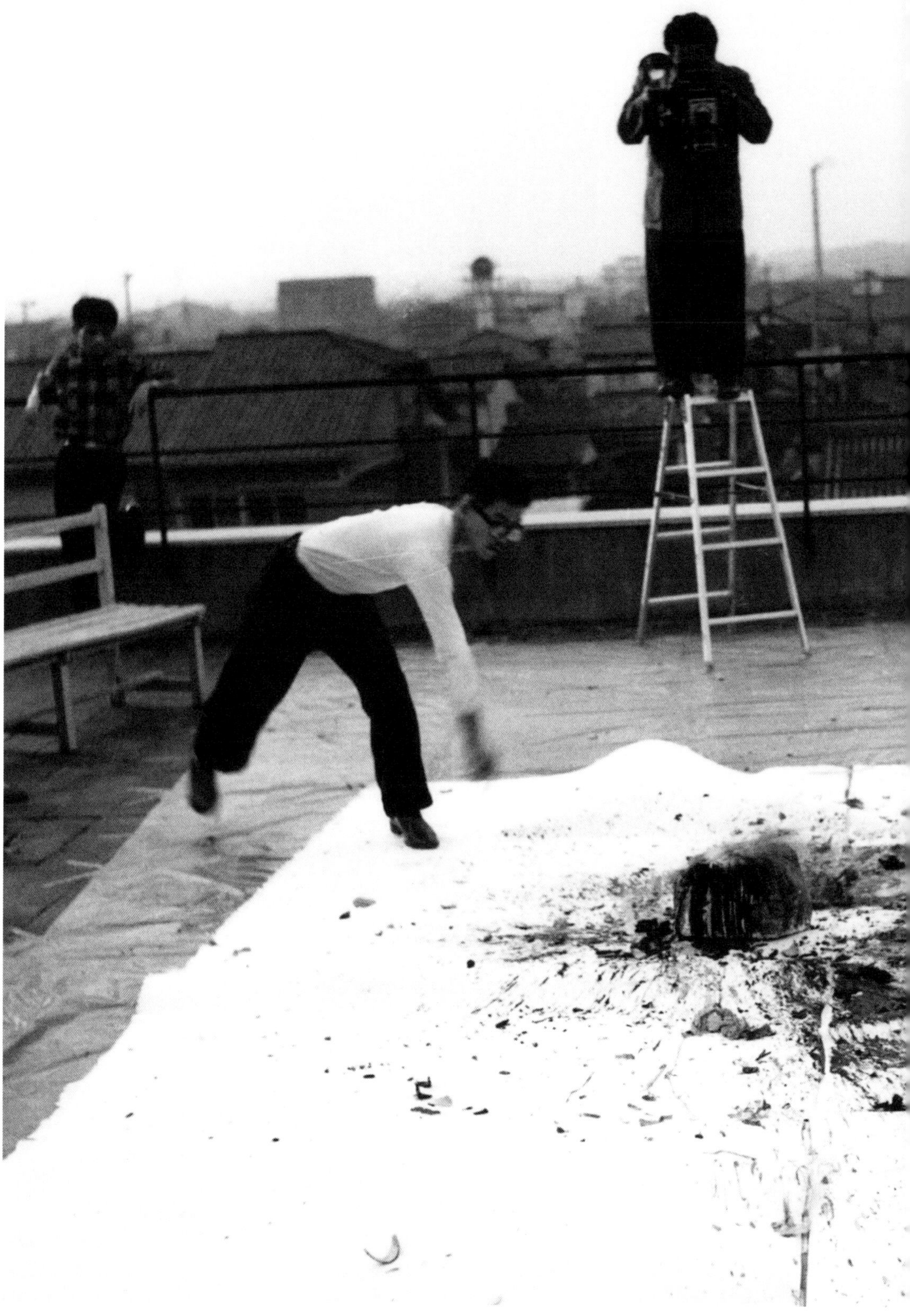

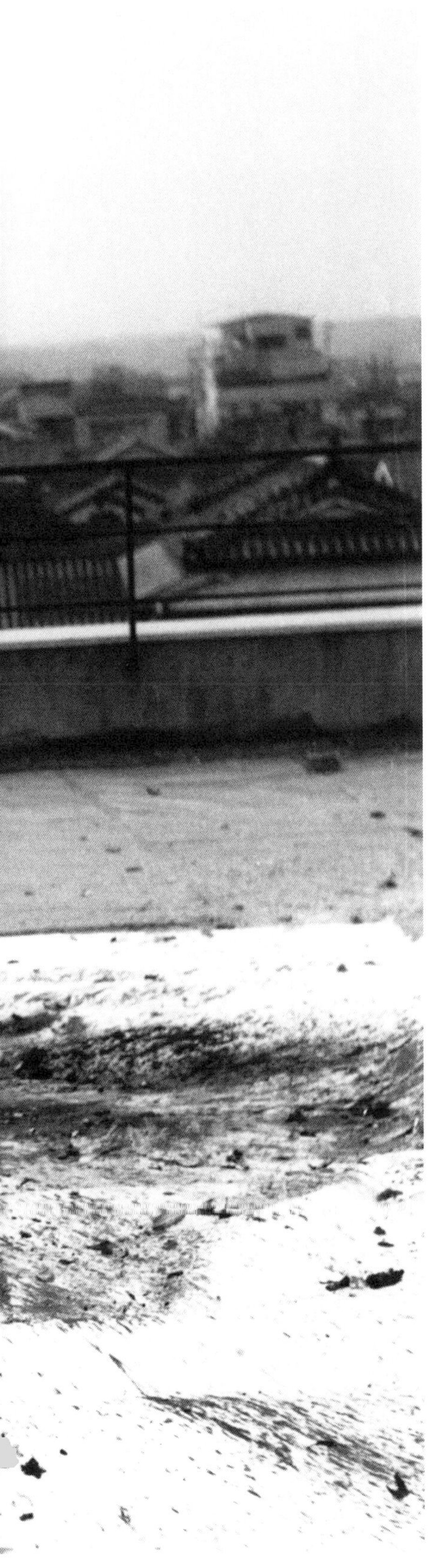

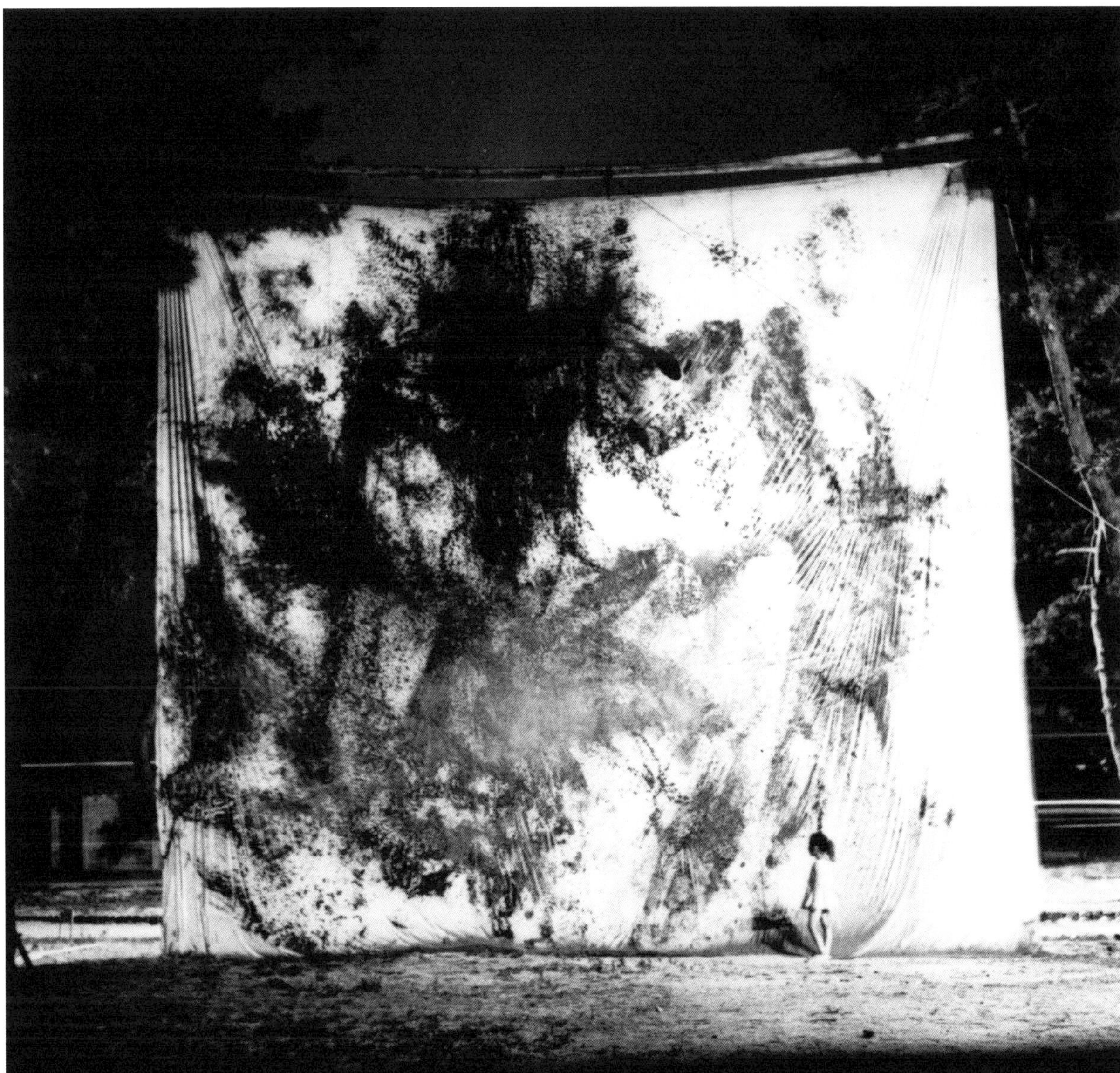

the center. There is a trace left where the rock sat, a hollow center from which the braids of color have spread. For Shimamoto, any premeditated intention or expression must be thought of merely as a means to provoke, rather than to define, the work. The artist's rough smashing of hundreds of bottles, very different from the throw of a seasoned baseball pitcher, along with the speed and force of the material impact, serves to disperse and refute any controlled effect. The result resonates with what Krauss identified as "a condition of the structure of the marker's having been cut away from himself; it is as though he had gone up to a mirror to witness his own appearing and had smashed the mirror instead."[17] This is the opposite of the process of signification in which the artist binds the work to a specific expressivity; instead, the work is turned back on the artist, to disintegrate any notion of intentionality or unification. Here we might describe Shimamoto's act not just as a new experimental technique to create a painting but as a form of gesture, which Roland Barthes referred to as the "surplus of an action." In connection with the divisibility of subjectivity and temporality in Twombly's work mentioned above, Barthes, writing about the idea of dispersion in Twombly's gestures, noted: "They are reversed, inadvertent effects which turn back upon him and thereupon provide certain modifications, deviation, mitigation of the line, of the stroke. Thus in gesture is abolished the distinction between cause and effect, motivation and goal, expression and persuasion. The artist's gesture—or the artist as gesture—does not break the causative chain of actions…but he blurs, confuses it, he starts it up again until it loses its meaning."[18] This follows Barthes' critique of the view that treats the artwork as a product of singular intentionality; he argues instead that the work is a product of multiplicity, which engages the spatiotemporal circumstances of both the producer (artist) and the reader (viewer).

This texture of multiplicity provides a crucial reference point for the repetitive yet shifting nature of Shimamoto's aesthetic strategies. Through the reenactments of piercing, puncturing, exploding, and smashing and our subsequent engagement with their ephemeral traces, what remains is a systematic cycle of erasure, rupture, and renewal. In the artist's deliberate blurring of the lines between creation and loss, production and consumption, and cause and effect, we witness a condition fundamental to Shimamoto's aesthetics of *dakai*: the visceral embodiment of destruction itself as a precondition for breaking through. In *Untitled* (1956), this process is fully captured in the physicality and violent impact of the detritus that strikes the canvas, compounded by our confrontation with the corporeal residue of the spherical void (the "surplus of an action") that lies at its center. Shimamoto's radicality here depends on the regenerative vitality of destruction—a condition that would link the practices of the next generation.

Anti-Art and the Spectacles of Expenditure
What did the precondition for the work's destruction mean in the larger artistic context that followed Shimamoto? This question situates the works in relation to historians such as Yoshikuni Igarashi, who argued that by the 1960s, society had managed to naturalize the process of forgetting by positing loss as the basis for Japan's postwar prosperity.[19] Tokyo in the 1960s witnessed a plethora of avant-garde art collectives that staged a battle against the mainstream establishment. The Yomiuri Indépendant (an annual exhibition sponsored by the Yomiuri newspaper)[20] was integral to the formation of collectives as a

site for performance and experimentation, particularly during the years 1960–63. The Yomiuri artists became coterminous with the "anti-art" generation, which encompassed a range of groups, most notably Neo-Dadaism Organizer (or simply Neo-Dada), Kyūshū-ha (Kyushu School), Zero Dimension, Jikan-ha (Time School), Group Ongaku (Group Music), and Hi Red Center, which explored art as an economy of excess and the activation of a public.

The works of Neo-Dada (founded in 1960) incorporate a vast storehouse of industrial and junk materials, assembled in allover formats, laid directly on the floor or pinned to the wall in high relief. The group's name references a "return" to avant-garde strategies, reflecting a growing parity with the Euro-American neo-avant-garde (for example, Rauschenberg's combines and Arman's junk accumulations) that recalled Dada and Surrealist practices and emerged as radical departures from the sublimity of Abstract Expressionism and the tactile existentialism of Informel. In fact, one could argue that Neo-Dada acknowledged Japan's own historical avant-garde group Mavo (active 1923–25), whose anarchic assemblages consisted of rifles, bottle caps, shoeboxes, and human vending machines.[21] Whereas Mavo disseminated their works through photographs published in their self-titled magazine from 1924 to 1925, Neo-Dada took advantage of Yomiuri's sponsorship by directly staging and disseminating their actions through the newspaper and various print media. Artist Yoshimura Masanobu infamously promoted Neo-Dada's exhibitions in the streets with flyers bearing the group's name wrapped around his entire body.

In *Boxing Painting Action* (1960–62), Neo-Dada's leader, Ushio Shinohara, performed his version of "action painting" by dipping a pair of boxing gloves into a bucket mixed with Japanese rice glue and *sumi* ink, and punching across a large sheet of canvas made from discarded packaging material.[22] His work often took the form of live performance, after which he would burn or discard his works in garbage dumps outside the museum. This insistence on the useless, the ephemeral, and the spectacular positions the works within an economy of excess, citing the artist's relationship to urban waste as a subject of Occupation culture. Symptomatic of the 1960 *Anpo* crisis stemming from the

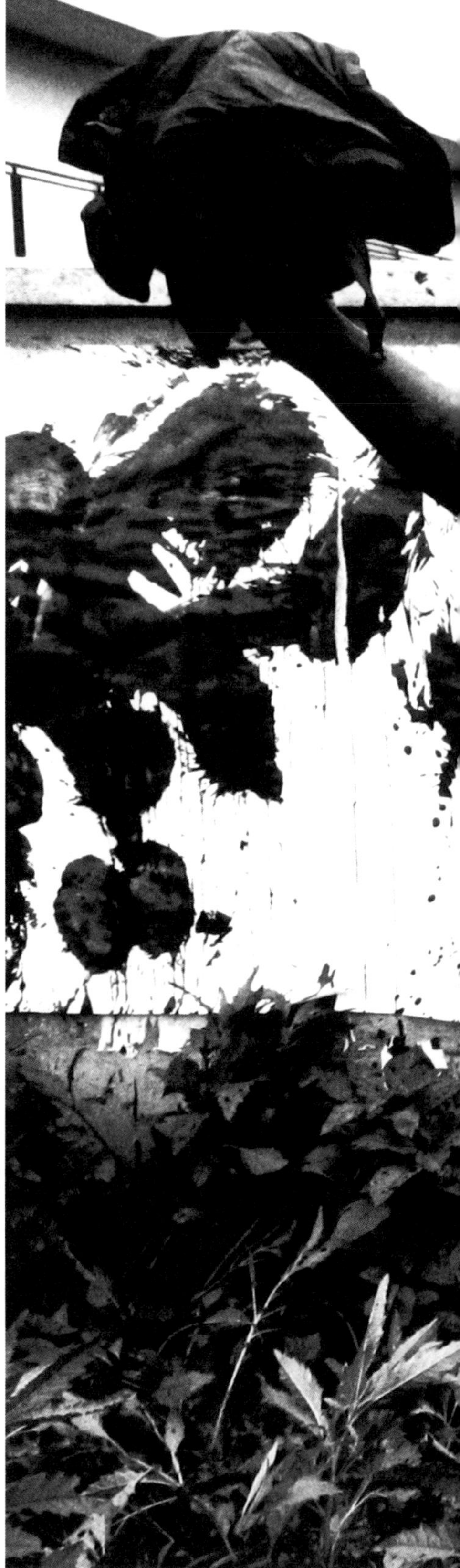

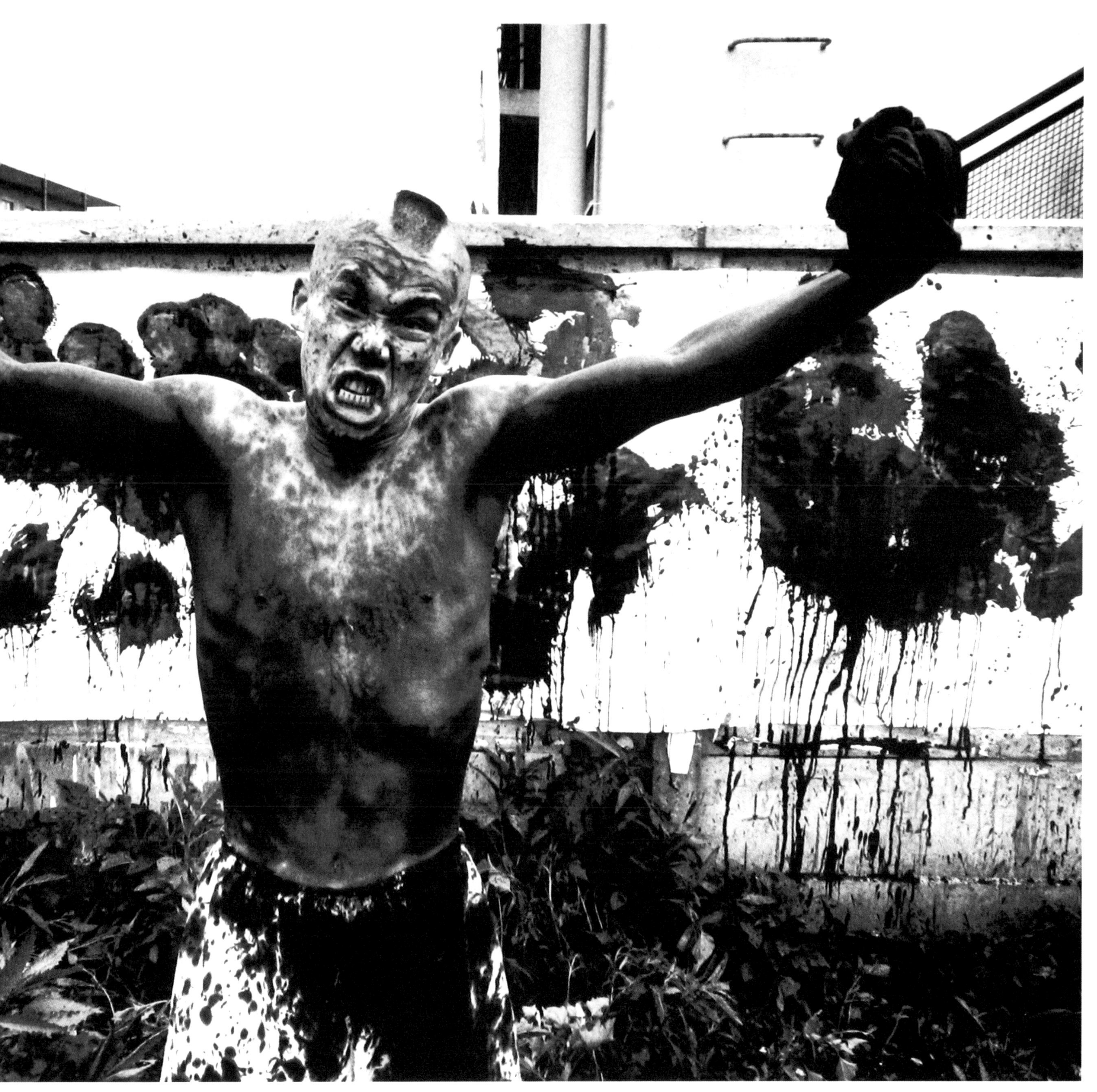

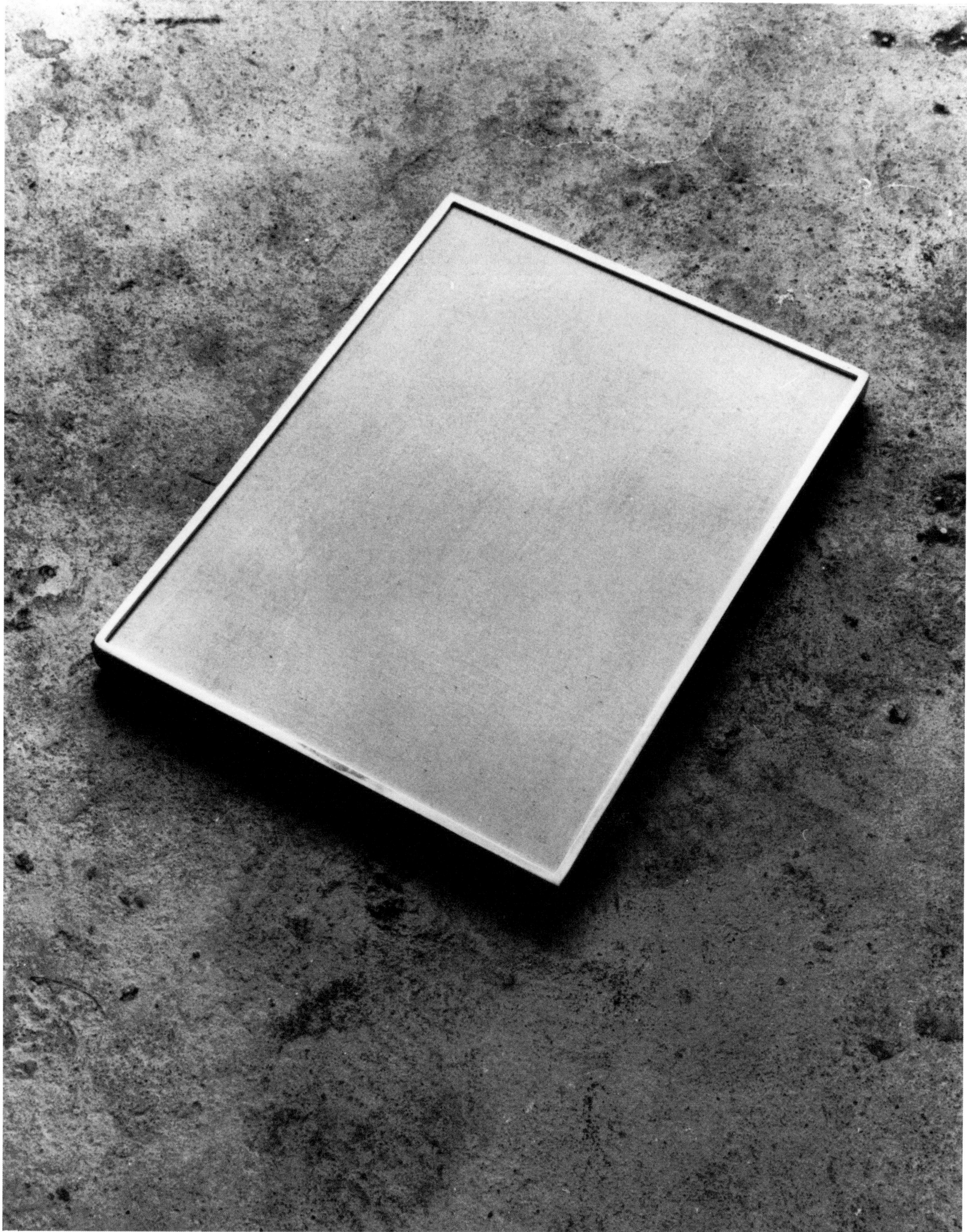

renewal of the U.S.-Japan Security Treaty,[23] the collapse of faith and humanism that coincided with massive economic reconstruction points to the artist's complex position amidst Japan's relationship to the United States, which can be characterized by conflicting extremes of democracy versus imperialism and international culture versus gross local materialism.

The term "anti-art" was first coined by the critic Tōno Yoshiaki in 1960 when he referred to appropriated junk assemblages exhibited at the 12th Yomiuri Indépendant as "anti-painting" and "anti-sculpture."[24] Tōno was one of the leading art critics of the period, along with Miyakawa Atsushi, who conceived anti-art in terms of ideas imported from the United States (namely, the neo-dadaist strategies of Rauschenberg and Johns) and theories stemming from French thinkers Gaston Bachelard and Maurice Blanchot.[25] Shinohara voiced his opposition to Tōno's term, stating that the work of these artists was not against painting or sculpture, but rather sought an *expansion* of art through daily life.[26] In a series of symposia and texts that followed, critics insisted on grounding the site of the work in the objects themselves. Whereas the critics saw these objects as attacks on the conventions of painting and sculpture, for the artists, their work constituted *acts* symptomatic of a larger transformation of culture.

The emergence of conceptually oriented groups in 1962, such as Jikan-ha, Group Ongaku, and Hi Red Center, led to yet another position that focused on elements of activating the public through direct participation. At the 14th Yomiuri Indépendant, in 1962, members of Jikan-ha left a bunch of colored rubber balls on the floor of a gallery, contained within roped stanchions, allowing viewers to kick and bounce the balls freely around the exhibition space, breaching into the territory of other works in the same gallery. The element of "play" here parallels experiments in chance and the visualization of sound that occupied the members of Group Ongaku, which comprised proto-Fluxus members such as Kosugi Takehisa, Shiomi Chieko (Mieko), and Yasunao Tone.[27] In Tone's *Geodesy for Piano* (January 1962), an audience member was provided with a topographic map that indicated various elevations from which to throw objects onto a piano. The map thus functioned as a piano score. Such

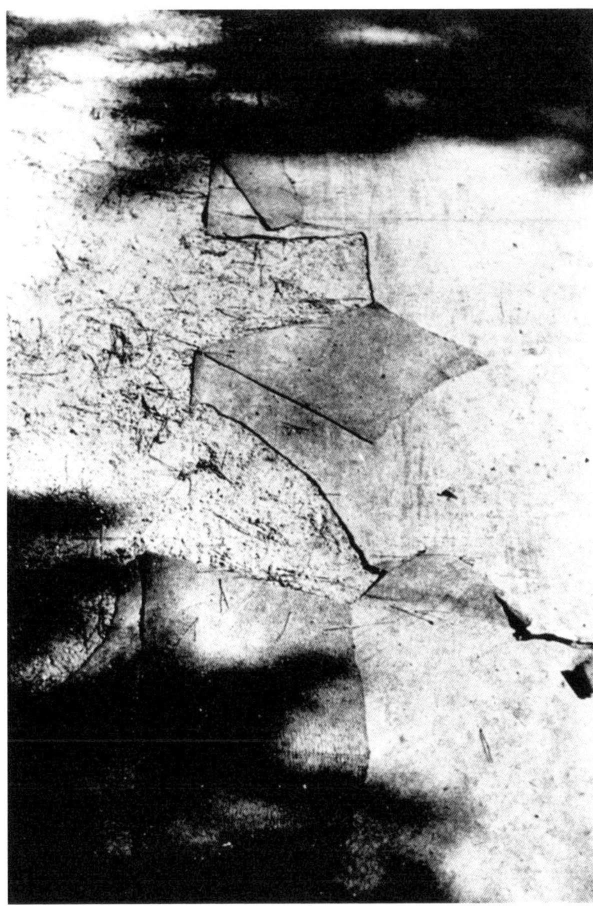

task-oriented events are exemplified by the instruction pieces of Yoko Ono, including *Painting to Be Stepped On* (1960) and *Painting to Hammer a Nail* (1961; page 29). In *Painting to Be Stepped On* in particular, the vertical/ horizontal inversions of the pictorial plane can be seen as a conceptual extension of Murakami's *Tearing* (1955), an early Gutai performance in which the artist ran across a strip of asphalt on the rooftop of a building.

Finally, in direct response to contemporary events, Hi Red Center used strategies of absurdist mockery through highly staged public events in their 1964 "Mixer Plan" performances.[28] Among their most iconic works was *Be Clean* (October 1964), in which they "sanitized" the streets of Tokyo as members of the group, dressed in lab coats and wearing face masks, meticulously cleaned the pedestrian walkways of Ginza in response to the city's preparation for the Tokyo Olympics. Their street Happenings revealed society's new inclination toward consumption and waste amidst Tokyo's

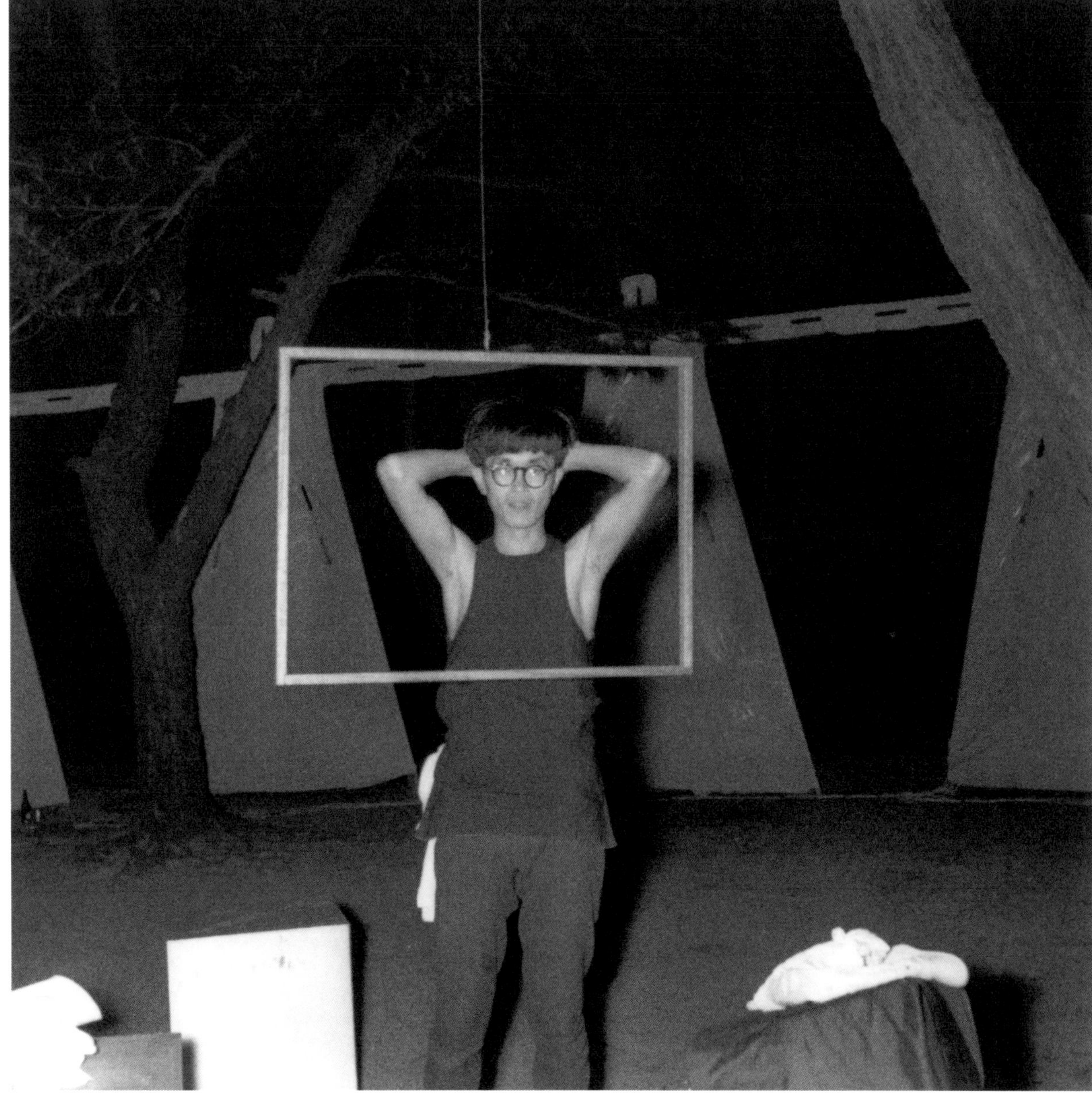

reconstruction, as well as the decaying historical memory of the city.

The positions of anti-art—art as an economy of excess and art as the activation of a public—suggest that the actions of these artists were not targeted against the unique categories of art sanctioned by the modern Japanese art establishment so much as they were aimed at undoing the classifications of "modern art" altogether.[29] That is, their conception of art consisted in a set of social relations among artist, action/event/object, site, and audience. The nature of these works—as spectacle, ritual, or instructions for a task or event—points to how these specific relations are particularized in the trajectories of Japanese modernity within concurrent Western practices. Shimamoto's legacy reveals *dakai* to be one of the central principles of ephemerality that focuses on the spirit of the object's existence rather than on the object itself and asserts the belief that neither experience nor object can be re-created, only re-performed.

Notes

Japanese personal names follow the tradition of listing the surname first. Exceptions apply to Japanese-born individuals who reside permanently abroad (e.g., Yoko Ono, Ushio Shinohara) or who are identified in the current exhibition using the westernized order of names (e.g., Shōzō Shimamoto, Saburō Murakami). Macrons are used to indicate long vowels with the exception of words that are standardized in the English language, such as Tokyo and Osaka. All quotes from Japanese sources have been translated by the author.

A very special thank-you to Ming Tiampo.

1. Shōzō Shimamoto, "Buttai no dakai" (Material Destruction), *Gutai*, no. 7 (July 15, 1957) [unpaginated]. Gutai's self-titled journal was published and printed in Shimamoto's studio. Issue 7 featured the *Gutai Art on Stage* exhibition in Osaka (May 29–July 17, 1957).

2. Alexandra Munroe, "Morphology of Revenge: The Yomiuri Indépendant Artists and Social Protest Tendencies in the 1960s," in *Japanese Art after 1945: Scream Against the Sky* (New York: Harry N. Abrams, 1994), 154. The ideas of French Surrealism were first introduced to Japan in the 1930s through Takiguchi Shūzo's translation of André Breton's *Le surréalisme et la peinture*. See Takiguchi, *Chōgenjitsu shugi to kaiga* (Tokyo: Koseikaku-shoten, 1930).

3. For an insightful account of Yoshihara and Tapié's exchanges and problems of cultural translation, see Ming Tiampo, "Gutai & Informel: Post-War Art in Japan and France, 1945–1965" (Ph.D. dissertation, Northwestern University, 2003).

4. Uemae Chiyu, *Jigadō* (Kobe: Kyōdō Publishers, 1985), 143. Diary entry of August 9, 1954. This book is a rare firsthand account by a former Gutai artist who documented the group's practices from the early days of its inception.

5. See Mizuho Kato and Ming Tiampo, *Electrifying Art: Atsuko Tanaka, 1954–1968* (Vancouver, BC: Morris and Helen Belkin Art Gallery, 2004).

6. According to literary critic Karatani Kōjin, Mishima's suicide in 1970, though appropriated by right-wing conservatives as an ultimate spectacularization of Japan's traditional spirit, represents a symbolic destruction of the postwar Shōwa emperor (Hirohito) rather than a resurrection. See Karatani, "The Discursive Space of Modern Japan," in *Japan in the World*, ed. Masao Miyoshi and H. D. Harootunian, special issue of *Boundary 2* 18, no. 2 (Fall 1991): 217.

7. Tashiro Yukitoshi, "Shōkyo: Shōkyo suru to iū kōi ni tsuite…" (Erasure: On the Act of Erasure…), in Shōzō Shimamoto, *AU no ronri* (The Theory of Art Unidentified) (Nishinomiya: Operations Research Ichibankan, 1980), 34.

8. Shōzō Shimamoto, "The Beginnings of Gutai," in *Shōzō Shimamoto Networking* (Nishinomiya, Hyōgo: Art Space, 1990), 26.

9. Many of the artists commonly used *Sakuhin* (Work) to title their works so as not to conjure a symbolic connotation and to maintain a committed interest in the spirit of raw materials themselves.

10. Anthony White, "Lucio Fontana: Between Utopia and Kitsch," *Grey Room*, no. 5 (Autumn 2001): 59.

11. Quoted in ibid., 73.

12. Alexandra Munroe, "To Challenge the Mid-Summer Sun: The Gutai Group," in *Scream Against the Sky*, 87.

13. Rosalind Krauss, "Six," in *Optical Unconscious* (Cambridge, MA: MIT Press, 1993), 259.

14. Roland Barthes, "Cy Twombly: Works on Paper" (1979), in *The Responsibility of Forms: Critical Essays on Music, Art, and Representation*, trans. Richard Howard (New York: Hill and Wang, 1985), 160–61.

15. In describing the process of arriving at the work, Shimamoto stated, "Before producing the cannon shots, I would feel a strange sensation that came from witnessing the ability to generate ash-colored grays, brushstrokes, and paint splashes never before imagined. I used this feeling as the basis for a new departure point to create the cannon works. Each time I repeated this process, I would discover a new self that had not existed in my prior self. What is most gratifying about producing artworks is the discovery of a self that we never even knew." See Shimamoto, "Taihō" (Cannon), in *AU no ronri*, 4.

16. Natsu Oyabe, "Human Subjectivity and Confrontation with Materials in Japanese Art: Yoshihara Jirō and Early Years of the Gutai Art Association, 1947–1958" (Ph.D. dissertation, University of Michigan, 2005), 175.

17. Krauss, "Six," 260.

18. Barthes, "Cy Twombly: Works on Paper," 160–61.

19. Yoshikuni Igarashi, "From the Anti-Security Treaty Movement to the Tokyo Olympics: Transforming the Body, the Metropolis, and Memory," in *Bodies of Memory: Narratives of War in Postwar Japanese Culture, 1945–1970* (Princeton, NJ: Princeton University Press, 2000).

20. The Yomiuri newspaper company sponsored the Yomiuri Indépendant, which was held annually between 1949 and 1963 at the Tokyo Metropolitan Museum of Art, one of the first venues to allow artists to freely exhibit their work without a presiding jury.

21. See Gennifer Weisenfeld, *Mavo: Japanese Artists and the Avant-Garde, 1905–1931* (Berkeley: University of California Press, 2002).

22. This was in direct reference to Informel artist Georges Mathieu, whose kimono-clad demonstration of "action painting" in Tokyo and Osaka stunned the Japanese art world in 1957. These gestures did not target Informel itself so much as the pervasiveness of Japan's amateur versions of Informel works.

23. *Anpo* is short for Anzen hoshō jōyaku, or the U.S.-Japan Security Treaty. The *Anpo* crisis refers to the widespread campaign by students and leftist movements against the U.S.-Japan Security Treaty, which was renewed in 1960. The treaty was first signed in September 1951 together with the San Francisco Peace Treaty, which ended the American Occupation and allowed Japan to enter the international community. However, the Security Treaty allowed the United States to continue stationing troops in Japan, which served as a military base during the Korean War. The renewal of the Security Treaty in 1960 was faced with intense antiwar sentiment from the left, which feared rearmament. Despite massive protests by hundreds of students, and even the death of one twenty-year-old female student, the Treaty was passed.

24. Tōno had just returned from a trip to the United States and Europe in 1960 and compared the works in the exhibition to those of the French Nouveaux Réalistes, Jasper Johns, and Robert Rauschenberg.

25. See Reiko Tomii, "Historicizing 'Contemporary Art': Some Discursive Practices in Gendai Bijutsu in Japan," *Positions: East Asia Cultures Critique* 12, no. 3 (Winter 2004): 611–41.

26. Ushio Shinohara, *Zen'ei no michi* (The Avant-Garde Road) (Tokyo: Bijutsu Shuppan-sha, 1968).

27. For further discussion of Group Ongaku, see Charles Merewether, "Disjunctive Modernity: The Practice of Artistic Expression in Postwar Japan," in *Art, Anti-Art, Non-Art: Experimentations in the Public Sphere in Postwar Japan, 1950–1970*, ed. Charles Merewether and Rika Iezumi Hiro (Los Angeles: Getty Research Institute, 2007).

28. The group's name was formed from the first characters of the three members' last names (Hi[gh]: Takamatsu, Red: Akasegawa, Center: Nakanishi). Although they began collaborating in 1962, they officially formed as a group in 1963 at the 15th Yomiuri Indépendant. This would serve as the last Yomiuri Indépendant exhibition, which was shut down in 1964 due to the artists' refusals to comply with the rules governing the display of works in the museum. As a result, artists boycotted the 1964 exhibition.

29. The art establishment was represented by the Nitten (short for Nihon Bijutsu Tenrankai, or Japan Art Exhibition). Nitten was the postwar reincarnation of the government-sponsored salon instituted in 1907 by the Imperial Art Academy. These annual exhibitions admitted members only on a juried basis. *Nihonga* and *yōga* artists who were already members of these organizations were able to display their works without being juried and presided at the top tier of the establishment. See Reiko Tomii, "Geijutsu on Their Mind: Memorable Words on 'Anti-Art,'" in *Art, Anti-Art, Non-Art*, 3.

Left: Saburō Murakami, *Every Possible Landscape*, 1956, shown at the *Outdoor Gutai Art Exhibition*, Ashiya Park, July 27–August 25, 1956. Ashiya City Museum of Art & History. (catalogue only)

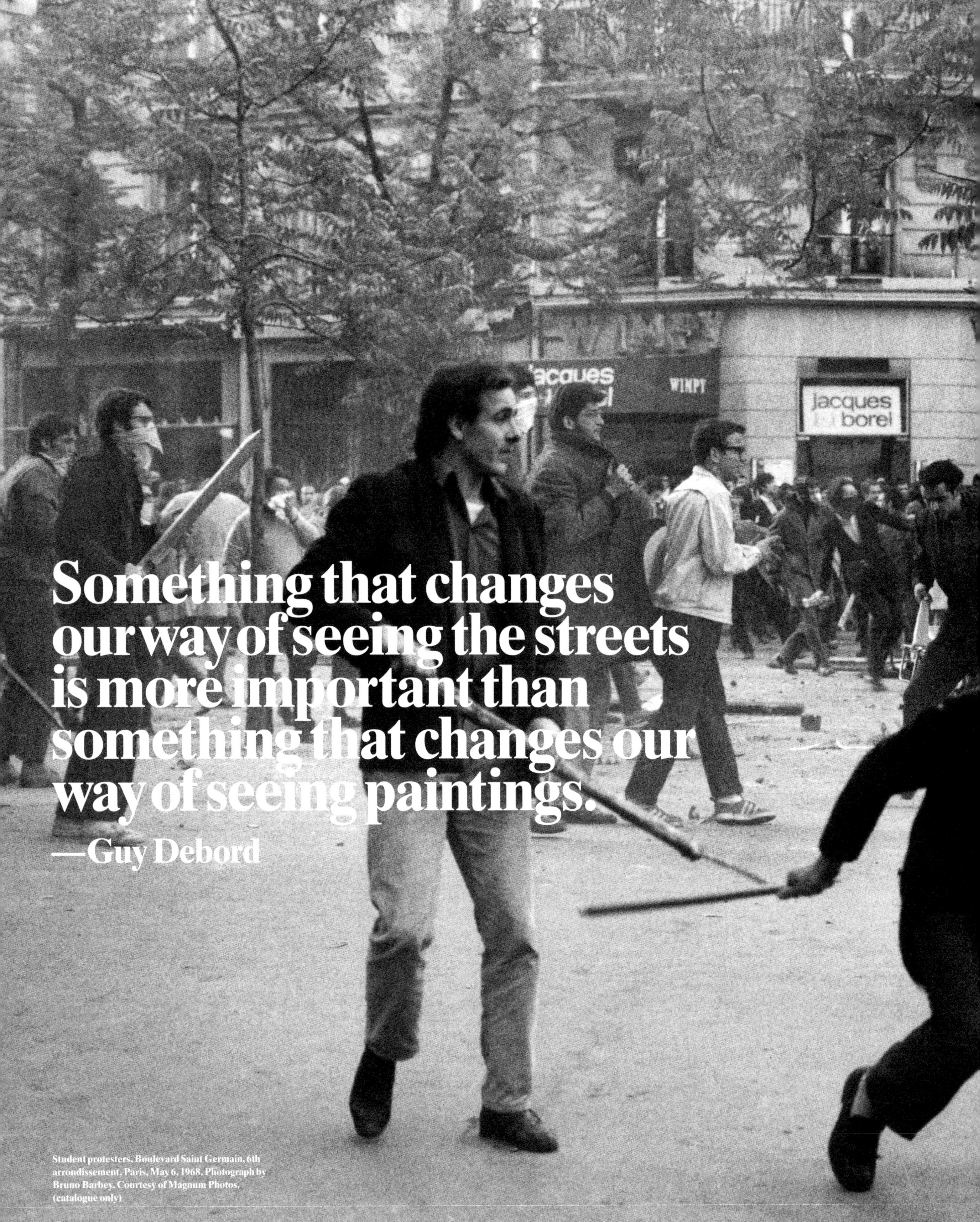

Student protesters, Boulevard Saint Germain, 6th arrondissement, Paris, May 6, 1968. Photograph by Bruno Barbey. Courtesy of Magnum Photos. (catalogue only)

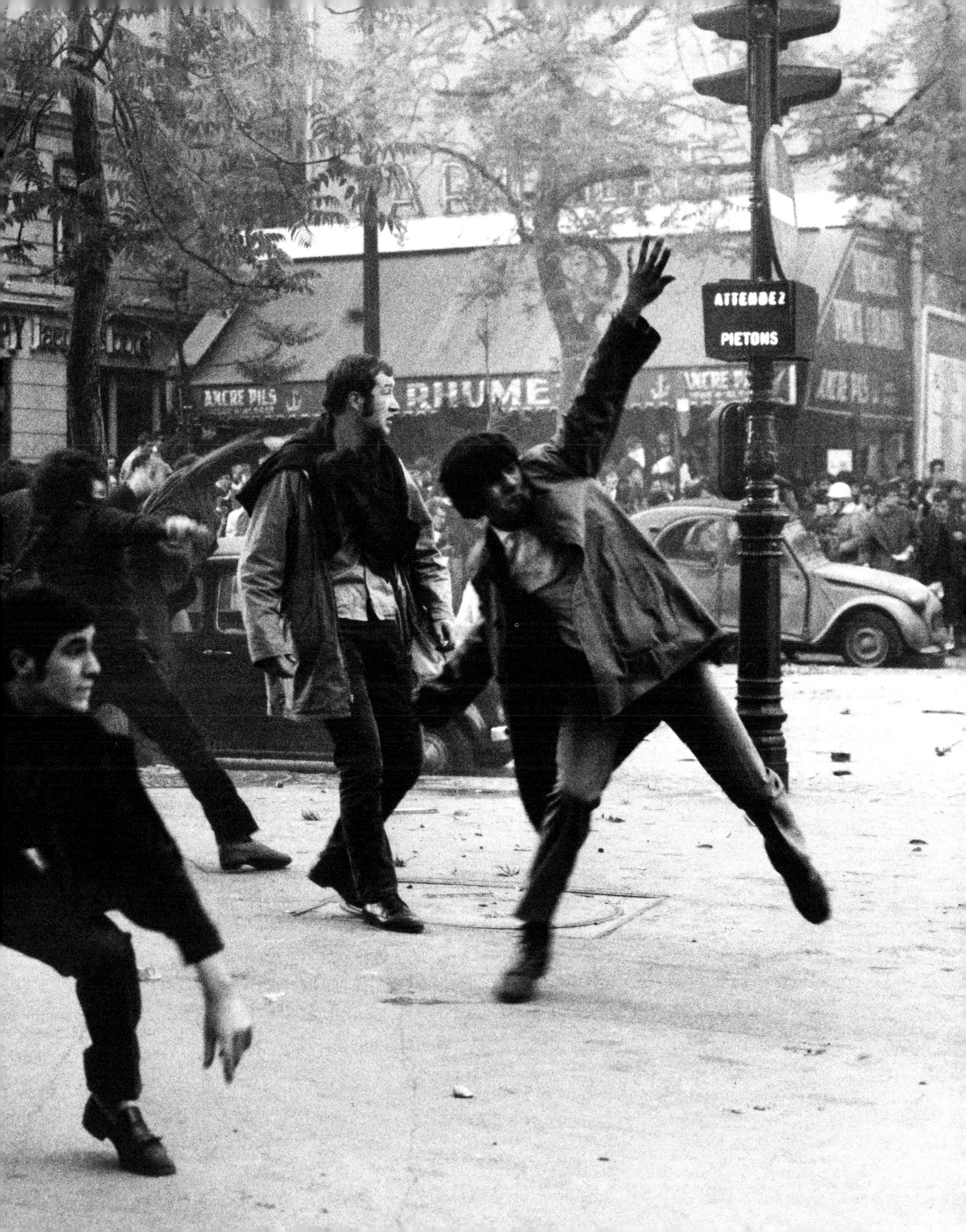

ATTENDEZ
PIETONS
ANCRE PILS
RHUME

Modern Painting, M[odern]
Iconoclasm

Graham Bader

odern

The history of painting is equally a history of iconoclasm. From the foundations of Western culture to today, painting has been shadowed by claims of its fraudulence, deviousness, and even dangerousness, and by calls—from philosophers, critics, politicians, and artists themselves—for its banishment and destruction. These calls are almost always connected to a striving for truthfulness, be it epistemological, religious, or political. In the modern era, however—that is, in the roughly two centuries since the dawn of the industrial revolution and concomitant birth of the idea of autonomous art—the truthfulness into whose service iconoclasm has most frequently been put has been *aesthetic*. The destruction of images, for one modern artist after another, has served as a means to renew the very project of image making. The present essay seeks to trace something of this history and to argue that such iconophilic iconoclasm (or iconoclastic iconophilia) in fact distills the dialectical structure of modernist painting itself—forever negotiating between obsolescence and innovation, decline and renewal, destruction and invention, image breaking and image making.

Before we consider the last two centuries, let's step back over two millennia, making brief stops in ancient Greece, Reformation Europe, and Revolutionary France. The iconoclastic arguments and actions of these three cultures help to contextualize the specific nature of iconoclasm in the modern period, which builds on but fundamentally differs from each of these precedents.

As Alain Besançon has argued, an iconoclastic impulse is present already at the origin of Western aesthetics, in Plato's writings of the fourth century B.C. For if Plato conceives of human experience, in Iris Murdoch's words, as a passage "from appearance to reality," he places painting, as all the mimetic arts, firmly on the side of the former.[1] Accordingly, Plato understands painting, in its distraction from the essential forms that constitute the good and the beautiful, as a *block* to human development. His most famous formulation of this position comes in the dialogue between Socrates and his pupil Glaucon that makes up the final book of Plato's *Republic*. There, Socrates asserts that imitative painting is necessarily three removes from the truth: taking the example of a bed, he argues that the bed exists as an essential form ("the nature of things") made by god, as a material object made by craftsmen and providing the sensual appearance of this ideal form, and finally as an imitation of this appearance in the work of the painter. "So the imitative art," he concludes, "is inferior, and having intercourse with an inferior begets inferiors."[2]

For Socrates—voicing the thoughts of Plato—this situation naturally leads to suspicion regarding the social role of the arts. "The imitator knows nothing worth mentioning about what he imitates," Socrates tells Glaucon, and hence "imitation is a kind of play, and not serious."[3] Even further, the "play" that constitutes the artist's work potentially acts as a destructive social force: for in obstructing our understanding of ideal forms, it keeps us farther from their divine author and thus from all those divine qualities—beauty, truth, reason—that are the primary goals of both individual and community. Plato refrains from advocating the banishment of painters, as the *Republic* infamously proposes for lyric poets, but does clearly suggest that an apprehension of the divine is possible only once art has been dismissed altogether. As Besançon writes:

> The nature of the divine makes the image of the divine impossible. Art has an upper-limit: it is confined to the earthly zone, where it performs a propaedeutic, educational, civic function. It prepares for its own dissolution. The lover of beauty relies on art in taking his first steps, then abandons it.[4]

Plato's aesthetic philosophy introduces, at the very origins of Western thought, the dialectical structure of iconoclasm that culminates in the modern era. Art, he contends, points toward but ultimately obscures the ideality of form; it seeks truth but is necessarily grounded in deception. In both cases, Plato is concerned with art's role in our desired apprehension of the divine—and claims it not only fails us but obstructs our very efforts toward this end.

It is just this logic—this time in practice, not theory—that motivated the iconoclastic purges of Byzantium in the eighth century and Reformation Europe eight centuries later. As Joseph Koerner has written of the impetus behind one

of the earliest episodes of Reformation iconoclasm, occurring in Zurich in 1523:

> Iconoclasts had numerous rationales:
> images contradicted the Old Testa-
> ment law, were a wasteful expenditure,
> exiled Christians from God's word,
> distracted the eye, symbolized the
> power of a corrupt Church, contra-
> dicted apostolic poverty, perpetrated
> fraud, etc. But in the sixteenth century,
> the most global objection was [that…]
> religion had to be purified from
> things of this world, and to achieve
> this, certain things that were not thus
> purified had to be eradicated…: to
> rid the heart of idols one must first
> banish them from the [eye]; *ab Aug,
> ab Herz.*[5]

The perceived incommensurability of image
and subject, then, raised the work of art in
sixteenth-century Zurich from distraction to
outright danger. Images not only failed to match
their sacred subjects but, by suggesting the
equivalence of divine absolute and man-made
imagery, actually denigrated them. The destruction of images was necessary because false
visions—which an image of the sacred inher-
ently was—engendered false belief.

Iconoclastic attacks, in Reformation Europe
as in ancient Greece, functioned to protect
divine truth from the falsities and contingencies
of everyday matter. If we jump forward two and
a half centuries to the French Revolution and
the dawn of the Enlightenment, we see similar
actions but a distinctly different logic at work.
Iconoclastic attacks on images and symbols of
the king were central to Revolutionary events;
but as Dario Gamboni has argued, these actions
were focused less on images themselves than
on their symbolic content.[6] It was not the fraudulence of images that was at issue (as in our
earlier examples) but rather the fraudulence of
those being depicted: the king and his allies and
enablers. Accordingly, the smashing of pictures
and symbols of Louis XVI became a means of
vicariously harming the sovereign himself. In
this, the Revolutionary destruction of images
both echoes and negates the iconoclastic arguments we have considered so far. Revolutionary
iconoclasts saw images as worthy of destruction

not for their separation *from* but rather because
of precisely their connection *to* their referents.

The central motivating force of French revolutionary iconoclasm, furthermore, was political
rather than religious. This follows the course
of art itself over the same period. As Peter
Bürger has outlined in his sketch of the emergence of autonomous art as a concept, three
general typologies can be traced throughout the
history of Western art: sacral art, such as that
of concern to Plato and Reformation iconoclasts, which was produced for religious ends
and served a cultic function; courtly art, such as
that under attack during the French Revolution,
which represented the royal court and served to
portray this society to itself; and, since the emergence of modern capitalism in the late nine-
teenth century, what Bürger terms bourgeois
art, in which art comes to be understood as an
autonomous sphere of practice separated from
the means-ends rationality of everyday life.[7]
Another term for this last category, of course,
is simply modern art—and another way to
describe its primary characteristic is to say that
works of art shifted from being in the service of
something else (almost always, as we have seen,
religious and courtly doctrine) to focusing on
their own means and materials. Accordingly,
the motivations and protagonists of iconoclastic
attacks and arguments changed as well: religious and political concerns were replaced by
aesthetic ones, and philosophers and worship-
pers were replaced above all by artists themselves. It is to these iconoclastic arguments and
actors that I now turn.

Contemplating the place of iconoclasm in the
history of modern art, our thoughts may initially
turn to the squelching of avant-garde practices
in the totalitarian regimes of Stalinist Russia
and Nazi Germany, both of which pursued aggressive cultural programs motivated by hostili-
ty toward modern culture in all its forms. Certainly, these are distinct and significant chapters
in any history of iconoclasm in the modern era,
and ones we will consider shortly. But more
essential to this history, and what I wish to
focus on in the following pages, is iconoclasm's
immanence to the logic of modern art itself.
Advanced painting since at least the 1880s has
been driven by relentless self-critique and historical awareness, and the immediate result of

both these motivating factors has been a history of works aspiring not only to formal innovation and historical newness but also to a literal assault on established image-making techniques and historical beliefs alike.

In this respect, Filippo Tommaso Marinetti's 1909 Italian Futurist manifesto—among the most extreme of avant-garde polemics—speaks directly to many of modern art's most essential impulses:

> Come on! Set fire to the library shelves! Turn aside the canals to flood the museums!... Oh, the joy of seeing the glorious old canvases bobbing adrift on those waters, discoloured and shredded!... Take up your pickaxes, your axes and hammers and wreck, wreck the venerable cities, pitilessly![8]

The Italian Futurists' words are arguably more forceful than their exhibited works, which for the most part remain traditionally mimetic compositions in oil on canvas and bronze. Kazimir Malevich, working at this same time in Russia and influenced by Futurist precedents, pursued their call for creation through destruction with considerably more force. His best-known work, and one of the seminal canvases of twentieth-century painting, is the appropriately named *Black Square* of 1915, first exhibited at the landmark *0.10* exhibition in Petrograd (today Saint Petersburg) in December of that year. The painting is, both literally and figuratively, about the clearest declaration of iconoclastic intent imaginable: its central black field not only *suggests* the eradication of another image beneath but is, in fact, painted over an earlier composition by the artist. For Malevich, the 1915 canvas functioned as a polemical attack against the "barbarism" of representation itself, which he regarded as antithetical to the cause of art. If critics and scholars have thus repeatedly described *Black Square* as a work of straightforward iconoclastic negation—in Boris Groys's words, as "a process of destruction and reduction…taken to the very end"—Malevich himself saw the piece as a passage *through* such destruction, one that necessarily led to a new era for painting.[9] As he wrote in the manifesto accompanying his work's inaugural exhibition, "I transformed myself into the zero of form and emerged from nothing to creation,

that is to Suprematism, to the new realism in painting—to non-objective creation."[10] And indeed, the painting was surrounded at the *0.10* show by heralds of this new art: canvases filled with carefully worked fields of flat color, each one devoid of even the faintest suggestion of figurative content.

Black Square's iconoclasm, in other words, was for Malevich a door both slamming shut and swinging open. And these actions neces-

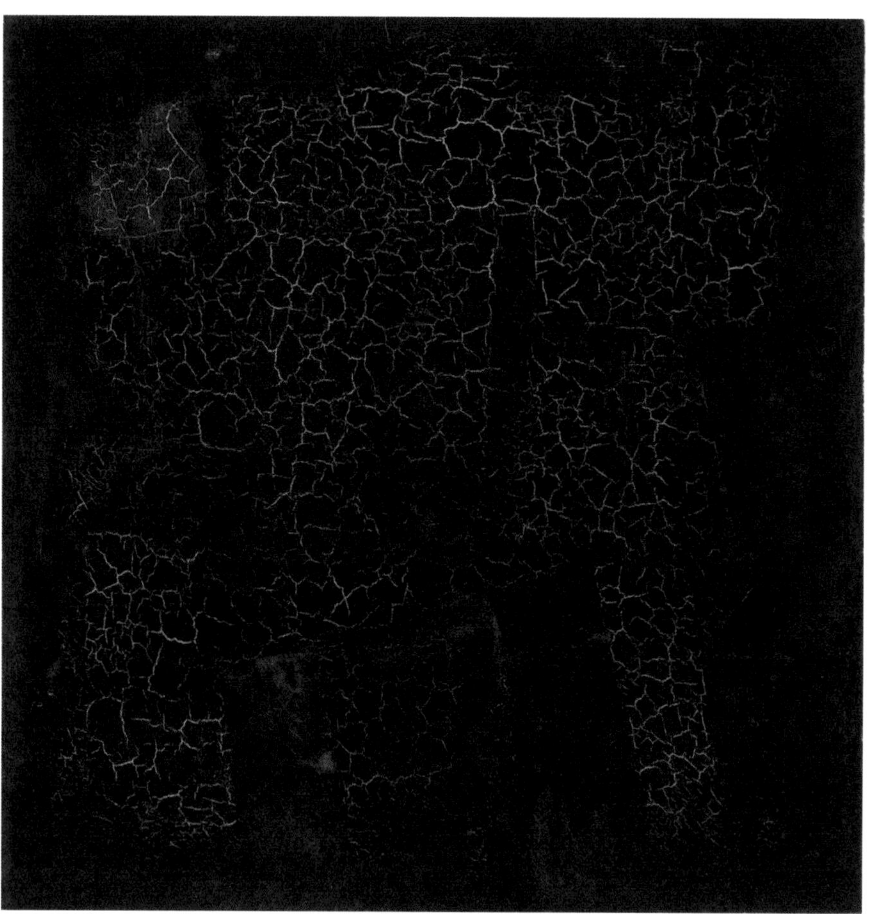

Below: Kazimir Malevich, *Black Square*, 1915. Oil on canvas, 21 x 21 in. (53.3 x 53.3 cm). The State Tretyakov Gallery, Moscow. (catalogue only)

Right: Hélio Oiticica, *B22 Bólide vidro 10 "Homenagem a Malevitch Gemini" 01*, 1965. Glass, painted plastic lids, and paint/pigment in water. Cesar and Claudio Oiticica Collection.

sarily belonged together: to inaugurate a new art—one committed, as Malevich described it, to "painted surface [as] a real, living form"—the obsolete means of the past had to be declaratively eradicated. There is an echo here, certainly, of the Futurists' celebration of shredded canvases and flooded museums. But perhaps a better antecedent through which to unpack Malevich's claims is the venerable Plato. For just as Plato understood the apprehension of the divine to be the truest aspiration of man

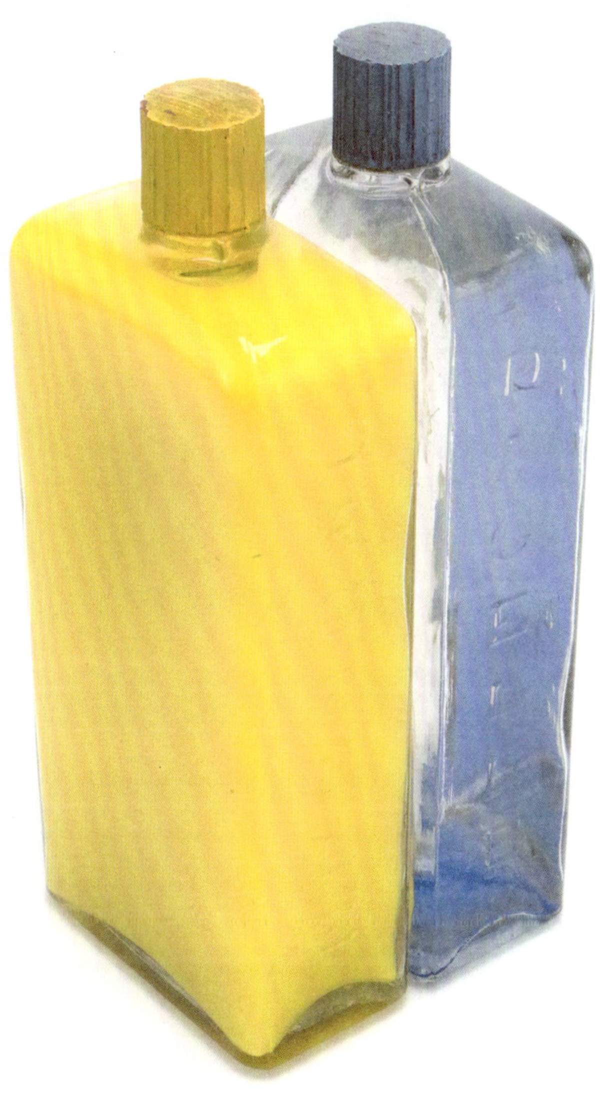

and saw the fallacies of art as an obstruction to this goal, so Malevich believed figuration—even that of such advanced practices as Cubism and Futurism—to be necessarily destructive to the cause of art, which occupied for him the absolute space that Plato had reserved for the sacred. (The artist explicitly invoked this connection, speaking of *Black Square*'s central form as analogous to the "face of God," and installing it at the *0.10* show in an upper gallery corner, a place traditionally reserved in Russian homes for the most sacred of icons.) As Malevich wrote in his 1915 manifesto, "color and texture are…the essence of painting, but this essence has always been destroyed by the subject."[11] Accordingly, the subject itself—figuration of any sort—had to be destroyed. *Black Square*, in short, declares iconoclasm's *necessity* for any reinvention of the icon—which is to say, of art itself. It is no mistake that Hélio Oiticica's 1965 *B22 Bólide vidro 10 "Homenagem a Malevitch Gemini" 01*, completed exactly five decades after Malevich's seminal canvas, was labeled by Oiticica as an homage to the Russian artist: consisting of two glass bottles containing pigment and water, the work distills Malevich's declarative materialism even further, presenting nothing other than color itself, bottled and ready for use.

Malevich came to Suprematism through collage, spurred by the masterful example of Picasso's and Braque's early experiments in the medium. Rosalind Krauss, in a brilliant reading of these works, has argued that they were motivated by an obliquely iconoclastic logic, one in fact endemic to collage as a practice. She writes:

> The collage element performs the occultation of one field in order to introject the figure of a new field, but to introject it *as* figure—a surface that is the image of eradicated surface. It is this eradication of the original surface and the reconstitution of it through the figure of its own absence that is the master term of the entire condition of collage as a system of signifiers.[12]

The very nature of collage, in other words—that is, of the image-making technique by which diverse two-dimensional materials are arranged and stuck to a backing—is that one pictorial field is covered over by another. The imported elements through which this covering-over is effected, furthermore—consisting, in the works of Picasso and Braque, primarily of newspaper and wallpaper fragments—serve to figure this very process of concealment. Picasso's early collages, in Krauss's analysis, utilize this fact to initiate an intricate examination of the nature of pictorial signification; they amount to, she writes, a "representation of representation" rooted in their occlusion of original surface.

Though we do not have the space here to further explore Krauss's densely formulated argument, she points us to the process by which artist after artist, from about 1915 to 1930, utilized collage to critique—indeed deface—dominant models of painting. This is above all the case in Dada, which was founded in Zurich in the midst of World War I and quickly spread to outposts across Europe. Dada responded to the horrors of war by critiquing the very foundations of what its practitioners perceived to be the sickened state of European culture at the time; as Leah Dickerman has written, "art as it was known was irretrievably implicated [for the Dadaists] in the cultural values that led to war."[13] And not just art; as Hugo Ball, a founding member of the Zurich Dada group, wrote at the time: "How can one get rid of everything that smacks of journalism, worms, everything nice and right, blinkered, moralistic, Europeanized, enervated? By saying Dada."[14] The goal, as Ball makes clear, was to *get rid* of things. Iconoclastic strategies, accordingly, were a primary method of Dada as a movement.

Two other key figures in the Zurich group, Hans Arp and Sophie Taeuber (later Sophie Taeuber-Arp), pursued such strategies in a remarkable series of collages and tapestries made between 1916 and 1920. Employing chance, geometric patterns, and craft techniques, their works in these years rejected every established aesthetic value: composition, tradition, individual touch, and the very notion of artistic volition. As Arp later wrote, he and Taeuber aspired to an "art of silence." In *Untitled (Duo-Collage)* of 1918, for instance—one of a series of similarly titled works produced in that year—the two artists randomly arranged machine-cut sheets of black and gray paper and silver leaf across a thirty-unit grid. In this way, they not only suppressed every sugges-

tion of individual authorship, narrative content, and compositional complexity but did so by *covering over* the very pictorial field in which these values were traditionally expressed. As Krauss suggests of collage more generally, Arp and Taeuber's gridded forms read not as figures set against a ground but as sheets blocking this ground from view. The work's silence, we could say, is equally a silencing, a negation of the space and means of art itself.

The artists associated with Zurich Dada set their iconoclastic sights not just on the visual arts but on communication across the board. This is perhaps best exemplified in Ball's sound poems, which, as T. J. Demos has written, "force verbal elements to behave as pure vocal sensation and aural phenomena, cut off from any clear purpose or communicative task."[15] Ball's 1916 poem "Karawane," for instance, which he performed live in June of that year while done up in a confining cardboard costume he described as that of a "magical bishop," begins: "jolifanto bambla ô falli bambla/*grossiga m'pfa habla horem*." This focus on the materiality of the voice, we can notice, is not far from Malevich's roughly simultaneous concern with the obdurate matter of the painted surface, as both are divorced from and set against any kind of narrative meaning. For Ball and other Dadaists, such "incommunicative communication" carried a distinctly political punch: to speak a language detached from semantic convention was to resist the instrumentalization of language itself, a process the Dadaists saw all around them in the jingoistic slogans and cheapened journalistic prose of wartime society. As Ball wrote in 1915: "The word has become commodity…[and] has lost all dignity." Accordingly, he noted a year later, the phonetic poems "totally renounce the language that journalism has abused and corrupted."[16]

A decade after the heyday of Zurich Dada, Arp pursued a more directly iconoclastic method in his *Torn Drawings* of 1930, made from ripped-apart fragments of his own earlier compositions. With their crudely torn image shards scattered across buckled grounds, these pieces are downright boisterous in their display of straightforward destruction. As Arp later recounted, the impetus for their creation was his late 1920s encounter with a set of earlier collages that had degraded over years of storage:

Right: Hans Arp and Sophie
Taeuber-Arp, *Untitled (Duo-Collage)*,
1918. Paper collage on cardboard
and silver foil on stick, 32¼ x 24⅜ in.
(82 x 62 cm). Nationalgalerie Staatliche
Museen zu Berlin, Berlin.
(catalogue only)

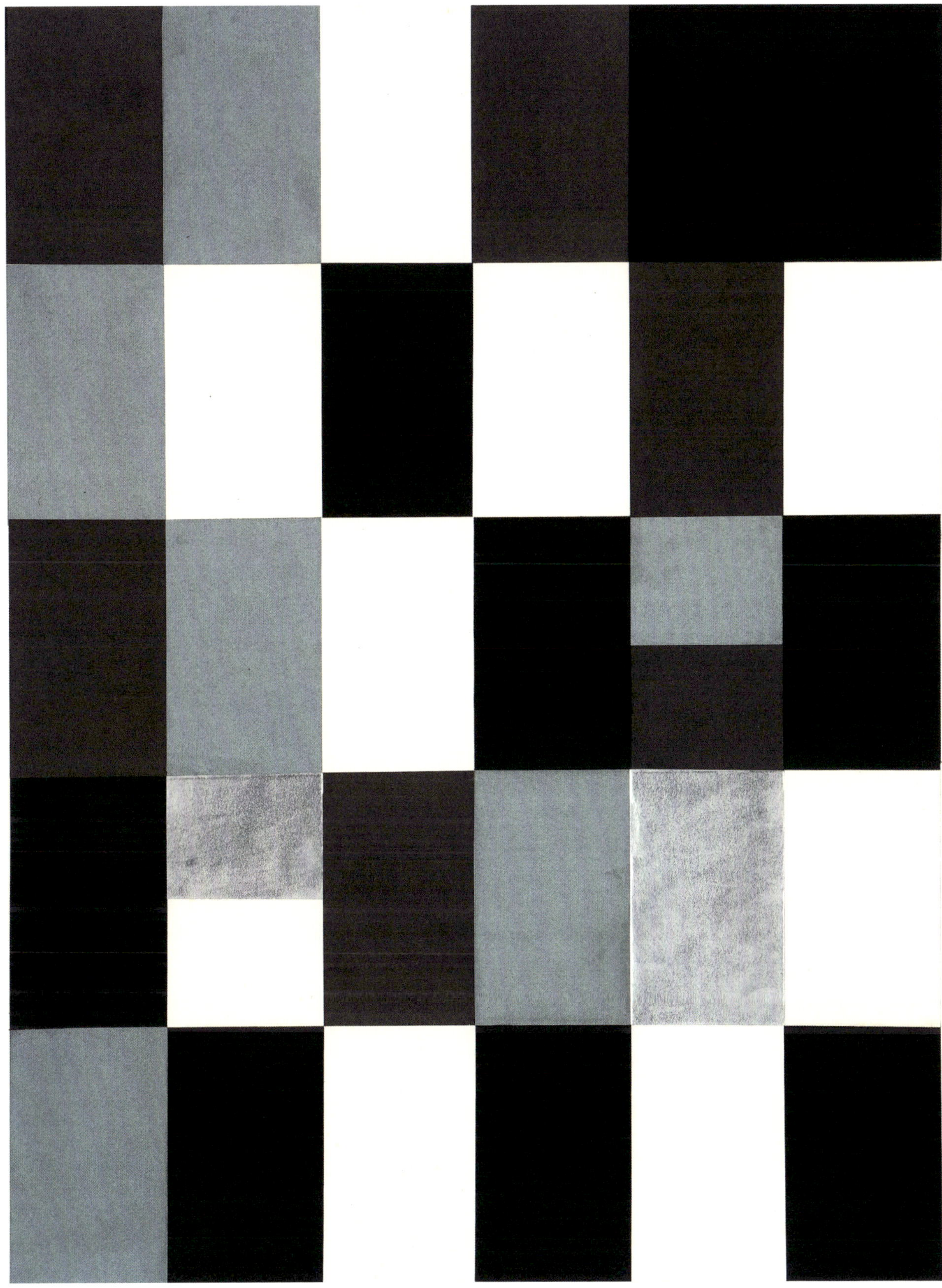

> We brought down the collages from the attic where they had been exposed for years to heat, cold, and dampness. Some of the papers had come unstuck, they were covered with spots, mould, and cracks, and between paper and cardboard blisters had formed that looked more loathsome to me than the bloated bellies of drowned rats.[17]

This is certainly dramatic language; it is not often that one hears an artist compare his work to drowned rats. Indeed, as Briony Fer has noted, Arp later described his 1930 collages as documentations of death itself, of the process by which "the work decomposes and dies."[18] Art's *degradation*, in other words, took the place of its composition for Arp; his 1930 series does not simply suggest but actively documents—indeed celebrates—artistic destruction.

Concomitant with Arp's production of these explicitly iconoclastic collages, John Heartfield was developing his own strategy of defacement—to very different ends—in Germany. His iconoclastic drive in fact began with his very own name: born Helmut Herzfelde, he chose his newly anglicized moniker in 1916 to protest wartime German jingoism. Active within Berlin Dada beginning in 1918, Heartfield, like Arp and so many others, embraced collage—and specifically photomontage, made from cut-apart scraps of newspapers and photographs—as a means to challenge painting's perceived obsolescence and corruption as an art form. (Like every other artist discussed in this essay, I should note, Heartfield began his career as a painter.) Indeed, for him, the notion of art itself was worthy of nothing but contempt. This is made clear in his 1920 broadside "The Art Scab," written with fellow Dadaist Georg Grosz to mock the Expressionist painter Oskar Kokoschka's earlier plea to remove then-common political street fights from the proximity of Dresden's Semper Gallery, housing the city's collection of Old-Master paintings. Declaring that "the title 'artist' is an insult," Heartfield and Grosz instead *celebrated* the bullets whizzing near the gallery's windows (and, in at least one case, through the windows and into paintings themselves) as an assault on the harmful boundary separating art from the realities of modern life. "With joy we welcome the news that the bullets are whistling through the galleries and palaces, into the masterpieces of Rubens," they wrote, "instead of into the houses of the poor in the working-class neighborhoods!"[19] Target practice, indeed.

Heartfield thought of his practice as fundamentally violent: his best-known slogan was "Use Photography as a Weapon!" and his most prominent self-portrait shows him, scissors in hand, snipping off the head of Berlin Police Commissioner Karl Zörgiebel, who

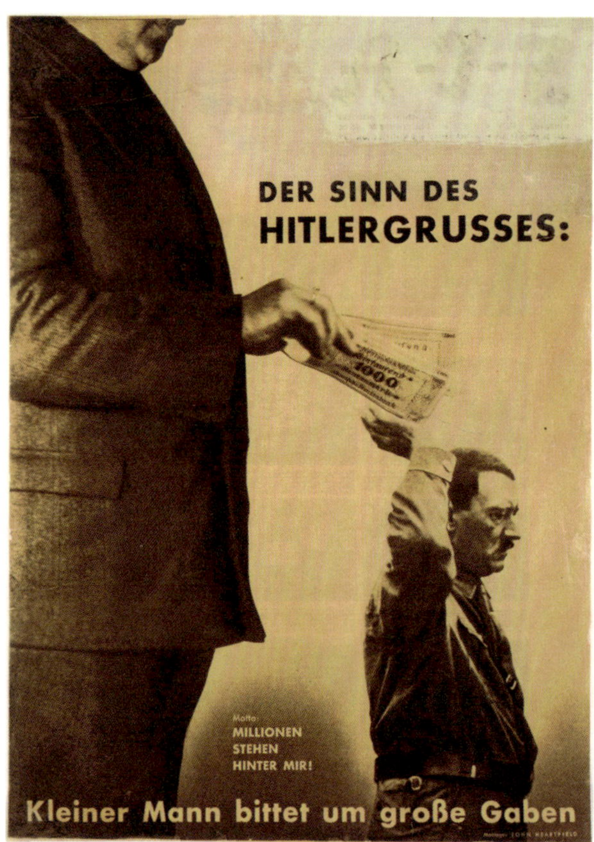

had condoned police brutality toward left-wing activists. Heartfield's destruction, like Arp's, was perfectly literal: he made images by destroying other images. Indeed, his work is *about* precisely this process. His 1932 photomontage *The Meaning of the Hitler Salute*, for instance, shows Hitler's upraised hand receiving a pile of cash from a portly industrialist, transforming the aspiring chancellor's phrase "Millions stand behind me!" into a commentary on the corporate money funding his drive to power. The picture creates meaning not only by highlighting Hitler's links to big industry but also—and above all—by using the future dictator's own image and words to demonstrate this. Presaging the dubs and mash-ups of our own day, Heartfield chops up existing images to turn them against themselves. He aims, furthermore, to engender a kind of iconoclastic vision through this process: to generate an enlightened skepticism in his viewers regarding the truth value of *all* images and to encourage these viewers to engage in a similar practice, chop-

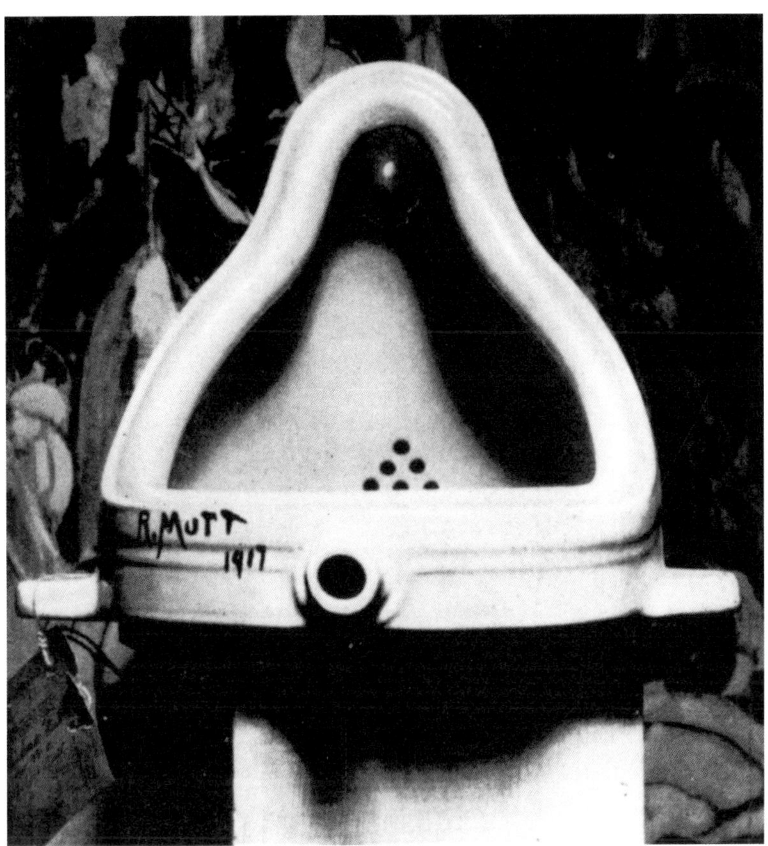

ping up and reconfiguring (either in actual fact or simply in their heads) the incessant media barrage that confronted them each day. In a manner not so distant from the iconoclasts of the French Revolution, Heartfield understood Hitler's power to be indelibly connected to his image; but rather than pursue a straightforward program of iconoclastic destruction, Heartfield sought to activate viewers' critical faculties toward an examination of images themselves, and of the increasingly image-saturated landscape of twentieth-century life.

From Malevich to Arp to Heartfield, the iconoclastic impulse was, by the 1920s and 1930s, arguably the central motivating force in advanced European art. There are far too many relevant practices to cover in this brief essay, but, before taking an even briefer look at the postwar period, I should note a few other examples. In Russia, Aleksandr Rodchenko exhibited three monochrome canvases titled *Pure Red Color*, *Pure Yellow Color*, and *Pure Blue Color* in September 1921, declaring them to be the end of painting. The three paintings (frequently cited as but not in fact a triptych) marked Rodchenko's conclusion of his own career in the medium; as he later wrote, "I reduced painting to its logical conclusion and…affirmed: it's all over. Basic colors. Every plane is a plane and there is to be no representation."[20] In New York, meanwhile, the recently arrived Frenchman Marcel Duchamp continued his assault on what he termed "retinal art" by submitting his infamous *Fountain*—a urinal turned on its side and signed "R. Mutt"—to the annual open exhibition of the Society of Independent Artists in 1917; the work was promptly rejected, leading Duchamp to voice his objections in a journal (which he coproduced) titled, not incidentally, *The Blind Man*. Four years before this incident, Duchamp (like Rodchenko) had dramatically withdrawn from painting, going so far as to propose using "a Rembrandt as an ironing board" as a means to challenge the modernist doctrine of autonomous art. As a last example, the Spaniard Joan Miró, though never fully abandoning painting, did declare his central aspiration in 1927 to be to "assassinate" it. For the Surrealist critic Georges Bataille, who himself considered modern painting to "be fashioned around a core of inner, underlying violence," Miró's subsequent work—including garishly stained canvases and collages made from materials such as garbage and nails—pushed decomposition "to the point where nothing remained but some formless blotches on the cover (or, if you prefer, on the gravestone) of painting's box of tricks."[21]

Each of these iconoclastic projects—and countless others—was motivated by the same concern that had inspired Plato's aesthetics more than two millennia before, namely, the potential for, and indeed the tendency of, images to lie. But whereas Plato's central focus was the false start provided by images in any attempt to apprehend the divine, these early twentieth-century pioneers all took *aesthetic* fraudulence as their target. Hence, the declarative materiality of Malevich's *Black Square* is directed above all at the outmoded transcendentalist rhetoric of Russian Symbolism; Arp and Taeuber's "silent" collages protest the bombastic colors and thickly laid-on paint of German Expressionism; the mocking playfulness of Duchamp's *Fountain* challenges the rigidified institutional framework of the doctrine of *l'art pour l'art*; and Heartfield's photomontages take aim at the political and mass-media manipulations that enabled Hitler's rise, as well as—and even primarily—the corruption of a German artistic culture that turned a blind eye to their threat. In every case, pictures and processes were literally or figuratively ripped apart so that both could be reconceived anew—only to be taken apart once more, in the logic of aesthetic contestation thus initiated, within a perpetual dialectic of modernist destruction and renewal.

This history, of course, was abruptly halted with the spread of Fascism and war across Europe in the 1930s. And if Hitler and Stalin introduced their *own*, infinitely more lethal iconoclastic practices—burning, selling, and storing away works of art; exiling artists; shutting down academies and galleries—these actions can ironically be understood as an iconoclasm directed against iconoclasm itself. For what the cultural authorities of Fascist Germany and Stalinist Russia sought to shut down above all was the rigorous process of self-criticism that underlies all the modernist iconoclasms we have just reviewed. Artists from Malevich to Miró, motivated by a dialectical skepticism that reaches back to Plato's own image critique of the fourth century B.C., adopted iconoclastic procedures as a means to call into question the truth-telling power of works of art. Hitler's and Stalin's regimes countered this skepticism by simply banning it and proposing new artistic cultures committed instead to the absolute truth of the dictators who commanded them, communicated through the most conventional sort of academic realism.[22] Totalitarian iconoclasm, that is, aimed to resuscitate the unquestioned icon—and considered the eradication of *modernist* iconoclasm, rooted in an incessant interrogation both of art and of images themselves, to be a necessary first step in this process.

This all changed—and yet remained oddly the same—with the end of World War II. For even as artists across Europe and the United States sought to redefine avant-garde practices in the wake of Fascism's defeat, they turned to a familiar idea in doing so: iconoclasm. Having been the primary target of Fascism's assault on images, art driven by modernist image critique regained the upper hand, with Hitler's anachronistic program of "Great German Art" becoming the model against which nearly every advanced artist chose to work. But more than any specific aesthetic program espoused by Hitler (or Stalin, Hitler's near twin in aesthetic matters among others, who in fact intensified the spread of Socialist Realism in the years immediately following World War II), it was the very idea of the seamless, inviolable image that artist after artist—particularly in Europe and Japan, where memories of wartime cultural propaganda were especially rich—took in their sights. Hence, the present exhibition offers such works as Lucio Fontana's *Concetto spaziale* of 1949 (page 20), Shōzō Shimamoto's *Work (Holes)* and *Untitled* of 1950 (pages 21, 111), Alberto Burri's 1955 *Sacco* (page 95), and Otto Muehl's slightly later *Untitled*, of 1963, in all of which the canvas is presented as a wounded, battered object, as far as could be imagined from the triumphant compositions that had filled many European and Japanese museums just a few years before.

Though such works—being precisely *about* the violation of images and, accordingly, the subversion of accepted cultural values—recall the collages of Arp and Miró or the anti-art ethos of Dada, between 1930 and 1950 the political and ideological stakes of such a practice had grown exponentially. The horrors of World War I were no match for the atrocities of the Holocaust, the bombings of Hiroshima and Nagasaki, and the global insanity of "mutually assured destruction" that soon followed. As the German-Jewish philosopher Theodor Adorno wrote in 1949, reflecting on the possibility of culture in the wake of Fascism's horrors, "to write poetry after Auschwitz is barbaric."[23] Adorno did not mean by this statement that culture as a concept was to be abandoned, but rather that any work of art—poetry and music as well as painting and sculpture—needed to pursue a program of dialectical self-criticism

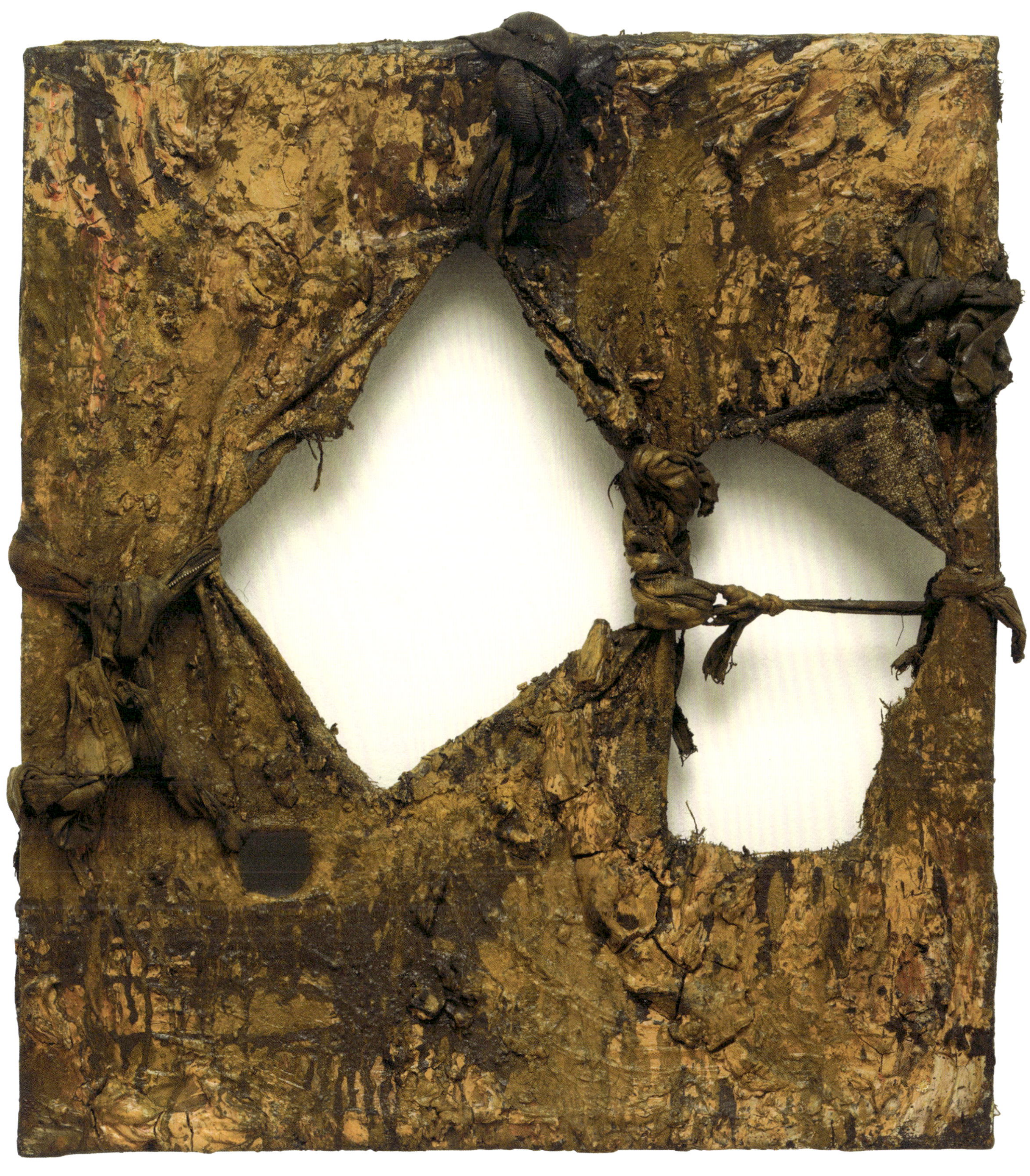

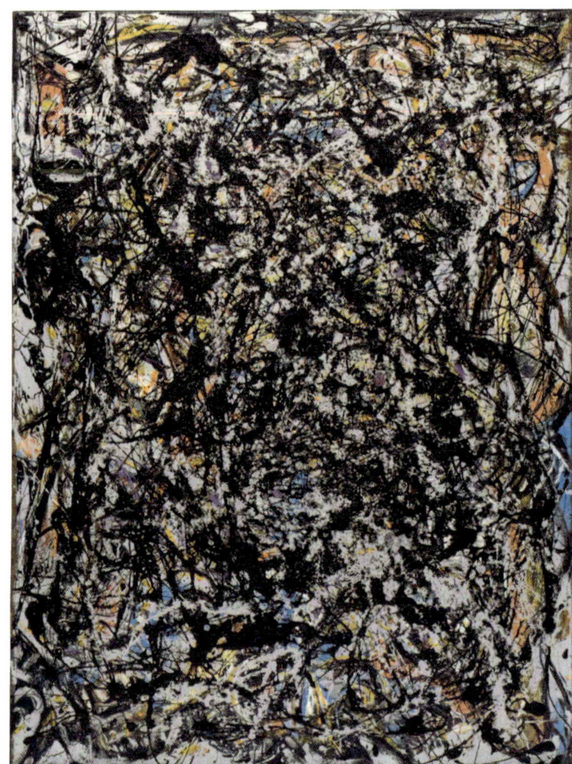

"until the notion of culture is itself negated, fulfilled, and surmounted in one." Culture, that is, was compelled to pursue its own negation in order to make itself anew; as Adorno wrote in the same essay:

> A successful work…is not one which resolves objective contradictions in a spurious harmony, but one which expresses the idea of harmony negatively by embodying the contradictions, pure and uncompromised, in its innermost structure.[24]

The negative program Adorno lays out here is in fact not so far removed from the precedents discussed in this essay. From Malevich to Arp to Heartfield to Miró, early twentieth-century artists engaged in explicitly iconoclastic strategies as a means to simultaneously negate and renew the practice of art, and most often saw this process (as did Adorno) as intimately connected to the political circumstances of the day. Hal Foster has discussed this pattern of repetition between early and late twentieth-century avant-garde practices (what have come to be referred to as the "historical" and "neo"

avant-gardes) as a form of deferred action. He writes: "historical and neo-avant-gardes are constituted…as a continual process of protension and retension, a complex relay of anticipated futures and reconstituted pasts…that throws over any simple scheme of before and after, cause and effect, origin and repetition."[25] In other words, the dialectical project of the historical avant-garde, including iconoclasm as a primary strategy, is not rejected or superseded in the postwar period but rather worked through and enacted, in its full theoretical complexity, for the very first time.

If this process of avant-garde repetition was less marked in the United States than in Europe in the early postwar decades, iconoclastic strategies were nevertheless central to American art of the period. As artist Allan Kaprow argued in his seminal 1958 essay "The Legacy of Jackson Pollock," Pollock's drip canvases of 1947–50 had effectively "destroyed painting."[26] Citing the older artist's radical subversion of conventions of painterly composition, form, scale, and space, Kaprow—the father of the Happening— argued that Pollock had laid the path for artists' direct engagement with the spaces, objects, and activities of everyday life itself. "Not satisfied with the *suggestion* through paint of our other senses," Kaprow concluded his essay, "we shall utilize the specific substances of sight, sound, movements, people, odors, touch…[as] materials for the new art."[27] Once again, we hear echoes here of earlier twentieth-century precedents; what is Kaprow suggesting, after all, but the passage "from nothing to creation" and the move toward a "real, living" art that Malevich heralded in 1915? But more noteworthy than Kaprow's connection to the past is his prophesy of the future. Many of the works in *Target Practice* take leave of painting as Pollock had known it to celebrate the materials and actions of life itself, including Robert Rauschenberg's materially heterogeneous assemblages; Daniel Spoerri's preserved dinner remains; Oiticica's participatory *Parangolés*; Richard Tuttle's and Sam Gilliam's loosely hanging sheets of stained canvas; the painting-as-performance works of Shigeko Kubota, Paul McCarthy, and others; and Yoko Ono's paintings to be hammered into or stepped on.

For the great art historian Meyer Schapiro, writing also in 1958, Pollock's work did not

Left: Jackson Pollock, *Sea Change*, 1947. Oil paint and pebbles on canvas, 58 x 44 in. (147.3 x 111.8 cm). Seattle Art Museum, Gift of Signora Peggy Guggenheim, 58.55. (catalogue only)

Right: Sam Gilliam, *Bow Form Construction*, 1968. Acrylic on canvas with aluminum powder and enamel. Whitney Museum of American Art, New York, Purchase with funds from the Friends of the Whitney Museum of American Art and the Howard W. Lipman Foundation, and gift of the Ford Foundation Purchase Program and an anonymous donor, by exchange, 2001.343.

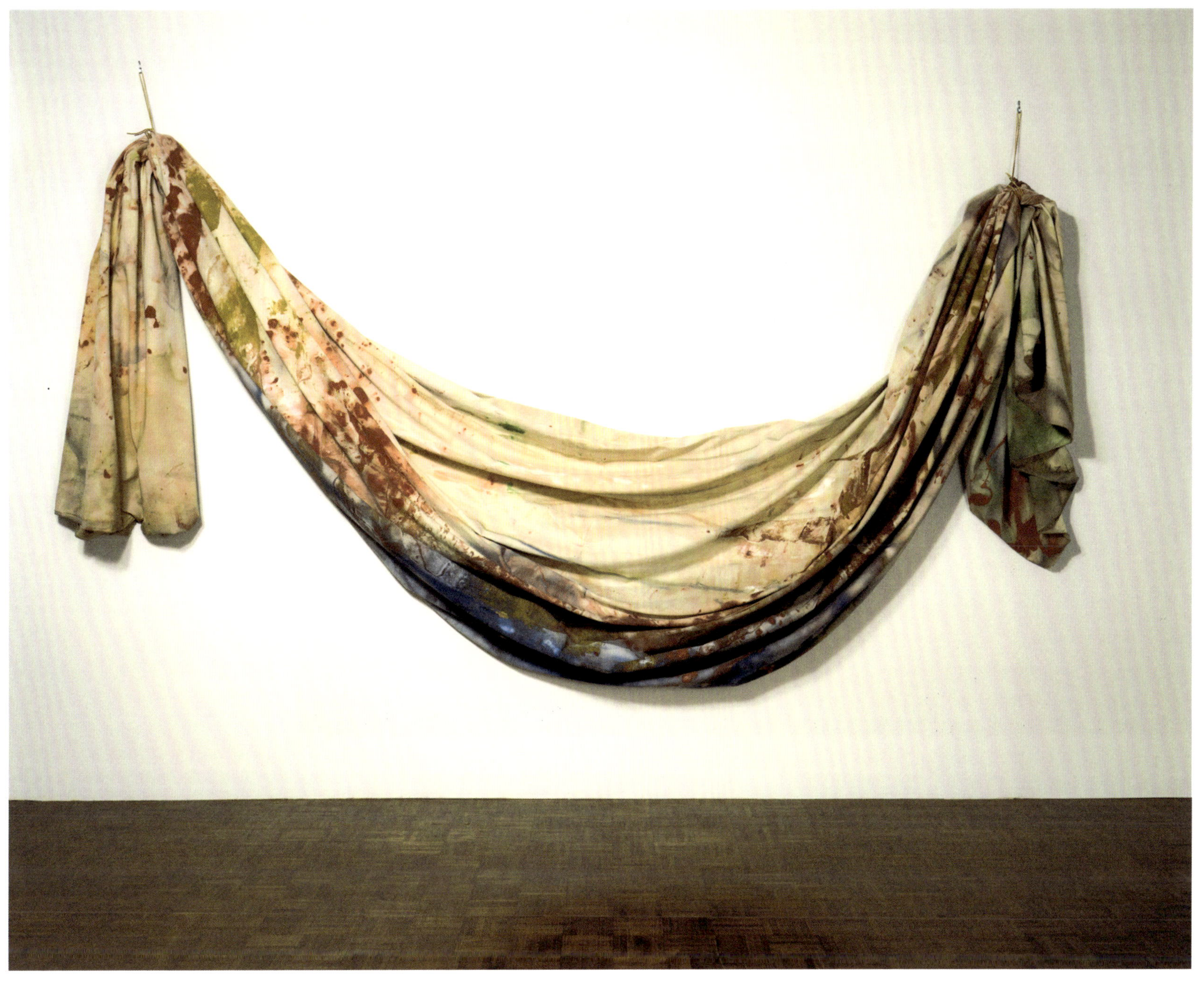

destroy painting so much as it self-consciously opposed the "culture of communication"—the dawning era of television, picture magazines, and ever-present advertising—that had so rapidly developed over the course of the 1950s. The abstractions of Pollock and his contemporaries, Schapiro wrote, aimed to *block* straightforward communication—just as had the earlier sound poems of Ball and collages of Arp—and thus to offer a more profound "communion with the work of another human being,… [with] another's perfected feeling and imagination."[28] Echoing and inverting Plato, Schapiro argued that it was postwar abstraction's radical *rejection* of mimesis that enabled it to attain a certain level of truth: it avoided what Plato had described as painting's necessary third-degree remove by refusing to pose as anything other than what it was, namely, paint applied to a flat surface. Schapiro championed such work as

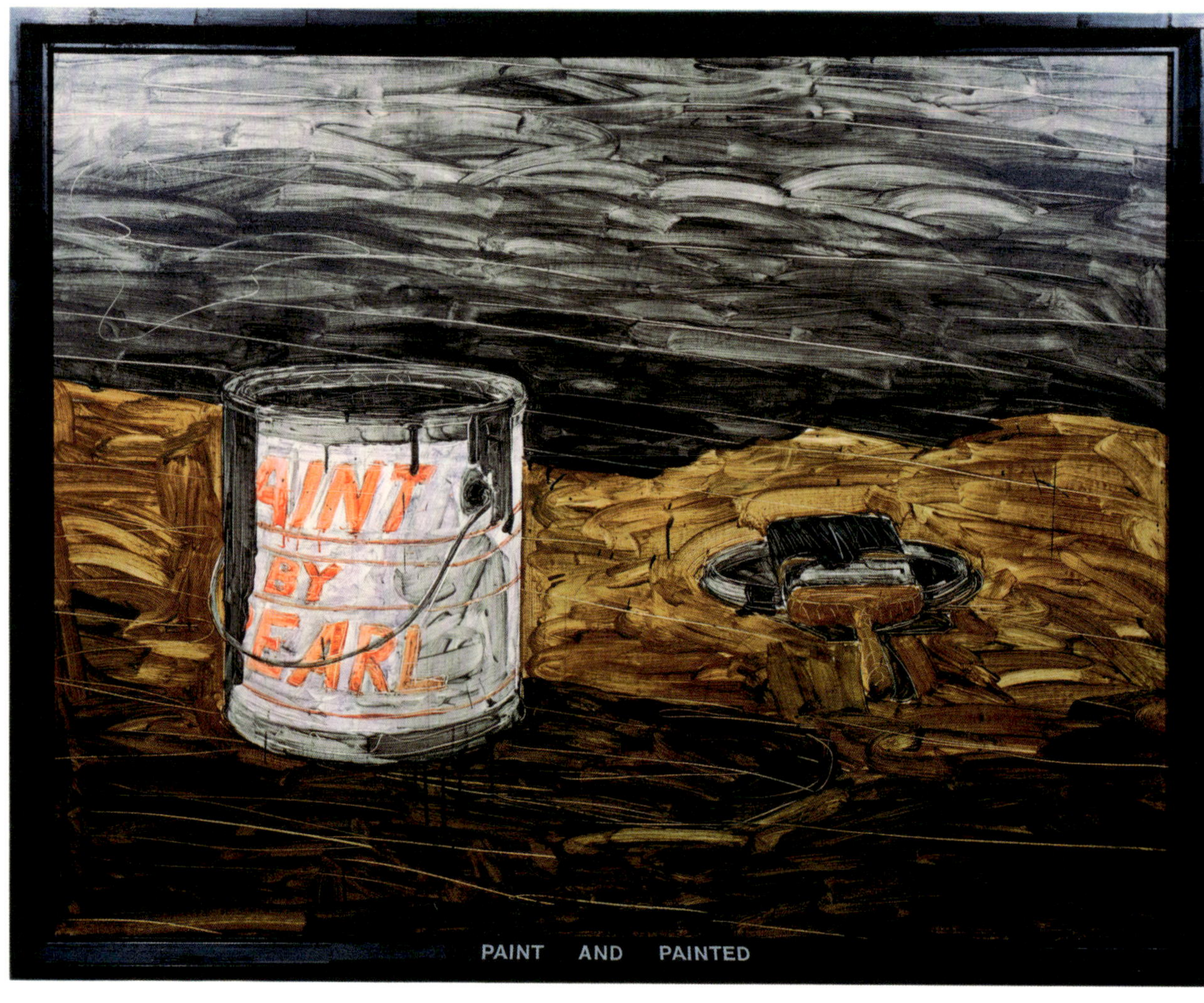

Left: Neil Jenney, *Paint and Painted*, 1969. Acrylic on canvas. Seattle Art Museum, Promised gift of the Virginia and Bagley Wright Collection, in honor of the 75th Anniversary of the Seattle Art Museum, T98.84.26.

Right: Frank Stella, *Die Fahne hoch!*, 1959. Enamel on canvas, 121½ x 73 in. (308.6 x 185.4 cm). Whitney Museum of American Art, New York, Gift of Mr. and Mrs. Eugene M. Schwartz and purchase, with funds from the John I. H. Baur Purchase Fund; the Charles and Anita Blatt Fund; Peter M. Brant; B. H. Friedman; the Gilman Foundation, Inc.; Susan Morse Hilles; The Lauder Foundation; Frances and Sydney Lewis; the Albert A. List Fund; Philip Morris Incorporated; Sandra Payson; Mr. and Mrs. Albrecht Saalfield; Mrs. Percy Uris; Warner Communications, Inc.; and the National Endowment for the Arts, 75.22. (catalogue only)

an implicit act of resistance to the overflow of images—specifically, orchestrated and deceptive images—that were increasingly dominating postwar American life, a position not far from Heartfield's pointed media critique of the 1920s and 1930s.

The most influential—and most directly iconoclastic—explication of postwar American abstraction was that of the critic Clement Greenberg, whose writings dominated American aesthetic discourse in the 1950s. For Greenberg, modernism as a cultural idea was rooted in self-criticism, the process by which disciplines analyze their characteristic means and procedures from within so as to entrench themselves more firmly in their distinct areas of competence. Thus, the task of artists is "to eliminate from the specific effects of each art any and every effect that might conceivably be borrowed from or by the medium of any other art."[29] So,

for Greenberg, properly modernist painting concerned itself with the three definitive qualities of the medium: "the flat surface, the shape of the support, the properties of the pigment."[30] Such work, then, necessarily entailed not just an abandonment *of* but an adamant opposition *to* figuration. History itself, in Greenberg's criticism, became a kind of iconoclastic cloak, positioning any kind of representational content as fundamentally antithetical to the tide of modernist progress.

The clearest demonstration of Greenberg's iconoclastic logic is to be found in the late 1950s work of an artist whom the critic himself never embraced: Frank Stella. For in his disarmingly simple series of Black Paintings produced in 1959–60, consisting of concentric bands of black paint that repeat the shape of their picture support and are separated by thin strips of exposed canvas, Stella restricts painting's task to a straightforward declaration of precisely those qualities delineated by Greenberg above: flatness, shape, color. A 1959 catalogue statement by Stella's close friend the Minimalist sculptor Carl Andre is noteworthy in this respect:

> Art is the exclusion of the unnecessary. Frank Stella has found it necessary to paint stripes. There is nothing else in his paintings. He is not interested in sensitivity or personality, either his own or those of his audience. He is interested in the necessities of painting.[31]

Painting, in short, is nothing but painting. What you see is what you see: the deliberate, broad strokes of color—specifically here, of *black*—that cover Stella's canvases from edge to edge and corner to corner.[32] Just as Malevich did in his *Black Square*, Stella here presents the "necessities of painting" as a calculated and emphatic process of covering over the space of representation. The motivations behind this process, Andre makes clear, are decidedly negative: art *excludes*; there is *nothing else*; Stella is *not interested*. As the artist responded when asked by the critic Bruce Glaser if he was trying to destroy painting: "It's not a question of destroying anything. If something's used up, something's done, something's over with, what's the point of getting involved with it?"[33]

I hate to sound like a broken record, but we are on utterly familiar ground here: the project of renewing painting by negating it or declaring it dead. Yve-Alain Bois, reflecting on the course of contemporary painting in an important essay of 1986, describes the medium's central project since the dawn of modernity as one of mourning—of repeatedly enacting and then deferring its own death, its own expiration, as a legitimate form of cultural expression:

> Indeed the whole enterprise of modernism, especially of abstract painting, which can be taken as its emblem, could not have functioned without an apocalyptic myth. Freed from all extrinsic conventions, abstract painting was meant to bring forth the pure *parousia* of its own essence, to tell the final truth and thereby terminate its course. The pure beginning, the

liberation from tradition, the "zero degree" that was searched for by the first generation of abstract painters could not but function as an omen of the end.[34]

This project, Bois writes, continues to the present day; and those who undialectically declare "the end of painting" as accomplished fact stand blind to its history: a history of renewal through negation that leads from Malevich and Rodchenko through Duchamp to Stella and beyond. Looking at the decades since Stella, we see artist after artist seemingly nullifying painting precisely to reinvent its parameters and possibilities: Robert Ryman reducing his practice to the repeated declaration of white surface in order to undertake an infinite dissection of the medium's component elements; Gerhard Richter turning to monochrome gray paintings from the mid-1960s on as a means to achieve what he described as a "lack of differentiation, nothing, nil, the beginning and the end"; and Daniel Buren restricting his production since 1966 to alternating 8.5-centimeter bands of white and a single color per work as a means to critique, with infinite variation, art's institutional parameters, to name just a few.[35]

We're coming to the end of this essay—necessarily somewhat abruptly, for to discuss iconoclasm's role in the art of the last fifty years, much less the entire modern period, would require (and has required) many books, not a single catalogue text. As a final example, Rauschenberg's *Erased de Kooning Drawing* of 1953 is arguably the most literal instance of iconoclasm in postwar art (page 26). As its title declares, Rauschenberg made the work by erasing an earlier drawing by the Abstract Expressionist master Willem de Kooning, given to him by the artist himself. At once a violent defacement of the older artist's work and an intimate embrace between the two men, Rauschenberg's erased sheet reminds us that for all the historical and epistemological abstractions undergirding it, modernist iconoclasm remains grounded in the simplest of questions: What can I draw? What can I paint? How do I make a new mark? Rauschenberg's act of *un*drawing enacts an extended and literal process of emulation—indeed, a kind of melancholy repetition—of de Kooning's earlier work, one whose resulting blankness unites its two "makers" as one.[36] Only by negatively mimicking his elder did Rauschenberg feel he could definitively move beyond him, beyond a cultural situation in which the very idea of original gesture had itself become suspect.[37] Once again, negation is fused here with the process of renewal, of one destroyed work enabling—even engendering—another.

Closing with Rauschenberg, of course, brings us nowhere near the end of our tale. Far from it; iconoclastic strategies have continued to drive work in painting, collage, sculpture, video, performance, installation, and myriad other practices over the last half century. But Rauschenberg's iconoclastic sheet *does* bring us near the beginning of this exhibition's own story. Indeed, nearly every artist in *Target Practice* could arguably be classified as an "iconoclast." But the exhibition's torn, nailed, stomped-upon, sliced, erased, shot, or merely blank or

reversed images are *not*—as should now be clear enough—gestures of simple negation or destruction. They are rather, like Malevich's simple black field of 1915, prompts for a new formulation of painting, as of art, itself. And as such they are part of a history that reaches back across the last century, and as far back as the philosophical debates of ancient Greece. There, Plato criticized images for always falling short of, and thus holding us back from, the truth. Modern art's incessant iconoclasm takes this position one step further: it demands pictorial truthfulness, but understands that the most genuine statement one can make is that absolute truth is always, necessarily, a falsehood.

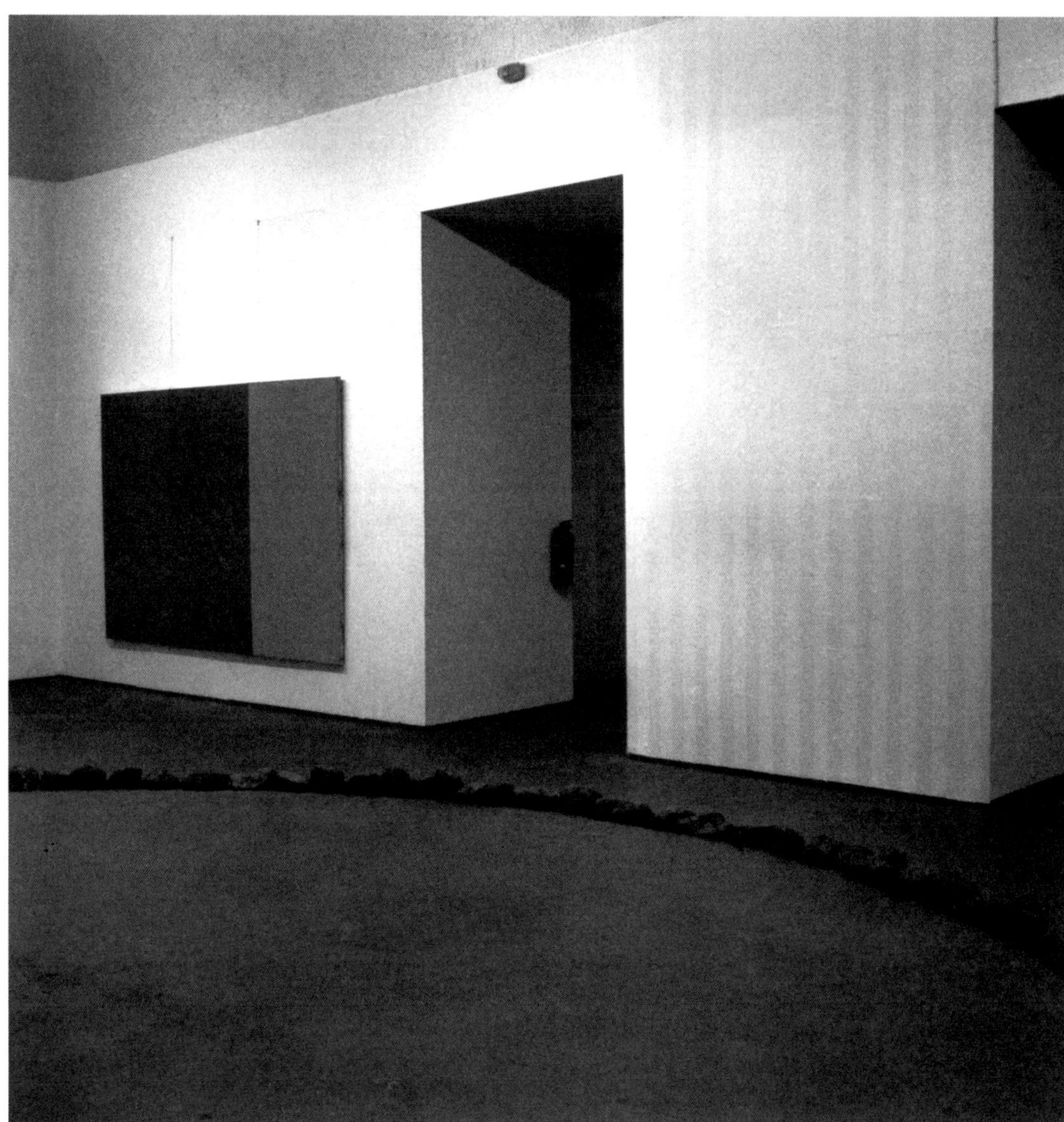

Above: Daniel Buren, *Photo-souvenir: Exposition d'une Exposition*, 1972. Printed wallpaper. Installation view at Documenta 5, Kassel, 1972, with works by Brice Marden and Richard Long. Courtesy of the artist and Bortolami Gallery, New York.

Notes

1. Iris Murdoch, *The Fire and the Sun: Why Plato Banished the Artists* (Oxford: Clarendon Press, 1977), 2.
2. Plato, *Republic*, trans. R. E. Allen (New Haven: Yale University Press, 2006), 337.
3. Ibid., 335.
4. Alain Besançon, *The Forbidden Image: An Intellectual History of Iconoclasm*, trans. Jane Marie Todd (Chicago: University of Chicago Press, 2000), 36.
5. Joseph Koerner, "The Icon as Iconoclash," in Bruno Latour and Peter Weibel, eds., *Iconoclash: Beyond the Image Wars in Science, Religion, and Art* (Karlsruhe, Germany: ZKM/Zentrum für Kunst und Medientechnologie, 2002), 168. I should note that Koerner's original passage reads "banish them from the heart," which is a false summary of the German phrase to which he refers and likely a typographical error; hence my license in altering the text.
6. See Dario Gamboni, *The Destruction of Art: Iconoclasm and Vandalism Since the French Revolution* (London: Reaktion Books, 1997), 31–36.
7. See Peter Bürger, *Theory of the Avant-Garde*, trans. Michael Shaw (Minneapolis: University of Minnesota Press), 47–54.
8. Filippo Tommaso Marinetti, "The Foundation and Manifesto of Futurism" (1909), reprinted in Charles Harrison and Paul Wood, eds., *Art in Theory, 1900–2000: An Anthology of Changing Ideas* (London: Blackwell, 2003), 149.
9. Boris Groys, *The Total Art of Stalinism*, trans. Charles Rougle (Princeton: Princeton University Press, 1992), 15.
10. Kazimir Malevich, *From Cubism and Futurism to Suprematism: The New Realism in Painting* (1915), reprinted in *K. S. Malevich: Essays on Art, 1915–1933*, vol. 1, ed. Troels Andersen, trans. Xenia Glowacki-Prus and Arnold McMillin (Copenhagen: Borgen, 1968), 37.
11. Ibid., 25.
12. Rosalind E. Krauss, "In the Name of Picasso," in *The Originality of the Avant-Garde and Other Modernist Myths* (Cambridge, MA: MIT Press, 1985), 37.
13. Leah Dickerman, *Dada: Zurich, Berlin, Hannover, Cologne, New York, Paris* (Washington, DC: National Gallery of Art, 2006), 7.
14. Hugo Ball, "Dada Manifesto" (1916), cited in ibid., 6.
15. T. J. Demos, "Zurich Dada: The Aesthetics of Exile," in Leah Dickerman and Matthew S. Witkovsky, eds., *The Dada Seminars* (Washington, DC: Center for Advanced Study in the Visual Arts, 2005), 9.
16. This and the previous quote are cited in ibid.
17. Hans (Jean) Arp, "Looking," in *Arp* (New York: Museum of Modern Art, 1958), 14. Cited in Briony Fer, *On Abstract Art* (New Haven and London: Yale University Press, 1997), 69.
18. Ibid., 73.
19. John Heartfield and Georg Grosz, "The Art Scab" (1920), reprinted in *The Weimar Republic Sourcebook*, ed. Anton Kaes, Martin Jay, and Edward Dimendberg (Berkeley: University of California Press, 1994), 485.
20. Aleksandr Rodchenko, "Working with Mayakovsky" (1939), cited in Magdalena Dabrowski, "Aleksandr Rodchenko: Innovation and Experiment," in *Aleksandr Rodchenko* (New York: Museum of Modern Art, 1998), 43. Ending his work in painting certainly did not mean that Rodchenko took leave of art altogether: after the concluding gesture of his monochromes, he pursued projects in photography, architecture, and design that would cement his place as one of the great figures of twentieth-century art.
21. For Bataille's comments on modern art, see his 1955 study *Manet*, trans. Austryn Wainhouse and James Emmons (New York: Rizzoli, 1983), 50–51; his comments on Miró, made in 1930, are cited in Hal Foster et al., *Art Since 1900: Modernism, Antimodernism, Postmodernism* (New York: Thames & Hudson, 2004), 246–47.
22. A full consideration of Soviet iconoclasm would include an examination of the strange relationship between Socialist Realist painting and photography under Stalin's rule. As Leah Dickerman has illustrated, official painting under Stalin was on the one hand based on historical photographs and on the other committed to an eradication of the same. To wit, Soviet cultural authorities commissioned monumental oil paintings based on well-known photographic sources, only to then suppress these original photographs as their (carefully edited) painted surrogates were widely displayed and reproduced. As Dickerman brilliantly argues, this project aimed to combine photography's "reality effect" with the monumental power of painting while controlling (and ideally canceling) the dangerous contingencies of photography itself. It sought, Dickerman writes, "to make history in a sense ahistorical" and thus unquestionable. See Leah Dickerman, "Camera Obscura: Socialist Realism in the Shadow of Photography," *October* 93 (Summer 2000): 139–53.
23. Theodor Adorno, "Cultural Criticism and Society" (1949), reprinted in *Prisms*, trans. Samuel and Shierry Weber (Cambridge, MA: MIT Press, 1981), 34.
24. Ibid., 32.
25. Hal Foster, *The Return of the Real* (Cambridge, MA: MIT Press, 1996), 29.
26. Allan Kaprow, "The Legacy of Jackson Pollock" (1958), reprinted in *Essays on the Blurring of Art and Life*, ed. Jeff Kelley (Berkeley: University of California Press, 1993), 2.
27. Ibid., 7.
28. Meyer Schapiro, "Recent Abstract Painting" (1957), reprinted in *Modern Art: 19th and 20th Centuries* (New York: George Braziller, 1979), 224.
29. Clement Greenberg, "Modernist Painting" (1960), reprinted in *Clement Greenberg: The Collected Essays and Criticism*, ed. John O'Brian, vol. 4, *Modernism with a Vengeance, 1957–1969* (Chicago: University of Chicago Press, 1993), 86.
30. Ibid.
31. Carl Andre, "Preface to Stripe Painting" (1959), reprinted in Harrison and Wood, *Art in Theory*, 820.
32. Stella famously used the phrase "what you see is what you see" to discuss his canvases in a 1964 interview with Bruce Glaser and Donald Judd, subsequently published in *Art News* in 1966. See Bruce Glaser, "Questions to Stella and Judd," reprinted in *Minimal Art: A Critical Anthology*, ed. Gregory Battcock (Berkeley: University of California Press, 1995), 158. As if to call our attention to the stripe paintings' representational blankness, Stella furthermore assigned them emphatically charged or referentially specific titles—such as *Die Fahne hoch*, a German phrase meaning "raise the flag high" and carrying unmistakable militaristic connotations—bearing no connection whatsoever to the material substance of the works.
33. Ibid., 57.
34. Yve-Alain Bois, "Painting: The Task of Mourning" (1986), reprinted in *Painting as Model* (Cambridge, MA: MIT Press, 1990), 230.
35. Richter's comments are from a 1977 letter to the critic and historian Benjamin H. D. Buchloh reprinted in *Gerhard Richter: The Daily Practice of Painting—Writings and Interviews, 1962–1993*, ed. Hans Ulrich Obrist, trans. David Britt (Cambridge, MA: MIT Press; London: Anthony d'Offay Gallery, 1995), 84–85.
36. For a dense but insightful consideration of the "coupling" that *Erased de Kooning Drawing* enacts, see John Paul Ricco, "Name No One Man," *Parallax* 11, no. 2 (April–June 2005): 93–103.
37. As William Rubin wrote in 1961 on the codification of gestural abstraction within fifties painting, "the dominant avant-garde mode of painting in the late fifties (substantially the same throughout the world though known by different and confusing names, e.g., Abstract Expressionism, Tachism, etc.) seems to have allowed for less variety, less inventiveness, and less individual profile than any other major style in the history of modern art." See William Rubin, "The International Style: Notes on the Pittsburgh Triennial," *Art International* 5, no. 9 (November 20, 1961): 26–34.

There was a fine line between just painting a wall and Painting. Only by pointing out the differences, do I make a change from one to another.

—John Baldessari

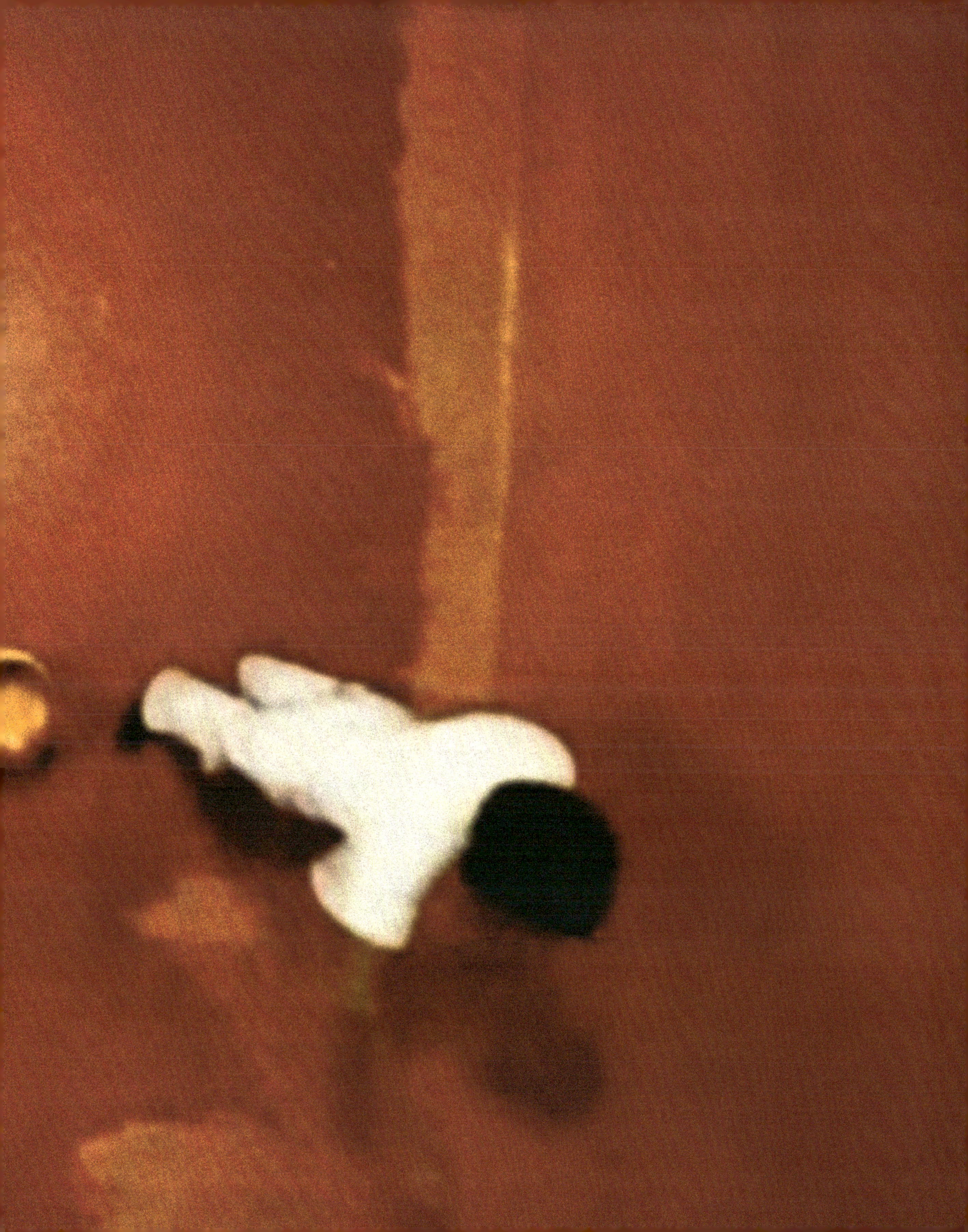

List of Works in the Exhibition

Arman
Ocher (Ochre), 1967
paint tubes and paint in synthetic resin
47¼ x 47¼ in. (120 x 120 cm)
Hirshhorn Museum and Sculpture Garden,
Smithsonian Institution, Washington, DC,
The Joseph H. Hirshhorn Bequest, 1981

John Baldessari
Composing on a Canvas, 1967–68
acrylic on canvas
114 x 96 in. (289.6 x 243.8 cm)
Museum of Contemporary Art San Diego,
Gift of the artist

John Baldessari
Six Colorful Inside Jobs, 1977
video projection, color, silent; 35 min.
dimensions variable
Courtesy of the artist and Electronic Arts Intermix,
New York

Iain Baxter
(since 2005 the artist has gone by the name
IAIN BAXTER&)
Standards: 24, 1962
acrylic on canvas
68½ x 61 in. (174 x 154.9 cm)
Collection of the artist and Corkin Gallery, Toronto.
Courtesy of Corkin Gallery

Iain Baxter
(since 2005 the artist has gone by the name
IAIN BAXTER&)
Still Life with 6 Colours, 1965
vacuum-formed plastic
32 x 37½ in. (81.3 x 95.3 cm)
Collection of the artist and Corkin Gallery, Toronto.
Courtesy of Corkin Gallery

Lynda Benglis
Baby Planet, ca. 1969
poured pigmented latex paint
106 x 24 x 1½ in. (269.2 x 61 x 3.8 cm)
Courtesy of the artist and Cheim & Read,
New York

Lynda Benglis
Chi, 1973
aluminum screen, bunting, plaster, silver paint,
enamel, and sparkles
27 x 13⅜ x 9 in. (68.6 x 34 x 22.9 cm)
Collection of James and Christina Lockwood

Mel Bochner
Theory of Painting, 1969–70
newspaper, spray paint, and vinyl text
dimensions variable
The Museum of Modern Art, New York,
Committee on Painting and Sculpture Funds, 1997

Marcel Broodthaers
Paintings/Peintures (serie l'art et les mots), 1973
oil on canvas
9 parts, 33½ x 39⅜ in. (85.1 x 99.9 cm) each
Tate: Purchased 1983

Marcel Broodthaers
Tableau Bateau, 1973
80-slide projection
dimensions variable
Collection of Pamela and Richard Kramlich

Günter Brus
Selbstbemalung, 1964
nine gelatin silver prints
9½ x 7 in. (24 x 8 cm) each
Archivio Conz, Verona

Daniel Buren
Exposition d'une Exposition, 1972
printed wallpaper
dimensions variable
Courtesy of the artist and Bortolami Gallery,
New York

Daniel Buren
One Piece in Four Parts on 2 Parallel Walls,
March 1973, March 1976
printed canvas
dimensions variable
Courtesy of the artist and Bortolami Gallery,
New York

Alberto Burri
Sacco, 1955
burlap, cardboard, muslin, and paint
35½ x 28¼ in. (90.1 x 71.8 cm)
Seattle Art Museum, Gift of Hester Diamond
in memory of Alberto Burri, 95.134

Ivan Cardoso
H.O., 1979
film transferred to DVD, color, sound; 13 min.
Courtesy of Ivan Cardoso

Karen Carson
Untitled, 1971
textile, cotton duck, and industrial zippers
95 x 83 in. (241.3 x 210.8 cm)
Los Angeles County Museum of Art, Purchased
with funds provided by the Pasadena Art Alliance
and Rosamund Felsen Gallery

Jim Dine
Vise, 1962
oil on canvas with wooden table and metal vise
overall: 80 x 36 x 30 in. (203.2 x 91.4 x 76.2 cm);
framed canvas: 51⅜ x 41⁵⁄₁₆ in. (130.8 x 104.7 cm)
Seattle Art Museum, Promised gift of the artist,
in honor of the 75th Anniversary of the Seattle
Art Museum, T2006.91

Dan Flavin
Untitled (to Bob and Pat Rohm), 1969
red, green, and yellow fluorescent lights
96 x 96 x 9 in. (243.8 x 243.8 x 22.9 cm)
Courtesy of Pace Wildenstein, New York

Lucio Fontana
Concetto spaziale (C.49B2), 1949
white paper mounted on canvas
39½ x 39½ in. (100.3 x 100.3 cm)
Fondazione Lucio Fontana, Milan

Lucio Fontana
Concetto spaziale, 1952
paint, powdered pigment, paper, linen, and
cardboard attached to a wooden stretcher
31½ x 31½ in. (80 x 80 cm)
The Rachofsky Collection

Lucio Fontana
Concetto spaziale, 1958
graffiti, cuts, and dye on paper mounted to canvas
39½ x 39½ in. (100.3 x 100.3 cm)
Fondazione Lucio Fontana, Milan

Sam Gilliam
Bow Form Construction, 1968
acrylic on canvas with aluminum powder
and enamel
118 x 330 in. (299.7 x 838.2 cm)
Whitney Museum of American Art, New York,
Purchase with funds from the Friends of the
Whitney Museum of American Art and the
Howard W. Lipman Foundation, and gift of the
Ford Foundation Purchase Program and an
anonymous donor, by exchange, 2001.343

Joe Goode
Torn Cloud Painting, 1975
oil on canvas
60 x 60 in. (152.4 x 152.4 cm)
Portland Art Museum Purchase: Funds provided
by the Contemporary Art Council

Richard Jackson
SAM, 1972–2009
canvas, wood, and acrylic paint
dimensions variable
Courtesy of the artist and Hauser & Wirth, Zurich
and London

Neil Jenney
Paint and Painted, 1969
acrylic on canvas
59 x 78 in. (149.9 x 198.1 cm)
Seattle Art Museum, Promised gift of the Virginia
and Bagley Wright Collection, in honor of the
75th Anniversary of the Seattle Art Museum,
T98.84.26

Jasper Johns
Canvas, 1956
encaustic and collage on wood and canvas
30 x 25 in. (76.2 x 63.5 cm)
Collection of the artist

Jasper Johns
Target, 1958
oil and collage on canvas
36 x 36 in. (91.4 x 91.4 cm)
Collection of the artist

Jasper Johns
White Numbers, 1958
encaustic on canvas
28 x 22 in. (71.1 x 55.9 cm)
Collection of Charles Simonyi, Seattle

Jasper Johns
Thermometer, 1959
oil on canvas with thermometer
51¾ x 38½ in. (131.5 x 97.8 cm)
Seattle Art Museum, Partial and promised gift
of Bagley and Virginia Wright, in honor of
the museum's 50th year, 91.97

Jasper Johns
Thermometer, 1960
charcoal and pastel on paper
22 x 15½ in. (55.9 x 39.4 cm)
Seattle Art Museum, Promised gift of the Virginia
and Bagley Wright Collection, in honor of the
75th Anniversary of the Seattle Art Museum,
T2006.65.70

Jasper Johns
Untitled (Cut, Tear, Scrape, Erase), 1964
graphite pencil on paper
11⅜ x 11⅜ in. (28.9 x 28.9 cm)
Collection of the artist

Asger Jorn
Détournement de paysage, 1959
oil on canvas
19½ x 25½ in. (49.5 x 64.8 cm)
Musée d'Art Moderne et Contemporain
de Strasbourg

William Klein
Boxer Painter, End, Tokyo, 1961
gelatin silver print
12 x 16 in. (30.5 x 40.6 cm)
© William Klein/Courtesy Howard Greenberg
Gallery, New York

Yves Klein
*Réalisation de peintures de feu au Centre d'essais
du Gaz de France, La Plaine Saint-Denis, France,
February 1961*, 1961
gelatin silver print
8 x 10 in. (20.3 x 25.4 cm)
Yves Klein Archives, Paris

Joseph Kosuth
'Title (Art As Idea As Idea)' ['PAINT-LESS'], 1968
photographic reproduction mounted to
museum board
46⅞ x 46⅞ in. (119.1 x 119.1 cm)
Collection of Diane L. Ackerman and
Kelly L. Ackerman

Edward Krasiński
Intervention, 1975/1981
acrylic paint, collage, and blue tape
28¼ x 28 in. (71.8 x 71.1 cm)
Courtesy of Anton Kern Gallery, New York

Yayoi Kusama
Self-Obliteration, 1967
16mm film transferred to DVD, color, sound; 23 min.
Courtesy of the artist, Victoria Miro Gallery,
Gagosian Gallery, Ota Fine Arts

KwieKulik (Przemyslaw Kwiek and Zofia Kulik)
Variants of Red and *The Path of Edward Gierek*,
1971
slide show transferred to DVD; 11:33 min.
dimensions variable
KwieKulik Collection

Roy Lichtenstein
Red Painting (Brushstroke), 1965
oil and magna on canvas
60 x 60 in. (152.4 x 152.4 cm)
Collection of Charles Simonyi, Seattle

Roy Lichtenstein
Stretcher Frame—Two Panels, 1968
oil and magna on canvas
48 x 104 in. (121.9 x 264.2 cm)
Collection of Charles Simonyi, Seattle

Alvin Loving
Untitled, ca. 1970s
torn canvas
80 x 60 in. (203.2 x 152.4 cm)
Guild Hall Museum, East Hampton, New York,
Gift of Maddy and Larry Mohr, in memory of
Robert M. (Mac) Doty

Lee Lozano
No title (idea that cannot be drawn, Nov. 16, 1968),
1968
ink and graphite on paper
11 x 9 in. (27.9 x 22.9 cm)
Private collection, New York. Courtesy of
Hauser & Wirth, Zurich and London

Lee Lozano
No title, 1970
gesso with graphite and perforations on canvas
42 x 62 in. (106.7 x 157.5 cm)
The Estate of Lee Lozano. Courtesy of
Hauser & Wirth, Zurich and London

George Maciunas
photodocumentation of Shigeko Kubota's
performance *Vagina Painting*, 1965
two gelatin silver prints
13¾ x 14³⁄₁₆ in. (35 x 36 cm) each
The Gilbert and Lila Silverman Fluxus
Collection, Detroit

Paul McCarthy
Face Painting—Floor, White Line, 1972
16mm film transferred to DVD, black and white,
sound; 2:02 min.
Courtesy of the artist and Hauser & Wirth,
Zurich and London

Hirata Minoru
Ushio Shinohara's *Cheerful Fourth Dimension,
Tokyo, 1963*, 1963
gelatin silver print
8¼ x 11¾ in. (21 x 29.8 cm)
Courtesy of Minoru Hirata

Otto Muehl
Untitled, 1963
sand, plaster, stockings, and emulsion on sackcloth
30⅜ x 28½ x 4 in. (77.2 x 72.4 x 10.2 cm)
Walker Art Center, Minneapolis, T. B. Walker
Acquisition Fund, 1999

Ugo Mulas
Lucio Fontana, 1964
four gelatin silver prints
10 x 8 in. (25.4 x 20.3 cm) each
Archivio Ugo Mulas, Milan

Saburō Murakami
At One Moment Opening Six Holes, 1955
gelatin silver print
8 x 10 in. (20.3 x 25.4 cm)
Ashiya City Museum of Art & History

Bruce Nauman
Art Make-Up, 1967–68
four 16mm films on video projected onto four
walls; 40 min. total:
No. 1, White, 1967 (16mm film on video, color
sound; 10 min.)
No. 2, Pink, 1967–68 (16mm film on video, color
sound; 10 min.)
No. 3, Green, 1967–68 (16mm film on video, color
sound; 10 min.)
No. 4, Black, 1967–68 (16mm film on video, color
sound; 10 min.)
Electronic Arts Intermix, New York

N.E. Thing Co.
*Paint into Earth, Simon Fraser University,
Vancouver, BC*, 1966–68
gelatin silver print, chromogenic print, lithograph
60¼ x 40⅜ x ¹¹⁄₁₆ in. (153 x 102.5 x 2 cm) (framed)
Vancouver Art Gallery, Vancouver Art Gallery
Acquisition Fund

Hélio Oiticica
P02 Parangolé bandeira 01, 1964
paint, canvas, tulle, plastic, and wooden pole
16⅛ x 31⅞ x 1 in. (41 x 81 x 2.5 cm)
Cesar and Claudio Oiticica Collection

Hélio Oiticica
*B22 Bólide vidro 10 "Homenagem a Malevitch
Gemini" 01*, 1965
glass, painted plastic lids, and paint/pigment
in water
8 x 3¼ x 3⅝ in. (20.3 x 8.3 x 9.2 cm)
Cesar and Claudio Oiticica Collection

Hélio Oiticica
*B38 Bólide Lata 01—Appropriação 02
"Consumitivo,"* 1966
photographic facsimile
4 x 3 in. (10.2 x 7.6 cm)
Cesar and Claudio Oiticica Collection

Yoko Ono
Painting to Be Stepped On, 1960/2009
canvas
24 x 36 in. (61 x 91.4 cm)
Collection of the artist

Yoko Ono
Painting to Hammer a Nail, 1961/2009
painted wood panel with 42-inch chain attached
with an eye screw and a container with 1½- to
2-inch small finishing nails
12 x 9 x 1½ in. (30.5 x 22.9 x 3.8 cm)
Collection of the artist

Nam June Paik
Zen for Head, 1962
film transferred to video, black and white, sound;
40 sec.
Courtesy of the Nam June Paik Art Center and
Hessischer Rundfunk

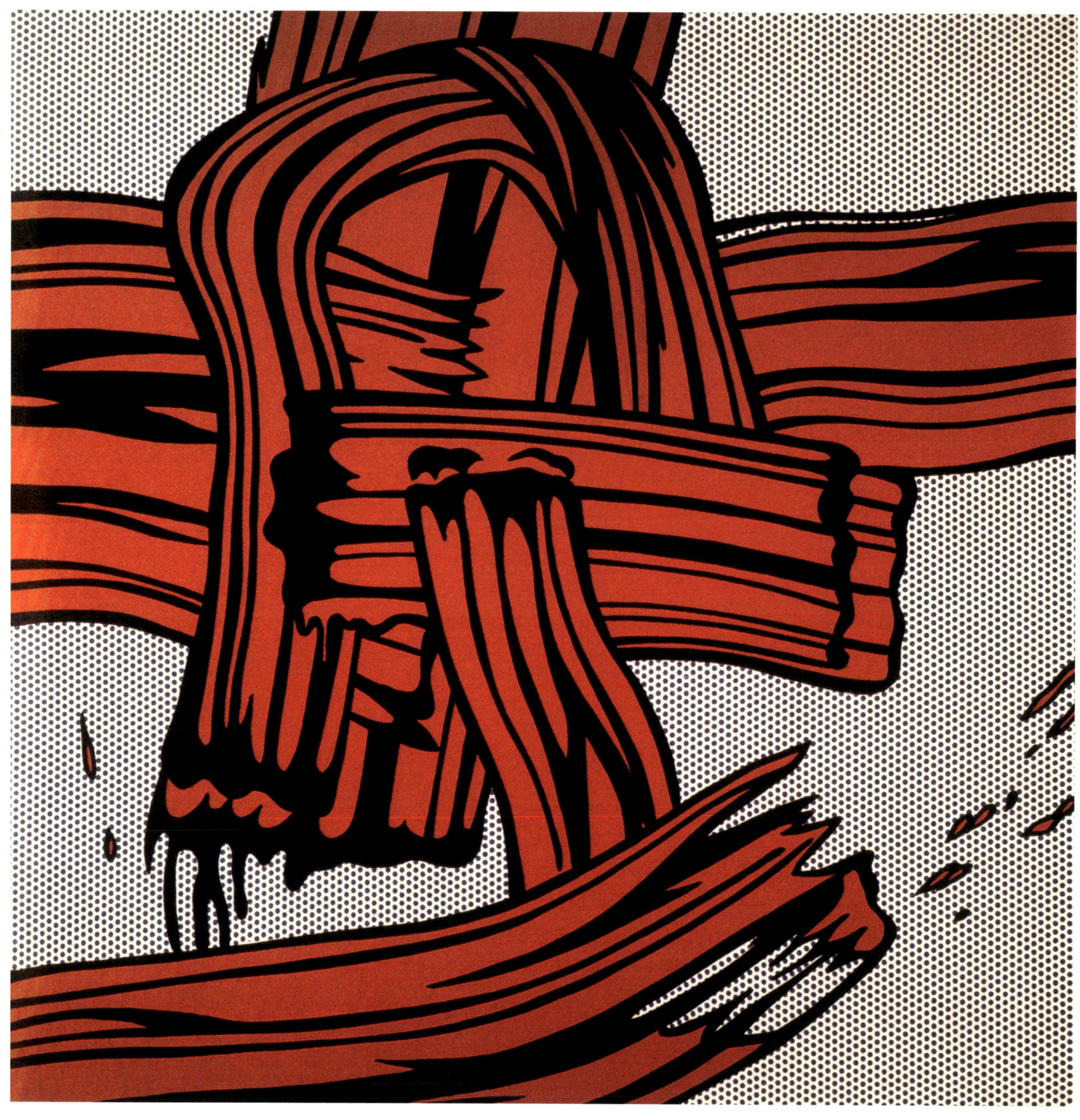

Giulio Paolini
Senza titolo, 1962
canvas and wood
19½ x 23½ in. (49.5 x 59.7 cm)
Titze Collection, Switzerland

Lygia Pape
Divisor, 1968–91
video projection, color, sound; 3 min.
Projeto Lygia Pape Collection

Richard Pettibone
Untitled (Train ran over tube of paint, October 25, 1963), 1964
acrylic, pencil, type, rubber stamp, and paint tube on canvas
diptych: 4½ x 11⅝ in. (11.4 x 29.5 cm) overall
Private collection, USA

Richard Pettibone
Andy Warhol, "Flowers," 1964 (rear view), 1974
oil on canvas
4¼ x 4¼ in. (10.8 x 10.8 cm)
Private collection, USA

Howardena Pindell
Untitled, 1968–70
canvas, enamel, grommets, and foam
144 x 144 in. (365.8 x 365.8 cm)
Mott-Warsh Collection, Flint, Michigan.
Courtesy of Sragow Gallery, New York

Howardena Pindell
Untitled (Study for Grommet Piece), 1970
oil stick, pencil, and ink with mixed media and collage on graph paper
17 x 22 in. (43.2 x 55.9 cm)
Courtesy of Sragow Gallery, New York

Robert Rauschenberg
Erased de Kooning Drawing, 1953
traces of ink and crayon on paper with mat and label on gold-leaf frame
25¼ x 21¾ x ½ in. (64.1 x 55.2 x 1.3 cm)
San Francisco Museum of Modern Art, Purchased through a gift of Phyllis Wattis

Robert Rauschenberg
Untitled, ca. 1954
oil, paper, fabric, newspaper, cardboard, wood, paint tube, and glass on wood
10 x 7¾ in. (25.4 x 19.7 cm)
Collection of Barney A. Ebsworth

Robert Rauschenberg
Octave, 1960
oil on canvas with assemblage (oil, paper, fabric)
77½ x 42¼ in. (196.9 x 107.3 cm)
Seattle Art Museum, Promised gift of the Virginia and Bagley Wright Collection, in honor of the 75th Anniversary of the Seattle Art Museum, T2006.65.123

Gerhard Richter
Farbtafel, 1966–78
lacquer on canvas
27½ x 25⅝ in. (69.9 x 65.1 cm)
The Museum of Contemporary Art, Los Angeles, Partial and promised gift of Blake Byrne

Edward Ruscha
Damage, 1964
oil on canvas
72 x 67 x 2 in. (182.9 x 170.2 x 5.1 cm)
Jeffrey and Susan Brotman Collection

Niki de Saint Phalle
Hors-d'oeuvre (Portrait of My Lover/Portrait of Myself), 1960
paint, plaster, and various objects (dartboard, darts, man's white shirt, buttons, metal objects) on plywood
32 x 24⅜ in. (81.3 x 61.9 cm)
Collection Niki Charitable Art Foundation, California, USA

Niki de Saint Phalle
Le moindre effort, June 26, 1961
35mm film transferred to video, black and white, sound, in French; 4 min.
Collection Niki Charitable Art Foundation, California, USA

Niki de Saint Phalle
[Niki de Saint Phalle Shooting a Tir], 1962
film transferred to video, color, sound, in English; 4:40 min.
Collection Niki Charitable Art Foundation, California, USA

Niki de Saint Phalle
Tir neuf trous, 1964
paint, plaster, and plastic on plywood
27⅞ x 20¾ in. (70.8 x 52.7 cm)
Private collection

Shōzō Shimamoto
Untitled, 1950
oil on newspaper intentionally pierced by the artist
18 x 15 in. (45.7 x 38.1 cm)
The Rachofsky Collection

Shōzō Shimamoto
Work (Holes), ca. 1950
paint and pencil on newspaper
76¾ x 51¾ in. (194.9 x 131.4 cm)
Museum of Contemporary Art, Tokyo

Shōzō Shimamoto
Exploding Red, 1961
color photograph
14⅟₁₆ x 20⅞ in. (35.7 x 53 cm)
Courtesy of Shōzō Shimamoto

Harry Shunk
Robert Rauschenberg firing at Tirs, sandpit near Stockholm, in conjunction with the exhibition "Rörelse I Konsten," Moderna Museet, Stockholm, May 23, 1961, 1961
gelatin silver print
8 x 10 in. (20.3 x 25.4 cm)
Collection Niki Charitable Art Foundation, California, USA

Harry Shunk
Visitors at the exhibition "Rörelse I Konsten" throw darts at Niki de Saint Phalle's dartboard works, Moderna Museet, Stockholm, May 27, 1961, 1961
gelatin silver print
10 x 8 in. (25.4 x 20.3 cm)
Collection Niki Charitable Art Foundation, California, USA

Daniel Spoerri
31 Variations on a Meal: Eaten by Bruce Conner, 1964
bread, dishes, flatware, ashtray, wrappers, cloth napkins, cigarette butts, match, plastic plant, and wood
21¼ x 25³⁄₁₆ x 11 in. (54 x 64 x 27.9 cm)
Walker Art Center, Minneapolis, T. B. Walker Acquisition Fund, 2001

Richard Tuttle
Untitled, 1967
dyed canvas
35⅟₁₆ x diag. 86½ in. (89 x 219.7 cm)
Seattle Art Museum, Gift of Sidney and Anne Gerber, 81.87

Günther Uecker
Grosse Wolke, 1965
paint and nails on canvas and particle board
68⅝ x 68¾ x 2⅞ in. (174.3 x 174.6 x 7.3 cm)
The Museum of Contemporary Art, Los Angeles, Gift of Lannan Foundation

Andy Warhol
Oxidation Painting, 1978
mixed media on copper metallic paint on canvas
twelve panels, each: 16 x 12 in. (40.6 x 30.5 cm); overall: 64 x 36 in. (162.5 x 91.4 cm)
Collection of Merrill Wright

Lawrence Weiner
An Amount of Paint Poured Directly Upon the Floor and Allowed to Dry [CAT #036], 1968
language and the materials referred to
dimensions variable
Public Freehold. Courtesy of the artist and Regen Projects, Los Angeles

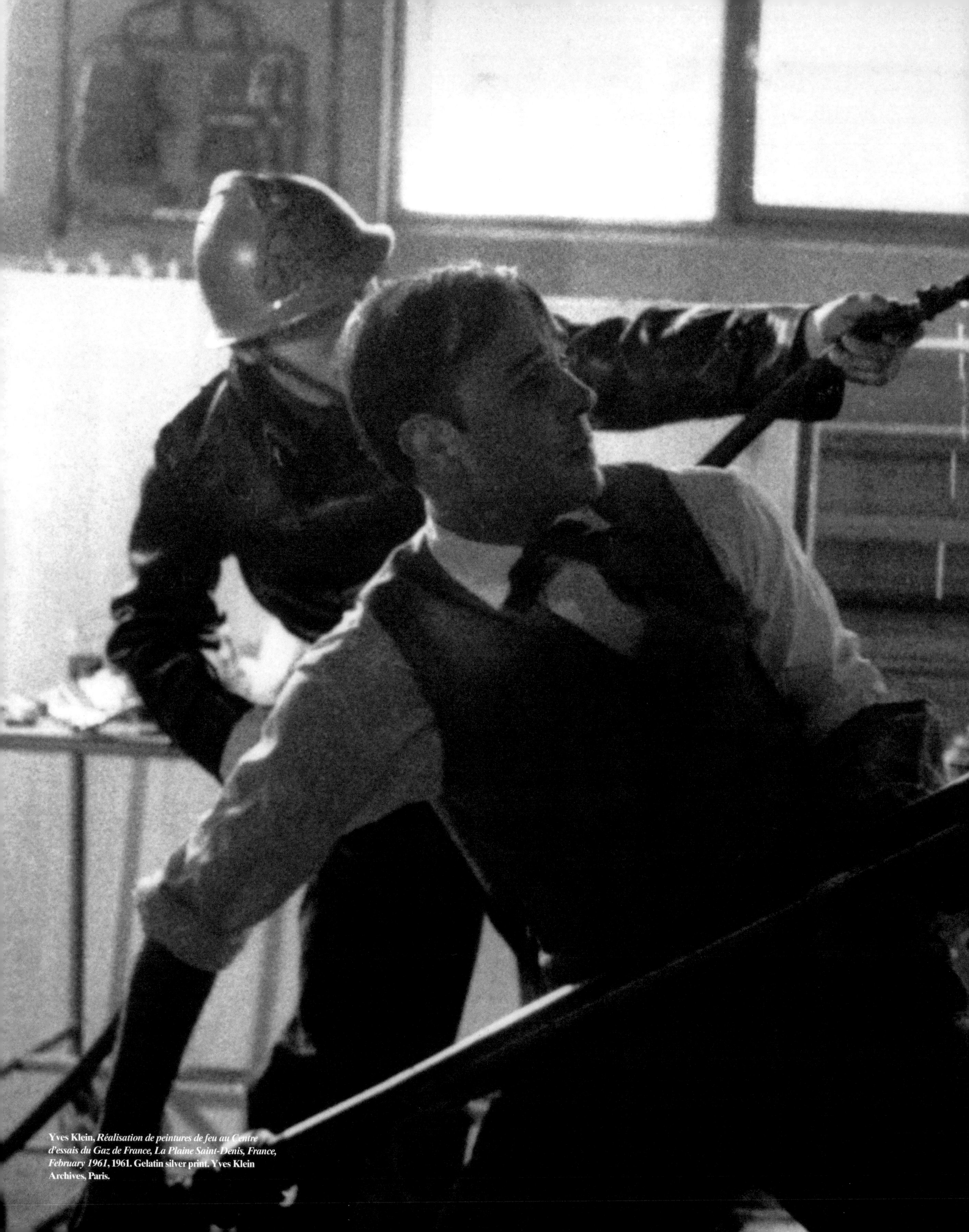

Yves Klein, *Réalisation de peintures de feu au Centre d'essais du Gaz de France, La Plaine Saint-Denis, France, February 1961*, 1961. Gelatin silver print. Yves Klein Archives, Paris.

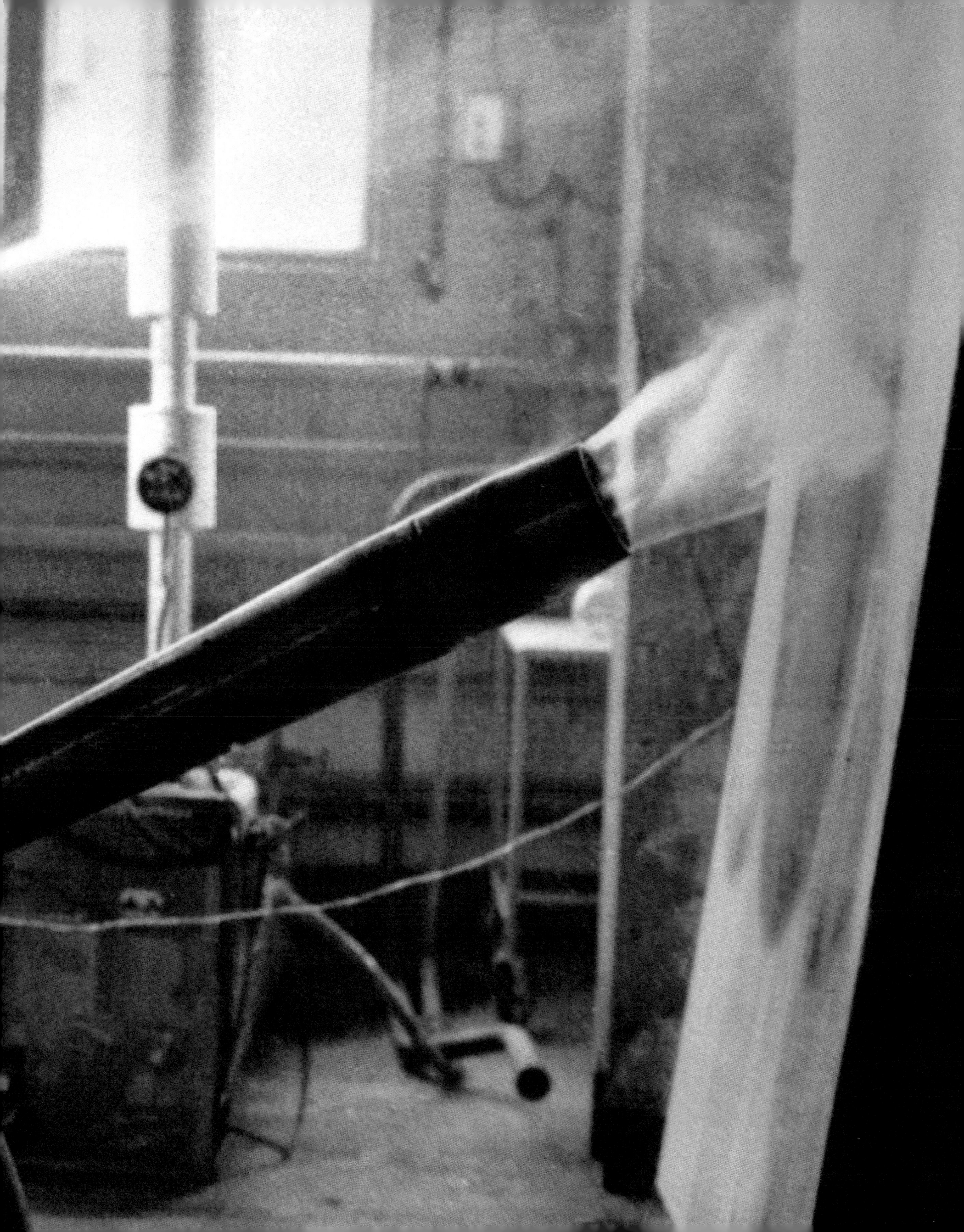

Selected Bibliography

Alberro, Alexander, et al. *Lawrence Weiner.* London: Phaidon, 1998.

Armstrong, Philip, Laura Lisbon, and Stephen Melville, eds. *As Painting: Division and Displacement.* Columbus, OH: Wexner Center for the Arts, 2001.

Auping, Michael. *Declaring Space: Mark Rothko, Barnett Newman, Lucio Fontana, Yves Klein.* Fort Worth, TX: Modern Art Museum of Fort Worth, 2007.

Bastian, Heiner, ed. *Andy Warhol: Retrospective.* London: Tate Publications, 2001.

Basualdo, Carlos, and Ellen Tepfer. *Painting Zero Degree.* New York: Independent Curators International, 2000.

Billeter, Erika. *Lucio Fontana, 1899–1968: A Retrospective.* New York: Solomon R. Guggenheim Foundation, 1977.

Binstock, Jonathan P. *Sam Gilliam: A Retrospective.* Berkeley: University of California Press, 2005.

Bois, Yve-Alain. *Painting as Model.* Cambridge, MA: MIT Press, 1991.

Bonito Oliva, Achille. "Avant-garde/Trans-avant-garde." In *Transavantgarde International,* 145–51. English translation by Dwight Gast and Gwen Jones. Milan: G. Politi, 1982.

———. *The Italian Transavantgarde.* Milan: G. Politi, 1980.

———. *Transavanguardia Italiana: Sandro Chia, Francesco Clemente, Enzo Cucchi, Nicola De Maria, Mimmo Paladino.* Buenos Aires: Proa Fundación, 2003.

Braga, Paula. *Fios Soltos: A arte de Hélio Oiticica.* São Paulo: Perspectiva, 2008.

Breitwieser, Sabine, ed. *Edward Krasiński: Les mises en scène.* Vienna: Generali Foundation, 2006.

Brett, Guy, and Luciano Figueiredo, eds. *Oiticica in London.* London: Tate Publishing, 2007.

Brett, Guy, et al. *Hélio Oiticica.* Rio de Janeiro: Centro de Arte Hélio Oiticica, 1997.

Broodthaers, Marcel, Manuel J. Borja-Villel, Michael Compton, and Maria Gilissen. *Marcel Broodthaers: Cinéma.* Barcelona: Fundació Antoni Tàpies, 1997.

Bruggen, Coosje van. *John Baldessari.* New York: Rizzoli, 1990.

Buchloh, Benjamin H. D. "Allegorical Procedures: Appropriation and Montage in Contemporary Art." *Art Forum* (September 1982): 43–56.

———. "Conceptual Art, 1962–1969: From the Aesthetic of Administration to the Critique of Institutions." *October* 55 (Winter 1990): 105–43.

Buren, Daniel. *Daniel Buren: Mot à mot.* Paris: Centre Pompidou, Éditions Xavier Barral, Éditions de La Martinière, 2002.

Burton, Johanna. *Mel Bochner: Language, 1966–2006.* Chicago: Art Institute of Chicago, 2007.

Butler, Cornelia, ed. *WACK! Art and the Feminist Revolution.* Los Angeles: Museum of Contemporary Art, 2007.

Carvajal, Rina, and Alma Ruiz. *The Experimental Exercise of Freedom: Lygia Clark, Gego, Mathias Goeritz, Hélio Oiticica, Mira Schendel.* Los Angeles: Museum of Contemporary Art, 1999.

Celant, Germano, ed. *The Italian Metamorphosis, 1943–1968.* New York: Guggenheim Museum; Rome: Progetti Museali Editore, 1994.

Christov-Bakargiev, Carolyn, ed. *Arte Povera.* London: Phaidon, 1999.

Clearwater, Bonnie. *Mythic Proportions: Painting in the 1980s.* North Miami: Museum of Contemporary Art, 2001.

Compton, Michael. *Marcel Broodthaers.* London: Tate Gallery, 1980.

Corral, María de, and John R. Lane, eds. *Fast Forward: Contemporary Collections for the Dallas Museum of Art.* Dallas: Dallas Museum of Art, 2007.

Crimp, Douglas. "The End of Painting." *October* 16 (Spring 1981): 69–86.

———. "On the Museum's Ruins." *October* 13 (Summer 1980): 41–57.

Crispolti, Enrico, ed. *Fontana.* Milan: Charta, 1999.

Davies, Hugh M., and Andrea Hales, eds. *John Baldessari: National City.* San Diego: Museum of Contemporary Art, 1996.

Duarte, Paulo Sergio. *Campo Ampliado.* São Paulo: Instituto de Arte Contemporânea, 2006.

Field, Richard S. *Mel Bochner: Thought Made Visible, 1966–1973.* New Haven: Yale University Art Gallery, 1995.

Gilman, Claire. "Asger Jorn's Avant-Garde Archives." *October* 79 (Winter 1997): 32–48.

Gilman, Claire, ed. "Postwar Italian Art: A Special Issue." *October* 124 (Spring 2008): 3–189.

Goldstein, Ann, and Anne Rorimer. *Reconsidering the Object of Art: 1965–1975.* Los Angeles: Museum of Contemporary Art, 1995.

Goldwater, Marge, Michael Compton, Douglas Crimp, Bruce Jenkins, and Martin Mosebach. *Marcel Broodthaers.* Minneapolis: Walker Art Center; New York: Rizzoli, 1989.

Govan, Michael, and Tiffany Bell. *Dan Flavin: A Retrospective.* New York: Dia Art Foundation, 2004.

———. *Dan Flavin: The Complete Lights, 1961–1996.* New York: Dia Art Foundation in association with Yale University Press, 2004.

Greene, Alison de Lima, and Pierre Restany. *Arman, 1955–1991: A Retrospective.* Houston: Museum of Fine Arts, 1991.

Gumpert, Lynn, Ned Rifkin, and Marcia Tucker. *Early Work: Lynda Benglis, Joan Brown, Luis Jimenez, Gary Stephan, Lawrence Weiner.* New York: New Museum, 1982.

Jackson, Richard, Harald Szeemann, Hans Ulrich Obrist, Walter Hopps, and Alberta Mayo. *Richard Jackson: Deer Beer.* Cologne: Oktagon; Zurich: Galerie Hauser & Wirth, 1998.

Joachimides, Christos M., Norman Rosenthal, and Nicholas Serota, eds. *A New Spirit in Painting.* London: Royal Academy of Arts, 1981.

Krane, Susan. *Lynda Benglis: Dual Natures.* Atlanta: High Museum of Art, 1990.

Krasiński, Edward, and Lena Kiessler. *Edward Krasiński.* Translated by Denis Bostock. Warsaw: Foksal Gallery Foundation, 2001.

Ledezma, Juan. *The Sites of Latin American Abstraction.* Miami: Cisneros Fontanals Art Foundation, 2006.

Lozano, Lee, and Adam Szymczyk. *Lee Lozano: Win First Dont Last, Win Last Dont Care.* Basel: Schwabe, 2006.

Manzoni, Piero. *Piero Manzoni: Paintings, Reliefs and Objects.* London: Tate Gallery Publications, 1974. Writings by Manzoni translated by Caroline Tisdall and Angelo Bozzola.

Marcadé, Bernard. "Daniel Buren." In *Luxe, calme et volupté: Aspects of French Art, 1966–1986: Daniel Buren, Robert Combas, Robert Filliou, Gérard Garouste, Pierre Klossowski, Jean LeGac, Annette Messager, Martial Raysse,* 16–17. Vancouver, BC: Vancouver Art Gallery, 1986.

Marshall, Richard. "New Image Painting." In *New Image Painting,* 7–13. New York: Whitney Museum of American Art, 1978.

McShine, Kynaston, ed. *Andy Warhol: A Retrospective.* New York: Museum of Modern Art, 1989.

Merewether, Charles, and Rika Iezumi Hiro, eds. *Art, Anti-Art, Non-Art: Experimentations in the Public Sphere in Postwar Japan, 1950–1970.* Los Angeles: Getty Research Institute, 2007.

Meyer, Ursula. *Conceptual Art.* New York: E. P. Dutton, 1972.

Mosset, Olivier. *Olivier Mosset.* Baden: L. Müller, 1990.

Munroe, Alexandra. *Japanese Art after 1945: Scream Against the Sky.* New York: Harry N. Abrams, 1994.

Nordland, Gerald. *Alberto Burri: A Retrospective View, 1948–1977.* Los Angeles: Frederick S. Wight Art Gallery, University of California, 1977.

Oiticica, Hélio, and Neville D'Almeida. *Cosmococa: Programa in Process.* Rio de Janeiro: Projeto Hélio Oiticica; Buenos Aires: MALBA Colección Costantini; Brumadinho, Brazil: Centro de Arte Contemporânea Inhotim, 2005.

Osaki, Shinichiro, ed. *Traces: Body and Idea in Contemporary Art.* Kyoto: National Museum of Modern Art, 2004.

Osbourne, Peter, ed. *Conceptual Art.* London and New York: Phaidon, 2002.

Pincus-Witten, Robert. *Circa 70: Lynda Benglis Louise Bourgeois.* New York: Chiem & Read, 2007.

Ramírez, Mari Carmen. *Hélio Oiticica: The Body of Color.* Houston: Museum of Fine Arts, 2007.

Ramírez, Mari Carmen, and Héctor Olea. *Inverted Utopias: Avant-Garde Art in Latin America.* New Haven and London: Yale University Press, 2004.

Rothfuss, Joan, and Elizabeth Carpenter, eds. *Bits & Pieces Put Together to Present a Semblance of a Whole: Walker Art Center Collections.* Minneapolis: Walker Art Center, 2005.

Saint Phalle, Niki de. *Niki de Saint Phalle: Monographie—Malerei, Tirs, Assemblages, Reliefs, 1949–2000/Monograph: Paintings, Tirs, Assemblages, Reliefs, 1949–2000/Monographie: Peintures, Tirs, Assemblages, Reliefs, 1949–2000.* Lausanne: Acatos, 2001.

Schimmel, Paul, et al. *Out of Actions: Between Performance and the Object, 1949–1979.* Los Angeles: Museum of Contemporary Art, 1998.

———. *Robert Rauschenberg: Combines.* Los Angeles: Museum of Contemporary Art, 2005.

Shinohara, Ushio. *The Avant-Garde Road.* Translated by Lyn Katsumoto. Tokyo: Bijutsu Shuppansha, 1968.

Siegel, Katy, David Reed, and Anna Chave. *High Times, Hard Times: New York Painting, 1967–1975.* New York: Independent Curators International and D.A.P./Distributed Art Publishers, 2006.

Venancio Filho, Paulo, and Annika Gunnarsson. *Time & Place: Rio de Janeiro, 1956–1964.* Stockholm: Moderna Museet, 2008.

Weiss, Jeffrey, et al. *Jasper Johns: An Allegory of Painting, 1955–1965.* Washington, DC: National Gallery of Art, 2007.

Zweifel, Stefan, Juri Steiner, and Heinz Stahlhut. *"In Girum Imus Nocte et Consumimur Igni"—The Situationist International (1957–1972).* Zurich: JRP/Ringier, 2006.

Photo Credits and Copyright Notices

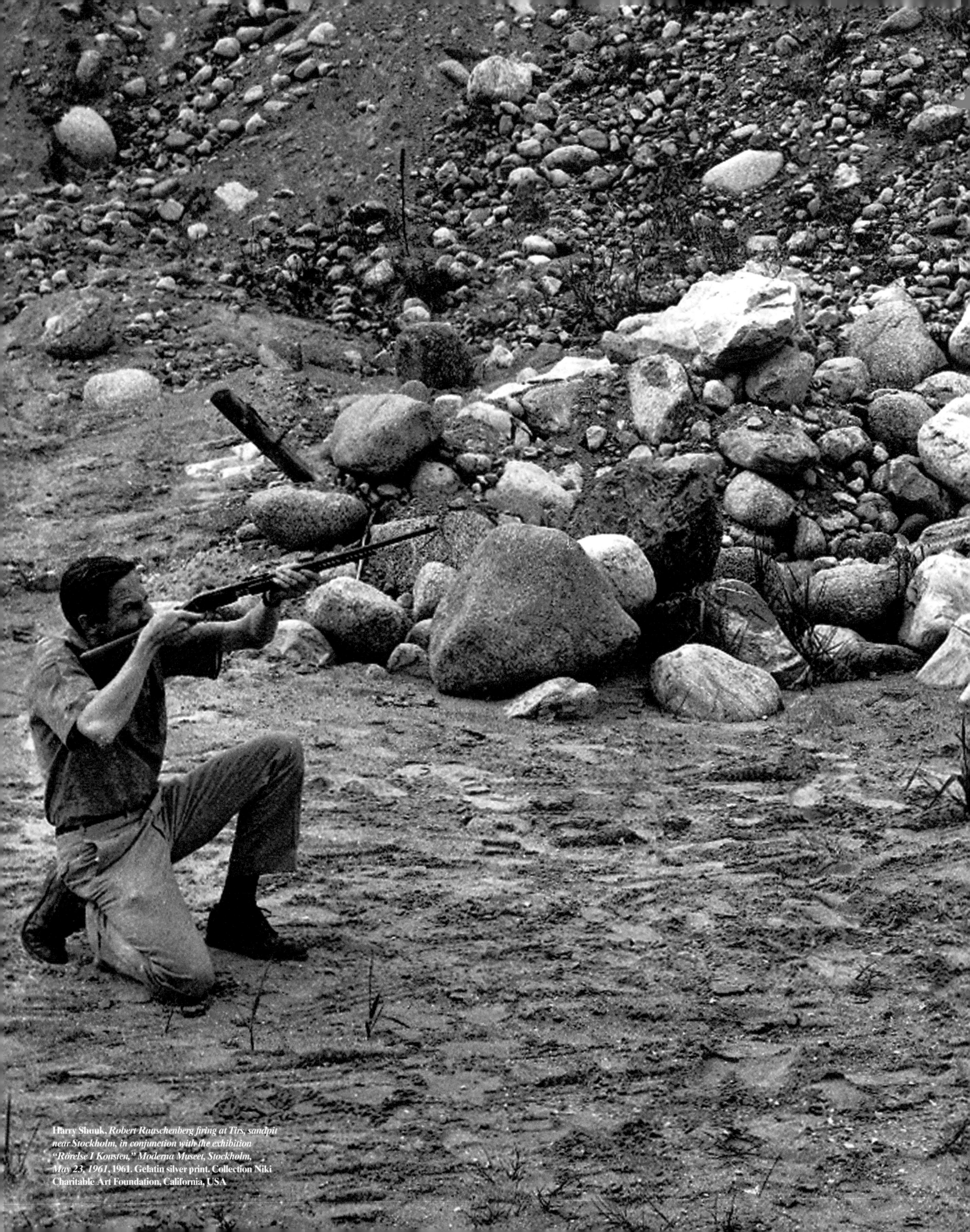

Harry Shunk, *Robert Rauschenberg firing at Tirs, sandpit near Stockholm, in conjunction with the exhibition "Rörelse I Konsten," Moderna Museet, Stockholm, May 23, 1961*, 1961. Gelatin silver print. Collection Niki Charitable Art Foundation, California, USA

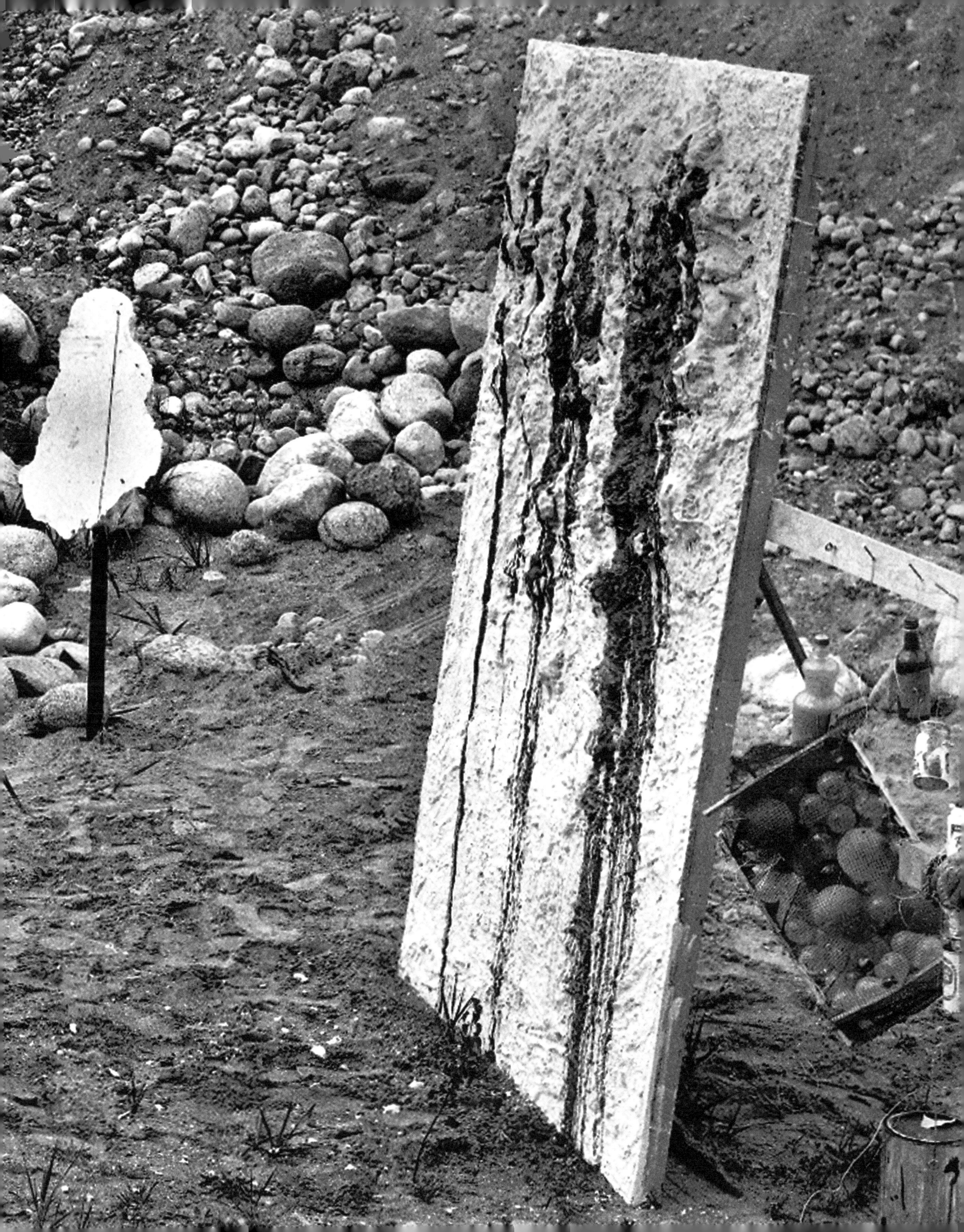

Contributors

Michael Darling has been the Jon and Mary Shirley Curator of Modern and Contemporary Art at the Seattle Art Museum since 2006. At SAM, he has organized exhibitions on the work of Su-Mei Tse, Oscar Tuazon and Eli Hansen, Enrico David, and Geoff McFetridge, in addition to forthcoming exhibitions on the work of Alexander Calder and contemporary artists inspired by Kurt Cobain. He was previously associate curator at the Museum of Contemporary Art, Los Angeles, where he organized exhibitions on the work of R. M. Schindler (with Elizabeth A. T. Smith), Roy McMakin, Sam Durant, and Ronan and Erwan Bouroullec, as well as group shows such as *Painting in Tongues* and *Superflat* (with Takashi Murakami).

Graham Bader is assistant professor of Art History at Rice University in Houston. His writing on modern and contemporary art has appeared in museum catalogues in Europe and the United States as well as in publications such as *Artforum*, *Grey Room*, *Art History*, and the *Oxford Art Journal*. His study of Roy Lichtenstein, *Hall of Mirrors: Roy Lichtenstein and the Face of Painting in the 1960s*, will be published by MIT Press in 2010, and he is currently at work on a study of the German Dada artist Kurt Schwitters.

Elizabeth Mangini is assistant professor of Visual Studies and Graduate Fine Arts at California College of the Arts in San Francisco. An art historian who specializes in social histories of postwar and contemporary art, her current research projects include a study of Arte Povera in Turin ca. 1968 and identity politics in American art of the 1980s and 1990s. She has held curatorial positions and postgraduate fellowships at the Museum of Modern Art, New York; the Walker Art Center, Minneapolis; and MASS MOCA, North Adams, Massachusetts.

Mika Yoshitake is a doctoral candidate in the Department of Art History at UCLA, specializing in postwar Japanese art, and project coordinator at the Museum of Contemporary Art, Los Angeles. She is a recipient of the 2007–2008 Japan Foundation Doctoral Fellowship, and her dissertation examines conceptual and process-based art practices in Japan during the 1960s and 1970s. Her writing has appeared in numerous publications, including *©Murakami* (2007), *First Light: Ai Yamaguchi* (2006), *X-TRA Contemporary Art Quarterly* (2006), and *(The World May Be) Fantastic: 2002 Biennale of Sydney*.